## PRAISE FOR THIS EDITION

*This publication is an invaluable tool for historians, history lovers and all those who are interested or engaged in the study of the history, culture and other aspects of Guyana. It updates the previous four (4) editions and will remain an irreplaceable reference tool for research on Guyana for future generations. It helps to fill the gap in the literature and is highly recommended for all libraries and your bookshelf.* – **Gwyneth George, University Librarian, University of Guyana.**

*A monumental tome, original and ground-breaking, which will be of considerable interest to both scholars and general readers. Lal Balkaran deserves a medal for his assiduous and patient scholarship.*
**– Professor David Dabydeen, Ambassador, Republic of Guyana; Hon. Fellow, Selwyn College, Cambridge University.**

*An invaluable and comprehensive Guyanese bibliography for any student, researcher, or curious readers alike. Significantly, the collection encompasses books, films, plays, and more, providing a diverse range of sources to deepen your understanding and appreciation of the country.*
**– Dr. Nigel Westmaas, Africana Studies, Hamilton College, New York.**

*This bibliography of Guyanese writers and writings is a remarkable and very valuable work of indefatigable research and compilation. What is also of interest is that it is an ongoing work subject to correction, elaboration and addition since the bibliographer's labours are never done. Lal Balkaran deserves our unstinted praise and thanks – and also our assistance when needed in his dedicated work of continuing to perfect and keep up to date his already unique achievement.*
**– Dr Ian McDonald, Literary Icon, Renowned Poet, Sportsman, and Columnist.**

*This is a monumental achievement that enriches our history and enhances our self-perception as a people – as Guyanese – however far or wide we may be dispersed.*
**– Dr. Clem Seecharan, Emeritus Professor of History and author of many books, London Metropolitan University.**

*This compilation of the Fifth Edition of an Updated "Bibliography of Guyana and Guyanese Writers" will remain a monumental masterpiece and invaluable resource for contemporary and future scholars. Mr. Balkaran's painstaking perusal of thousands of books, films and theatrical works is a tribute to his editorial skills and insightfulness, as it is a most welcome and invaluable possession for researchers and documentalists with interests across a wide expanse of Guyanese scholarship and learning. This Bibliography deserves to be as much in the libraries of institutions of higher learning as on the shelves and bedside of professionals, students and inquisitive readers.*
**– Dr. P.I. Gomes, former Secretary-General of the Organisation of Africa, Caribbean & Pacific States (OACPS).**

## PRAISE FOR THE LAST FOUR EDITIONS

*A wonderful and stimulating work that, for adepts and initiates alike, provides a continuing resource for and reference and learning......Lal Balkaran is to be warmly congratulated for his dedication to that place we hold as special - Guyana and its peoples...*
**– Dr. Neil L. Whitehead (1956-2012), Renowned Anthropologist, University of Wisconsin.**

*This is invaluable work for historians and other liberal arts scholars, and others far from those fields, as it covers a full spectrum of scholarship, from novels and poetry, other literary anthologies to scientific works. This is an invaluable resource for anyone who would want to know more about Guyana and its people. I recommend it highly.*
**– Professor Jan Carew (1920-2012), Guyanese literary icon.**

*Mr. Balkaran's book is a bold and exciting venture, pioneering in spirit, which seeks, for the first time, to compile a comprehensive list of publications about Guyana or by Guyanese.*
**– Dr. Frank Birbalsingh, retired Professor of English, York University.**

*An excellent contribution...Anyone perusing this volume is immediately struck by the monumental task that Lal Balkaran undertook and how well he accomplished the feat of putting together writings of Guyanese and about Guyana from a wide range of fields.*
**– Professor Stafford A. Griffith, University of the West Indies, Mona, Jamaica**

*The book itself is a welcomed addition to the growing interest and increasing scholarship in Guyanese literature... will further enhance and promote Guyanese literature and enrich the lives of litterateurs.*
**– Guyana Chronicle**

*It is astonishing how many authors Guyana, with its relatively small population, has produced. If one needed any proof of this, Lal Balkaran's 'Bibliography' provides it.*
**- Caribbean Camera**

*What you leave behind is not what is engraved in stone monuments, but what is woven into the lives of others.*

- Pericles

# Bibliography of Guyana & Guyanese Writers

**The Most Comprehensive Guide to Over 5,000 Books, Films, Documentaries, and Plays**

**By Lal Balkaran**

**FIFTH EDITION**

First published in 2004 by:
LBA Publications
18 Portsmouth Drive,
Scarborough, Ontario M1C 5E1, Canada

www.lbapublications.com

Library and Archives Canada Cataloguing in Publication

Title: Bibliography of Guyana & Guyanese writers / Lal Balkaran.
Other titles: Bibliography of Guyana and Guyanese writers
Names: Balkaran, Lal, author.
Description: Fifth edition. | "The most comprehensive guide to over 5000 books, films, documentaries, and plays" | Includes bibliographical references and index.
Identifiers: Canadiana 2023045576X | ISBN 9781738674817 (softcover)
Subjects: LCSH: Guyana—Bibliography. | LCSH: Guyana—Imprints.
Classification: LCC Z1791 .B34 2023 | DDC 015.881—dc23

## ALSO BY THE SAME AUTHOR

### BOOKS

**Business**

1. *A Practical Guide to Auditing and Related Terms*
2. *Accountants & Related Professionals: Reciprocal Memberships & Peer Acceptance*
3. *Directory of Global Professional Accounting & Business Certification Programs*
4. *Handbook of Global Professional Accounting Programs*
5. *Handbook of Global Professional Business Programs*
6. *Managerial Control Techniques*
7. *Professional Accounting & Business Programs: Effective Study and Examination Techniques*
8. *Dictionary of Risk, Governance, and Control*
9. *The Rise of Accounting, Auditing, and Finance*

**Guyana**

10. *Through Faith & Luck: The Story of an East Indian Family in Guyana*
11. *Immigrant #99840 and Canecutter #7074: The Story of an East Indian Family in Guyana*
12. *The Rupununi Savannas: A Visual Journey*
13. *Dictionary of the Guyanese Amerindians & Other South American Native Terms*
14. *Encyclopaedia of the Guyanese Amerindians & Other South American Native Terms*
15. *Timelines of Guyanese History: A Chronology of over 2000 Key Events in 30 Categories Since 1498*
16. *A Photojournal of the Guyanese Amerindians: Over 200 Photographs of Their Everyday Life and Cultural Activities*
17. *Biographical Dictionary of Guyana*

### DOCUMENTARIES

1. *A Photographic Journey of Guyana*
2. *A Photojournal of the Guyanese Amerindians*
3. *The Rupununi Savannahs: A Visual Journey*
4. *Stamps of British Guiana and Guyana*
5. *Georgetown: Guyana's Heartbeat – A Documentary*
6. *The Geography of Guyana – a 4-part series*

## *CONTENTS*

## *INTRODUCTION*

Since the first edition of this book came out in 2004, many other titles have been uncovered and requests for a revised edition have been increasing. A second edition came out in December 2006, a third in 2010, and a fourth in 2015. This is now a fifth edition in 2023 and it includes previously omitted titles as well as new ones in addition to corrections to those listed in the last four editions. Several authors submitted a wealth of information on their own publications as well as on others.

Many literary projects on Guyana over the years do cite other related books as sources of information. But such references are limited, and in some cases, incomplete and/or inaccurate. The major sources of information for this fifth edition were the 'Bibliography' section of previously published material, libraries of select institutions, and the internet. The annual *Guyana National Bibliography* that started in 1976 and ceased in 2016 published by the National Library of Guyana was a good source of literature on the country but this was restricted to material published in Guyana. Books published on other subjects (academic, business, reference, and otherwise) by Guyanese abroad are not contained in any one volume. No attempt was ever made to capture those publications. Also, there is no single reference that contains a bibliography of plays, documentaries, and films on Guyana and by Guyanese. In addition, with technological advancements, the explosion of the internet and self-publishing houses, quite a number of books on Guyana and by Guyanese on other subjects, that would have otherwise never been published by traditional publishing houses, came through these avenues. Some are egoistic, riddled with inaccurate information, poor language, style, and documentation standards in addition to self-aggrandizement. But they still met the criteria for inclusion in this bibliography and I went to great lengths to capture as many of these as possible – some of which were happily sent to me by the authors themselves.

So, that is what this guide is all about – a single reference that contains books, plays, documentaries, and films on Guyana by both Guyanese and non-Guyanese as well as those on other subjects by Guyanese. This book contains more than 4,300 book titles, 500 films, 400 plays, and 200 documentaries by well over 2,500 authors, playwrights, and producers. It is comprehensively organized into an *Index by Title* and five Appendices showing a listing by categories (Appendix A), documentaries (Appendix B), films (Appendix C), plays (Appendix D), and anthologies (Appendix E). Indeed, this is now the only broad-based bibliographical reference showcasing such a wide range of published works on Guyana and by Guyanese. In Appendix A, the titles are categorized into 80 subjects as follows:

**Afro-Guyanese; Agriculture; Amerindians; Amerindian Languages; Archaeology; Architecture; Art; Bibliography; Biography and Autobiography; Border Issues; Botany; Business; Caribbean; Cattle Ranching; Cheddi Jagan; Children; Chinese-Guyanese; Church History; Conservation; Cooking; Country Profile; Cultural Issues; Economic Development; Ecosystem; Education; El Dorado; Environment; Espionage; Family Life; Folk Tales; Foreign Interference; General; Geography; Geology; Global Issues; Government; Healthcare; History; Ichthyology; Immigration Issues; Indo-Guyanese; Jonestown; Language Studies; Legal History and Cases; Literature; Local Government; Mathematics; Media; Memoirs; Military Affairs; Mind, Body, and Spirit; Mining; Missionary Work; Music; Natural History; Novel; Ornithology; Philately; Photographic Scenes; Poetry; Political History; Politics; Pork Knockers; Portuguese-Guyanese; Prose; Race Relations; Ranching; Religion; Research; Social Studies; Sports; Trade Unions; Travel and Exploration; Walter Rodney; Women's Issues; and Zoology.**

There is no single source that captures such a cross-section of books, plays, films, and documentaries on such a wide range of subjects. This volume has therefore filled the void. However, it should not be considered an exhaustive one, as it is virtually impossible to ever compile a complete bibliography of such material to include every item there is to know about Guyana, especially where material has been written but not published. In summary, this fifth edition has been extensively revised and enlarged and is much more comprehensive. And as I mentioned before, submissions will be welcomed and used to enlarge future editions. A joint effort between readers and myself can only enrich the literary landscape of Guyana through future revisions of this volume and serve to instigate others to do the same for their own country where such an invaluable reference is lacking. I firmly believe that a work of this nature is of significant benefit to future generations. Sample reviews from authoritative sources given on the back cover attest to this assertion.

The volume contains books since Sir Walter Ralegh's volume on the country first appeared in 1596 as well as those written by Guyanese living in and out of Guyana on other subjects. Books that contain a few pages or whole sections on Guyana are also included, e.g., Arthur A. Schlesinger Jr's *A Thousand Days: John F. Kennedy in the White House* (Houghton Mifflin: New York, 1965) which has a few pages dealing with the role of Kennedy and the White House in undermining the democratically-elected government of Dr. Cheddi Jagan in the early 1960s.

A vast array of literature is out there containing information on the entries in this guide, but it is hardly likely that, in this era of information overload and constraints for time, anyone will have the time to go through even a portion of these to find a book, play, film, or documentary on a particular subject on the country. That was one main reason for compiling this guide. Many people, who always wonder where to go to look up a such and item on Guyana will find this volume informative. However, it will particularly appeal to the following:

- **Guyanese**: Whether living in or out of Guyana, Guyanese will find the book a good source of reference, one that will broaden their knowledge of the country;
- **Global**: Others from around the globe will find this book of special interest in helping them locate material of common interest;
- **Researchers:** They now have a good reference tool to aid in their research work;

- **Libraries:** The reference section of Libraries will now have a resource to help them source their collection; and
- **Teachers:** They can now quickly check up on the detail of a particular publication.

**How to use this book:**

The book is organized alphabetically by author and book title, followed by works they have edited, illustrated, or co-authored indicated by '_____;'. Each entry then lists the publisher's name, city or town, and date of publication in keeping with established documentation standard [*Chicago Manual of Style*]. Where either a publisher, city, or publication date is unknown, this is indicated by 'n.p.,' ' n.p.,' and 'n.d.' respectively. In addition to the sources mentioned earlier, research for this book included surfing the internet, contacting consulates, and searching the collections of select reference libraries. These included the British Library, National Library of Australia, National Library of Canada, Library of Congress, the Smithsonian Institution, the National Library of Guyana, and the University of Guyana Library. In addition, many others (too numerous to name) provided information for this fifth edition but the following in particular provided much more and I am therefore grateful for their kind assistance:

- The late Prof. Jan Carew – an icon in Guyanese and the Caribbean literary circles, for doing the *Foreword* to previous editions as well as providing information on other titles;
- Dr. Joy Gleason Carew for providing a complete list of the literary works of the Carew family (Jan Carew, Lisa St. Aubin de Teran, Iseult Teran, Denise Harris, and Wilson Harris), pointing out some omissions in the draft;
- Dr Ian McDonald (award-winning literary icon, renowned poet, sportsman, and columnist);
- Mr. Petamber Persaud (author and enabler of Guyanese literature);
- Mr. Ken Puddicombe (award-winning author and publisher);
- Ms. Gwyneth George, Chief Librarian at the University of Guyana;

- Ms. Emiley King, Chief Librarian, National Library of Guyana;
- Ms. Gem Madhoo-Nascimento, renowned actress;
- Mr. Nigel Westmaas, Africana Studies Department, Hamilton College (New York); and
- Ms. Hazel M. Woolford of the Guyana Institute of Historical Research (GIHR).

Finally, in any work of this nature, there will be books, plays, films, and documentaries that have not been captured. It is an intimidating and almost impossible task to include every such item on Guyana and by Guyanese. Also, given the wide range of subjects contained in this book, such a task becomes even more challenging. The omission is purely unintentional.

***Lal Balkaran,***
***Toronto, May, 2023***
***lalbalkaran@rogers.com***

*He who has profound knowledge often sees a lot where others see nothing.*

– James Smithson (c. 1765-1829)
Founding Donor of the Smithsonian Institution

# A

**ABDUL, Rahman**
*The Friend* (Ministry of Education: Georgetown, 1976).

**ABRAHAM, Sara**
*Labour and the Multiracial Project in the Caribbean: Its History and Its Promise.* (Lanham: Lexington Books, 2007).

**ABRAHAMS, Roger D.; and John F. Szwed, eds.**
*After Africa: Extracts from British Travel and Journals of the Seventeenth, Eighteenth, and Nineteenth Centuries concerning the Slaves, their Manners, and Customs in the British West Indies* (Yale University Press; New Haven, 1983).

**ABRAMS, Abioli**
*The Sacred Bombshell Handbook of Self-Love.* (El Dorado Publishing/Love University Press: New York, 2014).

**ABRAMS, Devon**
*Ananci Stories* (Free Press: Georgetown, 1999).

**ABRAMS, Ovid**
*Metegee: The History and Culture of Guyana* (El Dorado Publications: New York, 2000).

**ADAMS, John**
*Old Square – Toes and His Lady: The Life of James and Amelia Douglas* (Horsdal and Schubart: Victoria, 2001).

**ADAMS, Odel**
*A Gathering of Thoughts* (Magnet Printery: Georgetown, 1974).

**ADAMS-HAYNES, Beryl**
*Plaisance: From Emancipation to Independence and Beyond* (Beryl Adams-Haynes: Georgetown, 2010).

**ADAMSON, A.H.**
*Sugar Without Slaves: The Political Economy of British Guiana: 1838-1904* (Yale University Press: New Haven, 1972).

**ADARSH, Kumar Hari**
*An Educational Journey Against All Odds in Guyana, South America* (Workbook Plus: New York, 2022).

**ADI, HAKIM**
*Pan-Africanism and Communism: The Communist International, Africa and the Diaspora, 1919-1939* (Africa World Press: Trenton, 2013).

**ADONIS, Dennis E.**
*A Guide to Better Sex: A Sexual Improvement Guide* (Createspace: Seattle, 2014).

*An Introduction to Computers and the Internet – For Children ages 5 to 8* (Createspace: Seattle, 2012).
*An Introduction to Windows 8* (Createspace: Seattle, 2014).
*Anatomy of a Serial Rapist* (Createspace: Seattle, 2013).
*Boyhood Days, Book 2: A Caribbean Narrative* (Createspace: Seattle, 2014).
*How to Deal with Broken Relationships* (Createspace: Seattle, 2014).
*Sea of Sorrows: A Poetic Anthology* (Createspace: Seattle, 2013).
*Ten Letters to Obama* (Createspace: Seattle, 2014).
*The Pastor's Wife* (Createspace: Seattle, 2014).
*The Pregnancy Handbook for Inexperienced Mothers* (Createspace: Seattle, 2014).
*Tim and the Computer: A Computer Training Story for Toddlers Ages 2 to 4* (Createspace: Seattle, 2014).

**AGAMAH, June Wood**

*Caryl's Closet: A Journey of Faith and Love that Started in a village in Guyana and went around the world* (Carpenter's Son Publishing: New York, 2021).

**AGARD, C.N.**

*The Storm Within – An Anthology* (Xlibris: Bloomington, 2012).

**AGARD, John**

*A Stone's Throw from Embankment: The South Bank Collection* (Royal Festival Hall: London, 1993).
*All Sorts to Make a World* (Barrington Stoke Limited: London, 2014).
*Alternative Anthem* (Bloodaxe Books: London, 2009).
*Book* (Walker Book: London, 2014).
*Brer Rabbit: The Great Tug-o-war* (Barrons: New York, 1998).
*Calypso Alphabet* (Collins: London, 1990).
*Clever Backbone* (Bloodaxe Books: London, 2009).
*Dig Away Two-Hole Tim* (Bodley Head: London, 1981).
*Eat a Poem, Wear a Poem* (Heinemann Young Books: London, 1995).
*Einstein: The Girl That Hated Maths* (Hodder and Stoughton Children's Division: London, 2003).
*From the Devil's Pulpit* (Bloodaxe Books: London, 1997).
*Get Back, Pimple!* (Viking: London, 1996).
*Go Noah Go!* (Hodder & Stoughton: London, 1990).
*Granfather's Old Bruk-a-Down Car* (Bodley Head: London, 1994).
*Hello H20* (Hodder Children's Books: London, 2003).
*I Din Do Nuttin, and Other Poems* (Bodley Head: London, 1983).
*Laughter is an Egg: A Collection of Poems* (Penguin Books: London, 1991).

*Letters for Lettie, and Other Stories* (Bodley Head: London, 1979).
*Limbo Dancer in Dark Glasses* (Greenheart: London, 1983).
*Livingroom* (Black Ink: London, 1983).
*Loveliness for a Goat-Born Lady* (Serpent's Tail: London, 1990).
*Man to Pan* (Casa de las Américas: Havana, 1982).
*Mangoes and Bullets: Selected and New Poems* (Serpent's Tail: London, 1990).
*Oriki and the Monster Who Hated Balloons* (Longmans: London, 1994).
*Points of View with Professor Peekabo* (Bodley Head: London, 2000).
*Say it again, Granny! Twenty Poems from Caribbean Proverbs* (Magnet Books: London, 1989).
*Shoot me with flowers* (John Agard: Georgetown, 1968).
*The Emperor's Dan-dan* (Hodder & Stoughton: London, 1992).
*The Great Snakeskin* (Ginn: London, 1993).
*The Monster Who Loved Cameras* (Longmans: London, 1994).
*The Monster Who Loved Telephones* (Longmans: London, 1994).
*The Monster Who Loved Toothbrushes* (Longmans: London, 1994).
*We Animals Would Like a Word with You* (Bodley Head: London, 1996).
*Weblines* (Bloodaxe Books: London, 2000).

**_____, ed.**

*Hello New: New Poems for a New Century* (Orchard: London, 2000).
*Life Doesn't Frighten Me at All* (Heinemann: London, 1989).
*Poems in My Earphone* (Longmans: London, 1995).
*Why is the Sky* (Faber and Faber: London, 1996).

**_____, contr.**

*Another Day on Your Foot and I Would Have Died* (Macmillan Children's Books: London, 1996).
*Caribbean Poetry Now* (Hodder & Stoughton: London, 1984).
*Heinemann Book of Caribbean Poetry* (Heinemann: London, 1992).
*The Penguin Book of Caribbean Verse* (Penguin: London, 1986).

**_____; Jackie Kay; Grace Nichols; Nick Toczek; and Mike Rosen**

*Border Country: Poems in Progress* (Wood Wind Publications: London, 1991).
*Grandchildren of Albion* (New Departures: London, 1992).
*Number Parade: Number Poems from 0-100* (LDA: London, 2002).

**_____; and Adrienne Kennaway, ill.**

*Lend Me Your Wings* (Little Brown & Co: New York, 1989).

**_____; and Lydia Monks**

*Come Back to Me My Boomerang* (Orchard: London, 2001).

**_____; and Grace Nichols, co-eds.**

*Caribbean Dozen: Poems from Thirteen Caribbean Poets* (Walker Books Ltd: London, 2020).

*Collins Big Cat: Caribbean Tales* (Harper Collins: London, 2016).

*Equiano's Epigrams* (Windrush Foundation: London, 2009).

*Goldilocks on CCTV* (Frances Lincoln Children Books: London, 2014).

*Half-Caste and Other Poems* (Hodder Children's Books: London, 2005).

*From Mouth to Mouth* (Walker Books Ltd.: London, 2004).

*The Girl Who Hated Maths* (Hodder Wayland: London, 2003).

*The Young Inferno* (Frances Lincoln Children Books: London, 2009).

*Travel Light and Travel Dark* (Bloodaxe Books: London, 2013).

*Twinkle Twinkle, Firefly* (Harper Collins: London, 2010).

*Under the Moon and Over the Sea: A Collection of Caribbean Poems,* (Candlewick Press: Massachusetts, 2003).

*We Brits* (Bloodaxe Books; London, 2007).

*Wriggly Piggy Toes* (Frances Lincoln Children's Books: London, 2005).

**_____; Grace Nichols; and Cathie Felstead, ill.**

*A Caribbean Dozen: Poems from Caribbean Poets* (Candlewick Press: Massachusetts, 1994).

**_____; Grace Nichols; and Cynthia Jabar, ill.**

*No Hickory No Dickory No Dock: Caribbean Nursery Rhymes* (Candlewick Press: Massachusetts, 1994).

**_____; and J. Northway**

*Dig Away Two-Hole Tim* (Random House: New York, 1982).

**_____; Michael Rosen; and Robert Frost**

*A Child's Year of Stories and Poems* (Viking Children's Books: London, 2000).

**_____; Korky Paul**

*Brer Rabbit: The Great Tug-O-War* (Barrons Juveniles: London, 1998).

**AGARD, Rev. W. Oscar**

*Called to be more: Windows on the work and witness of the Anglican Church in the Diocese of Guyana* (W. O. Agard: Toronto, 1994).

**AGEE, Philip**

*Inside the Company: CIA Diary* (Stonehill Publishing Co.: New York, 1975).

**AGOSTINO, Malcolm A.**

*A Study of the Diploma in Education Curriculum, University of Guyana, in relation to the professional concerns of the 1969-1971 graduates* (SUNY: New York, 1972).

**AHMED, Rollo**

*I Rise: The Life Story of a Negro* (n.p.: London, 1937).

**AKHTAR, Shameen**

*British Guiana: A Study of Marxism and Racialism in the Caribbean* (Southern Methodist University Press: Dallas, 1962).

**ALERT, C.V.**

*Life and Work of Hubert Nathaniel Critchlow* (n.p.: Georgetown, 1949).

**ALEXANDER, J.E.**

*Transatlantic Sketches Comprising Visits to the Most Interesting Scenes in North and South America, and the West Indies* (Bentley: London, 1833).

**ALEXANDER, Lorri**

*Moongazer* (L. Alexander: Georgetown, 2006).

**ALEXANDER, Simone A James**

*African Diasporic Women's Narratives: Politics of Resistance, Survival, and Citizenship* (University Press of Florida: Miami, 2016).

*Mother Imagery in the Novels of Afro-Caribbean Women* (University of Missouri Press; 2001).

**_____; and Dorsia Smith Silva**

*Feminist and Critical Perspectives on Caribbean Mothering* (African World Press: Trenton, 2013).

**ALGOE, R Kirtie**

*Religion, Power, and Society in Suriname and Guyana: Hindu, Muslim, and Christian Relations* (Taylor & Francis: London, 2022).

**ALGU, Trevor**

*Unique Story Book for Children* (Red Thread Women's Press).

**ALI, Arif, ed.**

*Anguilla: Tranquillity Wrapped in Blue* (Hansib: Hertfordshire, 2003).

*Antigua & Barbuda: A Little Bit of Paradise* (Hansib: Hertfordshire, 1988, 1994, 1996, 1999, 2005, 2008, 2016).

*Barbados: Just Beyond Your Imagination* (Hansib: Hertfordshire, 2007).

*Barbados: Experience the Authentic Caribbean* (Hansib: Hertfordshire, 2007).

*Dominica: Nature Island of the Caribbean* (Hansib: Hertfordhsire, 1989, 2009).
*Grenada, Carriacou, Petit Martinique* (Hansib: Hertfordshire, 1994).
*Guyana* (Hansib: Hertfordshire, 2006, 2008).
*Guyana at 50: Reflection, Celebration and Inspiration* (Hansib: Hertfordshire, 2016).
*India: A Wealth of Diversity* (Hansib: Hertfordshire, 1997).
*Jamaica: Absolutely* (Hansib: Hertfordshire, 2010, 2012).
*Saint Lucia: Simply Beautiful* (Hansib: Hertfordshire, 1997).
*Third World Impact* (Hansib: Hertfordshire, 1982, 1984, 1986, 1988).
*Tobago: Clean, Green and Serene* (Hansib: Hertfordshire, 2005, 2012).
*Trinidad and Tobago: Terrific and Tranquil* (Hansib: Hertfordshire, 2000, 2007, 2012).
*Westindians in Great Britain* (Hansib: Hertfordshire, 1973, 1974, 1975). Renamed *Third World Impact* (1982).
*The Modern Book of Muslim Names* (Hansib: Hertfordshire, 2001).
**_____; and Catherine Hogben, eds.**
*Grass Roots in Verse* (Hansib: Hertfordshire, 1988)

**ALI, Ashmead**
*Don't Give Up On Us: A Rwandan Experience* (Ashmead Ali: Scarborough, 2008).
*Understanding Poverty and International Development Cooperation* (Ashmead A. Ali: Scarborough, 2012).

**ALI, Bashir**
*Jesus and the Gospel of the Kingdom of Heaven* (PublishAmerica: Baltimore, 2006).

**ALI, B.S.; et al**
*The New Wave: Poems* (Annandale Writers' Club: Annandale, 1974).

**ALI, E.**
*Muslims in America* (E. Ali: New York, 2002).
*Rise of the Phoenix* (E. Ali: New York, 1997).

**ALI, Grace Aneiza**
*Liminal Spaces: Migration and Women of the Guyanese Diaspora* (Open Book Publishers: Cambridge, 2020).

**ALI, Kamil**
*Benjamin, Prophet of the Apes* (Forthcoming).
*Gateway to the Dark Side: Final Book of The Appointed Collection* (eTreasures Publishing: Marianna, 2019).
*Phenomena* (Amazon Books: Bolton, 2020).
*Profound Vers-a-Tales* (Trafford Publishing – now Penguin: Vancouver, 2009).

*Supernatural* (Amazon Books: Bolton, 2016).
*The Beggar' s Diaries* (Amazon Books: Bolton, 2019).
*The Initiates: First Book of the Appointed Collection* (eTreasures Publishing: Marianna, 2013).
*The Order of the Mirror: Second Book of The Appointed Collection* (eTreasures Publishing: Marianna, n.d.).

**ALI, Khalil Rahman**

*Daughter of the Great River* (Hansib Publications: Hertfordshire, 2020).
*In Pursuit of Betterment* (Hansib Publications: Hertfordshire, 2017).
*Sugar's Sweet Allure* (Hansib Publications: Hertfordshire, 2013).
*The Domino Masters of Demerara* (Hansib Publications: Hertfordshire, 2015).

**ALLAHAR, Anton**

*Caribbean Charisma: Legitimacy and Political Leadership in the Era of Independence* (Ian Randle Publishers: Kingston, 2001).

**ALLI, Habeeb**

*Canadian Fiqh: Understanding Islam in Canada* (Blue Tree Publishing: Scarborough, 2006).
*Five White Roses and a Red, A Book of Poetry* (Blue Tree Publishing: Toronto, 2015).
*Hard Look at Contemporary Islam* (Blue Tree Publishing: Richmond Hill, 2008).
*Happiness: Naked Truths* (Blue Tree Publishing: Richmond Hill, 2009).
*Passions of El Dorado* (Blue Tree Publishing (Blue Tree Publishing: Scarborough, 2007).
*Realities Under the Stars* (Unique Remedy Publications: Georgetown, 2004).
*Red Coconut: Bridging the Racial Divide* (Blue Tree Publishing: Toronto, 2016).
*Roraima: An Anthology of Poetry from emerging Caribbean Canadian writers* (Blue Tree Publishing: Scarborough, 2011).
*Scaling Heights- Anthology of Poems by Pakaraima Writers* (MiddleRoad Publishers: Toronto, 2022).
*Underground Lines: 150+ Verses* (Blue Tree Publishing: Scarborough, 2017).
*Wild Lavender* (Blue Tree Publishing: Scarborough, 2018).

**ALLI, Shamshair**

*From Guyana to America: My Story* (Shamshair Alli: New York, 2013).

**ALLSOPP, Claire**

*Born in Adventure: A Glimpse of the Life and Works of a Guyanese Artist* (Claire Allsopp: Georgetown, 2022).

**ALLSOPP, J.**

*Teddy the Toucan* (n.p.: n.p., n.d.).

**ALLSOPP, Jeanette**

*Language, Cultural and Caribbean Identity* (University of the West Indies Press: Cave Hill, 2013).

*Caribbean Multilingual Dictionary of Flora, Fauna and Foods* (Arawak Publications, Kingston, 2012).

**_____; and John R. Rickford, eds.**

*Language, Culture and Caribbean Identity (UWI Press: Mona, 2012)*

*Language Education in the Caribbean: Selected Articles by Dennis Craig* (UWI Press: Mona, 2014).

*Dictionaries of Caribbean English: Agents of Standardization in the Cambridge Companion to English Dictionaries* (Cambridge University Press: Cambridge, 2013).

**_____; and Wendy Griffith-Watson, eds.**

*School Edition of the Dictionary of Caribbean English* (Cambridge University Press: Cambridge, 2013).

**ALLSOPP, Richard**

*Dictionary of Caribbean English Usage* (Oxford University Press: Oxford, 1996).

*Guyana Talk: Early Essays in the Study of a Caribbean Creole (*Carlex Language Consultancy: Bridgetown, 2002).

**ALLY, Hydar**

*Pragmatism or Opportunism? Guyana's Foreign Policy Behaviour (1964-1985)* (New Guyana Company Ltd.: Georgetown, 2014).

**ALLY, Dr. Shamir Andrew**

"A Look at the Watching Friends and Relatives Market Segment at the 2007 Cricket World Cup," in *Sports Event Management: The Caribbean Experience* (University of the West Indies: St. Augustine, 2010).

*Leading With Questions: How Leaders Find the Right Solutions by Knowing What to Ask* (Jossey-Bass: San Francisco, 2014).

*My Tenure as Guyana's Ambassador to Kuwait: Guyana's Image in the Middle East* (Forthcoming).

*Preparing Caricom for the Twenty-First Century Through Regional Economic Integration,* a 10-page article. ("Futurics"-A Journal of Futures Research: Saint Paul, 1996).

**ALPERS, E.A.; and Pierre-Michel Fontaine**

*Walter Rodney: Revolutionary and Scholar – A Tribute* (University of California: Los Angeles, 1982).

**ALPHONSO, Cassia**

*Black Cake Mix* (Cassia Alphonso: Georgetown, 2012). [Won the Guyana Prize for Literature in the 2012 Best Book of Poetry category jointly with Ian McDonald's *The Comfort of All Things*].

**ALTMAN, A.; and B. Swift**

*A Field Checklist of Birds of Guyana* (A. Altman: Great Barrington, 1989).

**ALVES, Malcolm**

*Roll Over* (Lulu Press: Raleigh, 2007).

**ALYAN, Lewiz**

*Giant of the Past* (Betty Lewis: Georgetown, 1988).

*Grass Roots of Guyana.* A Three-Part Series. Part One (Management Services Guyana Ltd.: Georgetown, 1985).

*Grass Roots of Guyana.* Part Two (Betty Lewis: Georgetown, 1991).

*Grass Roots of Guyana.* Part Three (Betty Lewis: Georgetown, 1994).

*Return of the Half Caste* (Betty Lewis: Georgetown, 1989).

*Straight and Narrow* (Betty Lewis: Georgetown, 1990).

*Sunset's Trail* (Betty Lewis: Georgetown, 1996).

*Tales Strange But True* (Betty Lewis: Georgetown, 1997).

**AMBROSE, Rupert, et al**

*Assessment of the Information Processing Needs for Agricultural Sector Planning in Guyana* (USAID: Washington, DC, 1979).

**ANAND, G.V.**

*Hungry Voices Cry: A Collection of Poems* (Guyana National Service Publications Centre: Georgetown, 1976).

**ANDAIYE (Sandra Williams)**

*The Point is to Change the World: Selected Writings of Andaiye* (Pluto Press: London, 2020).

**ANDERSON, Mickey**

*Hop Scotch: Some Guyanese Expressions* (M. Anderson: Georgetown, 1983).

*One Captain and Other Literary Works* (M. Anderson: Georgetown, 2009).

**ANDRADE, John, ed.**

*World Police and Paramilitary Forces* (Stockton Press: New York, 1985).

**ANDRÉ, Eugène**

*A Naturalist in the Guianas* (Smith, Elder, & Co.: London, 1904).

**ANDRIES, W.L.**

*Journey of Discovery: A Book of Poems* (Word for Word Publishing Co.: New York, 2005).

*The Key: Poems from the Heart* (Outskirts Press: Denver, 2009).

**ANGOY, W.A.**

*Guyana: A Nation on the Move* (Government of Guyana: Georgetown, 1966).

*Guyana Man: With Visions of Caribbean Integration* (Triumph Publications: Bridgetown, 1990).

**ANGUS, Richmond**

*A Kind of Living* (Casa de Las Americas: Havana, 1978).

*The Open Prison* (Hansib Publications: Hertfordshire, 1988).

**ANIM-ADDO, Joan, ed.**

*Framing the Word: Gender and Genre in Caribbean Women's Writing* (Whiting and Birch: London, 1996).

**ANTHONY, Ashley**

*Mysterious Association and the Virtu Gems* (Caribbean Press: Georgetown, 2002).

*Lia and Ellie talk about Coronavirus* (Amazon Books: 2020).

**ANTHONY, Michael**

*Bright Road to El Dorado* (Ian Randle Publishers: Kingston, 2007).

**ANTON, L.A., ed.**

*Caribbean Charisma: Reflections on Leadership, Legitimacy, and Populist Politics* (Lynne Rienner Publishers: Boulder, 2001).

**APPLE, Arnold**

*Son of Guyana* (Oxford University Press: Oxford, 1973).

*Bethany* (Chatto & Windus: London, 2003).

**ARBELL, Mordechai**

*Jewish Nation of the Caribbean: The Spanish-Portuguese Jewish Settlements in the Caribbean and the Guianas* (Gefen Publishing House: New York, 2002).

**ARBUTHNOT, Joan**

*More Profit than Gold* (Charles Scribner's Sons: New York, 1936).

**ARCHDIOCESAN PASTORAL CENTRE**

*Caribbean Personhood II: The Challenge of Violence* (Archdiocesan Pastoral Centre: St. Augustine, 2001).

**ARCHER, Beatrice**

*Poison of My Hate* (National Educational Company of Zambia: Lusaka, 1978).

**ARCHER, Fred**

*Sir Lionel. 232 murder trials…all 232 acquitted* (Gift Publications: Irvine, 1980).

**ARCHER, Mark Anthony**

*The Dark Horse: Letters From the Campaign Trail* (Mark Anthony Archer: Georgetown, 2021).

**ARCHER-PERSICO, Melva**

*Ink on Paper: Poems* (Amazon: New York, 2021).

*Ma Mae's Legacy* (Amazon: New York, 2019).

**ARJOON-MARTINS, Annette**

*Amerindian Women* (Conservation International: Washington, D.C.: 2011).

**ARJUNE, Frank**

*Retributions* (Stratton Press: New York, 2022).

*The Guyana Exodus* (Carlton Press: Cheshire, 1995).

**ARMITAGE, Christopher**

*Sir Walter Ralegh: An Annotated Bibliography* (University of North Carolina, Chapel Hill: Chapel Hill, 1987).

**ARNO, William Nicholas**

*History of Victoria Village, East Coast Demerara* (Guyana Heritage Society: Georgetown, 2000).

**ARNOLD, James A.**

*A History of Literature in the Caribbean* (John Benjamins Publishing: London, 1994).

**ASANTEWA, Michelle Yaa**

*Elijah* (Way Wive Wordz: London, 2015).

*Guyanese Komfa: The Ritual Art of Trance* (Way Wive Wordz: London, 2021).

*Mama Lou Tales: A Folkloric Biography of a Guyanese Elder* (Way Wive Wordz: London, 2016).

*Something Buried in the Yard* (Way Wive Wordz: London, 2022).

*The Awakening and Other Poems* (Way Wive Wordz: London, 2014).

**ASARE, Sardar**

*Courida Elegies* (S. Asare: Georgetown, 1991).

*Poems of Separation* (S. Asare: Georgetown, 1981).

**ASHBY, Timothy**

*The Bear in the Backyard: Moscow's Caribbean Strategy* (Lexington Books: Lexington, 1987).

**ASHTON, Nigel J.**

*Kennedy, Macmillan and the Cold War: The Irony of Independence* (Palgrave Macmillan: Houndmills, 2002).

**ASPINALL, Algernon E.**

*The Pocket Guide to the West Indies and British Guiana: British Honduras, Bermuda, the Spanish Main, Suriname and the Panama Canal* (Methuen: London, 1954).

**ATALLAH, Maria Teresa**

*The Secret of El Dorado City: The Tree of El* (A H Stockwell: Devon, 2022).

**ATKINS, Pope**

*South America into the 1990s: Evolving International Relationships in a New Era* (Westview Press: Boulder, 1990).

**ATKINS, Sharon**

*Classic Caribbean Cooking* (Hansib: Hertfordshire, 2005).

**ATKINSON, Katherine**

*Living My Dreams: Joseph 'Reds' Perreira* (AuthorHouse: Bloomington, 2011).

**ATTENBOROUGH, David**

*Zoo Quest to Guiana* (Pilot Books: London, 1956).

**AUGIER, F.R.; et al**

*Sources of West Indian History* (Longmans: London, 1962).

*The Making of the West Indies* (Longmans: London, 1960).

**AUGUSTE, Bryan**

*Love Math: A Book at Agate Love* (Imprimerie Omeane: 2016).

**AUSTIN, Ronald M; and Karla T. Pestana**

*Guyana Brazil Relations: 50 Years of Cooperation and Friendship* (Ministry of Foreign Affairs: Georgetown, 2018).

**AYEARST, Morley**

*The British West Indies: The Search for Self-Government* (George Allen & Unwin Ltd: London, 1962).

# B

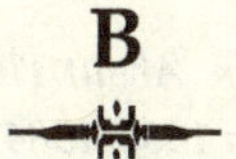

**BABB, V.**

*A Golden Eagle: How I Soared to Millions in $$$ in Sales* (Victor Babb: New York, 1988).

*How to Win Elections and Manage Political Process* (AuthorHouse: Bloomington, 2007).

**BABER, Colin**

*The Co-operative Republic of Guyana* (St. Martin's Press: New York, 1992).

**_____; and Henry B. Jeffrey**

*Guyana: Politics, Economics and Society* (Lynne Rienner Publishers: Denver, 1986).

**BACCHUS, M.K.**

*Education as and for Legitimacy. Developments in West Indian Education Between 1846 and 1895* (Wilfred Laurier University Press: Waterloo, 1994).

*Education for Development or Underdevelopment? Guyana's Educational System and Its Implications for the Third World* (Wilfred Laurier University Press: Waterloo, 1980).

*Educational and Social Change in the ex-British Caribbean Colonies: From Earliest Times to the 1940s* (PublishAmerica: Baltimore, 2006).

**BACCHUS, Nadeer**

*The Golden Arrowhead* (Nadeer Bacchus: Corriverton, 1978).

*Shattered Dreams* (Nadeer Bacchus: Corriverton, 1979).

**BACCHUS, Noel**

*Guyana Farewell: A Recollection of Childhood in a Faraway Place* (Noel Bacchus: New York, 2000).

*Where Cries the Kis-Ka-Dee* (Noel Bacchus: New York, 2009).

**BACCHUS, Rosaliene**

*The Twisted Circle* (Lulu Press: Morrisville, 2021).

*Under The Tamarind Tree* (Lulu Press: Morrisville, 2019).

**BACON, Margaret**

*Journey to Guyana* (Dennis Dobson: London, 1970).

*Journey to Guyana* (Hill House Publishers: London, 1988, 1993).

**BADRI-MAHARAJ, Sanjay**

*Armed Forces of the English-speaking Caribbean: The Bahamas, Barbados, Guyana, Jamaica, and Trinidad & Tobago* (Helion & Co.: London, 2022).

**BAGOT, Stella**

*A Troublesome Man: About The Life of Dr. Ptolemy Reid, Prime Minister of Guyana 1980-1984* (Balboa Press: Bloomington, 2018).

**BAHADUR, Gauitra**

*Coolie Woman: The Odyssey of Indenture* (University of Chicago Press: Chicago, 2013).

**BAILEY, A.C.**

*African Voices of the Atlantic Slave Trade* (Ian Randle Publishers: Kingston, 2007).

**BAILEY, B.; and E. Rhyme-Leo**

*Gender in the 21st Century* (Ian Randle Publishers: Kingston, 2004).

**BAIRD, Pauline**

*Dave and the Lime Tree* (Komaka Tree Books: New York, 2022).

*Encounters: An Afro-Caribbean Proverbs Journal* (Komaka Tree Books: New York, 2021).

*Morning Meditations Ah Village* (Komaka Tree Books: New York, 2021).

*Navel String* (Komaka Tree Books/Globunto: New York, 2020).

*The Move: The Diary of a 12 year-old girl from Brooklyn* (Komaka Tree Books: New York, 2021).

*To My Poppa and Gigi* (Komaka Tree Books: New York, 2022).

*Wah Dih Story She: An Oral Tradition in the Guyanese Village, Buxton* (Globunto Books: Johannesburg, 2019).

*Whispers in Our Ears: Afro-Caribbean Proverbs* (Komaka Tree Books: New York, 2018).

**_____; ed.**

*I am a Guyanese: Poems of Passion, Power, and Patriotism* (Oginga Productions: Silver Springs, 2022).

*I is a BV Man: Baronian and Proud* (Komaka Tree Books: New York, 2022).

*Poems of Consciousness* (Oginga Productions: Silver Springs, 2022).

*Tomorrow with the Rising Sun* (Komaka Tree Books: New York, 2021).

**_____; contr.**

'(Re)orienting borders with hybrid poetry in tertiary pedagogy' in Poetry in *Pedagogy: Intersections Across and Between the Disciplines* (Routledge: London, 2021).

**BAIRD, Wesley**

*Guyana Gold: The Story of Wesley Baird, Guyana's Greatest Miner* (Three Continents Press: Oxford, 1982).

**BAKSH, Ahamad**

*The mobility of degree level graduates of the University of Guyana* (Department of Sociology, University of Guyana: Turkeyen, 1973).

*The patterns of higher education at the University of Guyana, 1963-64 to 1971-72* (Department of Sociology, University of Guyana: Turkeyen, 1973).

**BAKSH, Imam**

*Children of the Spider* (Blue Moon Publishers: Stratford, 2016). [Winner of the 2015 Burt Award for Caribbean Literature].

**BALKARAN, Lal**

*A History of the Versailles Hindu Temple* (LBA Publications: Toronto, 2011).

*A Photojournal of the Guyanese Amerindians* (LBA Publications: Toronto, 2007).

*A Practical Guide to Auditing and Related Terms* (Lexis-Nexis, Butterworths: Markham, 2003).

*Accountants & Related Professionals: Reciprocal Memberships & Peer Acceptance* (LBA Publications: Toronto, 1997).

*Accounting, Auditing, Finance, & Related Programs: Cutting Edge Study & Examination Techniques*, 4th ed. (LBA Publications: Toronto, 2014).

*Bibliography of Guyana and Guyanese Writers* (LBA Publications: Toronto, 2004, 2006, 2009 (Seaburn Publishing: New York, 2009), 2015, 2023).

*Dictionary of Risk, Governance, and Control* (LBA Publications: Toronto, 2014).

*Encyclopaedia of the Guyanese Amerindians & Other South American Native Terms: An A-Z Guide to Their Anthropology, Cosmology, Culture, Exploration, History, Geography, Legend, Folklore, and Myth* (LBA Publications: Toronto, 2007).

*Directory of Global Professional Accounting & Business Certifications* (Wiley: Hoboken, 2007).

*Handbook of Global Professional Accounting Programs* (LBA Publications: Toronto, 1996).

*Handbook of Global Professional Business Programs* (LBA Publications: Toronto, 1996).

*Immigrant #99840 and Canecutter #7074: The Story of an East Indian Family in Guyana* (AuthorHouse: Bloomington, 2006).

*Managerial Control Techniques* (Chartered Institute of Management Accountants: London, 1989).
*The Rupununi Savannas: A Visual Journey* (AuthorHouse: Bloomington, 2005).
*Biographical Dictionary of Guyana* (LBA Publications: Toronto, 2022).
*The Rise of Accounting, Auditing, and Finance* (NOVA Publishers: New York, 2019).
**_____, contr.**
*Cutting Edge Internal Auditing* (Wiley: London, 2007).

**BAKSH, Kayume**
*Islam and Other Major World Religions* (Trafford Publishing: Vancouver, 2007).

**BANARJEE, G.R.**
*To Those Who Fought For Freedom* (n.p.; c. 1920s).
*Song Offerings to Lotus and God* (n.p.; c. 1920s).
*From Eternity for Peace* (n.p.; c. 1920s).

**BANCROFT, E.**
*An Essay on the Natural History of Guiana in South America: Containing a Description of Many Curious Productions in the Animal and Vegetable Systems of that Country together with an Account of the Religion, Manners, and…* (n.p.: London, 1769). Reprint. (Arno Press Inc: New York, 1971).

**BANCROFT, Parry W.**
*Blossoms and My Bullets As I Shoot My Mind: Poems and Short Stories* (n.p: n.p., 2007).

**BAROCAS, Deborah**
*Guyana's Tasting Exotic: Foods of Six People* (Xlibris: Bloomington, 2016).

**BARROW, C.; and R. REDDOCK, eds.**
*Caribbean Sociology: Introductory Readings* (Ian Randle Publishers: Kingston, 2001).
*Family in the Caribbean* (Ian Randle Publishers, Kingston, 1996).

**BARROW, Lloyd**
*A History of Film in Guyana* (n.p.; c. 1960s).

**BARROW, Wayne Westphal**
*Guyana's Elections 2020: The 153-Day Saga* (Wayne Barrow: New York, 2021).

**BARROW-GILES, Cynthia**
*Introduction to Caribbean Politics:* (Ian Randle Publishers: Kingston, 2006).

*Living at the Borderlines: Issues in the Caribbean Sovereignty and Development* (Ian Randle Publishers: Kingston, 2004).

*Women in Caribbean Politics* (Ian Randle Publishers: Kingston, 2011).

**_____; and Tennyson Joseph**

*General Elections and Voting in the English-Speaking Caribbean* (Ian Randle Publishers: Kingston, 2006).

**BARRY, William**

*Venezuela: A Visit to the Gold Mines of Guyana, and Voyage Up the River Orinoco During 1886, with a Brief Sketch of the Mineral Wealth and Resources of Venezuela, and Its History to the Present Time* (W. Barry: New York, 2021 – republished).

**BARTILOW, H.**

*The Debt Dilemma: IMF Negotiations in Jamaica, Grenada, Guyana* (Macmillan-Caribbean: London, 1997).

**BARTON, Lyndon O**

*Search and Find With Guyana in Mind* (Createspace Publishing: New York, 2015).

**BASCOM, Harold A**

*101 Words That Tell You're Guyanese* (Amazon KPD: 2016).

*Apata: The Story of a Reluctant Criminal* (Heinemann: London, 1986).

*How to get better reviews for your first novel: 11 Convos on the Basis of Fiction Writing for Self-Publishing* (Amazon KPD: 2019).

**BASDEO, Carol**

*KC & Kayla's Science Corner -The Apple Experiment* (Mindstir Media: New York, 2018).

*KC & Kayla's Science Corner - Matter! What's the Matter* (Mindstir Media: New York, 2019).

*KC & Kayla's Science Corner - The Life Cycle of an Apple* (Mindstir Media: New York, 2020).

*KC & Kayla's Science Corner - A Matter* (Mindstir Media: New York, 2020).

**BATES, H.W.**

*The Naturalist on the River Amazons*. 2 vols. (John Murray: London, 1863). Reprint. (John Murray: London, 1969).

**BAUGH, Ed**

*West Indian Poetry 1900-1970. A Study in Cultural Decolonisation* (Savacou Publication: London, 1974).

**BAYLEY, Jack**

*The Mudheads* (Peepal Tree Press: Leeds, 1990).

**BEACHY, R.W.**

*The British West Indies Sugar Industry in the Late Nineteenth Century* (Oxford University Press: Oxford, 1957).

**BEATTY, Paul B.**

*A History of the Lutheran Church in Guyana* (Paul B. Beatty: Georgetown, 1970).

**BEAUMONT, Joseph**

*The New Slavery: An Account of the Indian and Chinese Immigrants in British Guiana* (W. Ridgeway: London, 1897).

**BECKETT, John B.**

*Savage Interlude: Quest for Gold in the Guyana Jungle* (Travel Book Club: London, 1968).

**BECKLES, Hilary McD.**

*Cricket Without a Cause: Fall and Rise of the Mighty Weet Indian Cricketers* (Ian Randle Publishers: Kingston, 2018).

*Nation Imagined: First West Indies Test Team: The 1928 Tour* (Ian Randle Publishers: Kingston, 2006).

*The First West Indian Cricket Tour, Canada, and the U.S. 1886* (Canoe Press: Kingston, 2007).

**_____.; and V. Shephard, eds.**

*Caribbean Freedom* (Ian Randle Publishers: Kingston, 1993).

*Caribbean Slavery in the Atlantic World* (Ian Randle Publishers: Kingston, 1997).

*Caribbean Slave Society and Economy* (New Press: New York: 1993).

*Freedom Won: Caribbean Emancipation, Ethnicities, and Nationhood* (Cambridge University Press: Cambridge, 2007).

**BEDESSEE, Lional Moona**

*A Dynasty Created; A Legacy Ensured* (L. M Bedessee: Toronto, 2017).

**BEDIAKO, Kzembe Olugbala**

*Leaves of Life: Vol. 1. Select Medicinal Plants of Guyana with Healing Properties* (Shepsentchaas: Amsterdam, 2011).

**BEEBE, C.W.**

*Edge of the Jungle* (Duell, Sloan and Pearce: New York, 1950).

*Jungle Peace* (Copp Clark: Toronto, 1919).

*Tropical Wildlife in British Guiana: Zoological Contributions from New York Zoological Society* (New York Zoological Society: New York, 1917).

**_____.; and Mary B. Beebe**
*Our Search for a Wilderness: An Account of Two Ornithological Expeditions to Venezuela and to British Guiana* (Constable & Co.: London, 1910).

**BEGUM, Jameela**
*Cyril Dabydeen: Writers of the Indian Diaspora* (University of Maharashtra: Jaipur, 2000).

**BEISNER, Robert L., ed.**
*America Foreign Relations Since 1600: A Guide to the Literature,* 2nd ed., 2 vols (CABC-CLIO: Santa Barbara, 2003).

**BELNAVIS, George**
*Criminal Practice and Procedure in the Magistrates Courts in the Commonwealth Caribbean* (Ian Randle Publishers: Kingston, 2009).

**BELLON, Brian A.**
*Black Routes: Legacy of African Diaspora* (Hansib Publications: Hertfordshire, 2008).

**BENJAMIN, Anna**
*Freedom of Expression and the Birth of Stabroek News* (Guyana Publications Inc.: Georgetown, 2008).

**BENJAMIN, J.**
*They Came in Ships: An Anthology of Indo-Guyanese Writing* (Peepal Tree Press: Leeds, 1998).

**BENN, Denis**
*The Caribbean: An Intellectual History 1774-2003* (Ian Randle Publishers: Kingston, 2004).

**BENN-IRELAND, Tessa**
*Profiles of Afro Caribbean Canadians in York Region* (C. Pryce Publishing: Markham, 2003).

**_____; co-authored**
*Some Black Women: Profiles of Black Women in Canada* (Sister Vision Press: Toronto, 1993).

**BENNETT, Audrey Roth** (daughter of Vincent Roth)
*A Snake in My Shoe* (Book Guild Publishing: Leicestershire, 2017).

**BENNETT, George W.**
*An Illustrated History of British Guiana, Compiled from Various Authorities* (Richardson: Georgetown, 1866).

**BENNETT, Rev. Canon John Peter**
*An Arawak-English Dictionary: With an English wordlist* (Walter Roth Museum of Anthropology: Georgetown, 1994).
*The Arawak Language in Guyanese Culture* (Govt. of Guyana: Georgetown, 1986).

*Twenty-eight Lessons in Loko (Arawak): A Teaching Guide* (Walter Roth Museum of Anthropology: Georgetown, 1995).

**_____; and Richard Hart**

*Kabelhechino – A Correspondence on Arawak* (Demerara Publishers Ltd: Georgetown, 1991).

**BENNETT, Michael, ed.**

*Vincent Roth: A Life in Guyana, Vol. 1: A Young Man's Journey 1889-1923* (Peepal Tree Press: Leeds, 2002).

**BENNETT, Wendell C.; and C. Osgood**

*Excavations in the Cuenca Region, Ecuador, British Guiana Archaeology to 1945* (Yale University Press: New Haven, 1946).

**BENNETTE, Louise**

*Anancy and Miss Lou* (Sangster Publishing: Kingston, 1979).

**BENRALI** (Pen name for Aman Waseem Ben Ali)

*When I found a Moon of Chai* (Dreamworlds Beyond Time Co.: Basseterre, 2012).

*Manni From a World Beyond Star* (Dreamworlds Beyond Time Co.: Basseterre, 2010).

*The Turtles Dream & Keys®* (Only1Earth, LLC: Carson, 2008).

*The Turtles Dream & Keys®: Gardens Without End* (Dreamworlds Beyond Time Co.: Basseterre, 2014).

**BENTHAM, Ivan**

*A Second Slice* (Ivan Bentham: Georgetown, 2005).

**BAKSH, Ahamad**

*The mobility of degree level graduates of the University of Guyana* (Department of Sociology, University of Guyana: Turkeyen, 1973).

**BENTT, Vincent M.**

*The selection of university education in Guyana* (University of Guyana: Turkeyen, 1979).

**BERESFORD, Vanrick**

*Crown—The Analysis of Life* (V. Beresford: Georgetown, 2018).

*Guyana in Prophecy* (V. Beresford: Georgetown, 2018).

*Heavenly Wisdom—Mighty Words* (V. Beresford: Georgetown, 2018).

*The Poor Man's Wisdom* (V. Beresford: Georgetown, 2019).

*The Revelation of Jesus The Christ* (V. Beresford: Georgetown, 2018).

*The Seven Pillars of the Church* (V. Beresford: Georgetown, 2018).

**BERETON, Bridget; and Winston Dookeran, eds.**

*East Indians in the Caribbean: Colonialism and the Struggle for Identity* (Kraus: New York, 1982).

**BERNARD, Deryck**

*A New Geography of Guyana* (Macmillan-Caribbean: London, 1999).

*Going Home and Other Tales from Guyana* (Macmillan-Caribbean: London, 2002).

*Guyana Junior Atlas* (Macmillan-Caribbean: London, 2004).

**BERNARD Désirée Patricia**

*Reflections and Opinions* (Hansib: Hertfordshire, 2018).

**BERNAU, Rev. John Henry**

*Missionary Labours in British Guiana: With remarks on the manners, customs, and superstitious rites of the aborigines* (John Farquhar Shaw: Southampton, 1847).

**BERRANGE, J.P.**

*The Geology of Southern Guyana, South America* (HMSO: London, 1977).

**BERRIAN, Brenda F.**

*Bibliography of Women Writers from the Caribbean 1832-1986* (Three Continents Press: Washington: Oxford, 1989).

**BERRY, Lames, ed.**

*News for Babylon: The Chatto Book of West Indian British Poetry* (Chatto & Windus: London, 1984).

**BESS Harriet Alexis**

*The Story of a Great Warrior* (Lulu.com: 2021).

**BHAGWAN, Moses**

*Ancestors of the River* (n.p.; n.p., n.d.).

*Sources of Conflict in British Guiana* (International Union of Students: Prague, 1963).

**BHAGWANDIN, B.**

*I Hear Guyana Cry* (Writers Club Press: Denver, 2003).

*Wild Flowers* (Writers Club Press: Denver, 2001).

**BHAGWANDIN, D.**

*Georgetown Spies – A True Life Account of Espionage in a South American Country (Guyana) Involving the Russians and Americans* (Inside Publisher: New York, 1995).

*From Cubana to Santrina – The Secret Trail of Bambi-Caribbean and Latin American Most Notorious Terrorist* (Inside Publisher: New York, 2009).

**BHAGWANDIN, Dianand Denny**

*My Incredible Journey* (Authorhouse: Bloomington, 2014).

**BHATTACHARYA, Rahul**

*The Sly Company of People Who Care* (Picador: Bolton, 2011).

**BIBBY, Zorina Ishmail**

*Once a Guyanese Child* (Upfront Publishing: Leicester, 2009).

**BICKERTON, D.**

*Dynamics of a Creole System* (Cambridge University Press: Cambridge, 1975).

**BILLINGSBY,**

*The Bear with a Crinkled Ear* (Hansib: Hertfordshire, 2008).

**BIRBALSINGH, Frank**

*From Pillar to Post: The Indo-Caribbean Diaspora* (TSAR: London, 1997).

*Guyana: History and Culture* (Hansib: Hertfordshire, 2016).

*Guyana and the Caribbean* (Dido Press: London, 2004).

*Indian-Caribbean Test Cricketers and the Quest for Identity* (Hansib: Hertfordshire, 2014).

*Neil Bissoondath: Indo-Caribbean-Canadian Diaspora* (Rawat Publications: Jaipur, 2005).

*Novels and the Nation: Essays in Canadian Literature* (TSAR: Toronto, 1995).

*Passion and Exile: Essays in Caribbean Literature* (Hansib: Hertfordshire, 1988).

*Test Cricketers and the Quest for Identity* (Hansib: Hertfordshire, 2014).

*The People's Progressive Party of Guyana 1950-1992: An Oral History* (Hansib: Hertfordshire, 2007).

*The Rise of West Indian Cricket: From Colony to Nation* (Hansib: Hertfordshire, 1996).

*West Indian History and Literature* (Hansib: Hertfordhsire, 2016).

**_____, ed.**

*Frontiers of Caribbean Literature in English* (St. Martin's Press: London, 1996).

*Indenture and Exile: The Indo-Caribbean Experience* (TSAR: Toronto, 1989).

*Indo-Caribbean Resistance* (TSAR: Toronto, 1993).

*Jahaji – An Anthology of Indo-Caribbean Literature* (TSAR: Toronto, 2000).

*Jahaji Bhai – An Anthology of Indo-Caribbean Literature* (TSAR: Toronto, 1989).

**_____; and Clem Seecharan**

*Indo-West Indian Cricketers* (Hansib: Hertfordshire, 1988).

**BIRDLIFE INTERNATIONAL**
*Field Checklist of Birds of Georgetown* (Birdlife International: Cambridge, 2005).

**BISHOP, Myrtle D.; Robert W. Davenport; and Kenneth S. Flamm**
*A Definitional Study of the Private Sector in the Guyanese Economy* (M. Bishop: Georgetown, 1982).

**BISNAUTH, D.A.**
*A Short History of the Guyana Presbyterian Church* (Guyana Presbyterian Church: Georgetown, 1979).
*History of Religions in the Caribbean* (Kingston Publishers: Jamaica, 1989).
*In So Many Words* (Sheik Hassan Productions: Georgetown, 2002).
*The Settlement of Indians in Guyana: 1890-1930* (Peepal Tree Press: Leeds, 2000).

**BISSOON, Mahadeo**
*Guyana – For the Taking or the Making* (In Words Inc.: Mississauga, 2016).

**BISSUNDYAL, Churaumanie**
*A River Dreams Red* (Xlibris: Bloomington, 2009).
*Glorianna* (C. Bissundyal: Georgetown, 1976).
*Labaria Puraan* (Paddy Sheaves Books: Georgetown, 1995).
*Lotus in the Mud* (C. Bissundyal: Georgetown, 1996).
*Modern Western Fiction and Sanskrit Aesthetics and Theory: A Search for a Postcolonial concept* (Xlibris: Bloomington, 2009).
*The Cleavage* (C. Bissundyal: Georgetown, 2003).
*The Drums of Kassaku* (C. Bissundyal: New York, 2002).
*The Dumb and the Brave* (Caribbean Press: Georgetown, 2013).
*The Game of Kassaku* (GEICA: New York, 2002).
*The Labaria Palm* (C. Bissundyal: Georgetown, 1999).
*The Players of Kassaku* (C. Bissundyal: New York, 2002).
*The Presence* (Rooponandan Singh: Georgetown, 1997).
*The Ritual* (Paddy Sheaves Books: New York, 2000).
*The Stream of Red Tears* (C. Bissundyal: Georgetown, 2002).
*Whom the Kiskadees Call* (Peepal Tree Press: Leeds, 1994).

**BLACK, George**
*The Good Neighbour: How the United States Wrote the History of Central America and the Caribbean* (Pantheon Books: New York, 1988).

**BLACKBURN, Julia**
*Charles Waterton, 1782-1865: Traveller and Conservationist* (Bodley Head: London, 1989).

**BLAKE, Emmett R.**

*Birds of the Acary Mountains of Southern British Guiana* (Chicago Natural History Museum: Chicago, 1950).

**BLAKE, Renee**

*The Routledge Companion to the work of John R. Rickford* (Routledge: London, 2022).

**BLENESSEQUI, Omartalle**

*Cleavage: A Poem on East Indian Immigration to British Guiana* (C. Bissundayal: Georgetown, 1986).

*Glorianne* (C. Bissundayal: Georgetown, 1976).

*Labaria Puraan* (Paddy Sheaves Books: Georgetown, 1995).

**BLESSED, Brian**

*Quest for the Lost World* (Boxtree: London, 1999).

**BLOOD, William**

*A Mission to the Indians of Orialla, South America: To which is added A Narrative of the destruction by fire of the Amazon: with reflections by one of the survivors* (Partridge and Oakey: London, 1853).

**BLOUET, Olwyn M.**

*The Contemporary Caribbean: History, Life, and Culture since 1945* (Reaktion Books: London, 2007).

**BLUEBIRD BOOKS**

*Kids Travel Journal: My Trip to Guyana* (Lulu.com: 2014).

**BLUM, William**

*The CIA: A Forgotten History: US Global Interventions Since World War 2* (Zed Books: London, 1986).

**BODDAM-WHETHAM, J.W.**

*Roraima and British Guiana: With a glance at Bermuda, The West Indies, and the Spanish Main* (Hurst and Blackett: London, 1879).

**BOGGAN, J.; et al**

*Checklist of the Plants of the Guianas: Guyana, Surinam, French Guiana* (Smithsonian National Museum of Natural History: Washington, D.C., 1992).

**BOLINGBROKE, Henry**

*A Voyage to the Demerary, containing a statistical account of the settlements there, and of those on the Essequebo, the Berbice, and other contiguous rivers of Guyana* (Richard Phillips: London, 1807).

**BOLLAND, Nigel O.**

*The Birth of Caribbean Civilisation: A Century of Ideas About Culture and Identity, Nation and Society* (Ian Randle Publishers: Kingston, 2004).

*The Politics of Labour in the British Caribbean: The Social Origins of Authoritarianism and Democracy in the Labour Movement* (Ian Randle Publishers: Kingston, 2011).

**BONE, Olga Irene**

*Our Children, Our Schools* (Olga Bone: Georgetown, n.d.).
*Essays on School Management* (Olga Bone: Georgetown, n.d.).
*Revision Manual: Basic Calculation* (Olga Bone: Georgetown, n.d.).

**BOODHOO, Surendra L.**

*Procedure for the Evaluation of Public Investment Projects: Special Features for Guyana* (Our Knowledge Publishing: Lancaster, 2020).

**BOOKAL, D.O.**

*What is Man* (Toucan Publishing: Toronto, 2004).

**BOOKER, K.M.; and D. Juraga, eds.**

*The Caribbean Novel in English* (Ian Randle Publishers: Kingston, 2001).

**BOOKER, Malika**

*Pepper Seed* (Peepal Tree Press: Leeds, 2013).

**BOSMAN, L**

*Nieuw Amsterdam in Berbice (Guyana): de planning en bouw van een koloniale stad, 1764-1800* (Verloren: Amsterdam, 1994).

**BOSTON, A.M.**

*Unlock the True Wealth: Your Life will Change* (AuthorHouse: Bloomington, 2008).

**BOURNE, R., ed.**

*Shridath Ramphal: The Commonwealth and the World: Essays in Honour of His 80th Birthday* (Hansib: Hertfordshire, 2008).

**BOUSQUET, Ben; and DOUGLAS, Colin**

*West Indian Women at War: British Racism in World War* (Lawrence & Wishart: London, 1991).

**BOWIE, Robert R.; and Richard H. Immerman**

*Waging Peace: How Eisenhower Shaped an Enduring Cold War Strategy* (Oxford University Press: New York, 1998).

**BOWMAN, Fred**

*Reorientation of African Beliefs: A Prime Necessity* (Carleton Press: New York, 1981).

**BOWRY, Stephanie**

*A Splendid Dozen* (Stephanie Bowry: New Amsterdam, 2000).
*Esteem* (Stephanie Bowry: Georgetown, 2008).
*True-True Stories – Vol. 1* (Stephanie Bowry: New Amsterdam, 2011).

**BRADLEY, Lloyd**

*Sounds Like London: 100 Years of Black Music in the Capital* (Serpent's Tail: London, 2013).

**BRAILEY, J.**

*The Ghosts of November: Memoirs of an outsider who witnessed the carnage at Jonestown, Guyana* (J and J Publishing: n.p., 1998).

**BRAITHWAITE, Barrington**

*An Illustrated History of Pork Knockers* (Entertainment Graphics; Georgetown, 2010).

*Drums of Freedom: Saga of the Haitian Revolution* (Amazon Books: 2021).

*The Adventures of Brer Anancy: Voyage to the New World* (Entertainment Graphics: Georgetown, 2007).

*The Mighty Itanami: The Lore & Legends of the Gold Rush Come Alive When Least You Expect* (Entertainment Graphics: Georgetown, 2008).

**BRAITHWAITE, E.R.**

*A Kind of Homecoming* (Prentice-Hall: Englewood Cliffs, 1962).

*Billingsly: The Bear with the Crinkled Ear* (Hansib Publications: Hertford, 2008).

*Choice of Straws* (Bodley Head: London, 1965).

*Honorary White* (McGraw-Hill: New York, 1975).

*Paid Servant* (McGraw Hill: New York, 1968).

*Reluctant Neighbours* (Bodley Head: London, 1972).

*To Sir With Love* (Bodley Head: London, 1959) [Made into a movie by the same name].

**BRAITHWAITE, Makeda**

*An Anthology of Shivers* (M. Braithwaite: Georgetown, 2022).

**BRAITHWAITE, P.A.**

*Folksongs of Guyana: Queh-Queh, Chanties and Ragtime* (PA Braithwaite: Georgetown, 1964).

**BRANDT, Godfrey**

*Trail of the Lost Jaguar* (Austin MacCauley Publishers: London, 2021)

**BRASSINGTON, F.E.**

*Poems* (Argosy: Georgetown, 1941).

**BRAVEBOY-WAGNER, Jacqueline**

*The Venezuela-Guyana Border Dispute: Britain's Colonial Legacy in Latin America* (Westview Press: Boulder,1984).

**BRAY, Warwick**

*The Gold of El Dorado* (Benson & Hedges: London, 1978).

**BRERETON, Bridget; and Winston Dookeran, eds.**
*East Indians in the Caribbean: Colonialism and the Struggle for Identity* (Kraus: New York, 1982).
**_____; and Kevin A Yelvington, eds.**
*The Colonial Caribbean in Transition: Essays on Post-Emancipation Social and Cultural History* (University Press of Florida: Miami, 1999).

**BRETT, Rev. William Henry**
*Indian Missions in Guiana* (George Bell: London, 1851).
*Indian Tribes of Guiana: Legends and Myths of the Aboriginal Peoples of British Guiana* (Bell and Daldy: London, 1868).
*Legends and Myths of the Aboriginal Peoples of British Guiana,* 2nd ed. (William, Wells Gardiner: London, 1880). Reprint. (Kessinger Publishing: London, 2003).
*Mission work among the Indian Tribes in the Forest of Guiana* (SPCK: London, 1868).
*The Indian Tribes of Guiana: Their Condition and Habits: With Researches Into Their Past History, Superstitions, Legends, Antiquities, Languages* (Bell and Daldy: London, 1868).

**BRIDGES, Fr. John**
*Men of Faith* (Jesuit Missions: London, 1990).
*Rupununi Mission: The Story of Fr. Cuthbert Cary-Elwes: 1910-19* (Jesuit Missions: London, 1986).
*The Good News on the Wild Coast: Highlights of the Early Efforts of the Catholic Church: 1650s to 1850s* (Jesuit Missions: London, 1997).

**BRIJPAUL, Jay**
*Wealth Through Real Estate Investing* (Middle Road Publishers Toronto, 2021).

**BRILL, Marlene T.**
*Guyana: Enchantment of the World Series* (Scholastic Library Publishing: New York, 1994).

**BRINTON, Daniel Garrison**
*The Arawack Language of Guiana in its Linguistic and Ethnological Relations* (McCalla and Stavely: Philadelphia, 1871).

**BROCK, Stanley E.**
*Hunting in the Wilderness* (Robert Hale Ltd.: London, 1972).
*Jungle Cowboy* (Taplinger Publishing Company: New York, 1972).
*Leemo: A True Story of a Man`s Friendship with a Mountain Lion* (Taplinger Publishing Company: New York, 1967).
*More About Leemo: The Adventures of a Pet Puma and Her Friends* (Taplinger Publishing Company: New York, 1967).

**BRONKHURST, H.V.P.**

*Among the Hindus and Creoles of British Guiana* (n.p.: London, 1888).

*A Descriptive and Historical Geography of British Guiana* (Argosy Press: Georgetown, 1890).

*The Colony of British Guiana and its Labouring Population* (n.p.: London, 1883).

**BROSCOME, James**

*Guyana: Land of Many Waters – Images of Guyana* (Blurb: London, 2012).

**BROTHERSTON, Gordon**

*Image of the New World: The American Continent Portrayed in Native Texts* (Thames & Hudson: London, 1979).

**BROWN, C.B.**

*Canoe and Camp Life in British Guiana* (Edward Stanford: London, 1876).

**_____.; and W. Lidstone**

*15000 miles on the Amazon and its tributaries* (Edward Stanford: London, 1878).

**BROWN, Edith**

*The Life Story of Andrew Benjamin Brown* (n.p.: Georgetown, 1924).

**BROWN, H.H.**

*The Fisheries of British Guiana* (n.p.: Bridgetown, 1943).

**BROWN, Stewart**

*All Are Involved: The Art of Martin Carter* (Peepal Tree Press: Leeds, 2000).

**_____; and John Wickham**

*The Oxford Book of Caribbean Short Stories* (Oxford University Press: Oxford, 2002).

*Voiceprint: An Anthology of Oral and Related Poetry From The Caribbean* (Longman: London, 1995).

**BROWNE, Murphy**

*Berbician Griot* (Murphy Browne: Toronto, 2014).

**BRUMMELL, Roy**

*Halfway Tree (*Brummell & Family: New York, 2012*).*

*Mama's Boys* (Amazon: 2019).

*Ol' Time School Days* (Amazon: 2018).

*Sudden Jolts* (Amazon: 2018).

*Mih Buddyboy Mac (My Brother Mac) - Wordsworth McAndrew* (Caribbean Press: Georgetown, 2014).

*World Renowned Legend of the Saw: Dr. Moses Emanuel Josiah (Amazon: 2021).*

**BRUNNER, M**

*Major Timber Trees of Guyana* (Wagwingen: Amsterdam, 1994).

**BRYANT, Joshua**

*Account of an Insurrection of the Negro Slaves in the Colony of Demerara* (Colonial Government: Georgetown, 1824) [First Illustrated Locally Printed Book}.

**BUDHAN-MILLS, Christine T**

*Leela's Guyanese Anglo-Indian Inspired Recipes* (Amazon: Bolton, 2020).

**BUDHOS, M.T.**

*Ask Me No Questions* (Simon & Schuster: New York, 2006).

*Father's Tales* (Paradigm Press: Providence, 1989).

*Genesis and Other Stories* (Brown University: Providence, 1987).

*House of Waiting* (Global City Press: New York, 1995).

*Professor of Light* (G.P. Putnam: New York, 1999).

*Sugar Changed The World: A Story of Magic, Spice, Slavery, Freedom, and Science* (Clarion Press: Boston, 2010).

*The Professor of Light* (G.P. Putnam's and Sons: New York, 1999).

*Watched* (Random House: London, 2016).

**BUDHRAM, Angel**

*A Guyanese Alphabet: 26 Iconic Guyanese People To Know* (Bookbaby: New York, 2020).

**BULKAN, Arif; and Alissa TROTZ**

*The Survival of Indigenous Rights in Guyana. Transition* (University of Guyana: Turkeyen, 2014).

*Unmasking the State: Politics, Society and Economy in Guyana, 1992-2015* (Ian Randle Publishers: Kingston: 2019).

**BURN, W.L.**

*Emancipation and Apprenticeship in the British West Indies* (Jonathan Cape: London, 1937).

**BURNETT, D. Graham**

*Masters of all they surveyed: Exploration, Geography, and a British El Dorado* (University of Chicago Press: Chicago, 2000).

**BURNETT, Paula, ed.**

*The Penguin Book of Caribbean Verse in English* (Penguin: Harmondsworth, 1986).

**BURNHAM, L.F.S.**

*A Destiny To Mould: Selected Discourses by the Prime Minister of Guyana,* comps. C. A. Nascimento and R. A. Burrowes (Longman Caribbean: London, 1970).

*A Great Future Together* (Government Printery: Georgetown, 1968).

*Declaration of Sophia (*Peoples National Congress: Georgetown, 1974).

*Our Achievements in Perspective* (Peoples National Congress: Georgetown, 1976).

*Road to Socialism* (Peoples National Congress: Georgetown, 1975).

*Tribute to Dr. Martin Luther King, Jnr.* (Government of Guyana: Georgetown, 1968).

**BURNS, Sir Alan**

*History of the British West Indies* (Allen and Unwin: London, 1966).

**BURROWES, H.S.**

*Fifty Years of Flying* (Guiana Graphic: Georgetown, 1963).

**BURROWES, Reynold A.**

*I Never Said Goodbye* (Hansib: London, 2016).

*The Wild Coast: An Account of Politics in Guyana* (Schenkman Publishing Co. Inc.: Cambridge, 1984).

**BUTISINGH, R.**

*Love's Light* (R. Butisingh: Georgetown, 1972).

*Wild Flowers and Other Poems* (R. Butisingh: Georgetown, 1977).

**BUTT-COLSON, Dr. Audrey**

*Fr Cary-Elwes S.J. and the Alleluia Indians* (University of Guyana: Georgetown, 1998).

**_____; and Cesáreo de Armellada**

*El Origen Amerindio de la Etiologia de Enfermedades y su Tratamiento en la América Latina* (Universidad Católica Andrés Bello: Caracas, 1985). [A book written in Spanish on Amerindians].

# C

**CAIN, S.**

*Setting the Field for Your Financial Victory: Simple but Magical Ways of Cashing in on the World Cup Cricket Tournament in the Caribbean* (AuthorHouse: Bloomington, 2007).

**CALDWIN, J.**

*Let's Visit Guyana* (Macmillan: London, 1988).

**CAMBRIDGE, Joan**

*Clarise Cumberbatch wants to go home* (The Woman's Press: London, 1988).

**CAMBRIDGE, Vibert C.**

*Excuse Me! May I Offer Some Interpretations - A Collection of Poetry* (Wacacro Press: 1975).

*Musical Life in Guyana: History and Politics of Controlling Creativity* (University Press of Mississippi: Jackson, 2016).

*Immigration, Diversity and Broadcasting in the United States, 1990-2001 (Global & Comparative Studies* (Ohio University Press: Athens, 2004).

*Valerie Muriel Rodway, CCH, LRSM (1919-1970)* (Government of Guyana: Georgetown, 2018).

*Writings on Guyanese Music 2003-2004: Black Praxis: Special Edition* (Ohio University: Athens, 2004).

**_____; J.P. Jeter; K.R. Ramphal; and C.B. Pratt**

*Internationa Afro Mass Media: A Reference Guide* (ABC:CLIO, LLC: Santa Barbara, 1996).

**CAMERON, McR, J.**

*The Berbice Slave Uprising 1763* (Dido Press: London, 2007).

**CAMERON, Norman E.**

*150 Years of Education in Guyana With Special Reference to Post-Primary Education: 1808-1957* (n.p.: Georgetown, 1971).

*A Historical Survey of Christ Church* (n.p.: Georgetown, 1968).

*A History of the Queen's College of British Guiana* (n.p.: Georgetown, 1951). Reprint (Queen's College Association of Toronto: Toronto, 2009).

*Adoniya* (n.p.: Georgetown, 1943).

*Adventures in the Field of Culture* (Daily Chronicle: Georgetown, 1971).

*African Saga in Drama* (n.p.: Georgetown, n.d.).

*Algebra Revision* (n.p.: Georgetown, 1942).
*An Introduction to our Social Philosophy* (n.p.: Georgetown, 1963).
*Balthasar* (n.p.: Georgetown, 1931).
*Clearing the Political Air* (n.p.: Georgetown, 1963).
*Communism and British Guiana* (n.p.: Georgetown, 1964).
*Ebedmelech* (n.p.: Georgetown, 1952).
*Geometry Revision* (n.p.: Georgetown, 1944).
*Gilchrist Scholarships in the Caribbean* (n.p.: Georhgetown, 1963).
*Guianese Poetry* (n.p.: Georgetown, 1931). Reprint. (Kraus: Liechtenstein, 1970).
*Guide To The Published Works of a Guyanese Author and Playwright* (n.p.: Georgetown, 1966).
*Guyanese Library and Its Impact* (n.p.: Georgetown, 1971).
*Interlude: Original Poems* (Argosy: Georgetown, 1944).
*Jamaica Joe* (n.p.: Georgetown, 1946).
*Kayssa or Hear the Other Side* (n.p.: Georgetown, 1959).
*Price of Victory - 1960-61* (n.p.: Georgetown, 1965).
*Statics and Dynamics* (n.p.: Georgetown, 1942).
*The Evolution of the Negro,* Vol. 1 (n.p: Georgetown, 1929).
*The Evolution of the Negro,* Vol. 2 (n.p.: Georgetown, 1934).
*The Trumpet* (n.p.: Georgetown, 1968).
*Thoughts of Life and Literature* (n.p.: Georgetown, 1950).
*Thoughts on a Co-operative State* (n.p.: Georgetown, 1970).
*Thoughts on the Making of a New Nation* (n.p.: Georgetown, 1959).
*Three Immortals: Featuring Sabaco* (n.p.: Giorgetown, 1953).
*Trigonometry* (n.p,: n.p., 1942).
*Worrying Features in Our Politics* (n.p.: Georgetown, 1964).

**CAMERON, Pat**

*This is My Song* (Pat Cameron: New York, 2000).

**CAMERON, W., ed.**

*Guianese Poetry* (n.p.: Georgetown, 1931).

**CAMPBELL, David**

[Son of Stephen Campbell, who in 1957 became the first Amerindian to be elected to the Guyana Parliament. David is a self-taught and internationally acclaimed singer/song-writer, poet, painter, writer, and guitarist].

*A Caribbean Dozen* (Walker Books: n.p., n.d.).
*Between Songs* (Autonomy Press: Vancouver, 1992).
*Canada in us now* (NC Ltd: Toronto, n.d.).
*Covering Columbus* (Panrun Collective: n.p., n.d.).
*Search* (Galliard: n.p., n.d.).

*Through Arawak Eyes* (Develop Education Centre: Toronto, n.d.).

**CAMPBELL, Horace**

*Rasta and Resistance: From Marcus Garvey to Walter Rodney* (Africa World Press: Trenton, 1987).

**CAMPBELL, Ingrid Walter**

*HerSTory: A Magnificent Tale* (Zeruch Productions Inc.: New York, 2007).

**CAMPBELL, J.**

*5 and One-act Plays: For amateur performing groups* (J. Campbell: Georgetown, 1972).

*Our Own Poems* (J. Campbell: Georgetown, 1973).

*Poems For All* (Master Printery: Georgetown, 1971).

*Poems To Remember* (S.M. Sadeek: Georgetown, 1968).

*Sugar Cane: Hackia Sticks and Bullets: Resistance to the Plantation System* (J. Campbell: Georgetown, 1986).

**CAMPBELL, Lorna Ifill**

*Buxton Uprising* (n.p.: n.p., 2004).

**CANACHO-GINGERICH, Alina, ed.**

*Coping in America: The Case of Caribbean East Indians* (GEICA: New York, 2002).

**CANDLIN, Kit**

*The Last Caribbean Frontier, 1795-1815* (Palgrave-Macmillan: London, 2012).

**CAREW, Jan Rynveld**

*A Touch of Midas* (Coward-McCann: New York, 1958).

*Black Midas* (Secker & Warburg: London, 1958).

*Computer Killer* (Thomas Nelson Limited: London, 2007).

*Dark Night, Deep Water* (Longman Group: London, 2008).

*Dead Man's Creek: Two Stories* (Longman Group: London, 2008).

*Death Comes to the Circus* (Thomas Nelson: London, 2007).

*Don't Go Near the Water: Three Stories* (Longman Group: London, 2008).

*Eyam: Plague Village* (Thomas Nelson: London, 2008).

*Flowers of the Forest* (Pegasus: London, 2008).

*Footprints in the Sand* (Thomas Nelson: London, 2008).

*Fulcrums of Change: Origins of Racism in the Americas and Other Essays* (Africa World Press: Toronto, 1988).

*Green for Danger* (Harcourt Education: London, 2008).

*Green Winter* (Stein and Day: New York, 1964).

*Grenada: The Hour Will Strike Again* (International Organization of Journalists: Prague, 1985).

*High Impact Set B Plays: Green for Danger* (Heinemann (London, 2001).
*House of Fear: Two Stories* (Longman Group: London, 2007).
*Moscow is not my Mecca* (Secker & Warburg: London, 1964).
*No Entry* (Thomas Nelson: London, 2007).
*Potaro Dreams* (Hansib Publications: Hertford, 2014).
*Poulbot of Montmartre: Artist and Philanthropist* (Sterling Press: London, 2008).
*Rape of Paradise: Columbus and the Birth of Racism in America* (Seaburn Publishing Group: New York, 2006).
*Rape the Sun* (Third Press: New York, 1973).
*Return to Streets of Eternity* (Smokestack Books: London, 2015).
*Save the Last Dance for Me* (Prentice Hall: New York, 1976).
*Schooner* (Macmillan Caribbean: London, 2008).
*Shadow in the Glen: A Short Adventure Play* (SchoolPlay Productions Limited: London, 2007).
*Stranger than Tomorrow* (Longmans: London, 1979).
*The Cat People* (Longman Group: London, 2007).
*The Coming of Amalivaca* (Guyana Book Foundation: Georgetown, 1998).
*The Guyanese Wanderer* (Sarabande Books, Inc.: Louisville, 2007).
*The Last Barbarian* (Secker & Warburg: London, 1961).
*The Lost Love and Other Stories* (Longman: London, 2008).
*The Man Who Came Back* (Longman Group: London, 2008).
*The Riverman* (Seaburn Publishing: New York, 2015).
*The Sisters and Manco's Stories* (Macmillan-Caribbean: London, 2002).
*The Third Gift* (Little Brown & Co.: New York, 1974).
*The Wild Coast* (Secker & Warburg: London, 1958).
*Three Short Stories* (SchoolPlay Productions Limited: London, 2007).
*Timeloop* (Thomas Nelson: London, 2007).
*Voices in the Dark* (Thomas Nelson: London, 2008).
*Winter in Moscow* (Avon Books: New York, 1964).

**_____; Deo Dillon; and Diane Dillon, ills.**

*The Third Gift* (Little Brown & Co: Boston, 1974).
*Children of the Sun* (Little Brown & Co: Boston, 1980).

**_____; and C. Lusane**

*Black America: The Street and the Campus* (Institute of Race Relations: London, 2001).

**_____; and Malcolm X**

*Ghosts in Our Blood: With Malcolm X in Africa, England, and the Caribbean* (Lawrence Hill & Co.: Chicago, 1994). [Also published in German].

**_____; and Peter Gibson**

*Lost Love and Other Stories* (Pearson Education Limited: London, 2007).

**_____; et al**

*Fiery Spirits: A Collection of Short Fiction and Poetry by Canadian Writers of African Descent* (HarperPerennial: Toronto, 1994).

*West Indian Stories* (Faber & Faber: London, 1968).

**_____; Foreign Language Publications**

*Black Midas* [Georgian edition] (n.p.: Moscow, 1966).

*Children of the Sun* [Japanese Edition] (Hopy Shoppan Publishers: Tokyo, 1981).

*Geister in unserem Blut* [German edition of *Ghosts in Our Blood*] (Atlantik Verlags: Bremen, 1997).

*Invierno Verde* [Portuguese edition of *Green Winter*] (Distribuidora Record: Rio de Janeiro, 1971).

*Midas Negro* [Spanish edition of *Black Midas*] (Casa de Las Americas: Havana, 1983).

*Moskau ist nicht mein Mekka* [German edition of *Moscow is not my Mecca*] (List Verlag: Munchen, 1965).

*O Midas Negro* [Portuguese edition of *Black Midas*] (Editora Ulisseia: Lisboa, 1961).

*Prikosnoveniya Midasa* [Russian edition of *Black Midas*] (Gosudarstvenoye Isdatelstvo "Hudodjestvenoy Literaturi:" (Moskva, 1963).

*Schwartzer Midas* [German Edition of *Black Midas*] (List Verlag: Munchen, 1959).

*The Third Gift* [Japanese Edition] (Hopy Shoppan Publishers: Tokyo, 1985).

*Wilde Kuste* [German edition of *Wild Coast*] (List Verlag: Munchen, 1961).

**CAREW, Joy G.; and Jan Carew**

*Episodes of My Life: The Autobiography of Jan Carew* (Peepal Tree Press: Leeds, 2015).

**_____; and Hazel Waters**

*The Gentle Revolutionary: Essays in Honour of Jan Carew* (Institute of Race Relations: London, 2002).

**CARIBBEAN ASSOCIATION OF HOME ECONOMISTS**

*An Adventure in Caribbean Cuisine* (Macmillan-Caribbean: London, 2006).

**CARIBBEAN COMMON MARKET (CARICOM)**

*Caricom: Our Caribbean Community: An Introduction* (Caricom Secretariat: Georgetown, 2005).

*The Caribbean Trade and Investment Report* (Caricom Secretariat: Georgetown, 2001).

**CARMYN, L.**

*Guyana* (Marshall Cavendish Corp: 2000).

**CARNEGIE, Jeniphier R.**

*Critics on West Indian Literature: A Selected Bibliography* (UWI Press: Mona, 1979).

**CARNEGIE SCHOOL of HOME ECONOMICS**

*What's Cooking in Guyana* (Carnegie School of Home Economics: Georgetown, 2004).

*Taste of Carifesta: Recipes of the Caribbean, Latin and South America* (Carnegie School of Home Economics: Georgetown, 2008).

**CARPENTER and BALOW**

*Guyana; Enchantment of South America* (Children's Press: Chicago, 1970).

**CARR, E.A.; et al, eds.**

*Caribbean Anthology of Short Stories* (Pioneer Press: Kingston, 1953).

**CARR, Matthew**

*My Father's House* (Hamish Hamilton: London, 1988).

[Biography of the late Bill Carr, a one-time well known political and cultural personality in Guyana].

**CARTER, E.H.; et al**

*History of the West Indian Peoples*. Books I-IV. (Nelson: London, 1964).

**CARTER, Martin**

*Conversations* (Martin Carter: Georgetown, 1961).

*Jail Me Quickly* (Martin Carter: Georgetown, 1963).

*Poems of Affinity: 1978-80* (Release Publishers: Guyana, 1980).

*Poems of Resistance* (University of Guyana: Turkeyen, 1964).

*Poems of Resistance from British Guiana* (Lawrence and Wishart: London, 1954).

*Poems of Resistance from Guyana* (Release Publishers: Georgetown, 1979).

*Poems of Shape and Motion* (Martin Carter: Georgetown, 1955).

*Poems of Succession* (New Beacon: London, 1978).

*Poesias Escogidas* (Peepal Tree Press: Leeds, 1999).
*Selected Poems* (Demerara Publishers: Georgetown, 1989).
*Selected Poems* (Red Thread Press: Georgetown, 1997).
*The Hidden Man: Other Poems of Prison* (n.p.: Georgetown, 1953).
*The Hill of Fire Glows Red* (Master Printer: Georgetown, 1951).
*The Kind Eagle: Poems of Prison* (Martin Carter: Georgetown, 1952).
*To A Dead Slave* (Martin Carter: Georgetown, 1951).
*University of Hunger: Collected Poems and Selected Prose* (Bloodaxe Books: London, 2006).

**CARTER, Trevor**

*Shattering Illusions: West Indians in British Politics* (Lawrence & Wishart: London, 1986).

**CARTWRIGHT, Joshua Abraham-Paul**

*The Granny JJ Adventures: Guyana's Daily Detective. Vol.1* (Createspace: New York, 2017).

**CASE, Faye**

*Akawaio Basketry Techniques* (National Trust of Guyana: Georgetown, 2008).

**CASE, H.W.**

*On sea and land on creek and river. Being an account of experiences in the visitation of assembles of Christians in the West Indies and British Guiana: with reminiscences of pioneer missionaries and of the slave trade formerly carried on from Bristol* (Morgan and Scott: London, 1910).

**CASTELLO, Cedric**

*Rasta Lyrics* (Caribbean Press: Georgetown, 2013).

**CASTELLO, Michael E.**

*Cloud Warriors: A Pre-Historic Saga of the Warraus or the Alpha-Warraus Story* (M.E. Castello: Georgetown, 2019).
*Devildoer: Contemporary Stories Based on Real Life Incidents in the North West Region* (M.E. Castello: Georgetown, 2018).
*Riptide: A Cosmopolitan Short Story Collection* (M.E. Castello: Georgetown, 2017).
*Robberroadsters or Down Rubber Road* (M.E. Castello: Georgetown, 2019).
*ShadowWalkers: A Collection of Indigenous Short Stories from the North West Region of Guyana* (M.E. Castello: Georgetown, 2018) [A book written in tribute to the late Dr. Desrey Fox (1956-2009), an outstanding Amerindian academic who was a Minister within the Ministry of Education under the PPP/C Government].
*Twice Upon a Time* (M.E. Castello: Georgetown, 2019).

*Twice Upon 2* (A Sequel to the above) (M.E. Castello: Georgetown, 2018).

**CATEAU, H.; and R. Pemberton**

*Beyond Tradition* (Ian Randle Publishers: Kingston, 2006).

**CECIL, Gideon, S.**

*Songs of My Soul* (B&H Printers: Georgetown, 2002).

*The Revelation of Love* (Outskirts Press: Denver, 2009).

*Twenty-Five Poems of Guyanese Children* (Caribbean Press: Georgetown, 2014).

**CHAITRAM, Samantha S.S.**

*American Foreign Policy in the English-Speaking Caribbean* (Springer International Publishing: London, 2020).

**CHAMBERLAIN, David**

*Smith of Demerara: Martyr: Teacher of the Slaves* (London Missionary Society: London, 1924).

**CHAN, Brian**

*Expression* (n.p.: n.p., n.d.).

*Fabula Rosa* (Peepal Tree Press: Leeds, 1994).

*The Gift of Scream* (Peepal Tree Press: Leeds, 2006).

*Thief with Leaves* (Peepal Tree Press: Leeds, 1988).

**CHAND, Karan**

*A Will to Survive: Jim Jones' Justice and Other Short Stories* (Karan Chand: Belize City, 2012).

*From Bengal to Bush Lot to Belize: The Indentured Servants* (Karan Chand: Belize City, 2012).

*I Had a Dream: An Anthology of Poems* (Createspace: New York, 2014).

**CHANDERBALI, D.**

*A Patriot of Paternalism: Governor Henry Light of British Guiana 1838-1848* (Guyana National Service: Georgetown, 1994).

*Indian Indenture in the Strait Settlements: The Politics of Policy and Practice in the Strait Settlements* (Peepal Tree Press: Leeds, 2008).

*Kayman Sankar: The Ultimate Rice Magnate* (Kayman Sankar and Co.: Georgetown, n.d.).

**CHAPMAN, Walker**

*The Golden Dream: Seekers of El Dorado* (Bobbs-Merril: New York, 1967).

**CHARLES, B.**

*Our Dilemma* (B. Charles: Georgetown, 1972).

*The Alexin of Our Cure* (B. Charles: Georgetown, 1970).

**CHARLES, Kerwin K.; et al**

*Safeguarding Consumers Through Minimum Quality Standards: Milk Inspection and Urban Mortality* (National Bureau of Economic Research: Washington, D.C.: 2022).

**CHASE, Ashton**

*133 Days Towards Freedom in British Guiana* (People's Progressive Party: Georgetown, 1953).

*A History of Trade Unionism in Guyana 1900-1961* (New Guyana Co., Ltd.: Georgetown, 1964). Reprint. (Sheik Hassan Productions: Georgetown, 2006).

*Arise Africa* (Hansib Publications: Hertfordshire, 2007).

*Guyana: A Nation in Transit - Burnham's Role* (Ashton Chase: Georgetown, 1994).

*The Law of Workmen's Compensation* (Ashton Chase: Georgetown, 1954).

**CHASE, Audrey**

*The National Association of Agricultural, Commercial, and Industrial Employees: A History* (NAACIE: Georgetown, 1971).

**CHAUDHAHRY, Roop; and H.N. Rodney**

*Contract of Service and the Worker in a Caribbean Jurisdiction. With Special Reference to Guyana* (n.p.; n.p., n.d.).

**CHECKLAND, S.G.**

*The Gladstones: A Family Biography* (Cambridge University Press: Cambridge, 1971).

**CHEEKS, Patrick Noel**

*Heartsongs* (PN Cheeks: Georgetown, 2005).

*Progressively Through the Reservoir of God: The Evolution of Consciousness* (PN Cheeks: Georgetown, 2004).

**CHERNICK, Sidney E.**

*The Commonwealth Caribbean: The Integration Experience* (Johns Hopkins University Press: Baltimore, 1978).

**CHIDESTER, David**

*Salvation and Suicide - An interpretation of Jim Jones, the Peoples Temple, and Jonestown* (Indiana University Press: Indianapolis, 1988).

**CHIN, Godfrey**

*Nostalgias: Golden Memories of Guyana 1940 to 1980* (CKP Publishing: Miami, 2007).

**CHINAPEN, J.W.**

*Albion Wilds* (British Guiana Lithographic Co.: Georgetown, 1961).

**CHINAPEN, Joel**
*My Faith Looks Up to Thee* (Xulon Press: Bloomington, 2007).

**CHINAPEN, Karma**
*JW Chinapen, Educator and Poet* (Outskirts Press: Denver, 2009).

**CHOWTHI, B.N.**
*Enough is Enough: A Woman's Struggle with Abuse* (AuthorHouse: Bloomington, 2004).

**CHOY, T.; and M. Scott**
"Managerial Autonomy, Political Control, and the New Public Management: The Quest for a Corporate Culture at the Guyana Revenue Authority's Customs and Trade Administration" in *Rethinking the Reform Question* (Cambridge Scholars Publications: London, 2007).

**CHRISTIANI, Joan**
*A.J. Seymour: A Bibliography* (National Library: Georgetown: 1974).

**CHRISTIE, C.D**
*Autobiography – My Life* (C.D. Christie: Ottawa, 2000).

**CHUBB, Charles**
*The Birds of British Guiana, based on the collection of Frederick Vavasour McConnell.* 2 vols. (n.p.: London, 1921).

**CHUNASAMY, M.S.**
*MRI Guide for Technologists: A Step-by-Step Approach* (AuthorHouse: Bloomington, 2005).

**CIDR (Centro de Informação Diocesa de Roraima)**
*Indios de Roraima: Makuxi, Ingariko, Taurepang, Wapixana* (CIDR: Roraima, Brazil, 1999).
[A book in Portuguese that contains some historical and anthropological information of the Wapishanas, Makushis, and Arekunas of Guyana].

**CITIZEN'S COMMITTEE**
*Referendum: A Question of Human Rights* (Cedar Press: Bridgetown, 1978).

**CLAPP, Henry**
*With Raleigh to British Guiana* (Frederick Muller: London, 1965).

**CLARKE, Hazel**
*The Poem Book* (Xulon Press: Irving, 2011).

**CLARKE, H.D.; et al**
*Plant Diversity of the Iwokrama Forest Guyana* (University of Texas: Forth Worth, 2001).

**CLEARE, Laurence Delaney**

*British Guiana Nature Study Manual Book 1 – Birds* (The Argosy: Georgetown, 1940).

**CLEMENTI, Mrs. C.**

*Through British Guiana to the Summit of Roraima* (Dutton & Co: New York, 1916).

**CLEMENTI, Sir Cecil**

*A Constitutional History of British Guiana* (Macmillan: London, 1937).

*The Chinese in British Guiana* (Georgetown: Guyana, 1915).

**COCHRANE, Sharlene Voogd; M.A. Jones; and C. Koverola**

*Promoting Community Mental Health in Guyana: A Resource Guide for Practitioners* (Lul.com: 2017).

**COGGINS, Clarence**

*Auntie I Don't Want You To Get Married* (Clarence Coggins: New York, 2020).

*Six Magic Cans of Happiness: Danielle The Girl from New York* (Clarence Coggins: New York, 2021).

**COHEN, Stuart Bertie A**

*Women in the Caribbean: A Bibliography* (Royal Institute of Anthropology: London, 1979).

**COLCHESTER, M.**

*Forests for Sale: Guyana's Natural Resources, Going, Going, Goneé?* (World Rainforest Movement: London, 1992).

*Guyana: Fragile Frontier* (Latin American Bureau: London, 1997).

**COLLINS, Aubrey**

*The Achievements of Stephen Campbell* (The United Force: Georgetown, 1995).

**COLLINS-GONSALVES, Joanne**

*From Ashes to Ferro-Concrete: A History of the Immaculate Conception 1914-2014* (Guyana Heritage Society: Georgetown, 2014).

**_____; contr.**

*Dictionary of Caribbean and Afro-Latin American Biography* (Oxford University Press: Oxford, 2016).

**COMACHO-GIGERICH, Alina, ed.**

*Coping in America: The Case of Caribbean East Indians* (Guyana East Indians Civic Organization: New York, 2000).

**COMMISSIONG, Elaine**

*The Practice of Public Relations: A Caribbean Perspective* (Ian Randle Publishers: Kingston, 1998).

**COMMONWEALTH ADVISORY GROUP**
*Guyana: Economic Recovery and Beyond* (CAG: London, 1989).

**COMPTON, Jacques**
*The West Indians: Portrait of a People* (Hansib Publications: Hertfordshire, 2007).

**CONDE, Mary; and Thorunn Lonsdale**
*Caribbean Women Writers: Fiction in English* (Macmillan: London, 1999).

**CONNOLLY, Steve**
*Children of Watooka: A Story of British Guiana* (Hansib Publications: Hertfordshire, 2016).
*Journey Back to Watooka* (Friesen Press: Altona, 2016).

**CONSERVATION INTERNATIONAL**
*Biodiversity Assessment of the Eastern Kanuku Mountains, Lower Kwitaro River, Guyana* (Conservation International: Washington, D.C., 2002).

**CORBET, Marion**
*Naked Soul* (AuthorHouse: Bloomington, 2008).

**CORNETTE, Lennox W**
*The Development of Telecommunications in Guyana, Vol. 1 (1884-1994)* (F & H Printing Est., Georgetown, 2015).

**CORRIE, DAMON**
*Amazonia's Mythical and Legendary Creatures in the Eagle Clan Lokono-Arawak Oral Tradition of Guyana* (Damon Corrie: New York, 2019.
*Lokono-Arawaks* (Damon Corrie: New York, 2020).
*Understanding Spirituality, Dreams, Insights, Exorcisms, Visitations, and Shaman Healing* (Damon Corrie: New York, 2019).

**CORSBIE, Ken**
*Theatre in the Caribbean* (Longman: London, 1983).

**COSBERT, R.C.**
*Sex in the Scriptures of all places: Of course! Where else!* (Rivercross Publishing: Orlando, 1990).

**COSBERT, W.F.**
*Economics of Labour: Introduction to Wage Bargaining* (Honeywell & Todd: New York, 1989).

**COSTA, Emilia Viotti da**
*Crowns of Glory, Tears of Blood: The Demerara Slave Rebellion of 1823* (Oxford University Press: New York, 1994).

**COTT, E.B.**

*Destination – Green Hell: Davis Indians* (Review and Herald Publishing Association: Hagerstown, 1972).

*Jewels from Green Hell* (Review and Herald Publishing Association: Hagerstown, 1969).

**COUDREAU, H.**

*Voyage á Travers les Guyanes et l'Amazonie* (n.p.: Paris, 1887).

**COWELL, Noel; and Clement Branche**

*Human Resource Development and Workplace Governance in the Caribbean* (Ian Randle Publishers: Kingston, 2002).

**CRAIG, Deloris**

*Labba and Creek Water: Stories from the Caribbean* (Nelson Thornes Ltd.: Cheltenham, 2004).

**CRAHEN, M.E.; and F.W. Knight, eds.**

*Africa and the Caribbean: The Legacies of a Link* (Johns Hopkins University Press: Baltimore, 1980).

**CRANE, Alfred Victor**

*Law of Compulsory Motor Vehicle Insurance* (Guyana Printers Ltd.: Georgetown, 1975).

*Law of Workmen's Compensation* (The Argosy: Georgetown, 1943).

*Law of Unlawful Possession* (The Argosy: Georgetown, 1921).

*Manual Rating in Georgetown* (Guyana Printers Ltd.: Georgetown, 1976).

**CRANMORE, F.**

*The West Indies* (n.p.: n.p., n.d.).

**CRATON, Michael**

*Testing the Chains: Resistance to Slavery in the British West Indies* (Cornell University: New York, 2009).

**CREIGHTON, Al, ed.**

*Origins and Development of Mashramani* (Ministry of Culture, Youth, and Sport: Georgetown, 2012).

*The Pressures of Text* (Centre for West African Studies: Birmingham, 1996).

*Two Anthologies of Guyanese Plays* (Caribbean Press: Georgetown, 2013).

**CRESSAL, N.**

*From the Caribbean to England in Verse* (Ilfracombe: Devon, 1970).

**CROOKALL, Rev. Lawrence**

*British Guiana: Or Work and Wanderings among the Creoles and Coolies, the Africans and Indians of the Wild Country* (T. Fisher Unwin: London, 1898).

**CROSS, M.**

*The East Indians of Guyana and Trinidad* (Cultural Survival Press: Cambridge, 1980).

**_____; and Gad Heuman, eds.**

*Labour in the Caribbean: From Emancipation to Independence* (Macmillan: London, 1988).

**CRUICKSHANK, James Graham**

*Black Talk* (J.G. Cruickshank: Georgetown, 1916).

*Negro Humour* (J.G. Cruickshank: Georgetown, 1905).

*Pages from the History of the Scottish Kirk in British Guiana* (J.G. Cruickshank: Georgetown, 1921).

*Scenes From The History of the Africans in Guyana* (Free Press: Georgetown, 1999).

**CUDJOE, Selwyn Reginald**

*Caribbean Visionary – ARF Webber and the Making of Guyana* (University Press of Mississippi: Jackson, 2008).

*Caribbean Women Writers: Essays from the First International Conference* (Calaloux Publications: Wellesley, 1990).

*History, Fable and Myth in the Caribbean and Guianas* (Calaloux Publications.: Amherst, 1995).

*Pages from the History of the Scottish Kirk in British Guiana* (n.p.: Georgetown, 1930).

*Those That be in Bondage* (Calaloux Publications: Amherst, 2000).

**CUMBER, Dance Daryl**

*Conversations with Contemporary West Indian Writers* (Peepal Tree Press: Leeds, 1992).

**CUMMINGS, L.**

*Geography of Guyana* (Collins: London, 1976).

**CUMPTON, I.M.**

*Indians Overseas in British Territories 1834-1854* (Dawsons: London, 1969).

**CUNDALL, F.**

*Bibliography of the West Indies Excluding Jamaica* (The Institute of Jamaica: Kingston, 1909).

*Political and Social Disturbances in the West Indies: A Brief Account and Bibliography* (n.p.: Kingston, 1906).

**CUTRIGHT, P.R.**

*The Great Naturalists Explore South America* (Macmillan: New York, 1943).

**CUTTERIDGE, J.O.**

*Geography of the West Indies and Adjacent Lands* (Thomas Nelson: London, 1955).

**_____., ed.**

*Nelson's West Indian Readers Book 1* (Thomas Nelson: London, 1928).

*Nelson's West Indian Readers Book 2* (Thomas Nelson: London, 1928).

*Nelson's West Indian Readers Book 3* (Thomas Nelson: London, 1928).

*Nelson's West Indian Readers Book 4* (Thomas Nelson: London, 1928).

*Nelson's West Indian Readers Book 5* (Thomas Nelson: London, 1928).

*Nelson's West Indian Readers Book 6* (Thomas Nelson: London, 1928).

# D

**D'AGUIAR, Fred**

*Bethany Bettany* (Chatto and Windus: London, 2005).
*Bloodlines* (Chatto and Windus: London, 2000).
*British Subjects* (Bloodaxe Books: London, 1993).
*Dear Future* (Chatto and Windus: London, 1996).
*Explainer* (Race Today Publications: London, 1988).
*Feeding the Ghosts* (Chatto and Windus: London, 1997).
*Letters to America* (Carcanet Press: Manchester, 2020).
*Longest Memory* (Pantheon Books: New York, 1994).
*Mama Dot* (Chatto and Windus: London, 1985).

**D'OLIVEIRA, E.**

*Scattered Jewels* (Dido Press, London, 2003).

**DA COSTA, Emilia Viotti**

*Crowns of Glory, Tears of Blood: The Demerara Slave Rebellion of 1823* (Oxford University Press: Oxford, 1994).

**DABYDEEN, Cyril**

*A Chapbook* (Sheik Sadeek: Georgetown, 1969).
*A Shapely Fire: Changing the Literary Landscape* (Mosaic Press: Toronto, 1992).
*Another way to dance* (TSAR: Toronto, 1996).
*Berbice Crossing and Other Stories* (Peepal Tree Press: Leeds, 1996).
*Beyond Sangre Grande: An Anthology of Caribbean Literature* (TSAR Publications: Toronto, 2012).
*Beyond Sangre Grande: Caribbean Writing Today* (TSAR Publications: Toronto, 2011).
*Black Jesus and Other Stories* (TSAR: Toronto, 1996).
*Born in Amazonia* (Mosaic Press, Toronto, 1995).
*Coastland: New and Selected Poems* (Mosaic Press: Toronto, 1989).
*Crossing: And Other Stories* (Peepal Tree Press: Leeds, 1996).
*Dark Swirl* (Peepal Tree Press: Leeds, 1989).
*Discussing Columbus* (Peepal Tree Press: Leeds, 1997).
*Distances* (Fiddlehead Poetry Books: Fredericton, 1977).
*Drums of My Flesh* (Amazon Books: 2005).
*Elephants Make Good Stepladders* (Third Eye: New York, 1982).
*Glass Forehead* (Vesta Publications: Cornwall, 1987).
*Goatsong* (Mosaic Press/Valley Editions: Toronto, 1977).

*God's Spider* (Peepal Tree Press: Leeds, 2015).
*Heart's Frame* (Vest Publications: Cornwall, 1979).
*Imaginary Origins* (Peepal Tree Press, Leeds, 2005).
*Islands lovelier than a vision* (Peepal Tree Press, Leeds, 1986).
*Jogging in Havana: Short Stories* (Mosaic Press: Toronto, 1992).
*My Brahmin Days and Other Stories* (TSAR: Toronto, 2000).
*My Multi-Ethnic Stories and Other Stories* (Mosaic Press: Toronto, 2013).
*My Undiscovered Country: Short Stories* (Mosaic Press: Toronto, 2015).
*North of the Equator* (Beach Holme Publishing: Victoria, 2001).
*Play A Song Somebody; New and Selected Stories* (Mosaic Press: Toronto, 2004).
*Poems in Recession* (Sheik Sadeek: Georgetown, 1972).
*Selected Poems 1970-2002* (Peepal Tree Press: Leeds, 2004).
*Sometimes Hard* (Longman: London, 1994).
*Still Close to the Island* (Commoner's Publishing: Ottawa, 1980).
*Stoning the Wind* (TSAR: Toronto, 1994).
*The Wizard Swami* (Peepal Tree Press: Leeds, 1989).
*This Planet Earth (Poems)* (Mosaic Press: Toronto, 1979).
*To Monkey Jungle: Short Stories* (Mosaic Press: Toronto, 1992).
*Unanimous Night* (University of Windsor Press: Windsor, 2009).
*Uncharted Heart* (Brealis Press: Toronto, 2008).

**_____; Anita Nahal; B. Roy; E.E. Miller, et al**
*Soul Spaces: Poems on Cities, Towns, and Villages* (Authors Press: Pittsburgh, 2022).

**DABYDEEN, David**

*A Harlot's Progress* (Jonathan Cape: London, 1999). [Winner of the Guyana Prize for Literature].
*A Reader's Guide to West Indian and Black British Literature* (Hansib Publications: Hertfordshire, 1988).
*Black Writers in Britain 1760-1890* (Edinburgh University Press: Edinburgh, 1991).
*Caribbean Literature: A Teacher's Handbook* (Heinemann Educational: London, 1985).
*Cheddi Jagan: Selected Speeches 1992-1994* (Hansib Publications: Hertfordshire, 1995).
*Cheddi Jagan: Selected Correspondences 1947-1965* (Dido Press: London, 2003).
*Coolie Odyssey – Poems* (Hansib Publications: Hertfordshire, 1988).
*Disappearance* (Secker & Warberg: London, 1993).

*Ethnicity and Indian Identity in the Caribbean* (Macmillan-Caribbean: London, 2000).
*Guyana: Politics, Economics, and Society: Beyond the Burnham Era* (Columbia University Press: New York, 1986).
*Handbook for Teaching Caribbean Literature* (Heinemann: London, 1988).
*Hogarth, Walpole and Commercial Britain* (Hansib Publications: Hertfordshire, 1987).
*Hogarth's Blacks: Images of Blacks in Eighteenth Century English Art* (Dangaroo Press: London, 1987).
*Johnson's Dictionary* (Peepal Tree Press: Leeds, 2013).
[Winner of the 2014 Guyana Prize for Literature].
*Lutchmee and Dilloo: A Study of West Indian Life* (Edward Jenkins: London, 1877). Reprint. (Macmillan-Caribbean: London, 2002).
*Molly and the Muslim Stick* (Macmillan Caribbean: London, 2008).
*Our Lady of Demerara* (Dido Press: London, 2004). [Winner of the Guyana Prize for Literature].
*Slave Song: Poems* (Dangaroo Press: London, 1984). [Winner of the Commonwealth Poetry Prize and Quiller-Couch Prize].
*The Counting House* (Secker & Warberg: London, 1996).
*The Forgotten Colony* [A BBC Radio 4-Programme Exploring the History of Guyana] (BBC: London, 2001).
*The Intended* (Secker & Warberg: London, 1991). [Winner of the Guyana Prize for Literature].
*Turner – New and Selected Poetry* (Jonathan Cape: London, 1994); (Peepal Tree Press: Leeds, 2002).

**_____, ed.**

*Black Presence in English Literature* (Manchester University: Manchester,1985).
*Selected Poems of Egbert Martin* (Derek Walcott Press: London, 2007).

**_____; and John Gilmore**

*No Island is an Island: Selected Speeches of Sir Shridath Ramphal* (Macmillan: London, 2000).

**_____; John Gilmore; and Cecily James**

*The Oxford Companion to Black History* (OUP: Oxford, 2007).

**_____; Maria del Pillar Kaladeen; and Tina K. Ramnarine**

*We Mark Your Memory: Writings From the Descendants of Indenture* (University of Chicago Press: Chicago, 2019).

**_____; and Maria del Pilar Kaladeen, eds.**

*The Other Windrush: Legacies of Indenture in Britain's Caribbean Empire* (Pluto Press: London, 2021).

**_____; and Brinsley Samaroo, eds.**

*Across the Dark Waters: Indian Identity in the Caribbean* (Macmillan: London, 1996).

*India in the Caribbean* (Hansib: Hertfordshire, 1987).

**_____; Brinsley Samaroo; Jonathan Morley; Amar Wahab; and Brigid Wells**

*The First Crossing Being the Diary of Theophilus Richmond, Ship's Surgeon on the Hesperus 1837-1838* (Heaventree Press: Coventry, 2008).

**_____; and Nana Wilson-Tagoe**

*A Reader's Guide to West Indian and Black British Literature* (Hansib: Hertford, 1997).

**_____; Maria del Pilar Kaladeen; and Tina K. Ramnarine, eds.**

*We Mark Your Memory: Writings From the Descendants of Indenture* (Hansib: Hertfordshire, 2019).

**DABYDEEN, Leonard**

*Watching You, A Collection of Tetractys Poems* (Xlibris: 2012).

**DABYDEEN, Sally Ramage**

*An Introduction to Intellectual Property* (iUniverse Publishers: Bloomington, 2004).

*Civil Liberties in England and Wales (*iUniverse Publishers: Bloomington, 2004).

*Legal and Regulatory Framework for Business in the UK* (iUniverse Publishers: Bloomington, 2004).

*UK Steel Industry & International Trade* (iUniverse Publishers: Bloomington, 2004).

**DAGON, Jo**

*Cultivated Food Plants of the Rupununi* (McGill University: Montreal, 1967).

**DALGETY, William Thomas**

*PNC Burnham and Beyond: A Pocket Book Bible* (WT Dalgety: Georgetown 2009).

*Sacred Speeches on Africa: A Divine Story* (WT Dalgety: Georgetown, 2020).

**DALLEK, Robert**

*An Unfinished Life: John F. Kennedy, 1961-1963* (Little Brown: Boston, 2003).

**DALTON, Heny G.**

*The History of British Guiana,* 2 vols. (Longman, Brown, Green, and Longmans: London, 1855).

**DALRYMPLE, Henderson**

*50 Great West Indian Test Cricketers* (Hansib: Hertfordshire, 1983).

**DALRYMPLE, Kofi**

*Things Guyanese: A Collection of Short Stories* (K Dalrymple: Georgetown, 2007).

**DALY, P.H.**

*Historical and Biographical Essays* (n.p.: Georgetown, 19??).

*Stories of the Heroes* (The Argosy: Georgetown, 1949).

**DALY, V.T.**

*A Short History of the Guyanese People* (Longmans: London, 1966, 1970, 1978).

*Scenes from the History of the Chinese in Guyana* (MK Crawford: n.p., n.d.).

*The Making of Guyana* (Macmillan: London, 1974).

**DALZELL, Frank**

*Moments of Leisure* (Miniature Poet Series: Georgetown, 1952).

**DANCE, C.D.**

*Chapters from a Guianese Log Book: Or the Folklore and Scenes of Sea Coast & River Life in British Guiana* (Royal Gazette Establishment: Georgetown, 1881).

**DANIELS, Alicia**

*A Poet's Mind: A Collection of Inspiring Poems* (Alicia Daniels: Georgetown, 2021).

*My Book of Poetry 1* (Alicia Daniels: Georgetown, 2019).

**DANIELS, Elam J.**

*An Exposé of the King of the Cults: Inside Story Behind Suicide of Over 900 in Guyana* (Christ for the World Publishers: Orlando, 1979).

**DANIELS, Luke**

*Pulling the Punches: Defeating Domestic Violence* (Bogle l`Òverture: London, 2009).

**DANNS, George K.**

*Domination and Power in Guyana: A Study of the Police in a Third World Context* (University of Miami: Miami, 1982).

**_____; and Basmat Parsad Shiw**

*Domestic Violence within black families: A Study of wife abuse in Guyana* (University of Guyana: Turkeyen, 1988).

**_____; et al**

*Dynamics of Caribbean Diaspora Engagement: People, Policy, Practice* (University of Guyana: Turkeyen, 2018).

**DARROCH, Fiona**

*Memory and Myth: Post Colonial religion in Contemporary Guyanese Fiction and Poetry* (Rodopi: Amsterdam, 2009).

**DAS, Mahadai**

*A Leaf in the Air: Selected Poems* (Peepal Tree Press: Leeds, 2006).

*Bones* (Peepal Tree Press: Leeds, 1988).

*I Want to be a Poetess of My People* (Peepal Tree Press: Leeds, 1977).

*My Finer Steel Will Grow* (Peepal Tree Press: Leeds, 1982).

**DATHAN, P.W.**

*Bauxite, Sugar, and Mud* (Shoreline Press: Ste-Anne-de-Bellevue, 2006).

**DATHORNE, O.R.**

*African Literature in the 20th Century* (University of Minnesota Press: 1976).

*Africa in Prose* (Penguin: London, 1969).

*African Poetry for Schools and Colleges* (Macmillan: London, 1969).

*Asian Voyages: Two Thousand Years* (Greewnood Press: New Haven, 1996).

*Caribbean Verse* (Routledge: Oxford, 1967).

*Dark Ancestor: The Literature of the Black Man in the Caribbean* (Louisiana State Univeristy Press: Baton Rouge, 1981).

*Dele's Child* (Lynne Rienner Publishers Inc.: 1986).

*Dictionary of Guyanese Folklore* (National History and Arts Council: Georgetown, 1975).

*Dumplings in my soup* (Cassell: London, 1963).

*Imagining the World: Mythical Belief Versus Reality in Global Encounters* (Greenwood Press: New Haven, 1994).

*In Europe's Image: The Need for American Multiculturalism* (Bergin & Garvey: London, 1994).

*Songs for a New World* (Association of Caribbean Studies Press: 1988).

*The Black Mind: A History of African Literature* (University of Minnesota: Minnesota, 1975).

*The Scholar Man* (Cassell: London, 1964).

*Worlds Apart: Race in the Modern* (Greenwood Press: New Haven, 2001).

**_____., ed.**

*Caribbean Narrative* (Heinemann: London, 1966).

*Caribbean Verse: An Anthology* (Heinemann: London, 1967).

**DATT, Naraine**

*A Lonely Voice: A Book of 50 Poems* (N. Datt: Toronto, 2007). Republished by Dorrance Publishing: Pittsburgh, 2013.

**DAYFOOT, Rev. A., and Rev. R. Pierson**

*Bibliography of West Indian Church History* (Hansib Publications: Hertfordshire, 2004).

**DAVID, Wilfred**

*Economic Development of Guyana 1953-64* (Oxford University Press: Oxford, 1969).

**DAVIS, Benita**

*Kyle Learns About Freshwater* (Policy Forum Guyana: Georgetown, n.d.).

**DAVIS, Compton**

*City of Wooden Homes* (Merrell: London, 2017).

**DAVIS, L.C.**

*Eternal Tribute* (LC Davis: Georgetown, 1958).

*Invocation to Sivananda* (Adana Printing Service: Georgetown, 1957).

**DAVSON, Jr., George**

*Digging Through My Roots* (AuthorHouse: Bloomington, 2021).

**DAVSON, Victor**

*How the Warraus Came* (Ministry of Education, Georgetown, 1972).

**DE BARROS, Juanita L.**

*Order and Place in a Colonial Society: Patterns of Struggle and Resistance in Georgetown, British Guiana 1889-1924* (McGill-Queens University Press: Kingston, 2003).

**DE CAIRES, David.; and Miles Fitzpatrick**

*Twenty Years of Politics in Our Land* (GISRA: Georgetown, 1969).

**DE CAIRES, Dennis**

*Pictures for Georgetown, 1986-2009* (National Gallery of Art: Georgetown, 2009).

**DE HAARTE, Norma**

*Guyana Betrayal* (Sister Vision: Toronto, 1991).

*Mr. Jimmy the Black Pudding Man* (N. De Haarte: Toronto, 1997).

**DE RITTER, Frederica, trans.**

*Del Roraima al Orinoco.* 3 vols. (Ediciones del Banco Central de Venezuela: Caracas, 1982).

[Spanish translation of the original German of Theodor Koch-Grüberg's *Vom Roroima zum Orinoco*].

**DE VILLIERS, J.A.J.**

*The Rise of Guiana: Despatches of Laurens Storm van's Gravesande* (Hakluyt Society: London, 1911).

**DE WEEVER, Aloysius**

*A Textbook of the Geography of British Guiana, the West Indies, and South America for the Use of Schools* (The Argosy Co. Ltd.: Georgetown, 1903).

**DE WEEVER, Guy Egbert Leon**

*Children's Story of Guiana* (Education Department, Government of British Guiana: Georgetown, 1949).

*History of British Guiana 1831-1931 to mark the centenary of the union of three counties of Berbice, Demerara, and Essequibo* (Colonial Government: Georgetown, n.d.).

**De WEEVER, Jacqueline**

*Trailing the Sun's Sweat* (The Poet's Press: Providence, 2015).

**DEAN, Merrill; and Bonnie Thielmann**

*The Broken God* (DC Book Publishing: Colorado, 1979).

**DEANGELIS, Gina**

*Jonestown Massacre: Tragic End of a Cult* (Enslow Publishers Inc.: New York, 1984).

**DEBIDIN, Ade**

*Short Stories* (n.p.: n.p., n.d.).

*The Search* (n.p.: n.p., n.d.).

**DEDEAUX, Devra**

*The Sugar Reef Caribbean Cookbook* (n.p.: n.p., n.d.).

**DEEN, Mohamed Jamal**

**_____; contr.**

*Advanced Structured Materials* (Wiley: Hoboken, 2018).

*Advances in Imaging and Electron Physics* (Academic Press: New York, 1998, 1999, 2012).

*Bioelelectronics, Biointerfaces, and Biomedical Applications 2*, 210th ECS Meeting (ECS: Cancun, 2006).

*Cryogenic Operation for Low Temperature Electronics* (Academic Press: Amsterdam, 2001).

*Encyclopaedia of Electrical and Electronics Engineering* (Wiley: Hoboken, 1999, 2014).

*Fiber Optic Communications: Fundamentals and Applications* (Wiley: Hoboken, 2014).

*High Temperature Electronics* (IEEE Press: New York, 1998).

*Integrated Passive Component Technology* (IEEE Press: New York, 2003).

*Low Temperature Electronics: Physics, Devices, Circuits and Applications* (Academic Press: New York, 2001).
*Noise and Fluctuations Control in Electronic Devices* (American Scientific Publishers: New York, 2002).
*Optoelectronics and Photonics* (University of Saskatchewan: Saskatoon, 2000).
*Photodetectors: Materials, Devices, and Applications* (Woodhead Publishing: Cambridge, 2016).
*Photodetectors and Fiber Optics* (Academic Press: New York, 2001).
*Selected Topics in Electronics and Systems* (World Scientific Publishing: Singapore, 2002).
*Semiconductor Device-Based Sensors for Gas, Chemical, and Biomedical Applications* (Taylor and Francis: Boca Raton, 2010).
*Springer Handbook of Electronic and Optoelectronic Materials*, 2nd Ed. (Springer Science and Business Media Inc.: New York, 2016).

**_____; et al, eds.**
*Bioelelectronics, Biointerfaces, and Biomedical Applications 2*, 210th ECS Meeting (ECS: Cancun, 2006).
*Fiber Optic Communications: Fundamentals and Applications* (Wiley: Hoboken, 2014).

**_____; and C.H. Chen, eds.**
*ICNF 2011—IEEE Proceedings of 21st International Conference on Noise and Fluctuations* (IEEE: Toronto, 2011).

**_____; D. Misra; and J. Ruzyllo, eds.**
*Integrated Optoelectronics (First International Symposium)* (The Electrochemical Society: Pennington, 2002).

**_____; et al, eds.**
*Low Temperature Electronics and High Temp. Superconductivity*, Fourth International Symposium (ECS: Pennington, 1997).

**_____; E.A. Gutierrez-D; and C. Claeys, eds.**
*Low Temperature Electronics: Physics, Devices, Circuits and Applications* (Academic Press: New York, 2001).

**_____; Z. Celik-Butler; and M.E. Levinhstein, eds.**
*Noise in Devices and Circuits I, SPIE Proceedings Vol. 5113* (SPIE: Bellingham, 2003).

**_____; F. Danneville; F. Bonani; and M.E. Levinhstein, eds.**

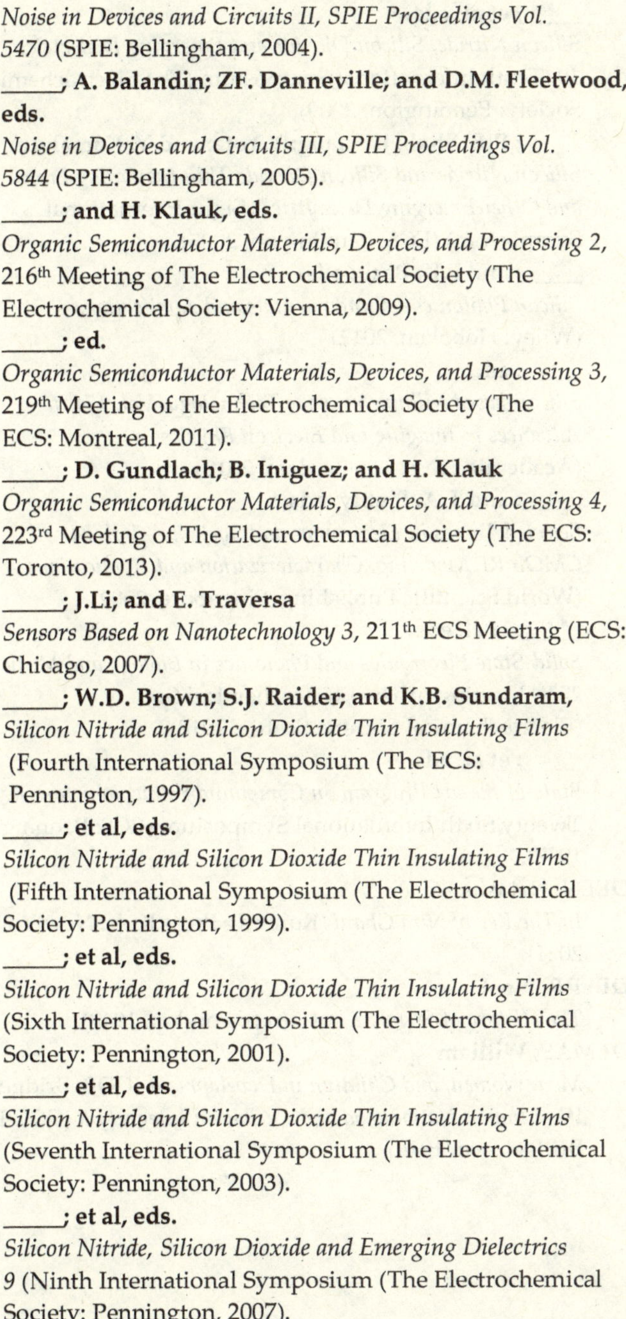

*Noise in Devices and Circuits II, SPIE Proceedings Vol. 5470* (SPIE: Bellingham, 2004).

**_____; A. Balandin; ZF. Danneville; and D.M. Fleetwood, eds.**

*Noise in Devices and Circuits III, SPIE Proceedings Vol. 5844* (SPIE: Bellingham, 2005).

**_____; and H. Klauk, eds.**

*Organic Semiconductor Materials, Devices, and Processing 2,* 216th Meeting of The Electrochemical Society (The Electrochemical Society: Vienna, 2009).

**_____; ed.**

*Organic Semiconductor Materials, Devices, and Processing 3,* 219th Meeting of The Electrochemical Society (The ECS: Montreal, 2011).

**_____; D. Gundlach; B. Iniguez; and H. Klauk**

*Organic Semiconductor Materials, Devices, and Processing 4,* 223rd Meeting of The Electrochemical Society (The ECS: Toronto, 2013).

**_____; J.Li; and E. Traversa**

*Sensors Based on Nanotechnology 3,* 211th ECS Meeting (ECS: Chicago, 2007).

**_____; W.D. Brown; S.J. Raider; and K.B. Sundaram,**

*Silicon Nitride and Silicon Dioxide Thin Insulating Films* (Fourth International Symposium (The ECS: Pennington, 1997).

**_____; et al, eds.**

*Silicon Nitride and Silicon Dioxide Thin Insulating Films* (Fifth International Symposium (The Electrochemical Society: Pennington, 1999).

**_____; et al, eds.**

*Silicon Nitride and Silicon Dioxide Thin Insulating Films* (Sixth International Symposium (The Electrochemical Society: Pennington, 2001).

**_____; et al, eds.**

*Silicon Nitride and Silicon Dioxide Thin Insulating Films* (Seventh International Symposium (The Electrochemical Society: Pennington, 2003).

**_____; et al, eds.**

*Silicon Nitride, Silicon Dioxide and Emerging Dielectrics 9* (Ninth International Symposium (The Electrochemical Society: Pennington, 2007).

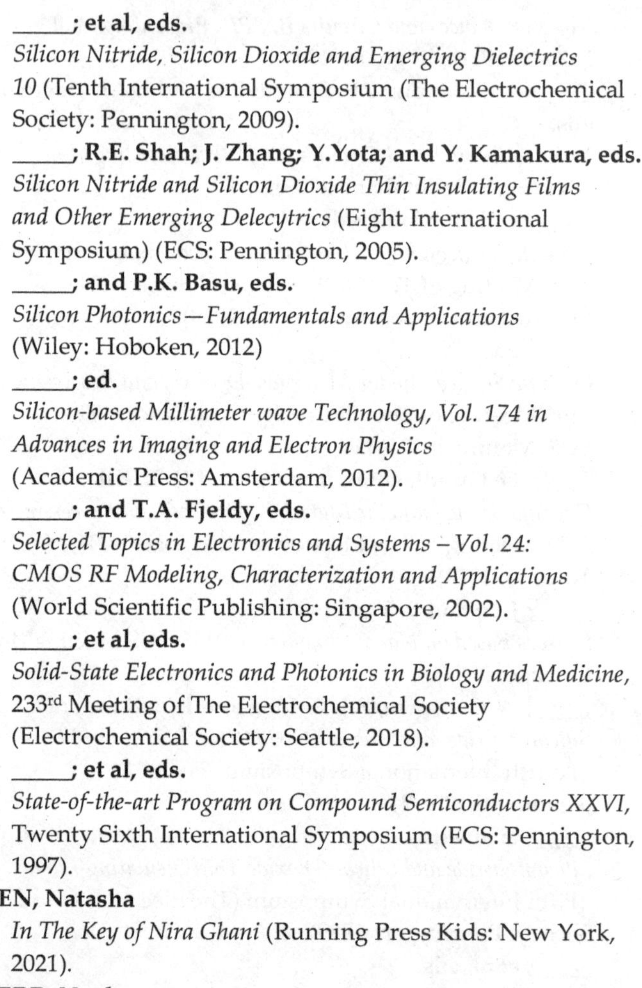

**_____; et al, eds.**
*Silicon Nitride, Silicon Dioxide and Emerging Dielectrics 10* (Tenth International Symposium (The Electrochemical Society: Pennington, 2009).

**_____; R.E. Shah; J. Zhang; Y.Yota; and Y. Kamakura, eds.**
*Silicon Nitride and Silicon Dioxide Thin Insulating Films and Other Emerging Delecytrics* (Eight International Symposium) (ECS: Pennington, 2005).

**_____; and P.K. Basu, eds.**
*Silicon Photonics—Fundamentals and Applications* (Wiley: Hoboken, 2012)

**_____; ed.**
*Silicon-based Millimeter wave Technology, Vol. 174 in Advances in Imaging and Electron Physics* (Academic Press: Amsterdam, 2012).

**_____; and T.A. Fjeldy, eds.**
*Selected Topics in Electronics and Systems – Vol. 24: CMOS RF Modeling, Characterization and Applications* (World Scientific Publishing: Singapore, 2002).

**_____; et al, eds.**
*Solid-State Electronics and Photonics in Biology and Medicine,* 233rd Meeting of The Electrochemical Society (Electrochemical Society: Seattle, 2018).

**_____; et al, eds.**
*State-of-the-art Program on Compound Semiconductors XXVI,* Twenty Sixth International Symposium (ECS: Pennington, 1997).

**DEEN, Natasha**
*In The Key of Nira Ghani* (Running Press Kids: New York, 2021).

**DEERR, Noel**
*The History of Sugar,* 2 vols. (n.p: London, 1949).

**DEMAS, William**
*Men, Women, and Children in Development* (CDB: Bridgetown, 1986).
*West Indian Nationhood and Caribbean Integration* (CCC Publishing: Bridgetown, 1974).

**DEODHARI, S.**

*Banglar Bow* (AuthorHouse: Bloomington, 2007).

**DEODAT, Rovin**

*From Word to Word* (Guyana National Newspapers Ltd.: Georgetown, 2002).

**DEONANDAN, Raywat**

*Sweet Like Salt Water* (TSAR: Toronto, 1999).

*Divine Elemental* (TSAR Publications: Toronto, 2003).

**DEPOO, T.; Prem Misir; and Basdeo Mangru; eds.**

*The East Indian Diaspora* (City University of New York: New York, 1993).

**DERBYSHIRE, Desmond C; and Geoffrey K. Pullum, eds.**

*Handbook of Amazonian Languages 3* (Mouton de Gruyter: Berlin, 1991).

**DESPRES, Leo A.**

*Cultural Pluralism and Nationalist Politics in British Guiana* (Rand McNally and Co.: Chicago, 1967).

**DES VOEAUX, Sir William**

*Experiences of a Demerara Magistrate 1863-69* (Daily Chronicle: Georgetown, 1948).

*My Colonial Service in British Guiana, St. Lucia, Trinidad, Fiji, Australia, Newfoundland, and Hong Kong With Interludes, Vol. 1* (John Murray: London, 1903).

**DEVEZE, Michel**

*Antilles, Guyanes, La Mer des Caraïbes de 1492 à 1789* (Société d'edition d'ensegnement superieur: Paris, 1977).

**DI, Morrissey**

*When the Singing Stops* (Macmillan: Sydney, 1996).

**DIECKMANN, Ed, Jnr.**

*Beyond Jonestown: Sensitivity Training and the Cult of Mind Control* (Legion for the Survival of Freedoms: Los Angeles, 1981).

**DINDAYAL, Vidur**

*A Life of Blessings* (Story Terrace: London, 2022).

*Guyanese Achievers in the UK* (Trafford Press: London, 2007).

*Guyanese Achievers USA & Canada: A Celebration* (Trafford Publishing: Bloomington, 2011).

**DIPCHAND, Cecil Ramnaraine; James C. Van Horne; and J. Robert Hanrahan**

*Fundamentals of Financial Management* (Prentice-Hall: Toronto, 1975).

[Stanford University's Dr Van Horne is the principal author of this book which was required reading for many college and university courses and business finance programs of professional accounting bodies. The late Dr. Dipchand, from Canal No. 1 on the West Bank Demerara, was a Guyanese who co-authored the 1975 edition.]

**_____; Migjia Ma; Yichun, Zhang**

*The Chinese Financial System and Its Management – Mandarin edition* (Social Science Press: Beijing, 1992).

*The Chinese Financial System* (Greenwood Press: New York, 1994).

**DOBSON, Michael**

*February 23: The Story of a Special Day* (M. Dobson: New York, 2016).

**DODD, David J.**

*The Wellsprings of Violence —Some Historical Notes on East Indian Criminality in Guyana* (University of Guyana: Turkeyen, 1976).

**DOHARRIS, Brenda**

*Calabash Parkway* (Tantaria Press: Washington, D.C., 2005).

*The Coloured Girl in the Ring: A Guyanese Woman Remembers* (Tantaria Press: Washington, D.C., 1997).

**DOLPHIN, Celeste**

*Children of Guyana* (Ministry of Education: Georgetown, 1953).

**DOLPHIN, Lynette**

*National Folksongs of Guyana and Twenty Amerindian Folksongs* (National History and Arts Council: Georgetown, 2000).

*National Songs of Guyana* (Ministry of Education: Georgetown, 1991).

*Ten National Songs of Guyana* (National History and Arts Council: Georgetown, 1969).

**DON, Thomas**

*Pious Effusions* (Royal Gazette: New Amsterdam, 1873).

**DONNELL, Allison**

*Twentieth-Century Caribbean Literature* (Routledge: London, 2006).

**DOOBAY, Kumar D.**

*A Little Hut in Heaven* (Kumar D. Doobay: Georgetown, 2010).

**DOOKERAN, Winston; and Bridget Bereton, eds.**

*East Indians in the Caribbean: Colonialism and the struggle for Identity* (Kraus: New York, 1982).

**DOOKHAN, Isaac**

*A History of the Virgin Islands of the United States* (Caribbean Universities Press for the College of the Virgin Islands: St. Thomas, 1974).

*A Pre-Emancipation History of the West Indies* (Collins-Caribbean: London, 1971).

*A Post-Emancipation History of the West Indies* (Collins-Caribbean: London, 1977).

*The United States in the Caribbean* (Collins-Caribbean: London, 1985).

**_____; and Ralph M. Paiewonsky**

*Memoirs of a Governor: A Man for the People* (New York University Press: New York, 1990).

**DORIE, Janet**

*360 Pieces of Diamond* (Janet Dorie: Georgetown, 2023).

**DORSI, E.**

*Fulfilment: Poems* (E. Dorsi: Georgetown, 1967).

*Guyana Drums* (E. Dorsi: Georgetown, 1972).

**DOUGLAS, Frank L.**

*Defining Moments of a Free Man from a Black Stream* (Dorrance Publishing: New York, 2018).

**DOUGLAS, Sybil**

*Fulfilment* (Sybil Douglas: Georgetown, 1967).

*Poems Old and New* (Sybil Douglas: Scarborough, 2009).

**_____; and P. Cameron**

*Guyana Drums* (n.p.: n.p., 1972).

**DOWDY, Homer**

*Christ's Witch-Doctor* (Vision House Publishing: Gresham, 1994). [Based on the Wai Wai Amerindian tribe].

*Christ's Jungle* (Vision House Publishing: Gresham, 1995).

**DOWNER, Maria; and David Gleave**

*The Walker Brothers and Their Legacy: Three Black Soldiers in World War One* (M. Downer: n.p., n.d.)

**DOYLE, Sir Arthur Conan**

*"The Lost World"* and *"The Poison Belt": Professor Challenger Adventures* (Chronicle Books: San Francisco, 1989).

**DRAKE, Sandra E.**

*Wilson Harris and the Modern Tradition: A New Architecture of the World - Contributions in Afro-American and African Studies* (Greenwood Press: Westport, 1986).

**DRAYTON, Harold**

*An Accidental Life* [His autobiography]. (Hansib: London, 2017).

**_____; contr.**

*University of Guyana: Perspectives on the Early History* (UG Guild of Graduates: Toronto, 2002).

**DRAYTON, Richard (son of Harold Drayton)**

*Commonwealth History in the Twenty-First Century — Cambridge Imperial and Post-Colonial Studies* (Palgrave Macmillan: London, 2021).

*Nature's Government: Science, Imperial Britain, and the Improvement of the World* (Yale University Press: New Haven, 2000).

**_____; C. Bayly; and R. Rathbone**

*Imperialism and Colonialism* (Routledge: London, 2022).

**DUFF, R**

*British Guiana: Being Notes on a Few of the Natural Productions, Industrial Occupations, and Social Institutions* (Thomas, Murray, and Stans: Glasgow, 1886).

**DUKE, Blanche E.**

*A History of the Anglican Church in Guyana* (Red Thread Women's Press: Georgetown, 2000).

*Diocesan Pot-Pourri* (n.p.: Georgetown, 2002).

**DUMONT, Maurice**

*Historical and Present Day Views of the Buildings of Guyana: With Notes on the Country's Cricketers and the Various Races* (Maurice Dumont: Toronto, 1998).

**DUMONT, R.**

*The State of Urban Planning in Guyana* (Government of Guyana: Georgetown, 1974).

**DUNDAS, Carl**

*Improving the Organization of Elections:* (Ian Randle Publishers: Kingston, 2006).

*The Integrationist: Observing Elections the Commonwealth's Way* (Ian Randle Publishers: Kingston, 2007).

**_____; et al**

*Caricom: Appropriate Adaptation to a Changing Global Environment* (Ian Randle Publishers: Kingston, 2005).

**DUNN, Katherine; and Alexis Rockman, ill.**

*Guyana* (Twin Palms: Santa Fe, 1996).

**DUNN, R.**

*Sugar and Slaves: The Rise of the Planter Class in the English West Indies: 1624-1713* (NYU Press: New York, 1972).

**DURRELL, G.**

*Three Singles to Adventure* (Penguin: London, 1984).

**DYAL, Karr**

*Sculptures, Paintings and Drawings* (n.p.: n.p., 2000).

**DYALRAM, Pooran**

*Reflections: An Anthology of Experiences in Guyana* (Createspace: New York, 2012).

**DYDE, B**

*The Empty Sleeve: The Story of the West Indian Regiment* (Hansib Publications: Hertfordshire, 1997, 2007).

# E

**EARP, Alan; et al**

*The University of Guyana: Perspectives on the Early History* (University of Guyana Guild of Graduates: Toronto, 2002).

**EBON, Martin, ed.**

*The Amazing But True Stories of Mysterious Sects from Around the World* (Signet Books: New York, 1979).

*The World's Weirdest Cults: From the Guyana Massacre to Secret Satanic Masses* (Signet Books: New York, 1979).

**EDAN, M.J.**

*The Savanna Ecosystem – Northern Rupununi, British Guiana* (Department of Geography, McGill University: Montreal, 1964).

**EDEN, K.**

*The Jonestown Massacre: The Transcript of Rev. Jim Jones's Last Speech in Guyana in 1978* (Temple Press: Nashville, 1993).

**EDEN, Michael J.**

*The Savanna Ecosystem of Northern Rupununi, British Guiana* (McGill University: Montreal, 1964).

**EDUN, A.M.**

*London's Heart Probe and Britain's Duty* (n.p.: London, n.d.).

**EDWARDS, H; and M.E. Scott**

*Equity Theory and Doping in Cycling* (University of Guyana: Turkeyen, 2015).

**EDWARDS, Walter F. ed.**

*A Brief Introduction of Some Aspects of the Language and Culture of the Guyana Arawak (Lokono)* (University of Guyana: Turkeyen, 1980).

*Focus on Amerindians* (University of Guyana: Turkeyen, 1980).

**_____.; and Elizabeth Charette**

*A Short Dictionary of the Warau Language of Guyana* (University of Guyana: Turkeyen, 1980).

**_____.; Kean Gibson; V. Bynoe; and K. Sugrim, eds.**

*A Short Grammar and Dictionary of the Akawaio and Arekuna Languages of Guyana* (University of Guyana: Turkeyen, 1980).

**_____.; Kean Gibson; and Daizal Samad, eds.**

*A Brief Introduction to Some Aspects of the Culture and Language of the Guyana Arawak (Lokono) Tribe* (University of Guyana: Turkeyen, 1980).

*An Annotated Glossary of Folk Medicines Used by Some Amerindians in Guyana* (University of Guyana: Turkeyen, 1978).

**_____; and H.R. Hubbard, eds.**

*Folk Tales and Legends of Some Guyana Amerindians* (University of Guyana: Turkeyen, 1980).

**EIGANMANN, C.H.**

*The Freshwater Fishes of British Guiana* (Linnaeus Press: Amsterdam, 1977).

**EISENBERG, John F.**

*Mammals of the Neotropics: The Northern Neotropics Col. 1 - Panama, Colombia, Venezuela, Guyana, Suriname, French Guiana* - (Oversize Paperback: New York, 1989).

**ELLIS, Deborah**

*The Greats* (Groundwood Books: Toronto, 2020).

**EMMERICK-HOGEN, Ferdinand**

*Die Kariben in Guayana* (n.p.: Regensburg, 1922).

**ENEAS, Godfrey**

*The New Caribbean: A Region in Transition* (AuthorHouse: Bloomington, 2008).

**ENNIS-TROTMAN, Adrian J.**

*I Remember That: A Collection of Cherished, Unforgettable and Lasting Memories* (iUniverse: New York, 2017).

**ENGLISH, Adrian J.**

*Armed Forces of Latin America* (Janes: London, 1984).

**ESKELUND, Karl**

*Revolt in the Tropics: Travels from Cuba to British Guiana* (Alvin Redman Ltd.: London, 1963).

**ESPOSITO, J. D**

*The Cold War and Decolonization in British Guiana: The Anglo-American Intervention and Guianese Nationalist Politics* (Proquest UMI Publishing: Ann Arbor, 2013).

**EUROMONITOR**

*South American Economic Handbook* (Euromonitor: London, 1986).

**EVANS, Clifford; and Betty J. Meggers**

*Archaeological Investigations in British Guiana* (Smithsonian Institution Press/ Bureau of American Ethnology: Washington, D.C., 1960).

**EVANS, W.W.**

*Biographical Portraits* (n.p.: Georgetown, 1909).

**EYTLE, Ernest**

*Frank Worrell* (Hodder & Stoughton: London, 1963).

# F

**FAIRRIE, Geoffrey**
*The Sugar Refining Families of Great Britain* (Tate & Lyle: London, 1951).

**FANSHAW, D.B.**
*Principal Timbers of British Guiana* (Government of Guyana: Georgetown, 1961).

**FARABEE, W.C.**
*The Central Arawaks* (University of Pennsylvania: Scranton, 1918). Reprint. (Anthropological Publications: Amsterdam, 1967).
*The Central Caribs* (University of Pennsylvania: Scranton, 1924).

**FARLEY, R.**
*Trade Unions and Politics in the British Caribbean* (n.p.: Georgetown, 1957).

**FARRAR, Thomas, ed.**
*Notes of the History of the Church in Guiana* (John Hadden & Co: New Amsterdam, 1892).

**FAURIOL, George A.**
*Foreign Policy Behavior of Caribbean States: Guyana, Haiti, and Jamaica* (University Press of America: Lanham, 1984).

**FEINSOD, Ethan**
*Awake in Nightmare – Jonestown: The Only Eyewitness Account* (W W Norton & Co.: New York, 1981).

**FELIX, Winston**
*Issues in Guyana's Development* (Lulu.com: 2012).
*The Shifting Foreign Policy of Venezuela Toward Guyana* (Lulu.com: 2015).

**FELTS, Shirley**
*The Iwokrama Forest* (Iwokrama Rain Forest: Georgetown, 2003).

**FENTY, Allan**
*A Plate-a-Guyana Cook-Up: A Collection of Guyanese Proverbs* (Allan Fenty: Georgetown, 2011).
*Stories of Protest* (Guyana National Service Publications: Georgetown, 1978).

**FERGUSON, J.**
*The Making of the Caribbean* (Ian Randle Publishers: Kingston, 2005).

**FERGUSON, Tyrone Robert**

*Structural Adjustment and Good Governance: The Case of Guyana* (Public Affairs Consulting Enterprise: Georgetown, 1995).

*The Third World and Decision-Making in the International Monetary Fund: The Quest for Full and Effective Participation* (St. Martin's Press: New York, 1988).

*To Survive Sensibly or to Court Heroic Death: Management of Guyana's Political Economy 1965-1985* (University Press of America: New York, 1993).

**_____; et al**

*Policy Transfer, New Public Management and Globalization Mexico and the Caribbean* (University Press of America: New York, 2002).

**FERNANDES, Robert J.**

*Amerindian Life in Guyana* (Robert J. Fernandes: Georgetown, 1983).

*An Introduction to Birds in Guyana* (Robert J. Fernandes: Georgetown, 1994).

*Shell Book of Guyana* (Robert J. Fernandes: Georgetown, 1999).

*Short and Sweet: A Collection of Guyanese Stories and Fables* (Hansib Publications: Hertfordshire, 2005).

*The Guyana Mosaic* (Robert J. Fernandes: Georgetown, 1990).

*The Seat at our Door* (Robert J. Fernandes: Georgetown, 1994).

*Visions of the Interior* (Robert J. Fernandes: Georgetown, 1977).

**_____.; and B. Singh**

*Birds of Guyana* (Macmillan-Caribbean: London, 2004).

**FERNANDEZ, Antonio de Pedro**

*La Historia y el Derecho en la Reclamación Venezolana de la Guayana Esequiba* (Edirial Mediterráneo: Caracas, 1969).

[A book in Spanish on Venezuela's claim over the Essequibo].

**FIEDLER, A.**

*The River of Singing Fish* (Hodder & Stoughton: London, 1951).

**FIEDTKOU, G.**

*River Ways* (n.p.: n.p., 2003).

**FIGUEIRA, Daurius**

*The East Indian Problem in Trinidad and Tobago 1953-1962: Terror and Race War in Guyana 1961-1964* (IUniverse Inc: Bloomington, 2009).

**FIGUEROA, J., ed.**

*Caribbean Voices. Vol. 1* (Evans: London, 1966).

*For the Fighting Front: An Anthology of Revolutionary Poems* (Peoples Progressive Party: Guyana, 1974).

**FISHER, Nigel**

*Harold Macmillan: A Biography* (St. Martin's Press: New York, 1971).

**FITTS, Norman R.**

*The Encounter* (Booksurge LLC: London, 2007).

**FITZPATRICK, Michelle**

*Murder So Sweet* (PublishAmerica: Baltimore, 2004).

**FLETCHER, Alan Mark**

*Land and Peoples of the Guianas* (J. B. Lippincott Co.: Philadelphia, 1966).

**FOCK, Niels**

*Waiwai: Religion and Society of an Amazonian Tribe* (The National Museum: Copenhagen, 1963).

**FORD, James**

*Notes of a Trip to South America* (Guardian Printing & Publishing: London, 1889).

**FORD, John Ronald Dipchandra (Deep)**

*Agricultural Trade Policy and Food Security in the Caribbean: Structural Issues, Multilateral Negotiations, and Competitiveness* (Food and Agriculture Organization: Rome, 2007).

**FORDE, A.N., ed.**

*Talk of the Tamarinds: An Anthology of Poetry for Secondary Schools* (Edward Arnold: London, 1971).

**FORRESTER, I**

*A Voice from Cuffy's Grave* (Ministry of National Development: Georgetown, 1976).

**FORSYTHE, Victor Leonard Consort**

*Survivals of Africanism and Creolese Language of Guyana* (University of Guyana: Turkeyen, 1988).

**FORTE, Janet**

*A Selective Reading List on Guyanese Amerindians* (University of Guyana: Turkeyen, 1995).

*About Guyana's Amerindians* (Janet Forte: Georgetown, 1996).

*Situation Analysis. Indigenous Use of the Forest With Emphasis on Region 1* (University of Guyana: Turkeyen, 1995).

*The Populations of Guyanese Amerindian Settlements in the 1980s* (University of Guyana: Turkeyen, 1990).

*Thinking About Amerindians* (Janet Forte: Georgetown, 1996).

**_____, ed.**

*Iwokramî pantoni: Stories about Iwokrama* (North Rupununi District Development Board: Georgetown, 2001).

*Makushi Lifestyles and Biodiversity Use* (Iwokrama International Rainforest Programme: Georgetown, 1996).
*Situation Analysis: Indigenous Use of the Forest with Emphasis on Region 1* (University of Guyana: Turkeyen, 1995).

**_____; and Ian Melville, eds.**

*Amerindian Testimonies* (Boise State University: Boise, 1989).

**_____; and Mark G. Plew, eds.**

*A Bibliography of Guyana Anthropology* (Boise State University: Boise, 1998).

**FORTUNE, Kito**

*The Zoo* (Kito Fortune: New York, 2019).

**FOURNIER, Alain, ed.**

*Waramadong: A Case Study for Amerindian Resettlement in the Upper Mazaruni Area, Guyana* (Upper Mazaruni Development Authority: Georgetown, 1978).

**_____; and Joel Benjamin, eds.**

*Bibliography of the Mazaruni Area, Guyana* (Upper Mazaruni Development Authority: Georgetown, 1978).

**FOWLER, R.D.**

*Subway Etiquette* (AuthorHouse: Bloomington, 2006).

**FOX, Desrey; and George K. Danns**

*Caught Within The Cracks: The Case of the Amerindian Women of Guyana* (University of Guyana: Turkeyen, 1991).
*Five Hundred Years After: Indigenous Women in the Caribbean Revisited* (University of Guyana: Turkeyen, 1992).
*The Indigenous Condition in Guyana: A Situation Analysis of the Mabura Great Falls Community* (University of Guyana: Turkeyen, 1993).

**FOX, John**

*Macnamara's Irish Colony and the US Taking of California in 1841* (MacFarland Inc. Publishers: Jefferson, 1942).
[Twenty six pages of this 230-page book deals with the Catholic missionary Eugene Macnamara's 1841-1844 mission and misadventures in British Guiana].

**FRANCIS, Claudette**

*Children's Bible Stories Workbook: Stories from the New Testament* (Claudette Francis: Toronto, 2006).
*Children`s Bible Stories Workbook – Teacher's Edition with Answers* (C&F Publishing: Toronto, 2013).
*Image Booster—24 Inspirational Messages For Young People of Faith* (AuthorHouse: Bloomington, 2012).

*Jesus is Risen—An Easter Play for Children* (AuthorHouse: Bloomington, 2009).
*Mystery of the Resurrection: An Inspirational Drama on the Resurrection of Jesus Christ* (AuthorHouse: Bloomington, 2008).
*Study Guide and Workbook—To Accompany the Mystery of the Nativity* (AuthorHouse: Bloomington, 2013).
*The Mystery of the Nativity – An Inspirational Drama on the Nativity of Jesus Christ* (Claudette Francis: Toronto, 2007).
[Author's Note: Ms. Claudette Francis, née Swan, taught yours truly, the author and his brothers at Malgre Tout School in the early 1960s.]

**FRANCIS, William; and John Mullin, eds.**
*The British Guiana Handbook* (n.p.: Georgetown, 1922).

**FRANCIS, Yvonne-Jackson**
*Come Walk with Me* (Xlibris: Bloomington, 2010).

**FRANKLIN, Sheila**
*Stray Leaves* (Lyn Frank Productions: London, 1997).

**FRASER, Gary**
*Ambivalent Anti-Colonialism: The United States and the Genesis of West Indian Independence, 1940-1964* (Greenwood Press: Westport, 1994).

**FRASURE, Lenny**
*A River Jungle Expedition: Guyana* (TCF Business: New York, 2019).

**FREDERICKS, Miriam Marietta**
*Lyrical Hues – The Colours of Inspiration* (Xlibris: Bloomington, 2006).
*One Leper's Heart: Expressions of Gratitude to God* (Outskirts Press: Parker, 2008).
**_____; John Lennon; Paul Mundy; and Janet Fredericks**
*Society and Health in Guyana: The Sociology of Healthcare in a Developing Nation* (Carolina Academic Press: Durham, 1986).

**FREEMANTLE, Lisa**
*Taste My Words* (Middle Road Publishers: Toronto, 2022).

**FREETH, Zahna**
*Run Softly Demerara* (Allen & Unwin: London, 1960).

**FROST, David**
*The Climate of the Rupununi Savannas: A Study in Ecological Climatology* (Department of Geography: McGill University, Montreal, 1967).

**FRSA, Godfrey L. Brandt**
*Madib and Other Poems* (AuthorHouse: Bloomington, 2014).

**FRYER, Peter**

*Staying Power: The History of Black People in Britain* (Pluto Press: London, 1984).

**FURTADO, Celso**

*Economic Development of Latin America,* 2nd ed. (Cambridge University Press: Cambridge, 1976).

# G

**GADDIS, John Lewis**

*We Now Know: Rethinking Cold War History* (Oxford University Press: New York, 1997).

**GAFAR, John**

*Guyana: From State Control to Free Market* (Nova Publishers: New York, 2003).

**GAFOOR, Ameena**

*Aftermath of Empire: The Novels of Roy A.K. Heath* (UWI Press: Mona, 2017).

*Evolution of Writing in English by and about East Indians of Guyana 1878-2018* (Hansib: Hertfordshire, 2018).

*Lantern in the Wind: A Fictional Memoir* (Hansib: Hertfordshire, 2021).

**GAFUR, Rudy**

*Cooperstown is My Mecca* (Toucan Publishing: Toronto, 1995).

*Stories from Guyana: A Collection of Jumbee Tales* (Toucan Publishing: Toronto, 2003).

**GALE, Laurence**

*Education and Development in Latin America with special reference to Colombia and Guyana, South America* (Praeger: New York, 1969).

**GALPERINA, Eu, ed.**

*The Time of Flambouy Trees: An Anthology of West Indian Poetry* (n.p.: Moscow, 1961).

**GAMPAT, Ramesh**

*Essays: Guyana—Economics, Politics, and Demography* (Xlibris: Bloomington, 2022).

*Domination by Region 4: Domestic Colonialism and Regionalization in Guyana* (Xlibris: Bloomington, 2023).

*Explorations and Reflections of an Indian Guyanese Hindu. Volume 1,* (Xlibris: Bloomington, 2019).

*Guyana – From Slavery to the Present, Vol. 1 – Health System* (Xlibris, Bloomington, 2015).

*Guyana – From Slavery to the Present Vol. 2 – Major Diseases* (Xlibris: Bloomington, 2015).

*Guyana's Great Economic Downswing, 1977-1990. Socio-Economic Impact of Co-operative Socialism* (Xlibris: Bloomington, 2020).

*Sanatana Dharma and Plantation Hinduism. Explorations and*
*Sanatana Dharma and Plantation Hinduism. Explorations and*
*Reflections of an Indian Guyanese Hindu.* Volume 2, Second Edition (Xlibris: Bloomington, 2020).

**______; and Anuradha Rajivan,**

*Perspectives on Corruption and Human Development (2009).* 2 vols. (Macmillan: London) 2009.

**GAR, Wilson**

*Phoenix Force No. 47: Terror in Guyana* (Gold Eagle: New York, 1991).

**GARNER, Steve**

*Ethnicity, Class & Gender: Guyana 1838-1985* (Ian Randle Publishers: Kingston, 2008).

**GARNETTE, Thelsa; and Donna Morrison**

*Passion! Healthy Recipes with Passion Fruit* (Peepal Tree Press: Leeds, 2008).

**GEORGE, Gwyneth, et al, eds.**

*University of Guyana: Heartbeat of a Nation* (Inspire Inc.: Georgetown, 2015).

**GEORGE, Mortimer**

*A Time in Our History: Berbice Cricket From 1939 to 2010* (George Mortimer: Georgetown, 2011).

**GEORGE, Neville B.**

*Singing Into Jesus in Songs and Carols at Christmas* (NB George: Georgetown, 2016).

**GHANY, Hamid A.**

*Constitutional Development in the Caribbean* (Ian Randle Publishers: Kingston, 2018).

**GIBBONS, R. Arnold**

*The Legacy of Walter Rodney in Guyana and the Caribbean* (University Press of America: Lanham, 2011).

*Race, Politics & the White Media: the Jesse Jackson campaigns* (University Press of America: Lanham, 1993).

*Walter Rodney and His Times.* (Guyana National Printers Ltd: Georgetown, 1994).

**GIBBS, Allan; and Christopher Barron**

*Geology of the Guyana Shield* (Oxford University Press: Oxford, 1993).

**GIBSON, Kean**

*Comfa Religion and Creole Language in a Caribbean Community* (State University of New York: New York, 2001).

*Sacred Duty: Hinduism and Violence in Guyana* (GroupFive Inc.: Georgetown, 2005).
*The Cycle of Racial Oppression in Guyana* (University Press of America: New York, 2003).

**GILBERT, Kwame**
*Transformational Leadership* (Xula Press: Toronto, 2012).

**GILES-BARROW, C., ed.**
*Introduction to Caribbean Politics: Text and Readings* (Ian Randle Publishers: Kingston, 2002).
**_____; and Joseph, T.S.D.**
*General Elections and Voting in the English-Speaking Caribbean 1992-2005* (Ian Randle Publishers: Kingston, 2006).

**GILKES, Michael**
*Couvade and a Pleasant Career* (Peepal Tree Press: Leeds, 2014).
*Echoes and Voices* (Vantage Press: New York, 1991).
*Frangipani House* (Heinemann: London, 1986).
*In Praise of Love and Children* (Peepal Tree Press: Leeds, 2002).
*Jonestown and Other Poems* (Peepal Tree Press: Leeds, 2002).
*Leaves in the Wind* (Mango Publishing: London, 2004).
*Racial Identity and Individual Consciousness in the Caribbean Novel* (Ministry of Information and Culture: Georgetown, 1974).
*The West Indian Novel* (Twayne Publishers: New York, 1981).

**GILLIN, J.**
*The Barama River Caribs: Papers of the Peabody Museum of American Archaeology and Ethnology* (Harvard University Press: Boston, 1936).

**GILROY, Beryl Agatha**
*A Visitor From Home* (Macmillan: London, 1973).
*Arthur Small* (Macmillan: London, 1976).
*Black Teacher* (Littlehampton: London, 1976). Reprinted by Faber & Faber: New York, 2021.
*Boy Sandwich* (Heinemann: London, 1989).
*Bubu's Street* (Macmillan: London, 1975).
*Carnival of Dreams* (Modern Curriculum Press: London, 1985).
*Grandpa's Footsteps, Aunt Olive's Wedding, and Elvira* (Macmillan: London, 1978).
*Frangipani House* (Heineman: London, 1986).
*Gather the Faces* (Peepal Tree Press: Leeds, 1994).
*In Bed* (Macmillan: London, 1975).
*In For a Penny* (Cassell Compers Books: London, 1980). Reprint. Holt Sanders: New York, 1982).

*Inkle and Yarico* (Peepal Tree Press: Leeds, 1994).
*Knock at Mrs. Harb* (Macmillan: London, 1973).
*New People At Twenty Four* (Macmillan: London, 1973).
*New Shoes* (Macmillan: London, 1976).
*No More Pets* (Macmillan: London, 1975).
*Once Upon a Time* (Macmillan: London, 1975).
*Outings for Everyone* (Macmillan : London, 1975).
*Paper Bag (Nippers)* (Macmillan : London, 1973).
*Praise of Love and Children* (Peepal Tree Press: Leeds, 1994).
*Rice and Peas* (Macmillan: London, 1975).
*Steadman and Joanna: A Love in Bondage* (Vantage: London, 1991).
*Sunlight on Sweet Water* (Peepal Tree Press: Leeds, 1994).
*The Green Grass Tango* (Peepal Tree Press: Leeds, 2001).
*The Present* (Macmillan: London, 1975).
*Yellow Bird* (Macmillan: London, 1975).

**GIMLETTE, John**
*Wild Coast: Travels on South America's Untamed Edge* (Profile Books Ltd: London, 2011).

**GIRDHARI, Gary**
*Education in Guyana with Special Reference to Science and Technology* (University of Guyana: Turkeyen, 1977).
*If Only the Gods Were Awake* (Gary Girdhari: New York, 2011).
*Reflections: On Politics, Human Conditions and Good Memories* (Guyana Journal: New York, 1998).

**GIRDHARRY, Arnold R.**
*Anthology of Caribbean Literature.* 2nd ed. (Acton: Copley, 2006).
*Country of New England: A Collection of Poems* (Bristol Banner Books: Bloomington, 1991).
*Marriage for Sale: Three One-Act Plays* (Geneva Books: New York, 1984).
*Poetry of Psycho-realism* (Notre Dame Foundations: New York, 1984).
*The Geometry of Marriage in Henry James* (UMI Press: Ann Arbour, 1982).
*The Indian and Indo-Guyanese Diaspora: A British Default* (Acton: Copley, 2006).
*The Wounds of Naipaul and the Women of India* (Acton: Copley, 2003).

**GITTENS, Cranston**
*Oreo: The Token Black Kid* (New Degree Press: Potomac: 2021).

**GIUSEPPI, N.; and U. Giuseppi**
*Backfire: A Collection of Short Stories from the Caribbean for Use in Secondary Schools* (Macmillan-Caribbean: London, 1973).

**GLAISHER, Ernest H.**
*A Journey on the Berbice River and Wieroonie Creek* (The Argosy Press: Georgetown, 1885).

**GLASGOW, Roy**
*Race and Politics Among Africans and East Indians* (Martinus Nijhoff: The Hague, 1970).

**GLASS, Ruth**
*Newcomers: The West Indians in London* (Allen & Unwin: London, 1960).

**GLOBAL FOREST WATCH**
*The State of Venezuela's Forests: A Case Study of the Guyana Region* (World Resources Institute: Washington, D.C., 2002).

**GOBLE, R., and Sandiford, K.A.P.**
*75 Years of West Indies Cricket* (Hansib Publications: Hertfordshire, 2004).

**GOEJE, C.H. De**
*The Arawak Language of Guiana* (Koninklijke Akademie van Wetenschappen: The Hague, 1928).

**GOLDSWORTHY, David**
*Colonial Issues in British Politics, 1945-1961: From Colonial development to 'Wind of Change'* (Clarendon Press: Oxford, 1971).

**GOMES, Joseph, ed.**
*Languages of the Guianas* (SIL, University of Oklahoma Press: Oklahoma City, 1972).

**GOMES, Mike**
*Piranha: The Falau Files (Createspace: New York, 2018).*

**GOMES, Patrick Ignatius**
*A Socio-economic Study of the Sub-watershed Area of the Castara, Community, Tobago* (UNDP: Port-of-Spain, 1988).
*Barbados: The Post-Independence Period 1966-1976* (UWI: St. Augustine, 1980).
*The OAS and Regional Development Planning in Saint Lucia: The Case of the Mabouya Valley* (OAS-GOSL, Natural Resources Management Project: Castries, 1988).
*The Marxian Populism of SLR James* (UWI: St. Augustine, 1980).

**_____; ed.**
*Rural Development in the Caribbean* (Heinemann: London, 1985).

**_____; et al**

*Report of a Commission of Inquiry into the Saint Lucia Banana Growers' Association* (St. Lucia Government: Castries, 1980).
*Report of a Land Reform Commission* (St. Lucia Government: Castries, 1981).

**_____; contr.**

"Agrarian Structures and Peasant Movements" in *A Sociology of the Contemporary Caribbean* (UWI: St. Augustine, 1981).
"Agriculture and Caribbean Económies: An Overview of Relations between Resources, Technology and State Policy in Trinidad and Tobago" in *Agricultures Pasaynnes Development: Caraibe-Amerique Tropicale* (SACAD: 1991).
"Transnational Capital, Food Dependency and Nutrition" in *Cornell Int. Nut. Series* (Cornell University: New York, 1988).
"Land Tenure Patterns in an Urban Periphery: Saint Lucia" in *Bull. Of Eastern Carib. Affairs* (ECS: Castries, 1991).
"The Political Context, Size and Structural Effects in the *New Public Administration: A Caribbean Perspective* (Seychelles/CAPAM/IASIA Conference: Victoria, 1997).
*Report of the World Bank/Government of Guyana/Public Administration Project, Regional Administrations and Local Government* (World Bank: Washington, D.C., 1999).
"In Pursuit of Public Sector Reform - Process and Products" in *Caribbean Journal of Public Sector Management* (Management Institute of Jamaica: Kingston, 1999).
"Report for the Guyana Forestry Commission Support Project, Diagnostic Study on Social Issues" in *Sustainable Forest Management, in collaboration with Natural Resources International* (NRI: London, 2000).

**____; and L.B. Coke**

"Critical Analysis of Agriculture Research and Development Institutions and their Activities" (UWI: ST. Augustine, 1982).

**_____; and T.H. Henderson**

"Family Structure, Attitudes and Decision-making among Caribbean Peasant Farmers" in *Agricultural Administration* (Caribbean Agro-Economics Society: Port of Spain, 1982).

**_____; T.H. Anderson; and M. Q. Patton**

"User -Focused Evaluation: A Caribbean Example" in *Studies in Educational Evaluation* (UWI: St. Augustine, 1983).

**_____; W.G. Clarke**

"Some Factors Affection the Adoption of Hand Tractors by Vegetable Farmers in Trinidad" in *Proc. Carib. Food Crops Soc* (CFCS: Port of Spain, 1984).

**_____; and R. Dumas**

"The CNIRD Initiative: Mobilising the NGO Sector for Rural Transformation" in *Caribbean Affairs* (New World Group: Mona, 1990).

**_____; and James Singh**

"Equity in Forest Policy and Practice" (Iwokrama International Conference: Georgetown, 2001).

" Ministries of Labour as Facilitators of Human Resource Development Strategies" in *Strategic Visions for Labour Administration in the Caribbean,* (ILO: Port of Spain, 2003).

" Rationalising Functions of Organs of the Community" (CARICOM 30th Anniversary Conference: Mona, 2003).

"Institutional Reforms for Better Governance: An Anglo-Caribbean Experience in Social Partnerships" in *Governance in Southern Africa and Beyond* (Macmillan: Gamsberg, 2004).

"The ACP Ambassadorial Working Group on Future Perspectives of the ACP Group" in *The ACP Group and the EU Development Partnership Agreement – Beyond the North-South Debate* (Palgrave Macmillan: London, 2017).

**GOODALL, Edward A.**

*Sketches of Amerindian Tribes 1841-43: With an Introduction by Sr. Mary Noel Menezes* (British Museum Publications: London, 1977). Reprint. (Macmillan-Caribbean: London, 2003).

**GOODRICH, Rev. Derek H.**

*A History of All Saints' Parish, New Amsterdam 1811-1979* (Derek Goodrich: Georgetown, 1979).

*A Short History of St. George's, Georgetown, Guyana* (Business Print: Georgetown, 1994).

*More Ramblings of a Parish Priest* (Derek Goodrich: Georgetown, 2010).

*Old-Style Missionary – The Ministry of John Dorman, Priest in Guyana* (Taverner Publications: Georgetown, 2003).

*The Ramblings of a Parish Priest* (Business Print: Georgetown, 1995).

*The Words and Works of Alan John Knight: Anglican Bishop of Guyana 1937-39. Archbishop of the West Indies 1950-79* (Business Print: Georgetown, 1999).

**GOODRIDGE, Sophia**

*The Spirit, The Passion and The Blood: A Nicky Porter Story* (S. Goodridge: Toronto, 2002).

**GOODWIN, Clay**

*West Indian at the Wicket* (Macmillan Caribbean: London, 1986).

**GOOLSARAN, Anand**

*Improving Public Accountability: The Guyana Experience, 1985-2007* (Outskirts Press: Parker, 2010).

**GOOLSARAN, Samuel Jerry**

*System of Industrial Relations in Guyana* (International Labour Organization: Geneva, 2003).

**GOOLSARRAN, Raj**

*Romancing a Goddess: Romantic verses for lovers* (Lulu Press: Raleigh, 2006).

**GOPAL, Madan M.**

*Notes on Race and Psychology* (n.p.: n.p., n.d.).

*Politics, Race and Youth in Guyana* (Edwin Meller Press: Lewiston, 1992).

*Schooldays in the Colony* (Edwin Meller Press: Lewiston, 2008).

*Stories from India for Children* ((n.p.: n.p., n.d.).

*Teachers and Students* (n.p.: n.p., n.d.).

**GOPAUL, N.K.**

*Ashton Chase: The Bengal Tiger* (NK. Gopal: Georgetown, 2012).

*Resistance and Change: The Struggles of the Guyanese Workers (1964 to 1994) with Emphasis on the Sugar Industry* (Inside News Publications: np., 1997).

**GOPAL, Paul**

*Alexander's Amazon Adventures (Xlibris: Bloomington, 2021).*

**GORDON, N.**

*Hunting for Gold* (AuthorHouse: Bloomington, 2006).

**GORDON, Shirley C.**

*A Century of West Indian Education* (Longmans: London, 1963).

**GOSINE, Mahin**

*The East Indian Odyssey: Dilemmas of a Migrant People* (Wilson Press: New York, 1994).

*The Legacy of Indian Indenture* (Africana Research Press: Port-of-Spain, 1987).

**GOSLINGA, Cornelis**

*The Dutch in the Caribbean and on the Wild Coast, 1580-1680* (Van Gorcum: Assesn, 1971).

*The Dutch in the Caribbean and the Guianas 1680-1791* (Van Gorcum: Assesn, 1985).

**GOTT, Richard**

*Land Without Evil: Utopian Journeys across the South American Watershed* (Verso: New York, 1993).

**GOVEIA, Elsa V**

*A Study of the Historiography of the British West Indies* (UWI, Mona, 1956).

*Slave Society in the British Leeward Islands at the End of the Eighteenth Century* (UWI Press: Mona, 1965).

**GOVERNMENT OF GUYANA**

*Amerindian Integration: A Brief Outline of the Progress of Integration in Guyana* (Guyana Government: Georgetown, 1970).

*Gazetteer of Guyana* (Guyana Government: Georgetown, 2001).

*Independence 10: Guyanese Writing 1966-76* (National History and Arts Council: Georgetown, 1976).

**GRAFF, Wendy**

*No Word in Guyanese For Me: A One-Woman Play* (Original Works Publishing: New York, 2014).

**GRAHAM, Ivy**

*Intransigence* (Ivy Graham: New York, 2018).

**GRANGER, Brigadier (r'td.), David A.**

*A Preliminary Study of Women Soldiers in the Anglophone Caribbean* (Free Press: Georgetown, n.d.).

*British Regiments in British Guiana* (Free Press: Georgetown: 2008).

*Crime Without Punishment: The Caribbean Case for Reparation Justice* (Free Press: Georgetown, 2016).

*Five-Thousand Day War: The Struggle for Haiti`s Independence, 1789-1904* (Free Press: Georgetown, 2004).

*Forbes Burnham and the Liberation of Southern Africa* (Free Press: Georgetown, 2013).

*Guyana Independence 1966* (Guyana Book Foundation: Georgetown, 2008).

*Guyana's Coinage, 1808-2008* (Free Press: Georgetown, 2009).

*Guyana's Golden Age: The Diversification of British Guiana's Economy 1880-1930* (Free Press: Georgetown, 2008).

*Guyana's Military Veterans* (Free Press: Georgetown, 1999).

*National Defence: A Brief History of the Guyana Defence Force 1965-2005* (Free Press: Georgetown, 2008).

*Public Security: Criminal Violence and Policy in Guyana* (Free Press: Georgetown, 2011).

*Scenes from the History of Africans* (Free Press: Georgetown, 1999).
*The British Guiana Volunteer Force, 1948-1966* (Free Press: Georgetown, 2008).
*The Emancipation Movement: The Pursuit of Dignity and Liberty* (Free Press: Georgetown, 2020).
*The Era of Enslavement, 1638-1838* (Free Press: Georgetown, 2011).
*The Guyana National Service, 1974-2000* (Free Press: Georgetown, 2008).
*The Guyana People`s Militia, 1976-1997*(Free Press: Georgetown, 2008).
*The Independence Movement 1946-1966* (Free Press: Georgetown, 2014)
*The New Road – A Short History of the GDF 1966-76* (Free Press: Georgetown, 2011).
*The Queen`s College Cadet Corps, 1889-1975* (Free Press: Georgetown, n.d.).
*The Village Movement, 1839-1889* (Free Press: Georgetown, n.d.).

**_____; ed.**
*Scenes from the History of the Africans* (Free Press: Georgetown, 1999).

**_____; and Barrington Braithwaite**
*The Era of Enslavement 1638-1838* (Free Press: Georgetown, 2008).

**_____; and Amera Jones, eds.**
*New Guyanese Publications* (Free Press: Georgetown, 1997).

**_____; and N. Westmaas**
*Guyana Periodicals* (Free Press: Georgetown, 1995).

**_____; and Winston McGowan; and James Rose, eds.**
*Themes in African-Guyanese History* (Hansib Publications: Hertfordshire, 2008).

**GRANNUM-SOLOMON, Victorine**
*Proverbial Wisdom from Guyana* (V. Grannum-Solomon: Georgetown, 1999).

**GRANT, C.H.; and R.M. Kirton, eds.**
*Governance, Conflict Analysis and Conflict Resolution* (Ian Randle Publishers: Kingston, 2003).

**GRANT, Cy**
*A Member of the RAF of Indeterminate Race* (Woodfield Publishing: Bognor Regis, 2006).
*Blackness and the Dreaming Soul* (Shoving Leopard:

Edinburgh, 2007).

*Ring of Steel: Pan Sound and Symbol* (Macmillan: London, 1999).

*Rivers of Time: Collected Poems* (Naked Light: London, 2006).

**GRANT, Kevin, ed.**

*The Art of David Dabydeen* (Peepal Tree Press: Leeds, 1997).

**GRANTHAM, D. R.; and R.F. Noel Paton**

*Geological Survey of British Guiana. Report on the Geology of the Superficial and Coastal Deposits of British Guiana* (Argosy: Georgetown, 1938).

*Guyana* (Chelsea House Publishing: Philadelphia, 1989).

*Let's Visit Guyana* (Macmillan: London, 1988).

**GRAY, Ashley**

*The Unforgiven: Missionaries or Mercenaries? The Untold Story of the Rebel West Indian Cricketers Who Toured Apartheid South Africa* (Pitch Publishers: Hove, 2020).

**GRAY, Caroline**

*The Promised Land and the Phoenix* (Pan Books: London, 1999).

*A woman of her time* (Paragon: New York, 1996).

**GREAVES, Stanley**

*Haiku* (Peepal Tree Press: Leeds, 2015).

*Horizons* (Peepal Tree Press: Leeds, 2002). [Won the Guyana Prize for Literature – 1st book of poems category].

*The Poems Man* (Peepal Tree Press: Leeds, 2009).

**_____; and Anne Walmsley**

*Art in the Caribbean: An Introduction* (2010)

**GREEN, Hamilton E.**

*Anthology of Georgetown and a Piece of the World* (Free Press: Georgetown, 2006).

*From Pain to Peace: Guyana 1953-1964* (Tropical Airways Inc.: Georgetown, 1987).

*Odyssey and Trials of the Georgetown Mayor and Councillors 1992-2012* (Hamilton Green: Georgetown, 2013).

**GREEN, Jeffrey**

*Black Edwardians: Black People in Britain 1901-1914* (Frank Cass: London, 2005).

**GREENE, J.E.**

*Race vs. Politics in Guyana: Political Cleavages and Political Mobilization in the 1968 General Election* (University of the West Indies: Kingston, 1974).

**GREENFIELD, Gerald M.; and Sheldon M. Maram, eds.**

*Latin American Labor Organizations* (Greenwood Press: Westport, 1987).

**GREENIDGE, Carl B.**

*Empowering a Peasantry in a Caribbean Context: The Case of Land Settlement Schemes in Guyana 1865-1985* (UWI Press: Kingston, 2001).

**GREGORY, Kyomi; J.B. Oetting; and J.R. Berry**

*Use of Linguistic Theory to Inform the Assessment and Treatment of Developmental Language Disorder Within African American English* (Routledge: New York, 2022).

**_____; and C. Chaney**

*President Obama: Code meshing and the power of speech in racial politic* (ABC-CLIO: Santa Barbara, 2017).

**_____; contr.**

*Clinical Applications of Linguistics to Speech Language Pathology: A Guide for Clinicians* (Routledge: New York, 2017).

*How the Obama Presidency Changed the Political Landscape* (ABC-CLIO: New York, 2017).

**GRIEVE, Robert**

*The Asylum, Volume 1* (Caribbean Press: Georgetown, 2013).

*The Asylum, Volume 2* (Caribbean Press: Georgetown, 2013).

**GRIFFITH, Charles L.**

*Comprehensive Quality Policy Thinking: A Means to Acquire Self-Determination* (C.L. Griffith: Georgetown, 2008).

**GRIFFITH, Ivelaw**

*Caribbean Security in the Age of Terror Challenge and Change* (Ian Randle Publishers: Kingston, 2002).

*Caribbean Security on the Eve of the 21st Century* (National Defense University Press: Washington, D.C., 1996).

*Challenged Sovereignty in the Caribbean: The Impact of Drugs, Crime, Terrorism and Cybercrime* (University of Illinois Press: Chicago, 2023).

*Drugs and Security in the Caribbean: Sovereignty Under Siege* (Penn State University Press: University Park, 1997).

*The Political Economy of Drugs in the Caribbean – International Political Economy Series* (Macmillan/Palgrave: London, 2000; St. Martin's Press: New York, 2000).

*The Quest for Security in the Caribbean: Problems and Promises in Subordinate States* (M.E. Sharpe: Armomnk, 1993).

**_____; ed.**

*Strategy and Security in the Caribbean* (ABC-CLIO: Santa Barbara, 1991).

**_____; et al**

*Democracy and Human Rights in the Caribbean* (Westview Press: Boulder, 1997).

*The Caribbean in the Pacific Century: Prospects for Caribbean-Pacific Cooperation* (Rienner Publishers: Lynne, 1993).

**GRIFFITH, Owen "Mitch"**

*Perseverance and Dignity* (Santa Clara Press: Santa Clara, 1987).

**GRIMBLE, Rosemary**

*Jonathan and Large* (Andre Deutsch: London, 1965. Reprint. Bobbs-Merrill: Indianapolis, 1966, 1967).

**GRITZNER, Charles F.**

*Guyana in Pictures* (Sterling: New York, 1975).

**GRUBB, Kenneth George**

*The Lowland Indians of Amazonia: A Survey of the Location and Religious Condition of the Indians of Colombia, Venezuela, the Guianas, Ecuador, Peru, Brazil and Bolivia* (World Dominion Press: London, 1927).

**GRUGEL, Jean**

*Politics and Development in the Caribbean Basin* (Indiana University Press: Indianapolis, 1995).

*Central America and the Caribbean in the New World Order* (Indiana University Press: Indianapolis, 1995).

**GUINN, Jeff**

*The Road to Jonestown: Jim Jones and Peoples Temple* (Simon & Schuster: New York, 2017)

**GULMAHAMAD, Hanif**

*Guyana Stories and Passages* (Createspace: New York, 2014).

*Stolen Hope and Stolen Dreams: Guyana 50 Years After Independence and Other Stories* (Xlibris: Bloomington, 2017).

*Stories and Poems by a Guyanese Village Boy* (Xlibris: Bloomington, 2009).

**GUNRAJ, Andrea**

*The Sudden Disappearance of Seetha* (Knopf: Toronto, 2009).

**GUPPY, Nicholas**

*A Young Man's Journey* (John Murray: London, 1973).

*Wai Wai: Through the Forests North of the Amazon* (John Murray: London, 1958).

**GUSKA**

*The Masses Create* (Guyana National Service Publications Centre: Georgetown, 1978).

**GUTHMAN, Edwin O.; and Jeffrey Shulman, eds.**

*Robert Kennedy in His Own Words: The Unpublished Recollections of the Kennedy Years* (Bantam Books: New York, 1988).

**GUTHRIE, Rev. William**

*A Woman of Valor, A Woman of Strength – The Latchmin Bridgelall Story* (Outskirts Press: Denver, 2017).

*Bartica – Gateway to the Interior of Guyana* (Outskirts Press: Denver, 2008).

*David and Jonathan - The Tale of Two Friends* (Outskirts Press: Denver, 2014).

*Speaking Truth to Power – An Anthology of Sermons* (Outskirts Press: Denver, 2015).

*Transformed and Renewed – The True Story of a Pastor's Struggle with Depression* (Outskirts Press: Denver, 2012).

**GUYADEEN, Indrani**

*Arshana* (In Our Words Inc.: Toronto, 2017).

**GUYANA HERITAGE SOCIETY**

*Aspects of European-Guyanese Heritage* (Guyana Heritage Society: Georgetown, 2017). [A Collaboration Between the European Union, Guyana Heritage Society, and the National Trust of Guyana].

*From Ashes to Ferro-Concrete: A History of the Cathedral of the Immaculate Conception* (Guyana Heritage Society: Georgetown, 2014).

**GUYANA INDIAN FOUNDATION TRUST**

*Report of the January 12, 1998 Violence Against Indians* (Guyana Indian Foundation Trust: Georgetown, 1999).

**GUYANA INFORMATION SERVICES**

*A Portrait of Guyana* (GIS: Georgetown, 1977).

**GUYANA INSTITUTE OF HISTORICAL RESEARCH (GIHR)**

*A Chronological History of Guyana, 1580-2004* (GIHR: Georgetown, 2004).

*David Leslie Lorain Melville: 1925-2015: An Autobiography* (GIHR: Georgetown, 2018).

*Leading Cause of Death During the Last 120 Years: Public Hospital New Amsterdam* (GIHR: Georgetown, 2019).

**GUYANA NATIONAL SERVICE (GNS)**

*This is Guyana National Service* (GNS: Georgetown, 1975).

**GUYANA WOMEN ARTISTS ASSOCIATION**

*60 Years of Women Artists in Guyana, 1928-1988: A Historical Perspective* (CIDA: Georgetown, 1988).

# H

**HAKLUYT, Richard**

*The Principal Navigations of the English Nations* (James MacLehose and Sons: Glasgow, 1904).

**HALDER, Peter**

*Jax and the Wizard of Zandar* (Proglen Trading Company, Ltd.: Bangkok, 2015).

*Quest for the Rod of Moses* (Proglen Trading Company, Ltd.: Bangkok, 2015).

*The Alligator and the Sun: And Other Rainforest Tales* (Proglen Trading Company, Ltd.: Bangkok, 2014).

*The Cat of Muritaro* (Franklin and Franklin: New York, 2012).

*The Dance of Death: Chilling Supernatural Tales of Guyana (Proglen* Trading Company, Ltd.: Bangkok, 2014).

*The Dead Don't Die: Macabre Supernatural Tales of Guyana* (Proglen Trading Company, Ltd.: Bangkok, 2014).

*The Doomsday Earthquake* (Proglen Trading Company, Ltd.: Bangkok, 2014).

*Hero the Warrior: Defender of the Forces of Good* (Proglen Trading Company, Ltd.: Bangkok, 2015).

*The Monkey Wife: Four Bizarre Tales of the Rainforest* (Proglen Trading Company, Ltd.: Bangkok, 2015).

*The Princess of the Forest: Two Heart Warming Fairy Tales* (Proglen Trading Company, Ltd.: Bangkok, 2015).

*The Rainbow's End: Two Super Fantasy Tales* (Proglen Trading Company, Ltd.: Bangkok, 2014).

*The Riddle: Four Enchanting Fairy Tales* (Proglen Trading Company, Ltd.: Bangkok, 2015).

*The Three Princes: Two Exciting Adventure Tales* (Proglen Trading Company, Ltd.: Bangkok, 2014).

*Tiger's Birthday Party: A Collection of Animal Tales* (Proglen Trading Company, Ltd.: Bangkok, 2014).

**HALL, Duncan H.**

*Commonwealth: A History of the British Commonwealth of Nations* (Van Nostrand Reinhold: London, 1971).

**HALL, Gwendolyn**

*Slavery and African Ethnicities in the Americas: Restoring Links* (The University of North Carolina Press: Chapel Hill, 2005).

*The Promised Land: Jonestown as American Cultural History* (Transaction Publishers: Somerset, 2001).

**HALL, John R.**

*Gone from the Promised Land: Jonestown as American Cultural History* (Transaction Publishers: Somerset, 2001).

**HALL, K.O.**

*Caribbean Imperatives: Regional Governance and Integrated Development* (Ian Randle Publishers: Kingston, 2005).

*Integrate or Perish* (Ian Randle Publishers: Kingston, 2003).

*Reinventing Caricom* (Ian Randle Publishers: Kingston, 2003).

*Survival and Sovereignty in the Caribbean Community* (Ian Randle Publishers: Kingston, 2004).

*The Caribbean Community: Beyond Survival* (Ian Randle Publishers: Kingston, 2001).

*The Caribbean Integration Process: A People-Centred Approach* (Ian Randle Publishers: Kingston, 2005).

**_____; and Benn, D.**

*Caribbean Initiatives* (Ian Randle Publishers: Kingston, 2008).

*Contending with Destiny* (Ian Randle Publishers: Kingston, 2000).

**_____; and Chuck-a-Sang, M., eds.**

*Caricom: Genesis and Prognosis* (Ian Randle Publishers: Kingston, 2007).

*Caricom: Policy Options for International Engagement* (Ian Randle Publishers: Kingston, 2010).

*Caricom Options: Towards Integration Into The World Economy* (Ian Randle Publishers: Kingston, 2003).

*Integration: Caricom's Key To Prosperity* (Ian Randle Publishers: Kingston, 2006).

*Intervention, Border and Maritime Issues in Caricom* (Ian Randle Publishers: Kingston, 2007).

*The Integrationist- Observing Elections in the Caribbean: The Early Years* (Ian Randle Publishers: Kingston, 2006).

*The Caribbean Community in Transit: Functional Cooperation as a Catalyst for Change* (Ian Randle Publishers: Kingston, 2008).

*The Caribbean Integration Process: A People Centred Approach* (Ian Randle Publishers: Kingston, 2007).

**_____; and Denis Benn**

*Caribbean Imperatives: Regional Governance & Integrated Development* (Ian Randle Publishers: Kingston, 2005).

*Contending With Destiny: The Caribbean in the 21st Century* (Ian Randle Publishers: Kingston, 2002).

*Governance in the Age of Globalisation: Caribbean Perspectives* (Ian Randle Publishers: Kingston, 2004).

**_____; and Rose Marie Cameron**

*Higher Education: Caribbean Perspectives* (Ian Randle Publishers: Kingston, 2002).

**HALL, Laura Jane**

*The Chinese in Guyana: The Making of a Creole Community* (Her Ph.D. Thesis) (University of California: Berkeley, 1995).

**HANIFF, Nesha Z.**

*The Pedagogy of Action: Small Axe Fall Big Tree* (Palgrave/Macmillan: London, 2022).

*Blaze A Fire: Significant Contributions of Caribbean Women* (Sister Vision: Toronto, 1988).

**_____; and Karen De Souza, ill.**

*60 Years of Women Artists in Guyana 1928-88: A Historical Perspective* (Guyana Women Artists' Association: Georgetown, 1988).

**HANLEY, Eric**

*Mechanized Rice Production: The Experience of an East Indian Rice Community in Guyana* (Government of Guyana: Georgetown, 1979).

*The Guyana Rice Industry and USAID* (USAID: Georgetown, 1981).

**HARCOURT, Robert**

*A Relation of a Voyage to Guiana Describing the Climate, Situation, Fertilitie, Commodities of That Country. Together with the Manner and Customes of the People. Performed by Robert Harcourt of Stanton Harcourt Esquier 1609. (1626)* (n.p.: n.p., 1613). Reprint. (Proquest, Eebo Edition: Ann Arbor, 2010).

**HARDING, Wesley**

*Terror Island* (Wesley Harding: Toronto, 2005).

**HARI, Adarsh Kumar**

*An Educational Journey: Against All Odds in Guyana, South America* (Xlibris: Bloomington, 2012).

**HARLEQUIN, J.B.**

*Georgetown: The Garden City of the West. A Description in Verse and Also A Souvenir of the Centenary 1831-1931* (Persick: Georgetown, 1931).

**HARLOW, Vincent T.**

*Ralegh's Last Voyage* (Argonaut Press: London, 1932).

**_____., ed.**

*Colonising Expeditions to the West Indies and Guiana, 1623-1667* (Hakluyt Society: London, 1925. Reprint. (Nendeln: Liechtenstein, 1967).

**_____.; and F. Madden**

*British Colonial Developments 1774-1834* (Clarendon Press: Oxford, 1953).

**HARPER, Douglas**

*My Life as a Musician* (B4Press; Stockholm, 2012).

**HARPER-WILLS, Doris**

*The Wings of Iere: Amerindian Legends* (Trafford Publishing: London, 2013).

**HARRIS, Bonita**

*Calabash in my hand* (n.p: n.p., n.d.).

*Calabash Parkway* (n.p: n.p., n.d.).

**HARRIS, C.A., ed.**

*A Relation of a Voyage to Guiana by Robert Harcourt* (Hakluyt Society: London, 1928). [Robert Harcourt's book above].

**_____.; and J.A.J. De Villiers, eds.**

*Storm Van's Gravesande: The Rise of British Guiana: Compiled from his Despatches,* 2 vols. (Hakluyt Society: London, 1911).

**HARRIS, Denise** [Wilson Harris's daughter]

*In Remembrance Of Her* (Peepal Tree Press: Leeds, 2004).

*Web of Secrets* (Peepal Tree Press: Leeds, 1996).

**HARRIS, Maggie**

*After a Visit to A Botanical Garden* (Mango Publishing: London, 2006). [Shortlisted Guyana Prize for Literature, 2011].

*Canterbury Tales on a Cockcrow Morning, Selected Poems 1999-2010* (Caribbean Press: Georgetown, 2012).

*From Berbice to Broadstairs: Poems* (Mango Publishing: London, 2006).

*In Margate By Lunchtime* (Cultured Llama: London, 2015).

*Kiskadee Girl – A Memoir* (Kingston University Press: Kingston, 2011). [Prize Winner Life Writing Competition KUP].

*Limbolands* (Mango Publishing: London, 1999). [Winner Guyana Prize for Literature, 2000].

*On Watching A Lemon Sail The Sea* (Cane Arrow Press: London, 2019).

*Selected Poems* (Caribbean Press: Georgetown, 2013).

*Sixty Years of Loving* (Cane Arrow Press: London, 2014). [Winner Guyana Prize for Literature, 2014].

*Writing on Water* (Seren: London, 2017).

**HARRIS, Mike**

*Rivers of Green* (Createspace: New York, 2017).

**HARRIS, P.**

*Like Father...Like Son* (P. Harris: Georgetown, n.d.).

**HARRIS, William I.**

*Joseph of Demerary* (n.p.: Georgetown, 2008).

*Managing a Great Woman: Things Men Need to Know About the Women in Their Lives* (n.p.: Georgetown, 2010).

**HARRIS, Wilson** [Jan Carew's brother in-law]

*An Angel at the Gate* (Faber and Faber: London, 1982).

*Ascent to Omai* (Faber and Faber: London, 1970), (Peepal Tree Press: Leeds, 2018).

*Black Marsden* (Faber and Faber: London, 1972).

*Carnival* (Faber and Faber: London, 1972).

*Companions of the Day and Night* (Faber and Faber: London, 1975).

*Da Silva's Cultivated Wilderness and Geneses of the Clowns* (Faber and Faber: London, 1977).

*Eternity to Season* (New Beacon Books, London, 1978).

*Far Journey of Oudin* (Faber and Faber: London, 1961).

*Fetish* (Master Printery: Georgetown, 1951).

*Fossil and Psyche* (University of Texas: USA, 1974).

*Heartland* (Faber and Faber: London, 1964).

*Infinite Rehearsal* (Faber and Faber: London, 1988).

*Jonestown* (Faber and Faber: London, 1996).

*Palace of the Peacock* (Faber and Faber: London, 1998).

*Resurrection at Sorrow Hill* (Faber and Faber: London, 1993).

*The Age of the Rainmakers* (Faber and Faber: London, 1971).

*The Angel at the Gate* (Faber and Faber: London, 1982).

*The Carnival Trilogy* (Faber and Faber: London, 1993).

*The Dark Jester* (Faber and Faber: London, 2001).

*The Eye of the Scarecrow* (Faber and Faber: London, 1965).

*The Four Banks of the River of Space* (Faber and Faber: London, 1990).

*The Ghost of Memory* (Faber & Faber: London, 2006).
*The Guyana Quartet (Comprising Palace of the Peacock; The Far Journey of Oudin; The Whole Armour; The Secret Ladder* (Faber and Faber: London, 1985).
*The Mask of the Beggar* (Faber and Faber: London, 2003).
*The Secret Ladder* (Faber and Faber: London, 1963).
*The Sleepers of Roraima: A Carib Trilogy* (Faber and Faber: London, 1970).
*The Tree of the Sun* (Faber and Faber: London, 1978).
*The Waiting Room* (Faber and Faber: London, 1967).
*The Whole Armour* (Faber and Faber: London, 1962).
*Tradition, the Writer and Society* (New Beacon: London, 1967).
*The Womb in Space: The Cross-Cultural Imagination* (Conn & London: Westport, 1983).
*Tumatumari* (Faber and Faber: London, 1968).
**_____; Foreign Language Publications**
*Der Palast der Pfauen* (Amman Verlag: Zurich, 1988).
*El palacio del pavo real* (Diagonal: Barcelona, 2003).
*Il palazzo del pavone* (Einaudi: Torino, 1989).
*L'ange sur le seuil* (Belfond: Paris, 1982).
*L'échelle secrete* (Belfond: Paris, 1981).
*Le palais du paon* (Edition des autres: Paris, 1979).
*Longa Jornado de Oudin* (Globo: Sâo Paulo, 1991).
*Palacio do Pavâo* (Globo: Sâo Paulo, 1990).
**_____; and S.R. Cudjoe**
*History, Fable and Myth in the Caribbean and Guianas* (Calaloux Publications: London, 1995).

**HARRISON, John**
*The Geology of the Gold Fields of British Guiana* (n.p.: n.p., 1908). Reprint. (eBooks: Cleveland, 2013).

**HARRY, Caryle**
*Critchlow: His Main Tasks and Achievements* (GTUC: Georgetown, 1976).

**HARRY, Lloyd Sylvester**
*Forests and Forestry: A Select Bibliography with Special Reference to Guyana* (National Science and Research Council: Georgetown, 1977).

**HART, Richard**
*From Occupation to Independence: A Short History of the Peoples of the English-Speaking Caribbean Region* (University of the West Indies Press: Kingston, 1998).

**HASSAN, Dolly Z.**

*V.S. Naipaul and the West Indies* (Peter Lang Publishing: New York, 1989).

**HASSANKHAN, Maurits S; et al**

*Islam, Muslims, and Indentured Labour: Diaspora Experiences of a Minority Group in Plural Societies* (Manohar Publishing: New Delhi, 2016).

*The Legacy of Indian Indenture: Historical and Contemporary of Migration and Diaspora* (Ian Randle Publishers: Kingston, 2016).

**HAYNES, Pat "Tricha"**

*WOW – Words of Wisdom – 100 Booster Shots for the Mind* (PPC Books: Reddyton Shores, 2005).

**HAZLEWOOD, Leyland**

*Chester Goes to Africa* (Xlibris: Bloomington, 2011).

*Chester Visits the Mountain Gorillas* (Dimpex Press: 2022).

*The Ultimate Guide to Doing Business in Africa* (Motivational Press: USA, 2016).

**HEAD, Harold, ed.**

*Canada in US Now: The First Anthology of Black Poetry and Prose in Canada* (NC Press Ltd.: Toronto, 1976).

**HEATH, Roy**

*Art and Experience* (Ministry of Education: Georgetown, 1983).

*From the Heat of the Day* (Persea Books: New York, 1994).

*Genetha* (Allison and Busby: London, 1981).

*Kwaku or the man who could not keep his mouth shut* (Allison and Busby: London, 1982).

*One Generation* (Allison and Busby: London, 1981).

*Orealla* (Allison & Busby: London, 1984).

*Shadows Round the Moon: Caribbean Memoirs* (Collins: London, 1991).

*The Angel at the Gate* (Allison and Busby: London, 1982).

*The Armstrong Trilogy: From the Heat of the Day, One Generation, Gentha* (Persea Books: London, 1994).

*The Ministry of Hope* (Marion Boyars Publishers: New York, 1997).

*The Murderer* (Persea Books: New York, 1992).

*The Shadow Bride* (Collins: London, 1988).

*The Tree of the Sun* (Allison and Busby: London, 1978).

**HELMAN, Albert**

*De foltering van Eldorado: een ecologhische geschiedenis van de vijf Guyana's* (Nijgh and Van Ditmar: Amsterdam, 1983).

**HELMS, Richard**

*A Look Over My Shoulder: A Life in the Central Intelligence Agency* (Random House: New York, 2003).

**HELLIUM, A.K.; and G. Nicholl**

*Trees of Guyana: A Seedling Identification Guide* (LP Publishing: Beaverton, 1994).

**HEMMING, John**

*Amazon Frontier: The Defeat of the Brazilian Indians* (Macmillan: London, 1987).

*Red Gold: Conquest of the Brazilian Indians* (Macmillan: London, 1978).

*The Search for El Dorado* (Dutton: New York, 1978).

**HENDERSON, Thomas**

*The Missionary's Wife: A Memoir of Mrs. M.A. Henderson of Demerara by Her Husband* (n.p.: London, 1855).

**HENFREY, C.**

*The Gentle People: A Journey among the Indian Tribes of Guiana* (Travel Book Club: London, 1964).

**HENFREY, Thomas**

*Wapishana Ethnoecology* (Lulu Publishers: Morristown, 2018).

**HENNINGSGAARD, William**

*The Akawaio, the Upper Mazaruni Hydroelectric Project and National Development in Guyana* (Cultural Survival: Cambridge, 1981).

**HENRY, C. Michael**

*Economics of Adoption of New Agricultural Technology: The Case for the Guyana Rice Sub--sector* (USAID: Georgetown, 1986).

**HENRY, Edgar**

*Guyanese Slang Alphabet* (Dorrance Publishing: Pittsburgh, 2022).

**HENRY, M.**

*Economics of Adoption of New Agricultural Technology – The Case of the Guyana Rice Sub-sectors* (Hansib: London, 1990).

**HENRY, Norman**

*Adversity is Temporary* (N. Henry: New York, 2005).

**HENRY, Zin**

*Labour Relations and Industrial Conflict in Commonwealth Caribbean Countries* (Columbus Publishers: Port of Spain, 1972).

**HENSHALL-MOMSEN, Janet**

*Women and Development in the Third World* (Routledge: London, 1991).

**HEPHAESTUS BOOKS**

*Guyanese Women* (Hephaestus Books: Richardson, 2011).

*Guyanese Literature* (Hephaestus Books: Richardson, 2011).
*Guyanese Writers* (Hephaestus Books: Richardson, 2011).

**HERGASH, Harry T.**
*A Collection of Indian-Guyanese Words and Phrases and Their Meanings* (Harry T. Hergash: Toronto, 2013).

**HERMAN, Marc**
*Searching for El Dorado* (Bantam Doubleday: New York, 1999).

**HERRIB, E.J.**
*Of Flesh and Blood—and God: A Collection of Poems* (E. J. Herrib: Georgetown, 1972).

**HETRAM, Charran**
*Doodnauth and Charran Hetram: It's the Journey That Matters: India-Guyana-Canada* (Amazon Books: Bolton, 2022).

**HEWICK, W.**
*A Post Slavery Nightmare* (AuthorHouse: Bloomington, 2006).

**HEYDORN, Bernard**
*Carnival Girl* (Learning Improvement Centre: Newmarket, 1996).
*Dialect and/or Cultural Interference in Language Arts* (Learning Improvement Centre: Newmarket, 1986).
*Heydorn Elementary Learning Profile: A Test of Basic Skills Grades 1-8* (Learning Improvement Centre: Newmarket, 1993).
*Longtime Days* (Learning Improvement Centre: Newmarket, 1999).
*Song of the West Indies: A Collection of Poems* (Learning Improvement Centre: Newmarket, 1986).
*Unlit Roads* (Learning Improvement Centre: Newmarket, 2000).
*Walk Good Guyana Boy* (Learning Improvement Centre: Newmarket, 1994).

**HEYDORN, Malcolm W.**
*Guyana at the Millenium Crossroads: A Psychosocial Perspective* (M & L Counselling: Markham, 2000).

**HEYWOOD, Theresa C.**
*I was There: My Stint in the Guyana National Service* (T.C. Heywood: Georgetown, 2004).

**HIGMAN, B**
*Slave Populations of the British Caribbean: 1809-1834* (Johns Hopkins University: Baltimore, 1984).

**HILHOUSE, William**
*Journal of a Voyage up the Massaroony in 1831* (Royal Geographical Society: London, 1834).

**HILL, Robert**

*Walter Rodney Speaks: The Making of an African Intellectual* (Africa World Press: Trenton, 1990).

**HILLMAN, Richard S.; and J. D'Agostino**

*Understanding the Contemporary Caribbean,* 2nd Ed. (Ian Randle Publishers: Kingston, 2009).

**HILLS, Theo L.**

*The Savanna Biome* (Department of Geography, McGill University: Montreal, 1976).

**HINCKSON, Oliver**

*Enemy Within* (Oliver Hinckson: Georgetown, 2007).

*Cry Havoc* (Oliver Hinckson: Georgetown, 2008).

**HINDS, David**

*Race and Political Discourse in Guyana* (Guyana-Caribbean Politics Publications: Georgetown, 2004).

*The Ethno-Politics and Power Sharing in Guyana: History and Discourse* (New Academia Publishing: Washington, D.C., 2011).

**HINDS, Roger**

*The Life and Works of Bill (Bhagee) Rogers and the Origin of the Shanto Music in Guyana* (Carifesta Secretariat: Georgetown, 2008).

**HINDS, Selwyn**

*Gunshots in my cook-up: Bits and Bites from a Hip-Hop Caribbean Life* (Atria Books: New York, 2002).

**HINGSTON, R.W.G.**

*A Naturalist in the Guiana Forest* (Edward Arnold & Co.: London, 1932).

**HINTZEN, P.C.**

*The Costs of Regime Survival: Racial Mobilization, Elite Domination and Control of the State in Guyana and Trinidad* (Cambridge University Press: Cambridge, 1989).

*West Indians in the West: Self Representations in a Migrant Community* (New York University Press: New York, 2001).

**_____; and Jean Muteba Rahier, eds.**

*Global Circuits of Blackness: Interrogating the African Diaspora* (University of Illinois Press: Urbana, 2010).

*Problematizing Blackness: Self-Ethnographies by Black Immigrants to the United States* (Routledge: New York, 2003).

**HODGSON, Stiedholme**

*Truths From the West Indies* (William Ball: London, 1828).

**HOGG, Ethel**

*Quintin Hogg: A Biography* (n.p.: London, 1904).

**HOLDER, Yvonne**

*Women Traders of Guyana* (ECLAC: Port of Spain, 1986).

**HOLLETT, David**

*Passage from India to El Dorado; Guyana and the Great Migration* (Farleigh Dickenson University Press: London, 1999).

**HOLLOWELL, Tom; Lynn J. Gillespie; V.A. Funk; and Carol L. Kelloff**

*Smithsonian Plant Collections, Guyana* (Smithsonian Institution: Washington, D.C., 2003).

**HOOPER, Andrew**

*Sons of God, Come Forth* (Essence Publishing: Belleville, 2007).

**HOOPER, Eddie**

*Down in Guyana* (Ministry of Information & Culture: Georgetown, 1975).

**HOPE, Kempe R.**

*Guyana: Politics and Development in an Emergent Socialist State* (Mosaic Press: Cincinnati, 1986).

*The Post-War Planning Experience in Guyana* (Latin American Studies Centre of Arizona State University: Tempe. 1978).

**HOPKINSON, Nalo**

*Brown Girl in the Ring* (Warner Books Inc.: New York, 2005).

**HOPKINSON, 'Slade' Abdur Rahman**

*Falling in Love with Hominids* (Tachyon Publications: San Francisco, 2015).

*Midnight Robber* (Warner Books: New York, 2000).

*Mojo: Conjure Stories* (Aspect: Southfield, 2003).

*Report from Planet Midnight* (PM Press: Oakland, 2012).

*Sister Mine* (Grand Central Publishing: New York, 2013).

*Skin Folk* (Aspect: Southfield, 2001).

*Snowscape with Signature* (Peepal Tree Press: Leeds, 1993).

*The Chaos* (Margaret K. McElderly Books: New York, 2013).

*The Four and Other Poems* (n.p.: n.p., n.d.).

*The Friend* (Government of Guyana: Georgetown, 1976).

*The Madwoman of Papine* (Government of Guyana: Georgetown, 1976).

*The New Moon's Arms* (Grand Central Publishing: New York, 2012).

*The Onliest Fisherman* (UWI Press: Mona, 1967).

*The Salt Road* (Grand Central Publishing: New York, 2004).

*Voiceprint* (Peepal Tree Press: Leeds, 1993).

**HORNE, Alistair**

*Harold Macmillan, Vol. 2, 1957-1986* (Viking: New York, 1989).

**HORNE, Charles**

*The Story of the London Missionary Society* (London Missionary Society: London, 1894).

**HORNUNG, Alfred**

*Colonialism and Autobiography: Michelle Cliff, David Dabydeen, Opal Adisa Palmer* (Rodopi: London, 1998).

**HOROWITZ, Michael, ed.**

*Peoples and Cultures of the Caribbean* (Natural History Press: New York, 1971).

**HOSEIN, Alim**

*Panorama: A Portrait of Guyana Images from the National Collection of Guyana* (Ministry of Culture and Sports: Georgetown, 2014).

**HOUSTON, Berkeley Bartrum**

*The Gathering: The Impending Re-Emergence of the Black Man (Nubian-New Being) The Hebrew: The Sons of God* (Bottom House Press: Georgetown, 1999).

**HOWE, Stephen**

*Anti-colonialism in British Politics: The Left and the End of Empire, 1918-1964* (Clarendon Press: Oxford, 1993).

**HOWES, Paul Grisworld**

*Photographer in the Rain-Forests* (Paul G. Howes and Associates: Chicago, 1969).

**HOYLES, Asher; and Martin Hoyles**

*Caribbean Publishing in Britain: A Tribute to Arif Ali* (Hansib Publications: Hertfordshire, 2011).

**HOYTE, Hugh Desmond**

*Economic Recovery Programme: Leadership, Will-power, Vision* (Free Press: Georgetown, 1997).

**HUBBARD, H.J.M.**

*Race and Guyana: The Anatomy of a Colonial Enterprise* (HJM Hubbard: Georgetown, 1969).

**HUDSON, W.H.**

*Green Mansions: A Romance of the Tropical Forest* (Classics Book: London, 1951). Republished in 2018 by Createspace, Scottsville.

**HUNT, E. Howard**

*Undercover: Memoirs of an American Secret Agent* (Berkeley Publishing: New York, 1974).

**HUNT, Michael H**

*Ideology and US Foreign Policy* (Yale University Press: New Haven, 1987).

**HUNTE, Cyril Kenrick**

*Freedom and Liberation Struggle in Southern Africa: Recognizing Guyana's Contribution* (Government of Guyana: Georgetown, 2016).

**HUNTLEY, E.L.**

*Come Lehwe Reason: A Journey of 50 years with Walter Rodney* (Bogle L'Ouverture Publications: London, 2018).

*Life and Times of Dr. Cheddi Bharrat Jagan* (Bogle-L'Ouverture Publications: London, 1994).

*Marcus Garvey: A Centenary, 1887-1987* (Friends of Bogle: London, 1988).

**HUSSAIN, Alicia**

*Black Guyanese Immigrant Women's Concepts of "Success": Four Stories in Canada* (LAP Lambert Academic Publishing: Toronto, 2011).

**HUTSON, Grace; Kristoff Wray, ill.**

*Black Watuh Tales, Vol. 1: Guyanese Folklore Saga* (Grace Hutson: Georgetown, 2023).

**HUTSON, Jesse**

*The Ol-Kai People: A Story from the Land of the Six Peoples* (Createspace; New York, 2013).

**HUTSON, Marcel Raymond**

*Born To Succeed: A Collaborative Approach To Developing The God-given Literacy Potential of Students in the Early Grades* (MR Hutson: Georgetown, 2020).

**HYBEL, Alex R.**

*How Leaders Reason: US Intervention in the Caribbean Basin and Latin America* (Cambridge University Press: Cambridge, 1994).

**HYMAN, Lennox**

*Me: A Book of Poetry* (L. Hyman: Georgetown, n.d.).

*Measurement for the Learner Who Knows Very Little Principles in Mathematics* (Unified Business Services: Georgetown, 2007).

*Measurement Made Simple for the Upper Primary Child* (Unified Business Services: Georgetown, n.d.).

*Poems of Thought* (United Business Services: Georgetown, 2021).

*Subject Integration* (Unified Business Services: Georgetown, n.d.).

*The Teaching of Mathematics Throughout Art and Craft for Pupils in Primary School* (Unified Business Services: Georgetown, n.d.).

# I

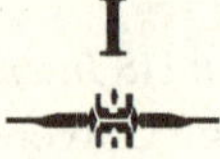

**IFILL, Owen**

*Blacka: Storythms* (Archway Publishing: New York, 2021).
*In Flux* (Goose River Press: Waldoboro, 2002).

**IM THURN, Sir Everard**

*Among the Indians of Guiana: Being Sketches Chiefly Anthropologic From the Interior of British Guiana* (Kegan Paul, Trench & Co: London, 1883). Reprint. (Dover Publications: New York, 1967).
*The Ascent of Mount Roraima* (Royal Geographical Society: London, 1885).

**IMHOFF, Janice**

*Chros Yuself: Using Creole to Explain Mental Health Issues* (Arawak Publishers: Kingston, 2021).
*Conversations: Pieces of the Truth – Demystifying Female Sexuality and Reproductive Issues* (Arawak Publishers: Kingston, 2012, 2015).
*Love Stretched!* (Janice Imhoff: Georgetown, 2020).
*Our Words will be there: Profiles of Female Cancer Survivors in Guyana* (Janice Imhoff: Georgetown, 2005, 2009).

**INNES, Catherine Lynette**

*A History of Black and Asian Writing in Britain 1700-2000* (Cambridge University Press: Cambridge, 2002).

**INSANALLY, Rudy**

*Dancing Between the Raindrops: A Despatch for a Small State Diplomat* (Createspace: Seattle, 2014).
*Multilateral Diplomacy – For Small States* (Rudy Insanally: Georgetown, 2013).
*The Guyanese Culture: Fusion or Diffusion* (Rudy Insanally: Georgetown, 2016).

**INSTITUTE OF INTERNATIOAL VISUAL ARTS (IIVA)**

*Aubrey Williams* (IIVA: London, 1998).

**INTER-AMERICAN DEVELOPMENT BANK**

*Economic and Social Progress in Latin America: Regional Integration* (IADB: Washington D.C., 1989).
*Ten Years of Caricom* (IADB: Georgetown, 1983).
*The Arts of Guyana: A Multicultural Caribbean Adventure* (IADB: Washington, D.C.: 2006).

**INTERNATIONAL BUSINESS PUBLICATIONS (IBP)**

*Guyana Electoral Political Parties Laws and Regulations Handbook – Strategic Information, Regulations, Procedures*

(IBP: New York, 2015).
*Guyana Information Strategy, Investment and E-Commerce Development Handbook – Strategic Information Programs, Regulations* (IBP: New York, 2015).
*Guyana Criminal Justice System Laws, Regulations and Procedures Handbook Vol. 1 Strategic Information and Regulations* (IBP: New York, 2015).
*Guyana: Doing Business Investing in Guyana Guide. Vol. 1 Strategic Practical Information Regulations, Contracts* (IBP: New York, 2015).
*Guyana Business Law Handbook Vol. 1 – Strategic Information and Basic Laws* (IBP: New York, 2015).

**IRELAND, W. Alleyne**
*Demerariana: Essays Historical, Critical, and Descriptive* (Baldwin and Company: Georgetown, 1897).

**IRWIN, Dorothy, ed.**
*Years of High Hopes: A Portrait of British Guiana 1952-1956 from an American Family's Letters Home: The Letters of Marian and Howard Irwin* (Hansib: London, 2016).

**ISHMAEL, Bibby Zorina**
*Once a Guyanese Child* (Upfront Publishing: Leicester, 2009).

**ISHMAEL, Odeen**
*Amerindian Legends of Guyana* (Artex Publishing: Sheboygan, 1995).
*Guyana Legends: Folktales of Indigenous Amerindians* (Xlibris: Bloomington, 2011).
*Problems of the Transition of Education in the Third World – The Case of Guyana* (University of Michigan: Ann Arbor, 1990).
*The Democracy Perspective in the Americas* (University Press of America: New York, 2010).
*The Guyana Story, Volume 1 – From the Earliest Inhabitants to British Colonisation* (Caribbean Press: Georgetown, 2013).
*The Guyana Story, Volume 2 – From the Workers` Struggle* (Caribbean Press: Georgetown, 2013).
*The Magic Pot* (Xlibris: Bloomington, 2010).
*The Trail of Diplomacy: The Guyana-Venezuela Border Issue, Vol. 1 of 3* (Xlibris: Bloomington, 2013).
*Towards Education Reform in Guyana* (New Guyana Company Ltd.: Guyana, 1993).

**ITWARU, Arnold**
*Body Rites: Beyond the Darkening* (TSAR: Toronto, 1991).

*Closed Entrances: Canadian Culture and Imperialism* (TSAR: Toronto, 1994).
*Critiques of Power* (Terebi: Toronto, 2001).
*Entombed Survivors* (Williams-Wallace: Toronto, 1987).
*Home and Back* (TSAR: Toronto, 2001).
*Mass Communication and Mass Deception* (Terebi: Toronto, 1989).
*Morning of Yesterday: Seven Stories* (Other Eye: Toronto, 1999).
*Negative Ecstasy* (Other Eye: Toronto, 2001).
*Shanti* (Peepal Tree Press: Leeds, 1988).
*Shattered Songs* (Aya Press: Toronto, 1982).
*The Invention of Canada: Literary Texts and the Immigrant Imagination* (TSAR: Toronto, 1990).
*The Sacred Presence* (Underwhich Editions: Toronto, 1986).

**IRVING, Brian, ed.**
*Guyana: A Composite Monograph* (Inter-American University Press: San Juan, 1972).

# J

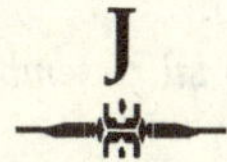

**JABAR, Bibi Sazieda**

*Guyanese Style Cooking* (iUniverse: Bloomington, 2011).

**JACKMAN, Yaphat**

*A Biographical Overview of Guyanese Filmmaking between 2002 and 2013* (LAP Lambert Academic Publishing: Sacramento, 2022).

**JACKSON, G.**

*Cuname, Curare, and Cool Aid* (n.p.: n.p.,1984).

**JACKSON, Rashleigh**

*Guyana's Diplomacy: Reflections of a Former Foreign Minister* (Free Press: Georgetown, 2003).

**_____.; et al**

*Intervention, Border, and Maritime Issues* (Ian Randle Publishers: Kingston, 2005).

**JACKSON, Shona**

*Creole Indigeneity: Between Math and Nation in the Caribbean* (University of Minnesota Press: Minneapolis, 2012).

**JACOBS, Mark**

*What a Friend We Have in Jesus* (Lulu Publishing: Morrisville, 2011).

**JAFFE, R.**

*The Caribbean Citizen* (Ian Randle Publishers: Kingston, 2005).

**JAGAN, Dr. Cheddi Berret**

[Author's Note: *Bharat* or *Bharrat* are used in some instances. E.g., Huntley, E.L., *Life and Times of Dr. Cheddi Bharrat Jagan* (Bogle-L'Ouverture Publications: London, 1994)].

*A New Global Human Order* (Harpy: Milton, 1999, 2001).

*A Time To Stand Up and Be Counted* (Cheddi Jagan: Georgetown, 1964).

*A West Indian State: Pro-imperialist or Anti-imperialist—14 Straight Talk Articles* (Cheddi Jagan: Georgetown, 1972).

*Address by Cheddi Jagan to 25th Anniversary Conference of PPP: On Critical Support* (PPP: Georgetown, 1975).

*Bitter Sugar 1953-1954* (Cheddi Jagan: Georgetown, 1954).

*British Guiana: The Case for Compromise—Letter to the British Prime Minister* (Cheddi Jagan: Georgetown, 1964).

*British Guiana's Future: Peaceful or Violent* (Cheddi Jagan: Georgetown, 1964).

*Cheddi Jagan: National Assembly Speeches, Vol. 1 1947-1951* (PPP: Georgetown, 1952).
*Cheddi Jagan: National Assembly Speeches, Vol. 2 1952-1953* (PPP: Georgetown, 1954).
*Cheddi Jagan: National Assembly Speeches, Vol. 3 1959-1964* (PPP: Georgetown, 1965).
*Cheddi Jagan: National Assembly Speeches, Vol. 4 1966-1968* (PPP: Georgetown, 1969).
*Cheddi Jagan: National Assembly Speeches, Vol. 5 1969-1972* (PPP: Georgetown, 1973).
*Cheddi Jagan: National Assembly Speeches, Vol. 6 1976-1980* (PPP: Georgetown, 1981).
*Cheddi Jagan: National Assembly Speeches, Vol. 7 1981-1987* (PPP: Georgetown, 1988).
*Cheddi Jagan: Select Speeches 1992-1994* (PPP: Georgetown, 1995).
*Fight For Freedom: Waddington Constitution Exposed* (National Printers: Georgetown, 1952).
*For a Revolutionary Democratic Alliance* (Cheddi Jagan: Georgetown, 1985).
*Forbidden Freedom: The Story of British Guiana*, 3rd ed. (Hansib Publications: Hertford, 1994). [First Published by the PPP in 1954].
*Guyana: A Bed of Thorns* (Cheddi Jagan: Georgetown, 1984).
*Is Imperialism Dead?* (Cheddi Jagan: Georgetown, 1953).
*Memorandum by President to IMF President Michel Camdessus* (Cheddi Jagan: Georgetown, 1994).
*My Credo—Here I Stand* (Cheddi Jagan: Georgetown, 1962).
*Non-Alignment as a viable alternative for Regional Cooperation* (Cheddi Jagan: Georgetown, 1982).
*Open Letter to Mr. Anthony Greenwood, Secretary of State for the Colonies* (Cheddi Jagan: Georgetown, 1965).
*Poverty: Cause and Cure in Developing Countries* (Cheddi Jagan: Georgetown, 1978).
*PPP Struggles for TUC Freedom 1978-1986* (Cheddi Jagan: Georgetown, 1987).
*Race, Class, and Ideology* ((Cheddi Jagan: Georgetown, 1974).
*Race, Class, and Nationhood: the Indo-Guyanese Experiences* (Cheddi Jagan: Georgetown, 1988).
*Rooting for Labour* (Cheddi Jagan: Georgetown, 1993).
*Speech by Premier at Freedom Rally* (PPP: Georgetown, 1964).
*Speeches of Cheddi Jagan* (PPP: Georgetown, 1957).
*Steps Towards Caribbean Unity* (Cheddi Jagan: Georgetown, 1989).

*The Bankrupt IMF Road* (Cheddi Jagan: Georgetown, 1987).
*The Caribbean Revolution* (Orbis Press Agency: Prague, 1979).
*The Coalition Exposed* (Cheddi Jagan: Georgetown, 1967).
*The IMF Takes Over Guyana* (Cheddi Jagan: Georgetown, 1981).
*The PPP and the Private Sector* (Cheddi Jagan: Georgetown, 1985).
*The State of the Free Press in Guyana* (Cheddi Jagan: Georgetown, 1980).
*The Struggle for a Socialist Guyana* (Cheddi Jagan: Georgetown, 1975).
*The Struggle for Independence* (New Guyana Company Ltd.: Georgetown, 1993).
*The Struggles of the PPP for Guyana's Independence* (Cheddi Jagan: Georgetown, 1966).
*The Truth About Bauxite* (Cheddi Jagan: Georgetown, 1971).
*The USA in South America* (Hansib Publications: Hertford, 1998).
The *West on Trial: My Fight for Guyana's Freedom* (Michael Joseph Ltd.: London, 1966). Reprinted 1967, 1971, 1975 and 1980 (Seven Seas Books: Prague), and 1997 (Hansib Publications: Hertford, 1997).
*Towards Independence* (Cheddi Jagan: Georgetown, 1958).
*Towards Understanding* (Cheddi Jagan: Georgetown, 1961).
*Tracing Our Path in a Changing World* (Cheddi Jagan: Georgetown, 1990).
*Tribute to Jawaharlal Nehru* (Cheddi Jagan: Georgetown, 1989).
*Unmasking Enemies of the Guyanese People* (Cheddi Jagan: Georgetown, 1984).
*US Intervention in Guyana* (Cheddi Jagan: Georgetown, 1966).
*What Happened in British Guiana* (Cheddi Jagan: Georgetown, 1954).

**_____; Clement Rohee; and Janet Jagan**
*A New Global Human Order* (Harpy: Milton, 1999).
*Development, Selected Speeches 1992-1997* (GAWU: Georgetown, 1998).

**_____.; Janet Jagan; Brindley Benn; and L.F.S. Burnham**
*British Guiana: A Challenge to Labour* (London Labour Publishing Society: London, 1952).

**_____; and Millette James**
*The Caribbean —Whose Backyard* (Cheddi Jagan: Georgetown, 1984).
**____; and Navin Chanderpal**
*President Cheddi Jagan Speaks on Environment and Development, Selected Speeches 1992-1997* (GAWU: Georgetown, 1998).

**JAGAN, Janet** [Dr. Cheddi Jagan's spouse]
*12 Years of the PPP* ((PPP: Georgetown, 1961).
*Workers of Guyana Reunite* (PPP: Georgetown, 1964, 2000).
*History of the PPP* ((PPP: Georgetown, 1963).
*The PPP in the Struggle for Independence* (PPP: Georgetown, 1963).
*The Phoney Two-thirds majority of the July 16th 1973 General Elections* (PPP: Georgetown, 1973).
*National Service: An Act of Coercion* (PPP: Georgetown, 1973).
*An Examination of National Service* (PPP: Georgetown, 1976).
*Anastasia the Anteater* (Peepal Tree Press: Leeds, 1997).
*Army Intervention in the 1973 General Elections in Guyana* (PPP: Georgetown, 1973).
*Patricia the Baby Manatee and Other Stories* (Peepal Tree Press: Leeds, 1995).
*The Alligator Ferry Service and Other Stories from Guyana* (Harpy: Milton, 2001).
*The Dog who Loved Flowers* (Peepal Tree Press: Leeds, 1997).
*When Grandpa Cheddi was a boy* (Peepal Tree Press: Leeds, 1993).
**_____, ed.**
*Children's Stories of Guyana's Freedom Struggles* (New Guyana Company Ltd.: Georgetown, 1995).
*The Lure of the Mermaid and Other Children's Stories* (Dido Press: London, 2002).
**_____, and Bernadette Persaud, eds.**
*Overcoming the Void* (Pavnik Press: Georgetown, 1997) [First publication of Castellani House].

**JAGAN-BRANCIER, Nadira** [Dr. Jagan's daughter]
*Cheddi Jagan – My Fight for Guyana's Freedom – With Reflections on My Father* (Harpy: Milton, 1997).
[7th Edition of The West on Trial].

**JAGDEO, Rory**
*Walk About: Searching for the Epic Life of a Guyanese Memoir* (Archway Publishing: New York, 2020).

**JAGDEO, Tribani**

*Guyana and Trinidad: A Comparative Analysis of Social Change* (University of Michigan Press: Ann Arbor, 2020).

**JAGESSAR, Rohit**

*Kiss and Breathe: Only The Broken Ones Will Rise* (Amazon: Efland, 2022).

**JAGMOHAN, Desmond**

*Dark Virtues: Booker T. Washington's Tragic Realism* (Princeton University: Princeton, 2022).

**JAIKARAN, Elizabeth**

*Trauma: A Collection of Short Stories* (Shanti Arts LLC: New York, 2017).

**JAHN, J.**

*A Bibliography of Neo-African Literature from Africa, America and the Caribbean* (Deutsch: London, 1965).

**JAILALL, Julie**

*Sharda* (Julie Jailall: Georgetown, 2011).

**JAILALL, Peter**

*Jottings: A Teacher's Logbook* (In Our Words Inc.: Toronto, 2014).

*Mother Earth: Poems for her children* (Natural Heritage Inc.: Toronto, 2009).

*Sacrifice: Poems on the Indian Arrival in Guyana* (In Our Words Inc.: Mississauga, 2010).

*Stop! Stop! Don't Be a Bully* (In Our Words Inc.: Mississauga, 2015).

*This Healing Place and Other Poems* (Natural Heritage Inc.: Toronto, 1993).

*Towards the Pebbled Shore* (MiddleRoad Publishers: Toronto, 2022).

*When September Comes: And Other Poems* (Natural Heritage Inc.: Toronto, 2003).

*Yet Another Home: Poems* (Natural Heritage Inc.: Toronto, 1997).

**______; and Ian McDonald**

*People of Guyana* (MiddleRoad Publishers: Toronto, 2018).

**JAIN, Jasbir; and S. Agarwal**

*Shifting Homelands Travelling Identities: Writers of the Caribbean Diaspora* (Ian Randle Publishers: Kingston, 2003).

**JAMES, C.L.R.**

*Party Politics in the West Indies* (Verdic Enterprises Ltd.: Port of Spain, 1962).

**JAMES, George**

*Stolen Legacy: Greek Philosophy was the offspring of the Egyptian Mystery System* (Digireads: New York, 2019).

**JAMES, R.W.; and H.A. Lutchman**

*Law and the political environment in Guyana* (University of Guyana: Georgetown, 1985).

**JAMESON, Kenneth P.**

*An Annotated Bibliography of Agricultural Development in Guyana* (USAID: Georgetown, 1977).

**JANKI, ROBERT**

*A Gift of Love: Poems* (Published by his daughter Jean Janki: Toronto, 2023).

**JARVIS, Carmen**

*From Seedtime to Harvest: An Autobiography* (Carmen Jarvis: Georgetown, 2016).

*History of Bishops' High School* (Carmen Jarvis: Georgetown, 2002).

**JARVIS, L.**

*An Econometric Model of the Guyanese Economy 1951-76* (University Press of America: New York, 1990).

**JAYAWARDENA, Chandra**

*Conflict and Solidarity in a Guianese Plantation* (The Athlone Press: London, 1963).

**JEAN, Norma**

*Fables and Tales of Guyana* (Lulu Press: Raleigh, 2005).

*Fables and Tales of Guyana,* Vol. 2 (Lulu Press: Raleigh, 2006).

**JEFFERSON-MILES, Andrew**

*Art of Navigation* (Peepal Tree Press: Leeds, 2003).

*Selected Essays of Wilson Harris* (Routledge: New York, 1999).

*The Timehrian* (Peepal Tree Press: Leeds, 2002).

**JEFFREY, Derrick "John"**

*Demerara* (Seawall Press: New York, 1992).

**JEFFREY, Henry B.**

*Cooperative Socialism: A Critical Review* (Institute of Development Studies, University of Guyana: Turkeyen, 1977).

*Problems of Development of Guyana* (Institute of Development Studies, University of Guyana: Turkeyen, 1991).

*Sustainable Development in the Guianas* (n.p., n.p.: 20??).

*Political and Ethnic Dominance in Guyana: Meaning, Consequences, and Solutions* (Createspace Publishing: Scotts Valley, 2015).

**_____; and Colin Baber**

*Guyana: Politics, Economics, and Society – Beyond the Burnham Era* (Rienner: Boulder, 1986).

**JENKINS, John Edward**

*Lutchmee and Dilloo* (Edward Jenkins: London, 1877).

*The Coolie: His Rights and Wrongs* (Routledge: New York, 1871).

**_____; and Bernadette Persaud, eds.**

**JENMAN, George Samuel**

*The Ferns and Fern Allies of the British West Indies and Guiana* (Royal Botanic Gardens: Port of Spain, 1881).

**JERMYN, Leslie**

*Guyana (Cultures of the World)* (Benchmark Books: Salt Lake City, 2000).

**JIN, Meiling**

*Gifts from my Grandmother* (Sheba Feminist Press: London, 1986).

*Song of the Boatwoman* (Peepal Tree Press: Leeds, 1996).

*Story of the Boatwoman* (Peepal Tree Press: Leeds, 2008).

*The Thieving Summer* (Hamish Hamilton: London, 1993).

**JOHN, Yvonne A; M.N. White; and Mack B. Marant, eds.**

*Guyanese Seed of Soul: How to prepare West Indian food* (R & M Publishing: Columbia, 1980).

*Guyanese Seed of Vegetables, Seafood, and Desserts: The Vegetarians`and Food Lovers`Paradise* (Rowland and Littlefield Publishing: London, 1985).

**JOHN-DORIE, Janet**

*The Break of Dawn: Poems* (J. John-Dorie: 2012).

**JOHNS HOPKINS UNIVERSITY**

*Modern Caribbean Politics* (Johns Hopkins University Press: Baltimore, 1994).

**JOHNSON, Christopher**

*British African Entrepreneurship Journey* (Austin McCauley Publishers: London, 2022).

*British Caribbean Enterprises: A Century of Challenges and Successes* (Austin McCauley Publishers: London, 2009).
*The Anatomy of British South Asian Enterprises* (Austin McCauley Publishers: London, 2016).

**JOHNSON, Mark**
*Caribbean Volunteers at War: The Forgotten Story of of the RAF's "Tuskegee Airmen"* (Pen and Sword Books: South Yorkshire, 2014).

**JOHNSON, Stacy**
*Beyond the Breaks* (Guyenterprise: Georgetown, 2021).
[Winner: Guyana Prize for Literature 2022 – Autobiography]
*Fictions* (Janus Books: Guelph, 2013).
*Collected Poems 2002-2012* (Janus Books: Guelph, 2013).

**JOHNSON-BHOLA, Linda**
*A Guide to the Principles and Practices of the Geography School-Based Assessment* (University of Guyana Press: Turkeyen, 2022).

**JONAS, Prior; and Joyce Jonas, eds.**
*Sportsmen and Sportsmanship - A compilation of articles* (n.p.: n.p., 2007).

**JONES, Edwin**
*Institutional Aspects of West Indian Development* (Ian Randle Publishers: Kingston, 1998).
*Coalitions of the oppressed* (UWI: Mona, 1987).

**JONES, Emerson J.**
*Dementia Careers Handbook: Practical Care and Coping Strategies for Careers and Families* (ShieldCrest Publishing Ltd.: Buckinghamshire, 2019).

**JONES, Wayne**
*Prophet Wills: The Walking Dictionary* (Damon Publishers: Georgetown, 1995).
*Great Guyanese Humour: Guyana's History Through Jokes* (Wayne Jones: Toronto, 2011).
*The Guyaspora in Canada: Guyanese Life in Canada* (Wayne Jones: Toronto, 2014).

**JORDAN, Michael**
*Kamarang: A Novel* (Michael Jordan: Georgetown, 2017).

**JOSA, F.P.L.**
*The Apostle of the Indians of Guiana: A Memoir of the Life and Labours of the Rev. W.H. Brett, B.D. For Forty Years a Missionary in British Guiana* (Wells, Gardner, Darton & Co.: London, 1888).

**JOSEPH, Cedric L**

*Anglo-American Diplomacy and the Re-Opening of the Guyana-Venezuela Boundary Controversy 1961-1966* (Trafford Publishing: London, 2008).

*The British West Indies Regiment 1914-1918* (Free Press: Georgetown, 2008).

**JOSEPH, Charles; et al**

*Poetic Tributes to Walter Rodney* (Bogle-L'Ouverture Publications: London, 1986).

**JOSEPH, Jane**

*The El Dorado Affair: A True Story of Pioneers in Rural Guyana, South America* (Sapodilla Press: London, 2015).

*Hussar: The Remarkable Life of Edwin "Joe" Joseph* (Sapodilla Press: London, 2017).

**JOSIAH, Barbara P**

*Migration, Mining, and the African Diaspora: Guyana in the 19th and 20th Centuries* (Palgrave Macmillan: London, 2011).

**JOSIAH, Henry**

*Tales of Makonaima's Children* (Roraima: Georgetown, 1994).

*Makonaima and Pia* (Roraima: Georgetown, 1966).

# K

**"K", Betty**

*Caribbean Cuisine* (Betty K: Toronto, 1990).

**KAHALAS, Laurie E.**

*Snake Dance: Unravelling the Mysteries of Jonestown* (Red Robin Press: New York, 1998).

**KALLI, Alwin**

*My Heritage: Memories of Growing Up in Guyana* (Createspace: Scotts Valley, 2018).

**KALLICHARAN, Laxmi**

*Hear the Ghunghrus Sing* [Her Only Book of Poetry] (Lakshmi Kallicharan: Georgetown, 1992).

*Shraadanjali: Anthology of Indo-Guyanese Poetry* (Lakshmi Kalicharran: Georgetown, 1986).

**_____; Ian Mcdonald; and Joel Benjamin, eds.**

*They Came in Ships: An Anthology of Indo-Guyanese Writing* (Peepal Tree Press: Leeds, 1998).

**KALLICHARRAN, Alvin; and Robert Caine, eds.**

*Colour Blind: Struggles, Sacrifice and Success of the Cricket Legend* (Notion Media Press: New York, 2019).

**KANHAI, Cyril**

*My New Guyana: A Collection of Poems* (Sheik Sadeek: Georgetown, 1969).

**KANHAI, Rohan**

*Blasting for Runs* (Souvenir Press: London, 1966).

**KANHAI, Terry** (Pen Name for Julia Theresa Kanhai)

*Backslider* (SBPRA Publishing: Boca Raton, 2013).

**KARRAN, Kampta**

*An Introduction to the Poetry of the East Indian Diaspora 1901-1991* (Offerings Publications: Georgetown, 1991).

*Offerings 3 Behold! A Decade of Thirty Poems 1977-1987* (Offerings Publications: Georgetown, 1988).

*Race and Ethnicity in Guyana* (Offerings Publications: Georgetown, 2000).

**_____, ed.**

*Racial Conflict Resolutions and Power Sharing in Guyana: Selected Readings* (Offerings Publications: Georgetown, 2004).

**_____; and Lyn Macedo, eds.**
*No Land, No Mother: Essays on the work of David Dabydeen* (Peepal Tree Press: Leeds, 2007).

**KARRAN, Kavita**
*Between Bible College, Church, and Community: Essays* (Offerings Productions: Georgetown, 2007).

**KARS, Marjoleine**
*Blood on the River: A Chronicle of Mutiny and Freedom on the Wild Coast* (New Press: New York, 2021) [Winner of the 2021 Cundell History Prize and the 2021 Frederick Douglas Book Prize. The book is based on the 1763 Berbice Slave Rebellion].

**KAY, Ernest**
*Dictionary of Latin American and Caribbean Biography* (Melrose Press Ltd.: London, 1971).

**KAYUM, Azeem**
*Wrestling with the Goddess – A Personal Odyssey* (AIF Publications: Toronto, 2004).

**KEARNS, Phil; and Doug Wead**
*People's Temple, People's Tomb* (Logos International: New Jersey, 1979).

**KEEGAN John**
*World Armies*, 2nd ed. (Gale Research: Detroit, 1983).

**KEITH, A.B., ed**
*Speeches and Documents on British Colonial Policy 1763-1917* (Oxford University Press: Oxford, 1961).

**KEITH, J.; S. Smith; K. Fawcett; et al**
*Secret and Suppressed: Banned Ideas and Hidden History* (Ferasl House: Portland, 1993).

**KELLOFF, C.L.; and V.A. Funk**
*Preliminary Checklist of the Plants of Kaieteur National Park, Guyana* (University of Guyana: Guyana, 1998).

**KELLY, M.; and Bain, B.**
*Education and HIV/AIDS in the Caribbean* (Ian Randle Publishers: Kingston, 2004).

**KEMPADOO, M.**
*Letters of Thanks* (Collins: London, 1969). Reprint. (Simon & Schuster: New York, 1986).

**KEMPADOO, O.**
*All Decent Animals* (Farrar, Straus and Giroux (Macmillan): London, 2013).

*Buxton Spice* (Phoenix House: London, 1998).
*Tide Running* (Picador: London, 2001).

**KEMPADOO, Peter**

*A-Z of Guyanese Words* (P. Kempadoo: Georgetown, 2000).
*Guiana Boy* (New Literature: Crawley, 1960). Re-published as *Guyana Boy* (Peepal Tree Press: Leeds, 2001).
*Old Thom's Harvest* (Eyre and Spottiswoods: London, 1965).

**KENSWIL, Federick W.**

*Children of the Silence. An account of the aboriginal Indians of the Upper Mazaruni River, British Guiana* (Interior Development Committee: British Guiana, 1946).

**KHALIDEEN, Rosetta**

*Leguan: A Collection of Poems* (R. Khalideen: Georgetown, 1979).
*Portrait in Poetry: A Collection of Poems* (R. Khalideen: Georgetown, 1989).

**KHAN, Abrahim H**

*Salighed As Happiness? Kierkegaard on the Concept: Salighed* (University of Waterloo Press: Waterloo, 1985).

**KHAN, Aliyah**

*Far From Mecca: Globalizing the Muslim Caribbean* (Rutgers University Press: Newark, 2020).

**KHAN, R.**

*The Unmuffled Voices of El Dorado* (Mekler and Deahl: Hamilton, 1997).

**KHAN, Yassin**

*Dreams: A Collection of Poems* (Yassin Khan: New York, 2020).

**KHAN, Yusuf S.**

*Anthology of Political Poems* (New Guyana Company Ltd: Georgetown, 1970).

**KHEMRAJ, Harischandra**

*Cosmic Dance* (Peepal Tree Press: Leeds, 1991).
*Our Wife and Other Stories* (Malthouse Press: Lagos, 1991).

**KHEMRAJ, Tarron**

*Banking and The Foreign Exchange Market in Emerging Economies* (Edward Elgar Publishing: Cheltenham, 2014).

**KHUBLALL, Nat**

*Compulsory Land Acquisition: Singapore and Malaysia* (Butterworths Asia: Singapore, 1994).
*Development Control and Planning Law: Singapore* (Longman: Singapore, 1991).

*Guyana: Politics and Oil Discovery* (Createspace: Scotts Valley, 2019).
*India: Ancient Influences and Superiority* (Createspace: Scotts Valley, 2016).
*India: Discovery and The Truth* (Createspace: Scotts Valley, 2018).
*India: Foreign Atrocities and Plunders* (Createspace: Scotts Valley, 2019).
*India: Invasions, Foreign Rule and Eurocentrism* (Createspace: Scotts Valley, 2015).
*India: Wisdom and Achievements: Ancient Wisdom and Achievements* (Createspace: Scotts Valley, 2014).
*Landlord and Tenant Law* (Createspace: Scotts Valley, 2015).
*Law of Compulsory Purchase and Compensation: Singapore and Malaysia* (Butterworths Asia: Singapore: 1991).
*Law of Real Property and Conveyancing* (Longman: Singapore, 1991).
*Law of Trusts* (Createspace: Scotts Valley, 2019).
*Make Your Own Will: Wills, Intestacy, Inheritance Tax and Administration* (Createspace: Scotts Valley, 2016).
*Peasant Farmer to Professor and Beyond: A Life Story* (Creatsepace: Scotts Valley, 2014).
*Revised Expectations* (Createspace: Scotts Valley, 2014).
*Strata Titles* (Butterworths Asia: Singapore, 1995).
*Taxation of Income and Capital* (Createspace: Scotts Valley, 2016).
*Teaching and Study Skills in Higher Education* (Createspace: Scotts Valley, 2014).
*Transmigration of Souls: Reincarnation* (Createspace: Scotts Valley, 2019).

**KILDUFF, Marshall; and Ron Javers**
*The Suicide Cult: The Inside Story of the Peoples Temple Sect and the Massacre in Guyana* (Bantam: New York, 1978).

**KING, Kenneth F. S**
*Land and People of Guyana* (Commonwealth Forestry Institute: Oxford, 1968).
*National Development Strategy* (Government of Guyana: Georgetown, 1992).
*Second Development Plan 1972-1976* (Government of Guyana: Georgetown, 1971).

**KING, Logan**
*Guyanese Easy-to-Follow Cookbook: With Bonus Recipes Guyanese Dessert and Sweet Treats* (Amazon Books: Bolton, 2022).

**KING, Sheila**

*Guyanese Stories for Children Everywhere* (Sheila King: Georgetown, 2008).

*Our Homes Spring Poetry* (Sheila King: Georgetown, 1993).

*Stories from Guyana* (Sheila King: Georgetown, 1967).

*The Cruellest Test* (Sheila King: Georgetown,1968).

**KING, Sonya Odele**

*Beautiful: Be Empowered, Be Inspired* (Amazon Books: Bolton, 2014).

*Drunk or Sober* (Amazon Books: Bolton, 2022).

*Four Women* (Amazon Books: Bolton, 2022).

*On a Prayer* (Amazon Books: Bolton, 2022).

*The First Time* (Amazon Books: Bolton, 2020).

*Wisdom Song* (Amazon Books: Bolton, 2013).

**KING-ARIBISAL, Karen**

*Our Wife and Other Stories* (Peepal Tree Press: Leeds, 2008).

*The Hangman's Game* (Peepal Tree Press: Leeds, 2007).

**KINNICK, B.J.**

*Crying for Guyana: Selected Poems and Prose* (Trade Paperback: Mukilteo, 1980).

**KIRKE, Henry**

*Twenty-five years in British Guiana* (Negro Universities Press: Westport, 1970).

**KIRKE, V.**

*Zorg: A Story of British Guiana* (Digby, Long, and Co.: London, *circa* 1800s).

**KIRKPATRICK, (nee Ting-a-Kee), Margerie**

*From the Middle Kingdom to the New World: Aspects of the Chinese Experience in Migrating to British Guiana* (Margerie Kirkpatrick: Georgetown, 1993).

*The Way We Were: Memories of a British Guiana Childhood* (Margerie Kirkpatrick: Georgetown, 2012).

**KISSOON, Frederick**

*Ethnic Power and Ideological Racism: Comparing Presidencies in Guyana* [Paper presented at the annual conference of the Guyana Historical Society] (Guyana Historical Society: Georgetown, 2010).

*Exodus and Authoritarianism: The Post-1992 State in Guyana* [Faculty of Social Sciences seminar paper] (University of Guyana: Turkeyen, 2008).

*Indian Attitudes toward the PPP and PNC in the forthcoming general elections* (Department of International Affairs, University of Guyana: Turkeyen, 2006).

*Self-Reflection: Is there an Indian racism in Guyana?* [Paper presented at the Inter-Guiana Conference] (University of Guyana: Turkeyen, 2002).

*The birth of the WPA: The context* [Paper presented at the annual conference of the Guyana Historical Society] (Guyana Historical Society: Georgetown, 2014).

*The failure of the Buxton Conspiracy* [Faculty of Social Sciences paper] (University of Guyana: Turkeyen, 2005).

*The great paradox in Guyanese politics: Indian attitudes to the PPP and PNC* [Sabbatical Report] (University of Guyana: Turkeyen, 2004).

*The more things change, the more they remain the same: An Analysis of Political Trends in Guyana* [Faculty of Social Sciences seminar paper] (University of Guyana: Turkeyen, 2005).

*The Small State in a Big World: The Foreign Policy Behaviour of the PRG in Grenada* (University of Guyana: Turkeyen, 1987).

**_____; contr.**

"African Extremism in an Age of Political Decay" in *Governance, Conflict Analysis and Conflict Resolution* by Cedric Grant and Mark Kirton, eds. (Ian Randle Publishers: Kingston, 2007).

**KISSOON, Gushka**

*The Masses Create* (Guyana National Service Publications: Georgetown, 1976).

**KISSOON, Tony**

*Tales of the Spirits* (Abbott Press: Bloomington, 2014).

**KLEIN, Herbert S.**

*African Slavery in Latin America and the Caribbean* (Oxford University Press: Oxford, 1988).

**KLEINSASSER, Cook Alice**

*The Onliest One Alive: Surviving Jonestown: Guyana* (M.K. Towne: New York, 1995).

**KLINEMAN, George; S. Butler; and D. Conn**

*The Cult that Died* (G. P. Putnam's Sons: New York, 1980).

**KLOB, Sinah T**

*Fabrics of Indianness: The Exchange and Consumption of Clothing in Transnational Guyanese Hindu Communities* (Palgrave Macmillan: London, 2011).

**KLOOS, Peter**

*The Situation of the Indian in South America* (WCC: Geneva, 1972).

**KNERR, M.E.**

*Suicide in Guyana* (Belmont Tower: New York,1978).

**KOCH-GRÜNBERG, Theodor**

*Vom Roroima zum Orinoco: Ergebnisse einer Reise in Nordbrasilien und Venezuela in den Jahren 1911-13.* 5 Vols. (Dietrich Reimer/Stuttgart; Strecker und Schröder: Berlin, 1916-28).

**KNOWLES, R.M.**

*The Rescue of Baby Meek Meek* (AuthorHouse: Bloomington, 2006).

**KNOWLES, Y.K.**

*The Town is Aaron* (Aegine Press: Charleston, 1989).

**KONWENBERG, S.**

*A Grammar of Berbice Dutch Creole* (Walter de Gruyte Inc.: n.p., 1993).

**KOEBEL, W.H.**

*British Exploits in South America* (The Century Co.: New York, 1917).

**KRAUSE, Charles A.**

*Guyana Massacre: The Eyewitness Account* (Pan Books: London, 1979).

**KULDIP, D.**

*The Best of Humanity* (AuthorHouse: Bloomington, 2006).

**KUMAR, K.**

*Caught in the Maelstrom. Teenage Dilemma*
(KD Publishing: Toronto, 2005).
*Falling Leaves* (KD Publishing: Toronto, 2000).
*Pure Gold and Other Poems* (KD Publishing: Toronto, 2001).
*The Face that Smiles* (KD Publishing: Toronto, 2000).
*Twiddling Thumbs* (KD Publishing: Toronto, 2014).

**KUNAR, Edith.**

*Rajkumari's Legacy: An Historical Novel* (York University: Toronto, 2017).

**KUNSTLER, Daniel**

*Passaic: The True Story of One Man's Journey Through American Immigration, Detention and Deportation* (Tamalpais Press: New York, 2014).

**KUSHNIR, Ian**

*Economy of Guyana* (Amazon Books: Bolton, 2019).

**KWAYANA, Eusi [formerly Sydney King]**

*A New Look at Jonestown: Dimensions From a Guyanese Perspective* (Caribbean Press: Georgetown, 2019).
*Buxton and Friendship in Print and Memory* (Red Thread Women's Press: Georgetown, 2000).

*Gang Gang: Thirty African Guyanese Proverbs* (Eusi Kwayana: Georgetown, 1997).

*Forward to the Democratic Republic* (Working Peoples' Alliance: Georgetown, 1985)

*Groovy Grammar* (Red Thread Women's Press: Georgetown, 1996).

*Guyana: Genesis of a Nation; The Indo-Guyanese Contribution to Social Change in Guyana* (n.p.: n.p., n.d.).

*Guyana: No Guilty Race* (Red Thread Women's Press: Georgetown, 2000).

*Next Witness: The Bauxite Strike and the Old Politics* (Eusi Kwayana: Georgetown, 1972).

*The Bauxite strike and the Old Politics* (Eusi Kwayana: Georgetown, 1972).

*The Morning After* (Free Press: Georgetown, 2005).

*Walter Rodney* (Calaloux Publications: Wellesley, 1991).

*Walter Rodney: His Last Days and Campaigns* (R. Ferdinand-Lalljie Publishers: Birmingham, 2010).

**___; Eric L. Huntley; and Ealing Race Equality Unit**

*Paul Robeson: 9th March 1898-23rd January 1976* (Bogle-L'Ouverture Publications: London, 1990).

**____; and Kwayana Tchaiko**

*Scars of Bondage: A First Study of the Slave Colonial Experience of Africans in Guyana* (Free Press: Georgetown, 2002).

**KWOK CRAWFORD, Marlene**

*Scenes from the History of Chinese in Guyana* (Demerara Publishers: Georgetown, 1989).

**KYTE, C.; and M. Scott**

*Caribbean Medicine Forward to Eden: A Sourcebook on the Healthy Modalities of Guyana, the Caribbean, and the Americas* (Centre for Sacred Healing Arts Publishing: n.p., 1988).

# L

**LA ROSE, J.F.O.**

*Poems of a British Guianese* (Persick: Georgetown, 1934).

**LA VARRE, William J.**

*Gold, Diamond and Orchids* (Fleming H. Revell Co.: New York, 1935).

*Up the Mazaruni for Diamonds* (Marshall Jones: Boston, 1919).

**LABASTIDE, Leon**

*Guyana in Color: Coloring Book* (Createspace: Scotts Valley: 2022).

*Pink Cover: Things That Are Important* (Createspace: Scotts Valley, 2016).

*We Are One: Poets are the People; Poetry is our Destiny* (Createspace: Scotts Valley, 2020).

**LABOUR RESEARCH DEPARTMENT**

*British Guiana? Who Owns it? What Are Wages and Conditions? What is the Meaning of Government's Policy* (Labour Research Department: London, 1953).

**LACEY, Robert**

*Sir Walter Ralegh* (Atheneum: New York, 1973).

**LACHMANSINGH, Reuben**

*A Dip in the Sangam* (Westbow Press: Bloomington, 2014).

**LAIDLAW, Keith; and Liz Laidlaw**

*The River Wolf* (Allen & Unwin: Boston, 1983).
[Giant Otter and the Guyana Wilds]

**LAKHAN, Dwarka**

*Winning Ways: Real World Strategies to Help You Reimagine Your Practice* (Telwell Talent: Toronto, 2020).

**LAKHAN, Vishnudutt Chris**

*Principles of Resource Management: An Introductory Text* (Geosphere Press: Toronto, 2012).

**LALBACHAN, Pamela; and Michelle Garrett, ill.**

*The Complete Caribbean Cookbook* (Charles E. Tuttle: Boston, 1995).

**LALL, G.H.K.**

*Birth of the Millenium: A Walk Through Life's Pathways* (Vantage Press: New York, 2000).

*Guyana: A National Cesspool of Greed, Duplicity and Corruption* (GHK Lall: Georgetown, 2012).

*Guyana Elections 2015: Hard Truths, Harder Challenges* (GHK Lall: Georgetown, 2015).

*Sitting on a Racial Volcano: Guyana Uncensored* (GHK Lall: Georgetown, 2013).

*Soaring into Magnificence – Cancer: From Illness to Holiness* (Publish America: Baltimore, 2011).

**LALL, Kissoon**

*Mapping in Guyana Since 1940: A Review and Its Relevance in National Development* (University of Guyana: Turkeyen, 1975).

**LALLJIE, Robert, ed.**

*A Bouquet Of Guyanese Flowers: Anthology of Guyanese Poetry* (R. Ferdinand-Lalljie Publishers: Birmingham, 2012).

*The Making Of The Caribbean Peoples & CLR James The Black Plato Of Our Generation* (R. Ferdinand-Lalljie Publishers: Birmingham, 2013).

*Sir Arthur Lewis Nobel Laureate: A Biographical Profile* (R. Ferdinand-Lalljie Publishers: Birmingham, 2013).

**LAMBERT, Leonard, ed.**

*Guiana Legends. Collected by the late William Henry Brett, B.D. Westminster* (Society for Propagation of the Gospel in Foreign Parts: London, 1931).

**LAMUR, Carlo**

*The American Takeover: Industrial Emergence and Alcoa's Expansion in Guyana and Suriname 1914-1921* (Foris Publications: Berlin, 1985).

**LANCASTER, Audrey**

*Trapped in the Middle* (n.p.: n.p., 2013).

**LANDAU, Nather**

*Heavenly Deceptor* (Sound of Music Publishing: New Jersey, 1994).

**LANE, Mark**

*The Strongest Poison* (Dutton: New York, 1979).

**LANTRY, E.**

*Jungle Adventure* (Pacific Press Publishing: Nampa, 1987).

**LARAQUE, Maja**

*A Jaguar Soul: My Guyanese-American Childhood* (Createspace: Charleston, 2013).

**LATIN AMERICAN BUREAU**

*Guyana: Fraudulent Revolution* (Latin American Bureau: London, 1984).

**LAURENCE, K.O.**

*A Question of Labour: Indentured Immigration into Trinidad and British Guiana 1875-1917* (Palgrave Macmillan: London, 1994).

*Immigration into the West Indies in the 19th Century* (Caribbean Universities Press: Kingston, 1971).

**LAWRENCE, Bridgette; and Ray Goble**

*The Complete Record of West Indian Test Cricketers* (ACL and Polar: Leicester, 1991).

**_____; and Reg Scarlett**

*100 Great Westindian Test Cricketers from Challenor to Richards* (Hansib: London, 1988).

**LAWRENCE, W.M.**

*Meditations: Thoughts in the Silence* (Daily Chronicle: Georgetown, 1929).

*The Poet of Guiana, Walter Mac A. Lawrence. Selected with a biography by P. H. Daly* (Daily Chronicle: Georgetown, 1948).

**LAYTON, Deborah**

*Seductive Poison: A Jonestown Survivor's Story of Life and Death in the Peoples Temple* (Doubleday: New York, 1998).

**LAYTON, Thomas N.; and S. Min Yee**

*In My father's House* (Henry Holt: New York, 1981).

**LEA, D.A.M.**

*A Socio-Demographic Analysis of St. Ignatius, Rupununi District* (Department of Geography, McGill University: Montreal, 1968).

**LEAN, J.H.**

*The Secret Life of Berbice Slaves* (University of Canterbury: Christ Church, 2002).

**LEE, Vivian**

*Super Seniors: Beyond 65 and Fully Alive* (Vivian J. Lee: Georgetown, 2005).

**LEGALL, Vania D**

*From Legall to Legal: A Guyanese Girl That Becomes an American Lawyer* (The Vision to Fruition Publishing House: New York, 2022).

**LEE-LOY, Anne-Marie**

*Reading Mr. Chin: Images of the Chinese in the West Indies* (Dido Press: London, 2006).

*The Godmother and Other Stories* (Peepal Tree Press: Leeds, 2004).

**LEO, E.M.**

*Poetical Works* (n.p.: n.p., 1883).

**LESLIE, Jermyn**

*Guyana* (Cavendish Square Publishing: New York, 2002). Reprinted, 2011 with Winnie Wong.

**LEVITT, K**

*Reclaiming Development* (Ian Randle Publishers: Kingston, 2005).

**LERNER PUBLICATIONS**

*Guyana in Pictures* (The Company: Minneapolis, 1988).

**LEVINE, Barry**

*The New Cuban Presence in the Caribbean* (Westview Press: Boulder, 1983).

**LEVINE, Robert**

*Race and Ethnic Relations in Latin America and the Caribbean: An Historical Dictionary and Bibliography* (Scarecrow Press: Boulder, 1980).

**LEVITT, Kari**

*Reclaiming Development Independent Thought and Caribbean Community* (Ian Randle Publishers: Kingston, 2005).

**LEWIS, Andrew Peter**

*The British West Indian Press in the Age of Abolition* (University of London: London, 1993).

**LEWIS, Betty (See Lewiz Alyan)**

**LEWIS, Gordon K.**

*Gather with the saint at the river: The Jonestown Guyana Holocaust 1978* (University of Puerto Rico: San Juan, 1979).

*The Growth of the Modern West Indies* (MacGibbon and Kee: London, 1968).

**LEWIS, Linden**

*Caribbean Sovereignty, Development and Democracy in an Age of Globalization* (Routledge: New York, 2015).

*The Culture of Gender and Sexuality in the Caribbean* (University Press of Florida: Gainesville, 2003).

**_____; et al**

*Color, Hair, and Bone: Race in the Twenty-First Century* (Bucknell University Press: Lewisburg, 2008).

**LEWIS, Pearl**

*Heads and Tails* (Pearl Lewis: Georgetown, 2022).

*Ovid the Octopus* (Pearl Lewis: Georgetown, 2022).

**LEWIS, Dr Rupert Charles**

*Walter Rodney's Intellectual and Political Thought* (Wayne State University Press: Detroit, 1999).

**LEWIS, W.A.**

*Aspects of Tropical Trade: 1883-1965* (Almqvist and Wiksells: Stockholm, 1969).

*Labour in the West Indies* (Allen & Unwin: London, 1939).

*Theory of Economic Growth* (Allen & Unwin: London, 1955).

*The Evolution of the Peasantry in the British West Indies* (Allen & Unwin: London, 1936).

**LEWIS, W.R.C.**

*Walter Rodney: 1968 Revisited* (University of the West Indies Press: Kingston,1998).

*Walter Rodney's Intellectual and Political Thought* (University of the West Indies Press: Kingston,1998).

**LIFTON, Judy**

*A Glimpse of the Other Americas: A Backpacker's Memoir* (Pentagon Gallery: Washington, D.C., 2022).

**LILLY, Melinda; and Charles Reasoner, ill.**

*The Moon People* (Rourke Publishing: Vero Beach, 1999).

**LINDFORS, B; and R. Sander, eds.**

*Twentieth Century Caribbean and Black African Writers* (Gale Research Inc.: Detroit, 1984).

**LINDSAY, Andrew O.**

*Illustrious Exile* (Peepal Tree Press: Leeds, 2006).

**LIVERPOOL, C.H.; and K.M. Campbell**

*Foundation of the Guyana Defence Force: A Soldier of Valour Story* (AuthorHouse: Bloomington, 2016).

**LIVERPOOL, Christine**

*Love and Gold* (Lulu Publishers: Morrisville, 2018).

**LIVINGSTONE, Kerwin A.**

*Exploring the Potential of Implementing E-Learning Practices at UG: A Case Study for the Adoption and Institutionalisation of Technology-Based Learning and Teaching in Higher Education* (Lambert Academic Publishing: London, 2022).

**LLC Books**

*Guyanese Politicians* (LLC Books: Memphis, 2010).

*Guyanese People by Occupation* (LLC Books: Memphis, 2012).

*Canadians of Guyanese Descent* (LLC Books: Memphis, 2010).

**LLOYD, Clive; and Tony Cozier**

*Living for Cricket* (Stanley Paul: London, 1980).

**LOCKE, William J**

*The Beloved Vagabond* (John Lane The Bodley Head: London, 1922).

**LOGAN, Terry J.**

*Roraima Gold* (Amazon Books: Bolton, 2014).

**LONCKE, Joycelynn**

*In the Shadow of El Dorado* (J. Loncke: Port of Spain, 1994).

*Norman Cameron: The Man and His Works* (Department of Culture: Georgetown, 1981).

**_____; ed.**

*Proceedings of the International Roundtable to Commemorate the 150th Anniversary of the Abolition of Slavery in the Anglophone Caribbean* (Guyana Commemoration Commission: Georgetown, 1985).

**_____; and Herman Snijders**

*One Hundred Years of Classical Music in the Guianas* (Government of Guyana: Georgetown, 2002).

**LONDON MISSIONARY SOCIETY**

*Report of the Proceedings Against the Late Rev. John Smith of Demerara* (Westley: London, 1824).

**LONDON, Philbert**

*The Law of Believing* (Philbert London: New York, 2013).

**LOOK LAI, Walton**

*Indentured Labour, Caribbean Sugar* (Johns Hopkins University Press: Baltimore, 1993).

*The Chinese in the West Indies 1806-1995: A Documentary History* (UWI Press: Mona, 1998).

**LORD, W.T**

*Guyanese Travel Talks* (W.T. Lord: Georgetown, 1957).

**LOVETT, Richard**

*The History of the London Missionary Society* (Henry Frowde: London, 1899).

**LOWE, Debra; and Syndrene Harris, eds.**

*National Bibliography of Guyana* (Ministry of Education: Georgetown, 2016).

**LOWE, Robson**

*The Great Stamp Collection of British Guiana* (Robson Lowe: London, 1970).

**LOXTON, R.F.; G.K. Rutherford; and J. Spector**

*Soil and Land-use in the Rupununi Savannas* (Imperial College of Tropical Agriculture: London, 1958).

**LUARD, E.C.; and Thorne, F.C., eds.**

*Overseer's Manual* (n.p.: Georgetown, 1882).

**LUCAS, Rex**

*Reflections of Our Homeland: Through My lens and My Life* (Rex Lucas: Arlington, 2020).

*Thoughts of an Old Barn* (Rex Lucas: Arlington, 2016)

**LUCKHOO, Lionel; and John R. Thompson**

*The Silent Witness* (Thomson Nelson: London, 1995).

**LUTCHMAN, Harold**

*A History of the Guyana Public Service Association* (GPSA: Georgetown, 1973).

*From Colony to Cooperative Republic* (Institute of Caribbean Studies, University of Puerto Rico: San Juan, 1976).

*Law and Political Environment in Guyana* (Institute of Development Studies, University of Guyana: Turkeyen, 1984).

*Planter Power in the Politics of Former British Guiana* (University of Guyana: Turkeyen, 1968).

*Some Aspects of the Crown Colony System of Government* (University of Guyana: Turkeyen, 1968).

*The 1891 Constitutional Change and Representation in the Former British Guiana* (Critchlow Labour College: Georgetown, 1970).

**LYNCH, M.A.**

*Mainly Personal* (n.p.: Georgetown, n.d.).

**LYTTLETON, Olivier (Viscount Chandos)**

*The Memoirs of Lord Chandos* (Bodley House: London, 1962).

# M

**MAAGA, Mary M.; and Catherine Wessinger**

*Hearing the voices of Jonestown - Religion and Politics.* (Syracuse University Press: Syracuse, 1998).

**MAAS, Sharon**

*Her Darkest Hour* (Bookouture: London, 2020).

*Of Marriageable Age* (HarperCollins: London, 1999). Reprinted by HarperCollins in 2014.

*Peacocks Dancing* (HarperCollins: London, 2001).

*The Children of Berlin* (Bookouture: London, 2023).

*The Darkest Hour: Two sisters torn apart by war* (Bookouture: 2021).

*The Far Away Girl* (Bookouture: London, 2021).

*The Girl From Jonestown* (Bookouture: London, 2022).

*The Girl from Lamaha Street* (Bookouture: London, 2022).

*The Girl from the Sugar Plantation* (Bookouture: London, 2017).

*The Lost Daughter of India* (Bookouture: London, 2017).

*The Mahabharat: Sons of God* (Bookouture: London, 2011).

*The Orphan of India* (Bookouture: London, 2017).

*The Secret Life of Winnie Cox* (Bookouture: London, 2015).

*The Small Fortune of Dorothea Q* (Bookouture: London, 2015).

*The Soldier's Girl* (Bookouture: London, 2018).

*The Speech of Angels* (HarperCollins: London, 2003).

*The Sugar Planter's Daughter* (Bookouture: London, 2016).

*Those I Have Lost* (Bookoutore: London, 2021).

*The Violin Maker's Daughter* (Bookouture: London, 2019).

**MACEOIN, G.**

*Colombia and Venezuela and the Guianas* (Life World Library, Time Life Books: New York, 1965).

**MACINNES, H.**

*Climb to the Lost World* (Hodder and Stoughton: London, 1974).

**MACMILLAN, ed.**

*The West Indies Past and Present with British Guiana and* (W.H. Collingridge: London, 1938)

**MACMILLAN, Allister**

*The Red Book of the West Indies* (n.p.: London, 1909).

**MACMILLAN, Harold**

*At the End of the Day, 1961-1963* (Harper & Row: New York, 1973).

*Pointing the way, 1959-1961* (Harper & Row: New York, 1972).

**MACPHERSON, John**

*Caribbean Lands: A Geography of the West Indies* (Longmans: London, 1963).

**MADHOO-BIPA, Juliet**

*Myrtle Turtle Can Too* (Liferich: New York, 2014).

**MADHOO-NASCIMENTO, Gem, ed.**

*Guyana: Where and What: Everything You need to Know, Every Place You Need to Go* [Also in Spanish and Portuguese] (Ministry of Tourism: Georgetown, 2014).

**MAES-JELINEK, Hena, ed.**

*Commonwealth Literature and the Modern World* (Didier: Brussells: 1975).

*Wilson Harris: Explorations: A Selection of Talks and Articles 1966-1981* (Twayne Publishers: Boston, 1982).

**MAGDALENE, Sister Rose**

*Amerindian Stories for Young Guyanese* (Department of Culture: Georgetown, 1985).

**MAHABIR, Kumar**

*Indian Diaspora in the Caribbean* (Serials Publishing: New Delhi, 2009).

**MAHABIR, Somdat; and Yashwant V. Pathak, eds.**

*Nutraceuticals and Health: Review of Human Evidence* (CRC Press: London, 2013).

**MAHADEO, Jag B.**

*The Heart of the Sun: A Collection of Stories of Childhood Memories and Personal Poems Based on a Young Boy's Actual Experiences in No. 66 Village* (Authorhouse: Bloomington, 2011).

**MAHARAJ, Niala**

*Like Heaven* (Random House: London, 2006).

**MAHASE, Radica**

*Why Should We Be Called 'Coolies'? The End of Indian Indentured Labour* (Manohar Publishers: New Delhi, 2020).

**_____; et al**

*Global Indian Diaspora: Charting New Frontiers* (Manohar Publishers: New Delhi, 2022).

*Legacy of Indian Indentured Labour* (Manohar Publishers: New Delhi, 2016).

*Social and Cultural Dimensions of Indian Indentured Labour and Its Diaspora: Past and Present* (Manohar Publishers: New Delhi, 2016).

**MAHASE, B. Richard**

*Footprints of a Farmer: Biography of Ken Subraj* (Amazon Books: Bolton, 2022).

**MAHASE, Joseph**

*An Intimate Journey: A Pomeroon Destiny Uncovered* (Friesen Press: Winnipeg, 2021).

**MAHESH, R.**

*A Pilgrimage to the Place of my Birth* (R. Mahesh: New York, 1995).

*Glimpses of Living Guyanese-American Poetic Images:* Part One (R. Maharaj: New York, 2012).

**MAIR, John**

*Morse The End of the Road?* (Bight-sized Books: London, 2023).

*Jericho Oxford* (CAP: London, December 2022).

*Boris Johnson Media Creation, Comic, Casualty* (MGM: London, August 2022).

*Morse, Lewis, Endeavour and Oxford. 35 years on screen. A guide* (Bite-Sized Books: London, November 2021).

*Oil Dorado: Guyana's Back Gold* (Bight-sized Books: London, 2019, 2020, 2021, 2022, 2023).

*Pandemic: Where are we still going wrong?* (Bite-Sized Book: London, November 2020).

*Populism and the Media* (Abramis: London, July 2021).

*Reporting the War in Ukraine. A first draft of history* (Abramis: London, June 2022).

*Ten Oxford Authors, ten literary walks* (Bite-Sized Books: London, February 2022).

*The BBC at 100 - Will It Survive?* (Bite-Sized Books: London, July 2021).

*What Price Channel Four NOW?* (Abramis: London, November 2021).

**MAISON, Stephen**

*Taken Without Consent: A True Story* (Createspace: Scotts Valley, 2015).

**MAJEED, Halim**

*Forbes Burnham, National Reconciliation and National Unity 1984-85* (Global Communications: New York, 2005).

**MAKHANLALL, David P**

*A Pilgrimage to the Place of my Birth* (R. Mahesh: New York, 1995).

*Brer Anansi and the Boat Race: A Folk Tale from the Caribbean* (Peter Berick Books: London, 1992).
*Brer Anansi Joy Ride and Other Stories* (Blackie Children's Books: London, 1992).
*Brer Anansi Strikes Again* (Blackie Children's Books: London, 1976).
*Brer Anansi's Bag of Tricks* (Blackie Children's Books: London, 1978).
*Brer Anansi's Luck Escape and Other Stories* (Blackie Children's Books: London, 1992).
*Further Adventures of Brer Anansi* (Blackie Children's Books: London, 1980).
*Invincible Brer Anansi* (Blackie Children's Books London, 1974).
*Long Live Brer Anansi* (Blackie Children's Books: London, 1979).
*The Best of Brer Anansi* (Blackie & Sins: London, 1973).

**MANDLE, Jay**

*Plantation Economy: Population and Economic Change in Guyana 1838-1960* (Temple University Press: Philadelphia, 1973).
*The Venezuela-Guyana Border Dispute: Britain's Colonial Legacy in Latin America* (Westview Press: Boulder, 1983).

**MANGAR, Tota**

*A Brief History of the Guyana Forestry Commission, 1925-2004: 79 Years of Service to the Nation* (University of Guyana: Georgetown, 2008).
*European Exploration of the Guianas, 16th and 17th Centuries* (University of Guyana: Georgetown, 2005).
*History of the Demerara Tobacco Company, 1934-1990* (University of Guyana: Georgetown, 1994).
*Rural and Interior Development Policy of Henry Irving, 1882-1887* (University of Guyana: Georgetown, 1992).

**MANGRU, Basdeo**

*A History of East Indian Resistance on the Guyana Sugar Estates 1869-1948* (Edwin Mellen Press: New York, 1996).
*Benevolent Neutrality: Indian Government Policy and Labour Migration to British Guiana 1854-1884* (Hansib: Hertfordshire, 1987).
*Champions of Indo-Guyanese Welfare: 1838-1938* (Adams Press: Chicago, 2017).
*Colonial Emigration from the Bengal Presidency* (Hansib Publications: Hertfordshire, 2014).
*Impressions of British Guiana, 1930: An Emissary's Assessment* (Adams Press: Chicago, 2007).

*In Search of Paradise* (University Press of America: New York, 2005).

*Indenture and Abolition: Sacrifice and Survival on the Guyanese Sugar plantations* (TSAR: Toronto, 1993).

*Indians in Guyana: A Concise History from their Arrival to the Present* (Adams Press: Chicago, 2000).

*Kanpur to Kolkota: Labour Recruitment for the Sugar Colonies* (Hansib Publications: Hertfordshire, 2014).

*The Elusive El Dorado: Essays on the Indian Experience in Guyana* (University Press of America: New York, 2005).

**_____; P. Misir; and T. Depoo**

*The East Indian Diaspora: 150 Years of Survival, Contributions, and Achievements* (Queen's College, CUNY: New York, 1983).

**MANLEY, Robert H.**

*Guyana Emergent: The Post-Independence Struggle for Nondependent Development* (GK Hall: Boston, 1979).

**MANNINGTON, George**

*The West Indies with British Guiana and British Honduras* (Eveleigh Nash & Grayson Ltd.: London, 1930).

**MANRAJ, A.S.**

*In Pursuit of Justice: Fifty Years as Criminal Defense Attorney* (NdueCzon Publishing Group: Tampa, 2004).

*The Law of Speeding and Radar* (Butterworths: Toronto, 1985).

**MANUEL, P.; et al**

*Caribbean Currents: Caribbean Music from Rumba to Reggae* (Temple University Press: Philadelphia, 1995).

**MARCHETTI, V.; and J.D. Marks**

*The CIA and the Cult of Intelligence* (Dell Publishing: New York, 1975).

**MARGAIN, Eduardo**

*Development Challenges and Cooperation in the Commonwealth Caribbean* (IADB: Washington D.C., 1983).

**MARK, Francis L.**

*Organized Labour in British Guiana* (Caribbean Institute: San Juan, 1965).

**MARKHAM, A., ed.**

*Penguin Book of Short Stories* (Penguin Books: London, 1997).

**MARKS-MENDONÇA, Maureen**

*Legend of the Swan Children* (Macmillan: London, 2009).

**MARRAT, Jabez**

*In the Tropics: Scenes & Incidents of West Indian Life.* 2nd ed. (Wesleyan Conference Office: London, 1881).

**MARRYSHOW, T.A.**

*Cycles Of Civilisations* (R. Ferdinand-Lalljie Publishers: Birmingham, 2013).

**MARS, Joan R.**

*Deadly Force, Colonialism, and the Rule of Law: Police Violence in Guyana* (Greenwood Publishing: Westport, 2002).

**MARS, Perry**

*Caribbean Labour and Politics: Legacies of Cheddi Jagan and Michael Manley* (Wayne State University Press: Detroit, 2004).

*Ideology and Change: The Transformation of the Caribbean Left* (UWI Press: Kingston, 1998).

**MARSHALL-RADCLIFFE, Rex**

*Venezuela, Guyana, French Guiana and Surinam: The Americas* (Macmillan: London, 1988).

**MARTIN, Cheryl**

*A Collection of Poems: More Cooked Up Poetry* (Toplink Publishing: New York, 2018).

**MARTIN, E.**

*Leo's Local Lyrics* (E. Martin: Georgetown, 1886).

*Leo's Poetical Works* (W.H.L. Collingridge Printers: London, 1883).

*Scriptology: A Collection of Four Short Stories* (E. Martin: Georgetown, 1885).

**MARTIN, Helena**

*Walk Wit' Me…All Ova Guyana: Memoir of Helena Martin* (Balboa Press: Bloomington, 2013).

**MARTIN, Robert**

*History of the West Indies: British Guiana, Barbados, St. Vincent, St. Lucia, Dominica, Montserrat, Antigua, St. Christopher* (Ansdesite Press: Amsterdam, 2017).

**MARTIN, Tony**

*Caribbean History: From Pre-Colonial Origins to the Present* (Pearson: London, 2013).

**MARTIN-COMBS, Claire; and Paula Matthews-Halewood**

*When We Grew Up in the Land of the Mighty Roraima circa 1930s-1960s* (Xlibris: Bloomington, 2007).

**MAS, Kar**

*Cooking Book Guyana: Self-Writing Cookbook for the Guyanese Cuisine* (Amazon Books: Bolton, 2020).

**MASSIAH, Marilyn A.**

*Black Paradox: The Folly Over Skin Colour* (Dorrance Publishing: Pittsburgh, 2022).

**MASUDA, Hirokuni**

*The Genesis of Discourse Grammar: Universals and Substrata in Guyanese, Hawaii Creole, and Japanese* (Peter Lang Publishing: New York, 2000).

**MATTAI, Bansraj**

*Aiming High and the Yogas of Self-Realization, Revisiting the Dharmic Scriptures of India* (Createspace: Scotts Valley, 2018).

*Hinduism: On the Nature of Religious Experience, Moral and Spiritual Value, and Human Conduct (Createspace:* Scotts Valley, 2009).

*The Hindu Concept of God and Use of Symbols (Createspace:* Scotts Valley, 2017).

**MATTHEWS, Lear.**

*English-Speaking Caribbean Immigrants: Transnational Identity* (University Press of America: Lanham, 2014).

**_____; and S.C.Lee**

*Forms of Matrucentrality: The Matrilineal Ashanti and the Matrifocal Guyanese* (American Sociological Association: New York, 1975).

**MATTHEWS, Marc**

*A Season of Sometime* (Peepal Tree Press: Leeds, 1992).

*Guyana My Altar* (Karnak House: London, 1987)

*Just Deserts* (Trafford Publishing: London, 2005).

**MAY, Jacques Meyer**

*The Ecology of Malnutrition in Eastern South America: Venezuela, Guyana, Surinam (and the Netherland Antilles), French Guiana, Brazil, Uruguay, Paraguay* (Hafner Press: New York, 1974).

**MCANDREW, Rosie**

*Wordsworth's White Wife: Living in Guyana 1968-1973* (Berforts Ltd: London, 2015).

**MCANDREW, Wordsworth**

*Blue Gaulding* (Miniature Poet Series: Georgetown, 1952).

*More Poems* (W. McAndrew: Georgetown, 1970).

*Poems* (W. McAndrew: Georgetown, 1969).

*Poems of St. Agnes* (W. McAndrew: Georgetown, 1962).

*Poetry. Introduction 3* (Faber and Faber: London, 1975).

*Selected Poems* (Erbar Press: Georgetown, 1966).

**MCCONNELL, Ro**

*Land of Waters: Explorations in the Natural History of Guyana, South America* (Book Guild Ltd: Sussex, 2000).

**MCCRACKEN, Jean**

*Aknoro Kaan Nakihtotho* [Wai Wai Primer] (n.p.: n.p., n.d.).

**MCDONALD, Ian**

*A Cloud of Witnesses* (Caribbean Press: Georgetown, 2013).

*A Love of Poetry* (Caribbean Press: Georgetown, 2013).

*AJS at 70: A Celebration on His 70th Birthday of the Life, Work, and Art of A. J. Seymour* (Ian McDonald: Georgetown, 1984).

*An Abounding Joy: Essays on Sports* (Hansib: Hertfordshire, 2019).

*Bedrock of a Nation: Cultural Foundations of West Indian Integration* (West Indian Commission: Port-of-Spain, 1992).

*Between Silence and Silence* (Peepal Tree Press: Leeds, 2004). [Winner Guyana Prize for Literature 2004].

*Essequibo* (Peterloo Poets: London, 1952). [Winner Guyana Prize for Literature 1992].

*Jaffo the Calypsonian* (Peepal Tree Press: Leeds, 1994).

*Mercy Ward* (Caribbean Press: Georgetown, 2010).

*Poetry Introduction 3* (Faber and Faber: London, 1975).

*River Dancers* (Hansib: Hertfordshire, 2016).

*Selected Poems* (Labour Advocate: Georgetown, 1984).

*Selected Poems* (Macmillan Caribbean: London, 2008).

*Sugar in B.G.: Challenge and Change* (New World Publications: Georgetown, 1965).

*The Bowling was Superfine: West Indian Writing and West Indian Cricket* (Peepal Tree Press: Leeds, 2009).

*The Comfort of All Things: A Collection of Poems* (Moray House Trust: Georgetown, 2012) [Winner of the Guyana Prize for Literature in 2012].

*The Garden: Poems* (MiddleRoad Publishers: Toronto, 2021).

*The Hummingbird Tree* (Heinemann: London, 1969) and (Macmillan: London, 2004). [Turned into a BBC film in 1992]

*The Tramping Man* (UWI School of Continuing Education: St. Augustine, 1969) [a one-act play published in a collection of eight Caribbean Plays titled *A Time and a Season*].

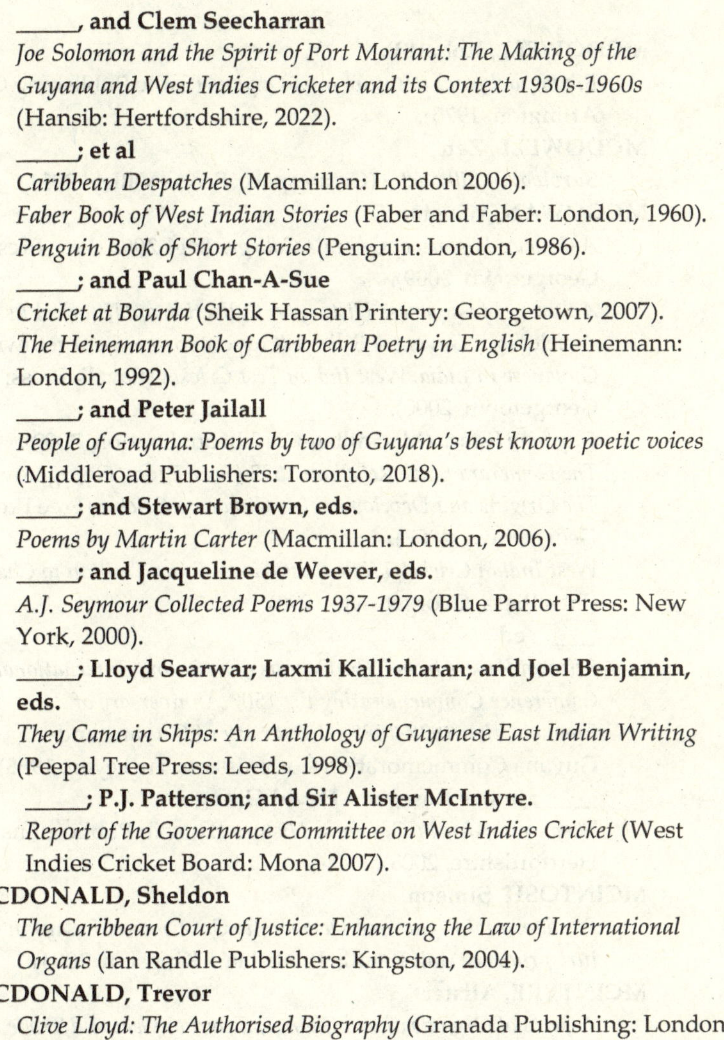

**_____, and Clem Seecharran**

*Joe Solomon and the Spirit of Port Mourant: The Making of the Guyana and West Indies Cricketer and its Context 1930s-1960s* (Hansib: Hertfordshire, 2022).

**_____; et al**

*Caribbean Despatches* (Macmillan: London 2006).

*Faber Book of West Indian Stories* (Faber and Faber: London, 1960).

*Penguin Book of Short Stories* (Penguin: London, 1986).

**_____; and Paul Chan-A-Sue**

*Cricket at Bourda* (Sheik Hassan Printery: Georgetown, 2007).

*The Heinemann Book of Caribbean Poetry in English* (Heinemann: London, 1992).

**_____; and Peter Jailall**

*People of Guyana: Poems by two of Guyana's best known poetic voices* (Middleroad Publishers: Toronto, 2018).

**_____; and Stewart Brown, eds.**

*Poems by Martin Carter* (Macmillan: London, 2006).

**_____; and Jacqueline de Weever, eds.**

*A.J. Seymour Collected Poems 1937-1979* (Blue Parrot Press: New York, 2000).

**_____; Lloyd Searwar; Laxmi Kallicharan; and Joel Benjamin, eds.**

*They Came in Ships: An Anthology of Guyanese East Indian Writing* (Peepal Tree Press: Leeds, 1998).

**_____; P.J. Patterson; and Sir Alister McIntyre.**

*Report of the Governance Committee on West Indies Cricket* (West Indies Cricket Board: Mona 2007).

**MCDONALD, Sheldon**

*The Caribbean Court of Justice: Enhancing the Law of International Organs* (Ian Randle Publishers: Kingston, 2004).

**MCDONALD, Trevor**

*Clive Lloyd: The Authorised Biography* (Granada Publishing: London, 1985).

**MCDONNELL, Alex**

*Considerations on Negro Slavery With Authentic Reports Illustrative of the Actual Condition of the Negro in Demerara* (Longman, Hurst: London, 1825).

**MCDOUGALL, Russell; and Iain Davidson, eds**

*The Roth Family, Anthropology and Colonial Administration* (Left Coast Press Inc: London, 2012).

**MCDOWELL, Robert E.**

*Bibliography of Literature from Guyana* (Sable Publishing Corp.: Arlington, 1975).

**MCDOWELL, Zen**

*Survival in Silhouette* (Createspace: Scotts Valley, 2011).

**MCGOWAN, Winston F.**

*A Concise History of Queen`s College, 1844-2009* (Free Press: Georgetown, 2009).

*A Survey of Guyanese History: A Collection of Historical Essays and Articles by a Guyanese Scholar* (Guyentrprise: Georgetown, 2018).

*Guyanese in India, West Indian Test Cricket* (Pavalk Press: Georgetown, 2000).

*Guyana History* (Macmillan-Caribbean: London, 2002).

*The Demerara Slave Rebellion 1823* (Free Press: Georgetown, 1998).

*The Origins and Development of Guyanese Cricket* (Free Press: Georgetown, 2007).

*West Indian Cricket Triple Centurions: From Tarilton to Chanderpal* (Free Press: Georgetown, 1998).

**_____; ed.**

*Selected Papers from "The Genesis of a Nation" International Conference Commemorating the 150th Anniversary of Emancipation 1938-1988* (University of Guyana and Guyana Commemoration Commission: Turkeyen, 1988).

**_____; James Rose; and David Granger**

*Themes in African-Guyanese History* (Hansib Publications: Hertfordshire, 2008).

**MCINTOSH, Simeon**

*Fundamental Rights and Democratic Governance: Essays in Caribbean Jurisprudence* (Ian Randle Publishers: Kingston, 2004).

**MCINTYRE, Alister**

*Aspects of Organisational Change, External Debt and Trade in Guyana in the Context of Adjustment* (Ministry of Finance: Georgetown, 1987).

**MCINTYRE, W.D.**

*Colonies into Commonwealth* (Blandford Press: London, 1966).

**MCKAW, Rev. J.D.**

*Under the Southern Cross: A Story of the East Indian Indenture in British Guiana* (HMS Eastern Division: London, 1914).

**MCKENZIE, V.M.**

*Domestic Violence in America* (Brunswick Publishing Corporation: Lawrenceville, 1995).

**MCLEWIN, P.J.**

*Power and Economic Change: The Response to Emancipation in Jamaica and British Guiana 1840-1865* (Garland Publishing: New York, 1987).

**MCLYMONT, Rosalind**

*The Guyana Contract* (New York Journal Communications Inc.: New York, 2015).

**MCPHERSON, A.**

*Like Heaven* (Random House: London, 2006).

*Short History of US Intervention in Latin America and the Caribbean* (Wiley-Blackwell: London, 2006).

**MCPHOY, Jared**

*By Grace Through faith: A Journey of Self-Discovery* (Priceless Publishing: Lauderhill, 2022).

**MCRCAMERON A.J.**

*The Berbice Uprising 1763* (Caribbean Press: Georgetown, 2013).

**MCRAE, M.V.**

*Shades of Life* (MV McRae: Georgetown, 2008).

**MCTURK, M.**

*Essays and Fables – Written in the Vernacular of British Guiana* (A.W.B. Long: London, 1899).

**MCWATT, Mark**

*Interiors* (Dangaroo Press: Sydney, 1989).

*Light Transports: Intercity* (Route Publishing: London, 2014).

*Suspended Sentences: Fictions of Atonement* (Peepal Tree Press: Leeds, 2005).

[Winner of a Commonwealth Writers' Prize in 2006, as well as the Casa de las Americas Prize for best book of Caribbean Literature in English or Creole].

*The Caribbean Short Story: Critical Perspectives* (Peepal Tree Press: Leeds, 2011).

*The Journey To Le Repentir* (Peepal Tree Press: Leeds, 2009).

*The Language of El Dorado* (Dangaroo Press: Sydney, 1994).

**_____; Stewart Brown, eds.**

*Oxford Book of Caribbean Verse* (Oxford University Press: Oxford, 2005).

**_____; Hazel Simmons-Brown, eds.**

*A World of Poetry for CXC* (Heinemann: London, 2005).

**MCWATT, Tessa**

*Dragon's Cry* (Riverbank Press: Toronto, 2000).

*Higher Ed* (Random House: Toronto, 2015).

*Luminous Ink* (Cormorant Books: Toronto, 2018).

*Out of My Skin* (Riverbank Press: Toronto, 1998; and Cormorant Books: Toronto, 2012).

*Shame on Me* (Random House: Toronto, 2020).

*Step Closer* (HarperCollins: Toronto, 2009),

*The Snow Line* (Random House: Toronto, 2021 and Scribe: London, 2021).

*There's No Place Like...* (Cormorant Books: Toronto, 2004).

*This Body* (HarperCollins: Toronto, 2004, and Macmillan Caribbean: London, 2005),

*Vital Signs* (Random House: Toronto, 2011 and William Heinemann: London, 2012).

*Where are you Agnes* (Groundwood Books: London, 2020)

**MEAD, Stella**

*Bim: A Boy in British Guiana* (The Oprion Press: Selsey, 1947).

**MEDFORD, Nikita**

*Yearnings of a Woman Poems* (N. Medford: Georgetown, 2005).

**MEEKS, B., ed.**

*Caribbean Reasonings* (Ian Randle Publishers: Kingston, 2005).

**MEGGERS, B.J.**

*Amazonia: Man and Culture in a Counterfeit Paradise* (Aldine-Atherton: Chicago, 1971).

*Prehistoric America* (Aldine Publishing: Chicago, 1972).

**MEIERS, Michael**

*Was Jonestown a CIA Experiment? A Review of the Evidence* (Edwin Mellen Press: New York, 1988).

**MELVILLE, Collette**

*Wapishana-English Dictionary* (Amerindian Peoples Association: Georgetown, 2005).

**MELVILLE, Edwina**

*This is the Rupununi: A Simple Story Book of the Savannah Lands of the Rupununi* (Government Information Service: Georgetown, 1956).

**MELVILLE, Leslie**

*A Voice Crying in the Wilderness* (Richter Publishing: Clearwater, 2015).

**MELVILLE, Pauline** [Edwina Melville's daughter]

*Eating Air* (Telegram Books: London, 2009).

*Shape-Shifter: A Collection of 12 short stories* (The Women's Press: London, 1990).

[Her first book. Winner of the Guardian Fiction Prize, the Macmillan Silver Pen Award, and the Commonwealth Writers Prize for the best first book].

*The Master of Chaos and Other Fables* (Sandstone Press: Ross-Shire, 2021).

*The Migration of Ghosts* (Bloomsbury: London, 1998).

*The Ventriloquist's Tale* (Bloomsbury: London, 1997).

**MENEZES, Sister Mary Noel**

*A Guide to Historical Research* (University of Guyana: Turkeyen, 1978).

*Amerindian Life in Guyana* (Ministry of Education: Georgetown, 1983).

*British Policy Towards the Amerindians in British Guiana: 1803-1873* (Oxford University Press: Oxford, 1977). Reprint. (Caribbean Press: Georgetown, 2011).

*Goodall's Sketches of Amerindian Tribes* (British Museum Publications: London, 1977). Reprint (Macmillan-Caribbean: London, 2003).

*Guyana and the Wider World: A Collection of Essays and Addresses* (Guyenterprise: Georgetown, 2017).

*How to do better research* (Demerara Publishers: Georgetown, 1990). Reprint. (Sheik Hassan Production: Georgetown, 2001).

*Scenes From The History of the Portuguese in Guyana* (M.N. Menezes: Georgetown, 1986).

*The Amerindians and the Europeans* (Collins Ltd: Glasgow, 1982).

*The Amerindians of British Guiana: 1803-1873: A Documentary History* (Frank Cass: London, 1979).

*The Portuguese in Guyana: A Study in Culture and Conflict* (Jesuit Missions: London, 1998).

**_____, ed.**

*William Hilhouse's Indian Notices 1825* (National Commission for Research Materials on Guyana: Georgetown, 1978). Reprint. (Caribbean Press: Georgetown, 2010).

**MENTORE, George**

*Killing, Eating and Compassion: Skeptical Anthropology* (University of Nebraska Press: Omaha, 2005).

*Of Passionate Curves and Desirable Cadences: Themes on Wai Wai Social Being* (University of Nebraska Press: Omaha, 2009).

*The Relevance of Myth* (Department of Culture: Georgetown, 1988).

**METCALFE, Fr. A.**

*The Flying Priest: A Journal* (Fr. A. Metcalfe: Georgetown, 1994).

**MIERS, Henry A.; and S.F. Markham**

*Directory of Museums and Art Galleries in Canada, Newfoundland, Bermuda, the British West Indies, British Guiana, and the Falkland Islands* (Museums Association: London, 1931).

**MILLAR, Carl E.**

*Wanda, the White Jaguar of the Cannibal Jungle* (Createspace: Scotts Valley, 2022).

**MILLER, E.W.; and R.M. Miller**

*The 3rd World: Colombia, Venezuela, Guyana, Surinam, French Guiana: A Bibliography* (Vance Bibliography: n.p., 1990).

**MILLIROUX, Felix**

*Demerara: The Transition from Slavery to Liberty* (n.p.: London, 1877).

**MILNE, R.S.**

*Politics in ethnically bipolar states: Guyana, Malaysia, Fiji* (University of British Columbia Press: Vancouver, n.d.).

**MILLER, E.W.; and R.M. Miller**

*The 3rd World: Colombia, Venezuela, Guyana, Surinam, French Guiana: A Bibliography* (Vance Bibliography: n.p., 1990).

**MILLS, Janet**

*Quamina, do you hear this? Revisiting the Demerara Slave Rebellion, 1823* (Dalhousie University Press: Dartmouth, 2018).

**MINISTRY OF EDUCATION**

*Heroes of Our Nation: 50 Nation Builders of Guyana* (Ministry of Education: Georgetown, 2017).

*More Amerindian Stories* (Ministry of Education: Georgetown, 1977).

*National Songs Composed by Valerie Rodway* (Ministry of Education: Georgetown, 1978).

*One Hundred Folk Songs of Guyana* (Ministry of Education: Georgetown, 1999).

*Small Enterprise Development for Blind and Visually Impaired Workers, Guyana Project Report 1986* (Ministry of Education: Georgetown, 2022).

**MINISTRY OF FOREIGN AFFAIRS**

*A Time For Action To Create a New International System. Addresses by Minister of Foreign Affairs, Mr. Fred Wills at the Conference of Non-Aligned Countries, Lima, Peru, August 25, 1975; the seventh special session of the UN General Assembly, September 8, 1975; and the 30th session of the UN General Assembly, Oct 1, 1975* (Ministry of Foreign Affairs: Georgetown, 1975).

*The New Conquistadors: Venezuelan Challenge to Guyana's Sovereignty* (Hansib: Hertfordshire, 2017).

**MINISTRY OF INFORMATION AND CULTURE**

*Amerindian Integration: A Brief Outline of the Progress of Integration* (Government of Guyana: Georgetown, 1970).

**MISIR, P.**

*Aspirations of Teachers in Guyana: A Comparative Analysis* (University of Guyana: Georgetown, n.d.).

*Cultural Identity and Creolisation in National Unity: The Multi-Ethnic Caribbean* (University Press of America: Lanham, 2006).

*Ethnic Cleavage and Closure in the Caribbean Diaspora* (Caribbean Diaspora Press: New York, 1999).

*HIV and AIDS Knowledge and Stigma in Guyana* (UWI Press: Kingston, 2013).

*Leadership Behaviour and the Compliance Structure in Education: A Sociological Study of Ideology and Social Change in Guyana* (Caribbean Diaspora Press: New York, 1998).

*Racial Ethnic Imbalance in Guyana Public Bureaucracies: The Tension between Exclusion and Representation* (Edwin Miller Press: New York, 2010).

*The Political Mass Media Racial Complex* (Caribbean Diaspora Press: New York, 2002).

*Work Commitment in Education: An International Perspective* (Reliance Publishing House: New Delhi, 1995).

*Workers Participation in Management: Case of Nationalised Enterprises in Guyana*, 2nd ed. (Reliance Publishing House: New Delhi, 1993).

**MISIR, Roop**

*OAC Biology Workshop Teachers' Guide* (Ministry of Education: Toronto, 1996).

**MITCHELL, Harold**

*Caribbean Patterns: A Political and Economic Study of the Contemporary Caribbean* (W&R Chambers: London, 1967).

*Contemporary Politics and Economics of the Caribbean* (Ohio University Press: Columbus, 1969).

**MITCHELL, William; et al**

*Area Handbook for Guyana* (GPO: Washington, D.C., 1969).

**MITRASING, F.E.M.**

*The Border Conflict Between Surinam and Guyana* (Kersten: Fort Dodge, 1975).

**MITTELHOLZER, Edgar**

*A Morning at the Office* (Hogarth Press: London, 1950). Reprinted by Peepal Tree: Leeds, 2010).

*A Morning in Trinidad* (Doubleday: London, 1950).

[His second book which was first published under the title *A Morning in the Office*].

*A Swarthy Boy: A Childhood in British Guiana* (Putnam's: London, 1963). [Reprinted by Peepal Tree Press: Leeds, 2023].

*A Tale of Three Places* (Secker and Warburg: London, 1957).

*A Tinkling in the Twilight* (Secker and Warburg: London, 1959).

*Children of Kaywana* (Secker and Warburg: London, 1956).

*Corentyne Thunder* (Eyre and Spottiswoode: New York, 1941).

*Creole Chips* (Edgar Mittleholzer: New Amsterdam, n.d.).

*Eltonsbrody* (Secker and Warburg: London, 1960).

*Kaywana Blood* (Secker and Warburg: London, 1958).

*Kaywana Stock* (Secker and Warburg: London, 1959)

[Originally published in 1954 under the title *The Harrowing of Hubertus*, the second in the author's *Kaywana Trilogy*, three works of historical fiction set in the author's British Guiana].

*Latticed Echoes* (Secker and Warburg: London, 1960).

*Life and Death of Sylvia* (John Day and Co.: New York, 1954).

*Mittelholzer, Edgar Austin*: [Bibliography of works of Mittelholzer and works on him, with tributes by Martin Carter, William Dow, Daisy Hahnfeld, Edward V. Luckhoo, Lucille Mittelholzer, Arthur J. Seymour] (National Library: Georgetown, 1968).

*My Bones and My Flute: A Ghost Story in the Old-Fashioned Manner* (Secker and Warburg: London 1955).

*Of Trees and the Sea* (Secker and Warburg: London, 1956).

*Shadows Move Among Them* (Peter Neville: New York, 1951). Reprint. (Peepal Tree Press: Leeds, 2010).

*The Adding Machine: A Fable for Capitalists and Commercialists* (Pioneer Press: Kingston, 1954).

*The Aloneness of Mrs. Chatham* (Library 33: London, 1965).

*The Harrowing of Hubertus* (Secker and Warburg: London, 1954).

*The Jilkington Drama* (Abelard-Schuman: London, 1965).

*The Life and Death of Sylvia* (Secker and Warburg: London, 1953). Reprint. (Peepal Tree Press: Leeds, 2010).
*The Mad MacMullochs* (Secker and Warburg: London, 1961).
*The Piling of Clouds* (Putnam's: London, 1961).
*The Weather Family* (Secker and Warburg: London, 1958).
*The Weather in Middenshot* (Secker and Warburg: London, 1952).
*The Wounded and the Worried* (Putnam: London, 1962).
*Thunder Returning* (Secker and Warburg: London, 1961).
*Uncle Paul* (MacDonald: London, 1963).
*With a Carib Eye* (Secker & Warburg: London, 1958).

**MITTERMEIER, Russell, et al**
*The Monkeys of the Guianas* (Conservation International: Washington, DC: 2008).

**MOHABIR, Philip**
*Building Bridges* (Hodder & Stoughton: London, 1988).

**MOHABIR, Rajiv**
*Antiman: A Hybrid Memoir* (Restless Books: New York, 2022).

**MOHABIR, Veda Nath**
*Under Attack! The Caribbean Indian: Rebutting and Educating UWI's Dr. Kean Gibson for Vilifying Hindus* (VN Mohabir: Toronto, 2009).

**MOHADEO, Jog B**
*The Heart of the Sun: A Collection of Stories of Childhood Memories and Personal Poems Based on a Young Boy's Actual Experiences at No. 66 Village, Corentyne* (AuthorHouse: Bloomington, 2011).

**MOHAMED, K.**
*A Tapestry of Life* (K. Mohamed: Scarborough, 2009).

**MOHAMED, Paloma**
*A Man Called Garvey* (Majority Press: Dover, 2001).
*Caribbean Mythology and Modern Life: 5 Plays For Young People* (Majority Press: Dover, 2004).
*Condones by Our Silence: Issues Impacting the Abuse of Children in Guyana* (UNICEF: Georgetown, 2000).
*Come Fiah: Poems* (Pavnik Press: Georgetown, 1991).
*Communication, Power and Change in the Caribbean* (Hansib Publications: Hertfordshire, 2013).
*Duenne* (Caribbean Press: Georgetown, 2013).
*Laura in the Linchkit Liyyerer: A Children's book on the Environment* (Creatspace: Scotts Valley, 2004).
*Listen Up: A Sourcebook on the Environment for Secondary School Students* (PRIMA-IADB: Georgetown, 2004).
*Marlee the Manatee* (Caribbean Press: Georgetown, 2013).

*Notes of a Red Woman, Slightly Sane: Collected Poems of Paloma Mohamed-Martin* (Createspace: Scotts Valley, 2017).
*Notes on the Media of Guyana* (Lambert Academic Publishing: Berlin, 2012).
*Preparing a Dramatic Production: A Handbook for Students and Novice Directors* (Ministry of Education: Georgetown, 2000).
*Song: Poems* (The Majority Press, Dover, 2000).
*The Adventures of Marlee the Manatee: Two Children's Stories About Moral Courage* (Creatspace: Scotts Valley, 2014).
*The Massacuraman: A Folk Play for Young People* (Createspace: Scotts Valley, 2014).
*What Every Woman in Public Life Should Know: Networking, Media Handling and Basic Communications for Agenda Setting* (OAS and Guyana Bar Association: Georgetown, 2002).

**MOHAMMED, Yusuf**

*A Bitter Harvest of Love: Poems for Young Hearts* (Y. Mohammed: Georgetown, 1981).
*When Kiskadees Sang: A Collection of Poems* (Y. Mohammed: Georgetown, 1981).
*Where the Wild Grass Whispers: A Collection of Poems* (Y. Mohammed: Georgetown, 1980).
*Wild Flowers and Water-Lilies* (Y. Mohammed: Georgetown, 1979).

**MONAR, R.**

*Backdam People* (Peepal Tree Press: Leeds, 1987).
*Estate People* (Roraima: Georgetown, 1994).
*High House and Radio* (Peepal Tree Press: Leeds, 1992).
*Janjhat* (Peepal Tree Press: Leeds, 1989).
*Koker* (A Collection of his Poems) (Peepal Tree Press: Leeds, 1987).
*Poems for Guyanese Children* (R. Monar: Georgetown, 1972).
*Ramsingh Street* (Guyana Writers' Association: Georgetown, 1998).
*Tormented Wives* (Guyana Writers' Association: Georgetown, 1999).

**MONROE, T.; and R. Lewis**

*Readings in Government and Politics in the West Indies* (University of the West Indies: Kingston, 1971).

**MOORE, B.L.**

*Cultural Power, Resistance and Pluralism. Colonial Guyana 1838-1900* (McGill University Press: Montreal, 1995).

*Race, Power, and Social Segmentation in Colonial Society* (Routledge: New York, 1981).

*Slavery, Freedom, and Gender: The Dynamics of Caribbean Society* (University of the West Indies Press: Mona, 2001).

**_____; and S.R. Wilmot, eds.**

*Before and After 1865: Education, Politics and Regionalism in the Caribbean* (Ian Randle Publishers: Kingston, 1999).

**MOORE, Nicole**

*Born Between the Lines: An Autobiography* (Lulu Publishers: Morrisville, 2016).

**MOORE, R.**

*A Sympathetic History of Jonestown: The Moore Family Involvement in Peoples Temple* (Edwin Mellen Press: New York, 1985).

**MOORE, Rebecca; M. Fielding; et al.**

*New Religious Movements, Mass Suicide, and Peoples Temple: Scholarly Perspectives on a Tragedy; Studies on American Religions* Vol. 37. (Edwin Meller Press: New York, 1989).

**MOORE, Renate A.**

*Just Eat: Pure and Simple Cooking* (Spark Publications: Charlotte, 2019).

**MOORE, Robert James "Bobby"**

*Slave Rebellions in Guyana* (University of Guyana: Georgetown, 1971).

*Third World Diplomats in Dialogue with the First World* (International Development Research Centre: Ottawa, 1984).

**_____; et al**

*Audacious Anglicans: Heroes of the Anglican Communion* (Blue Jay Publishing: Ottawa, 2008).

**MORGAN, Cecil Booker**

*Marriage is God's Gift* (Xulon Press: Maitland, 2010).

**MORGAN, Owen**

*Health Issues in the Caribbean* (Ian Randle Publishers: Kingston, 2005).

**MORGAN, Ted**

*A Covert Life: Jay Lovestone, Communist, Ant-Communist, Spymaster* (Random House: New York, 1999).

**MORIAH, R.**

*Moriah's Journey* (AuthorHouse: Bloomington, 2006).

**MORLEY, John G**

*Life of Gladstone* (Macmillan: London, 1903).

**MORRIS, George**

*CIA and American Labour: The Subversion of the AFL-CIO's Foreign Policy* (International Publishers: New York, 1967).

**MOORE, John G.**

*Poetry of People, Places, Politics, Philosophy: Roraima* (Book-Broker Publishing: Port Charlotte, 2021).

**MORRIS, Mervyn**

*Making West Indian Literature* (Ian Randle Publishers: Kingston, 2007).

**_____; and C. Allen, eds.**

*Writing Life: Reflections by West Indian Writers* (Ian Randle Publishers: Kingston, 2005).

**_____; and J. Carnegie, eds**

*Lunchtime Medley: Writings on West Indian Cricket* (Ian Randle Publishers: Kingston, 2008).

**MORRISON, Fr. A.**

*Justice: The Struggle for Democracy in Guyana 1952-1992* (Andrew Morrison: Georgetown, 1998).

**MORRISON, John**

*Fathers and Founders of London Missionary Society* (Fisher: London, 1844).

**MORRISON, Marion**

*Guyana* (Enchantment of the World Series, Children's Press: Minneapolis, 2003).

**MOTELALL, Sham**

*Marble, Grass, and Glass* (Xlibris: Bloomington, 2021).

**MOTILALL, Ashti A.**

*Growing Up Guyanese: A Memoir About Growing Up First Generation Indo-Caribbean in America* (Xlibris: Bloomington, 2017).

**MUNROE, Andrew Adrian**

*Caribbean Stories: Supernatural Tales of Guyana* (Golden Grove Publications: Georgetown, 1994).

**MUNSLOW, B.**

*Guyana: Microcosm of Sustainable Development Challenges* (Avenury: London, 1988).

**MURRAY, R.N.**

*Lest We Forget: The Experiences of World War II West Indian Ex-Service Personnel* (Hansib: London, 2007).

**MURUGAN, Joseph P.**

*Fulfilling a Vision: The Man, The Message and the Mission* (Diakonia Christian Institute: Miami, 2020).

**MUSGRAVE, George; and G.H. Mathieson**
*The Great Republic: A Political Phantasy* (Lightship Guides and Publications: New York, 2018).

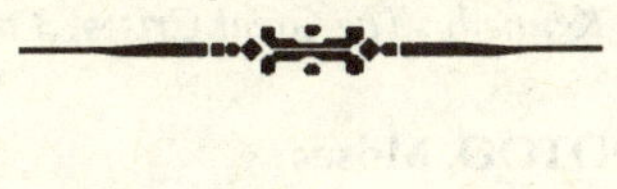

# N

**NAFTALI, Timothy; Philip Zelikow; and Ernest May, eds.**
*John F. Kennedy: The Great Crises, 3 vols.* (W.W. Norton: New York, 2001).

**NAGAMOOTOO, Moses**
*Anthology of Revolutionary Poems* (New Guyana Company Ltd.: Georgetown, 1976).
*Emancipation: The African Resistance* (Government of Guyana: Georgetown, 2018).
*Fraud: A Synopsis of Guyana's 1980 Elections* (New Guyana Company Ltd: Georgetown, 1981).
*Hendree's Cure: Scenes from Madrasi Life in a New World* (Peepal Tree Press: Leeds, 2000).
*Paramountcy of the Media in Guyana* (New Guyana Company Ltd.: Georgetown, 1990).
*The Three Trials of Arnold Rampersaud: A True Story Narrative* (New Guyana Company Ltd.: Georgetown, 1978).
*The Way Forward – Towards a Political Solution in Guyana* (New Guyana Company Ltd.: Georgetown, 1998).

**_____; and Cheddi Jagan**
*Race, Class, and Nationhood* (New Guyana Company Ltd.: Georgetown, 1991).
*State of the Free Press in Guyana* (New Guyana Company Ltd.: Georgetown, 1980).

**NAGEER, Sherlina**
*Thumbelina and the Yarrow* (Lulu Press: Raleigh, 2013).
*Toco the Terrible: How Toco Got a New name and a New Tail* (Lulu Press: Raleigh, 2013).

**NAGUIRE, John; and Mary Lee Dunn**
*Hold Hands and Die* (Fitzhenry & Whiteside: Dale, 1978).

**NAIDU, J.**
*Rainwater* (Greenheart Press: Toronto, 2005).
*Sacred Silence* (Hansib Publications: Hertford, 2009).
*Winged Heart: Poems* (Greenheart Press; Toronto, 1999).

**NAIN, G.T.; and Bailey, B., eds.**
*Gender Equality in the Caribbean: Reality or Illusion* (Ian Randle Publishers: Kingston, 2003).

**NAIPAUL, Balkrishna**

*Arc on the Horizon* (Xlibris Corporation: Philadelphia, 2002).

*Legends of the Emperor's Ring* (Xlibris Corporation: Philadelphia, 2003).

**NAIPAUL, Shiva**

*A Hot Country* (Penguin Books: London, 1983).

*Black and White* (Hamish Hamilton: London, 1980).

*Journey to Nowhere: A New World Tragedy* (Simon & Schuster: New York, 1981).

**NAIPAUL, V.S.**

*Middle Passage: Impressions of 5 Societies – British, French and Dutch – in the West Indies and South America* (Andre Deutsch: London, 1967).

*The Loss of El Dorado: A History* (Andre Deutsch: London, 1969).

**NAJHRAM, Shirley**

*Layers of the Rainforest* (Tate Publishing: Mustang, 2006).

**NANCOO, S.E.; Robert S. Nancoo; and Stephen N. Nancoo**

*Indo Caribbean Canadians, Who's Who, Profiles of Achievements* (Canadian Educators' Press: Mississauga, 2005).

**NARAIN, Denise DeCaires, ed.**

*Contemporary Caribbean Women's Poetry: Making Style* (Routledge: London, 2001).

**NARAIN, Frank**

*Historical Information Events and Dates on the Parliament of Guyana From 1718 to 2006* (F.A. Narain: Georgetown, 2007).

**NARAIN, Harry**

*Grass-root People: Thirteen Stories in one Theme* (Ediciónes Casa de las Americas: Havana, 1985).

*Old Thom's Harvest* (Eyre and Spottiswoods: London, 1965).

**NARAYAN, Ongkar**

*Welcome to a New Guyana* (Keysha Publishers: Toronto, 2006).

**NARAYAN, Rudy**

*Barrister for the Defence* (Hansib: Hertford, 1985).

**NARINE, Dhanpaul**

*America in Crisis: Glimpses from a Troubled Nation* (Vitasta Publishing Pvt. Ltd.: Kolkata, 2010).

*Shitty People* (AuthorHouse: Bloomington, 2023).

**_____; and Mahine Gosine, eds.**

*Sojourners to Settlers: Indian Immigrants in the Caribbean and the Americas* (Windsor Press: Hamburg, 1999)

**_____; et al**

*Community Participation, Social Development and the State* (Routledge: New York, 1986).

**NARINE, G.**

*Field Checklist of Birds of Georgetown* (Birdlife International: Cambridge, 2005).

**NARINE, Nirmala**

*In Nirmala's Kitchen: Everyday World Cuisine* (Lake Isle Press: New York, 2006).

**NASCIMENTO, C.A.**

*Birth of the Cooperative Republic of Guyana, February 23rd 1970: Speeches by the Prime Minister of Guyana on the Occasion of Guyana Becoming a Republic* (Peoples National Congress: Georgetown, 1970).

*The Achievement of National Unity Under the Peoples National Congress* (Design and Graphics: Georgetown, 1973).

**_____; and R.A. Burrowes, eds.**

*Forbes Burnham: A Destiny to Mould: Selected Discourses by the Prime Minister of Guyana* (Longman Caribbean: London, 1970).

**NASTA, Susheila, ed.**

*Motherlands: Black Women's Writing from Africa, the Caribbean, South Asia* (Women's Press: London, 1991).

**NATH, Dwarka**

*A History of Indians in British Guiana* (Governor's Office: Georgetown, 1950).

*A History of Indians in Guyana* (Dwarka Nath: London, 1970).

*A West Indian Hindi Primer* (Dwarka Nath: London, 1972).

*The Making of a President* (Dwarka Nath: London, 1982).

**NATIONAL HISTORY AND ARTS COUNCIL**

*Dictionary of Guyanese Folklore* (Ministry of Sports and Culture: Georgetown, 1975).

**NATIONAL LIBRARY OF GUYANA**

*Bibliography of the Africans in Guyana* (National Library of Guyana: Georgetown, 197?).

*Guyanese National Bibliography* (National Library of Guyana: Georgetown, 1966-2016).

**NEDD, Rioianne**

*50 Women: 50 Years: Celebrating 50 Years of Womanhood in Guyana* (Roi Jelly K Ltd.: London, 2016).

**NEHUSI, Kimani**

*A People's Political History of Guyana 1838-1964* (Amazon Books: Bolton, 2018).

*Language in the Construction of Afrikan Unity: Past, Present and Policy in Mammo Muchie* (Adonis-Abbey Publishing House: London, 2003).

*Libation: An Afrikan Ritual of Heritage in the Circle of Life* (UPA Press: Kuala Lumpur, 2015).

*The Making of Africa-Nation: Africanism and the African Renaissance* (Adonis-Abbey Publishing House: London, 2002).

**_____; and Pauline F. Baird**

*Wah Dih Story Seh? An Oral Tradition in the Guyanese Village, Buxton* (Amazon Books: Bolton, 2019).

**_____; et al**

*Ah Come Back Home: Perspectives on the Trinidad and Tobago Carnival* (Original World Press: New York, 2000)

**NEIHOFF, A and J**

*East Indians in the West Indies* (Public Museum: Milwaukee, 1960).

**NERO, Shondel**

*Dialects, Englishes, Creoles, and Education* (Routledge: New York, 2006).

*Englishes in Contact: Anglophone Caribbean Students in an Urban College* (Hampton Press: New York, 2001).

**_____; and Dohra Ahmad**

*Vernaculars in the Classroom: Paradoxes, Pedagogy, Possibilities* (Routledge: New York, 2014).

**NETSCHER, P.M.**

*History of the Colonies: Essequebo, Demerary, and Berbice: From the Dutch Establishment to the year 1888,* trans. By W.E. Roth (Daily Chronicle: Georgetown, 1931).

**NETTLES, K.D.**

*Guyana Diaries: Women's Lives Across Difference* (Left Coast Press: Walnut Creek: 2008).

**NEW, W.**

*Critical Writings on Commonwealth Literatures: A Selective Bibliography to 1970, with a List of Theses and Dissertations* (Pennsylvania State University Press: Scranton, 1975).

**NEWMAN, Peter**

*British Guiana: Problems of Cohesion in an Immigrant Society* (Oxford University Press: Oxford, 1964).

**NEWTON, A.P.**

*The European Nations in the West Indies: 1493-1688* (Black: London, 1966).

**NEUMAN, Stephanie G., ed.**

*Small States and Segmented Societies* (Praeger: New York, 1976).

**NIAMATALI, Stanley**

*Mira and Other Poems of Guyana* (Mountain Arbor Press: Alpharetta, 2017).

*The Hinterlands* (Mountain Arbor Press: Alpharetta, 2017).

**NICHOLL, Charles**

*The Creature in the Map: A Journey to El Dorado* (William Morrow & Co.: Chicago, 1995).

**NICHOLLS, Lawrence T**

*I was born to learn to love to run: And I ran and ran* (Createspace Publishing: Scotts Valley, 2020).

**NICHOLS, Grace**

*A Wilful Daughter* (Hodder and Stoughton: London, 1983).

*Asana and the Animals: A Book of Pet Poems* (Walker: London, 1997)

*Baby Fish and Other Stories from Village to Rainforest* (Islington Community Press: London, 1983).

*Come on into My Tropical Garden* (A & C Black: London, 1988 and Lippincott: Philadelphia, 1990).

*Cosmic Dance* (Frances Lincoln: London, 2013).

*Everybody's Got a Gift: New and Selected Poems* (A & C Black: London, 2005).

*Freedom From Fear and Panic* (Christian Faith Publishing: Meadville, 2007).

*Give Yourself a Hug* (A & C Black: London, 1994).

*I Have Crossed an Ocean: Selected Poems* (Bloodaxe Books: London, 2010).

*I is a Long Memoried Woman* (Karnak House: London, 1984). [Winner of the Commonwealth Poetry Prize].

*Lazy Thoughts of a Lazy Woman, and Other Poems* (Virago: London, 1989 and Random House, New York, 1990).

*Leslyn in London* (Hodder and Stoughton: London, 1984).

*Paint Me a Poem: New Poems Inspired by Art in Tate* (A and C Black: London, 2004).

*Marriage, Sex and the Bedroom: Marriage is Honourable, The Bed is Undefiled* (Amazon Books: London, 2018).

*No More Drama Relationships: Overcoming the Insanity of Drama in Relationships* (More Than Conquerors: London, 2018).

*No, Baby, No!* (Bloomsbury: London, 2011).
*Paint Me a Poem: Poems Inspired by Art in the Tate* (A&C Black: London, 2004).
*Passport to Here and There* (Bloodaxe Books: London, 2020).
*Picasso: I want my face back* (Bloodaxe Books: London, 2009).
*Poetry Jump-up: A Collection of Black Poetry* (Puffin: Harmondsworth, 1990).
*Pumpkin, Grumpkin* (Walker: London, 2011).
*Startling the Flying Fish* (Virago Press: London, 2005).
*Sun Time Snow Time* (A & C Black: London, 2013).
*Sunrise* (Virago: London, 1996).
*The Discovery* (Macmillan: London, 1986).
*The Fat Black Woman's Poems* (Virago: London, 1990).
*The Insomnia Poems* (Bloodaxe Books: London, 2017).
*The Poet Cat* (Bloomsbury: London, 2000).
*Tiger Dead! Tiger Dead! Stories From the Caribbean* (Collins: London, 1990).
*Trust You, Wriggly!* (Hodder and Stoughton: London, 1980).
*Whoa, Baby, Whoa* (Bloomsbury: London, 2012).
*Whole of a Morning Sky* (Virago: London, 1989).

**_____; et al**

*We Couldn't Provide Fish Thumbs* (Macmillan: London, 1997).

**_____; ed.**

*Black Poetry* (Penguin: Harmondsworth, 1989).
*Can I Buy a Slice of Sky? Poems from Black, Asian, and American Cultures* (Blackie: London, 1991).

**_____; and John Agard, eds.**

*From Mouth to Mouth: Oral Poems from Around the World* (Walker: London, 2004).

**NICOLE, Christopher**

*Amyot's Cay* (Jarrolds: London, 1964).
*Blood Amyot* (Jarrolds: London, 1964).
*Dark Noon* (Jarrolds: London, 1964).
*Off White* (Jarrolds: London, 1959).
*Ratoon* (Jarrolds: London, 1962).
*Shadows in the Jungle* (Jarrolds: London, 1961).
*The Amyot Crime* (Jarrolds: London, 1964).
*The Falls of Death* (Canongate Books: London, 2005).

*The Longest Pleasure* (Jarrods: London, 1970).
*The Self Lovers* (Heinemann: London, 1968).
*The Thunder and the Shouting* (Hutchinson: London, 1969).
*The West Indies: Their People and History* (Hutchinson: London, 1965).
*White Boy* (Hutchinson: London, 1969).

**NILLAND, Elly**
*Bone Soup and Other Stories* (MJN Press: London, 2016).
[Winner of the Guyana Prize for Literature, Best First Book of Fiction, 2022].
*Cornerstones* (Dido Press: London, 2005).
[Winner of the Guyana Prize for Literature, 2006].
*East of Centre* (Dido Press: London, 2008).
*Guyana Classics* (Caribbean Press: Georgetown, 2011).
*In Retrospect: A Collection of Poetry* (Dido Press: London, 2003).
*Selected Poems* (Caribbean Press: Georgetown, 2013).
*The Fog* (BBC: London, 2005).

**NINVALLE, C**
*Stereotypes* (Toucan Publishing: Toronto, 2005).

**NKOFI, Accabre**
*Rebirth of the Blackman* (A. Nkofi: Georgetown, 2007).
*The Black Resurgence* (A. Nkofi: Georgetown, 2008).

**NOBLE, Sherene**
*Intertwined: A Collection of Short Stories* (Amazon Books: Morrisville, 2007).

**NOBREGA, Cecile**
*Soliloquies: In Verse* (Master Printery: Georgetown, 1967).
*Japan* (Cecile Nobrega: Georgetown, 1970).
*The Butterfly* (Cecile Nobrega: Georgetown, 1970).
*Stories from Guyana* (Cecile Nobrega: Georgetown, 1972).

**NOEL, Sonia**
*7 Days Healthy Thoughts Challenge: A Transformational Journey* (Createspace: Scotts Valley, 2020).
*Compilation Beyond the Runway* (Createspace: Scotts Valley, 2018).
*Living With Intention: Create, Contribute, Celebrate* (Createspace: Scotts Valley, 2017).
*Women Across Borders* (Createspace: Scotts Valley, 2019).

**NOKTA, Harripersaud**

*A Journey, A Challenge* (H. Nokta: Georgetown, 2013).

*Genesis of the Pakaraima Mountain Safari* (H. Nokta: Georgetown, 2010).

**NORTHCOTT, Cecil**

*Slavery's Martyr: John Smith of Demerara and the Emancipation Movement 1817-24* (Epworth Press: London, 1976).

**NORTHRUP, David**

*Indentured Labour in the Age of Imperialism, 1834-1922* (Cambridge University Press: Cambridge, 1995).

**NORWOOD, V.C.G.**

*A Hand Full of Diamonds: Further Adventures in the Jungles and Diamond Fields of Guiana and Brazil* (Boardman: London, 1960).

*Jungle Life in Guiana* (Robert Hale Ltd: London, 1964).

**NUGENT, John P.**

*White Night: The True Story of What Happened Before and After – Jonestown* (Wade Publishers: New York, 1979).

**NUNEZ-TESHEIRA, Kara**

*Non-Contentious Probate Practice in the English-speaking Caribbean,* 2nd ed. (Ian Randle Publishers: Kingston, 2004).

*The Legal Profession in the English-Speaking Caribbean* (Ian Randle Publishers: Kingston, 2002).

# O

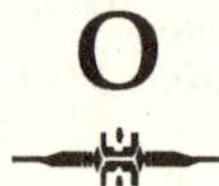

**O'GRADY, W.**

*Princess Marie Minnehaha of Manoa, Guiana* (Stockwell: London, 1934).

**O'MARDE, Dorbrene**

*Send Out You Hand* (Hansib: Hertfordshire, 2013).

**O'TOOLE, Brian**

*Educational Leadership: A Guyanese Perspective* (Baha'i Books: Sydney, 2018).

**ODIE-ALI, Stella**

*Zinc* (PublishAmerica: Frederick, 2006).

**ODLE, Maurice A**

*The Evolution of Public Expenditure: The Case of a Structurally Dependent Economy, Guyana* (University of the West Indies: Mona, 1976).

**OGINGA, Kwesi**

*A Few Things Our Sons and Daughters Should Know* (Xlibris: Bloomington, 2008).

*Divinity: A Heart That's Convicted* (Kulon Press: New York, 2016).

*Generational Curse: She Cut The Leash* (iUniverse: Bloomington, 2007).

*I am a Guyanese* (Xlibris: Bloomington, 2008).

*My Life is Literally and Long Love Poem* (Oginga Productions: Silver Springs, 2022).

*Poems of Preparation* (Oginga Productions: Silver Springs, 2022).

*Send Me My Eve: Reflections of a Grown Man* (Strategic Book Publishing: New York, 2014).

*Touching the Hem of His Garment* (Xlibris: Bloomington, 2014).

**OJER, Pablo**

*Robert H. Schomburgk: Explorador de Guyana y sus lineas de frontera* (Universidad Central de Venezuela: Caracas, 1969).

[Book in Spanish on Robert Schomburgk's exploration].

**ORMONDE HARROP-WILLIAMS, Kingsley**

*Poetry of K.O. Harrop: Reflections on Life, History, Injustice, Resistance, Civil Rights, and Guyana* (AuthorHouse: Bloomington, 2013).

**ORRETT, W.A.**
*The History of the British Guiana Police* (n.p.: Georgetown, 1951).

**OORSBORNE, Skipper**
*The Voyage of the Girl Pat: An Authentic Account by Skipper Orsborne and his crew* (Hutchinson & Co.: London, 1937).

**OSWALD, A.**
*It happened in British Guiana: Stories by an Overseer on a Sugar Estate* (Ilfracombe, Devon: Stockwell, 1955).

**OVERTON, Winston**
*Wall Street Scandals: Greed and Trading on Wall Street the American Way* (Xlibris: Bloomington, 2013).

**OWEN, R; and B. Sutcliffe, eds.**
*Studies in the Theory of Imperialism* (Longman: London, 1972).

# P

**PALMER, Colin A.**

*Cheddi Jagan and the Politics of Power – British Guiana's Struggle for Independence* (University of North Carolina Press; Chapel Hill, 2011).

*The Political History of Caricom* (Ian Randle Publishers: Kingston, 2008).

**PALMER, H.L.**

*Village Economics and Polity: A Study of the Parochial Administration of British Guiana* (n.p.: Georgetown, 1924).

**PALMER, Ransford W.**

*Caribbean Dependence on the United States Economy* (Praeger: New York, 1979).

*Problems of Development in Beautiful Countries: Perspectives on the Caribbean* (North-South Publishing: Lanham, 1984).

**PANTIN, Dennis, ed.**

*The Caribbean Economy* (Ian Randle Publishers: Kingston, 2005).

**PARASRAM, Kaila Narayan**

*Hot Mouth Gyal: A Collection of Short Stories* (Createspace: Scotts Valley, 2015).

**PARIAG, Florence; and Kojovi Dawes**

*East Indians in the Caribbean* (Arawak Publications: Kingston, 2014).

**PARKER, Jason C.**

*Brother's Keeper: The United States, Race, and Empire in the British Caribbean, 1937-1962* (Oxford University Press: Oxford, 2008).

**PARKER, Samuel J.**

*Red Snapper* (Mercom Associates Ltd.: New York, 2012).

**PARRIS, William Haslyn**

*Metanoia for Guyana: Post Parris Electoral Conjectures* (Trafford Publishing: Vancouver, 2013).

*Parris Electoral Conjectures and Governance in Guyana* (Trafford Publishing: Vancouver, 2011).

*Ribald Tales of Guyana* (Trafford Publishing: Victoria, 2002).

*The Constitution of Guyana: What Will It Look Like* (Trafford Publishing: Vancouver, 2013).

**PARRY, J.H.; and P.M. Sherlock**

*A Short History of the West Indies* (Macmillan: London, 1971).

**PASCOE, C.F.**
*Two Hundred Years of the SPG*, Vol. 1 (n.p.: London, 1901).
**PATRICK, Vivian E.**
*Little Savings Grow* (Ministry of Education: Georgetown, 1972).
**PATTERSON, Sam H.**
*World Bauxite Resources* (Forgotten Books: London, 2022).
**PAUL, Compton L.**
*Sorghum Agronomy* (ICRISAT: Andhra Pradesh, 1990). [In Spanish]
**PAUL, Roy** [brother of Dr Compton L. Paul mentioned above]
*Raiders of the Rupununi* (Harpy Publications: Georgetown, 2010).
*Stories of the Wilds: True Adventures in the Jungles of Guyana* (Harpy Publications: Georgetown, 2002).
*Tears of a Patriot* (Harpy Publications: Georgetown, 2000).
**PAUL, Sydney, ed.**
*Sandow's Gymnasium: A Brief History of Weightlifting and its Achievements in Guyana from 1936-2008* (n.p.: n.p. 2008).
**PAUL, Una**
*Citizenship Education for Small States: Guyana* (Commonwealth Secretariat: London, 2003).
**PAYNE, Anthony; and Paul Sutton, eds.**
*Dependency under Challenge: The Political Economy of the Commonwealth Caribbean* (Butler and Tanner: London, 1984).
*Modern Caribbean Politics* (Johns Hopkins University Press: Baltimore, 1993).
*The Political History of Caricom* (Ian Randle Publishers: Kingston, 2003).
*The Politics of the Caribbean Community 1961-1979: Regional Integration Amongst New States* (Manchester University Press: Manchester, 1980).
**PAYNE, H.**
*10 days in August 1834 that changed the world* (Caribbean Diaspora Press: New York, 2001).
**PEACE CORPS**
*Guyana in Depth* (Createspace: Scotts Valley, 2014).
**PEAKE, L.; and D. Alissa Trotz**
*Gender, Place and Ethnicity: Women and Identities in Guyana* (Routledge: London, 1999).
**_____; et al**
*Global Cities – Local Places: Issues in Urban Sustainability* (Black Rose Books: Toronto, 1996).

*Resource Sustainability and Caribbean Development* (University of the West Indies Press: Kingston, 1998).

*Self-Help Housing, the Poor and the State in the Caribbean* (University of the West Indies Press: Kingston, 1997).

*Sun, Sex and Gold: Tourism and Sex Work in the Caribbean* (Rowman and Littlefield: Boulder, 1999).

*Women and Change in the Caribbean* (Macmillan: London, 1993).

*Women, Human Settlements and Housing* (Tavistock: London, 1987).

**PEARCE, Jenny**

*Under the Eagle: US Intervention in Central America and the Caribbean* (South End Press: Cambridge, 1982).

**PEARSON, J.G.**

*New Overseer's Manual; or The Reason Why of Julius Juggler* (n.p.: Georgetown, 1890).

**PEOPLE'S PROGRESSIVE PARTY (PPP)**

*The People's Progressive Party Celebrating 50 Years of Independence* (PPP: Georgetown, 2016).

*Yes to Marxism* (PPP: Georgetown, 1986).

**PERCIVAL, Exley**

*Wild Flowers of Georgetown* (E. Percival: Georgetown, 1889).

**PEREZ, Maya; Jess Stern; and Terry A. Latterman**

*Born with a Veil* (Hampton Roads Publishing Co.: London, 1991).

**PERKINS, R.; and Hosken, J.**

*Gold Fields on the Barima* (Government Printery: Georgetown, 1895).

**PERREIRA, 'Reds' Joseph**

*Living My Dreams* (AuthorHouse: Bloomington, 2011).

**PERRY, E.**

*A New Morn* (E. Perry: Georgetown, 1970).

*Black Mahogany and Other Poems* (Bovell's Printery: Georgetown, 1971).

*Guyana's Child* (E. Perry: Georgetown, 1973).

**PERRY, Melvin**

*Guyana Redux* (Createspace: Scotts Valley, 2016).

**PERRY, Philippa**

*B.G. Bhagee: Memories of a Colonial Childhood* (CreateSpace: Vancouver, 2011).

**PERSAUD, Anthony**

*Secrets Unfold* (Dorrance Publishing: Pittsburgh, 2004).

**PERSAUD, Bishnodat**

*Caribbean in a Changing World* (University of the West Indies Press: Mona, 1997).

**_____; and Vincent Cable**

*Developing with Foreign Investment* (Routledge: London, 1987).

**PERSAUD, Brahmdeo**

*For The Millions* (B. Persaud: Georgetown, 1972).

**PERSAUD, Christopher H.K.**

*Contending for the Faith: 22 Methodical Arguments for Biblical Truth* (Xulon Press: Maitland, 2013). [ Winner of the 2013 Christian Writers Award in the 'Theology category'].

*Evolution: Beyond the Realm of Real Science* (Xulon Press: Maitland, 2008). [ Winner of the Grand Prize at the 2008 Christian Choice Book Awards.]

*God in our Midst: Making the Most Important Decision of Your Life* (Xlibris Corporation: Philadelphia, 2003).

*The Da Vinci Code Revisited: A Conclusive Refutation of the Widespread, Sinister Lie* (Xulun Press: Maitland, 2010). [Winner of the First Prize in the 'Theology' category at the 2010 Christian Writers Awards].

**PERSAUD, Harry McDonald**

*Butterfly in a Bamboo Grove: Poems in Transcendence* (CreateSpace: Charleston, 2011).

*Collection of Short Stories* (Createspace: Charleston, 2000).

*Why I Looked for the Divine and what I Have Found* (Amazon Books: New York, 2017).

**PERSAUD, Indar M.H.**

*Poems on Guiana* (P.A. Braithwaite: Georgetown, 1965).

**PERSAUD, J.K.**

*Famous Short Stories* (Sugar Cane Publishing: Markham, 2004).

**PERSAUD, Joseph S.**

*Across Three Continents: An Indo-Guyanese Family Experience* (Palm Tree Enterprises: Chicago, 2002).

*Beguiled Again* (Palm Tree Enterprises: Huntley, 2009).

*Florence and Adam* (Palm Tree Enterprises: Chicago, 2000).

**PERSAUD, Lakshmi**

*For the love of my name* (Peepal Tree Press: Leeds, 2000).

**PERSAUD, Narayan**

*African American Contributions to Criminology and Criminal Justice* (Cengage Publishing: Cleveland, 2007).

*African American Contributions to Sociology* (Cengage Publishing: Cleveland, 2006).
*Guardian Angels Along My Homeless Path* (AuthorHouse: Bloomington, 2006).
*Mentoring with a Humane Face* (Cengage Publishing: Cleveland, 2006).
*Recollections of Bath Estate: Lingering Childhood Memories of a Community built and destroyed by Colonials* (Amazon Books: New York, 2002).

**PERSAUD, Nowrang**

*A Proud Product of Guyana's Bitter-Sweet Sugar* (Book Venture Publishing: Ann Arbor, 2018).

**PERSAUD, M.O.**

*Twenty-Four Poems* (M.O. Persaud: Georgetown, 2006).

**PERSAUD, Navin**

*Life of an Immigrant* (Amazon Books: 2022).

**PERSAUD, O.**

*Book Smart* (Amazon Books: 2022).

**PERSAUD, Petamber**

*An Anthology of Caribbean Poetry for Carifesta* (Ministry of Culture, Youth, and Sport: Georgetown, 2008).
*An Anthology of Contemporary Guyanese Verse* (Petamber Persaud: Georgetown, 2013).
*An Introduction to Guyanese Literature* (Petamber Persaud: Georgetown, 2013).
*From Utopia to Paradise* (Petamber Persaud: Georgetown, 1976).
*Guyanese Writers of Indian Ancestry: A Centenary End to Indentureship Publication* (Petamber Persaud: Georgetown, 2017).
*Kal AAj Aur Kal* (Petamber Persaud: Georgetown, 2008).
*Lest we forget: 101 Poems about the Child* (Petamber Persaud: Georgetown, 2006).
*Made in Guyana* (Petamber Persaud: Georgetown, 2016).
P*lain Taak: A Collection of Poems in Creolese* (Petamber Persaud: Georgetown, 2006).
*The Balgobin Saga* (Hansib Publications: Hertfordshire, 2008).

**______, ed.**

*A Handbook of Guyanese Literature* (Guyenterprise Ltd.: Georgetown, 2007).
*An Anthology of Short Stories From Guyana* (Dido Press: London, 2007).

*Everest Centenary Souvenir Magazine* (Everest Cricket Club: Georgetown, 2014).

*St. Stanislaus 140th Anniversary Souvenir Magazine* (AMS: Georgetown, 2007).

*The Guyana Annual 2004-2005* (Guyenterprise Ltd.: Georgetown, 2004).

*The Guyana Annual 2005-2006* (Guyenterprise Ltd.: Georgetown, 2005).

*The Guyana Annual 2006-2007* (Guyenterprise Ltd.: Georgetown, 2006).

*The Guyana Annual 2007-2008* (Guyenterprise Ltd.: Georgetown, 2007).

*The Guyana Annual 2008-2009* (Guyenterprise Ltd.: Georgetown, 2008).

*The Guyana Annual 2009-2010* (Guyenterprise Ltd.: Georgetown, 2009).

*The Guyana Annual 2010-2011* (Guyenterprise Ltd.: Georgetown, 2010).

*The Guyana Annual 2011-2012* (Guyenterprise Ltd.: Georgetown, 2011).

*The Guyana Annual 2012-2013* (Guyenterprise Ltd.: Georgetown, 2012).

*University of Guyana 40th Anniversary Souvenir Magazine* (Guyenterprise Ltd.: Georgetown, 2004).

**PERSAUD, Pradeep**

*Fidel Castro is Dead: A Novel* (Pradeep Persaud: New York, 2014).

**PERSAUD, R.B.**

*Counter Hegemony and Foreign Policy: The Dialectics of Marginalized and Global Forces in Jamaica* (State University of New York: New York, 2001).

**_____; and N. Kumarakulasingam, eds.**

*Violence and The Third World in International Relations* (Routledge: New York, 2019).

**_____; and Alina Sajed, eds.**

*Race, Gender, and Culture in Internal Relations: Postcolonial Perspectives* (Routledge: New York, 2018).

**_____; contr.**

'Frantz Fanon, Race and World Order' in *Innovation and Transformation in International Studies* (Cambridge University Press: Cambridge, 1997).

'Human Security in Washington, D.C.' *in Human (In) Security in the Networks of Global Security* (CHS Press: Tokyo, 2008).
'North-South relations' in *Encyclopaedia of Globalization* (Routledge: New York, 2006).
'Power, Production, and the Racialization of Global Labour Recruitment and Supply in *Power, Production, and Social Reproduction* (Palgrave-Macmillan: London, 2003).
'Re-Envisioning Sovereignty: Marcus Garvey and the Making of a Transnational Identity' in *Africa's Challenge to International Relations* (Macmillan: London, 2001).
'Situating Race in International Relations: The Dialectics of Civilizational Security in *American Immigration in Power in a Postcolonial World: Race, Gender and Class in International Relations* (Routledge: London, 2002).
'Social Forces and World Order Pressures' in *The Making of Jamaican Multilateral Policies in Changing State/Society Perspectives in the United Nations System* (United Nations University Press: New York, 1995).
'The End of Bandung: Third World Foreign Policy in the Age of Globalization' in *New Directions in Third World Foreign Policies* (L. Rienner: Boulder, 2003).

**PERSAUD, R.N.**
*Scraps of Prose and Poetry* (Lutheran Press: New Amsterdam, 1933).

**PERSAUD, Raj (Mr.)**
*Simply Irresistable: The Psychology of Seduction* (Bantam Books: New York, 2007).

**PERSAUD, Raj (Mrs.)**
*Living with Purpose – Pt Sirju's Spirited Journey* (Raj Persaud: Toronto, 2014).

**PERSAUD, Roopnarain**
*Essays on Contemporary Conscience* (RDS Multiservices: Miami, 2019).

**PERSAUD, S.N.**
*Keeper of Souls* (AuthorHouse: Bloomington, 2006).

**PERSAUD, Sasenarine**
*A Surf of Sparrows' Songs - A Poemjali* (TSAR: Toronto, 1997).
*A Writer Like You* (TSAR Publications: Toronto, 2002).
*Between the Dash and the Comma* (S. Persaud: Toronto, 1989).
*Canada Geese and Apple Chutney* (TSAR Publications: Toronto, 1998).
*Dear Death* (Peepal Tree Press: Leeds, 1989).

*Demerary Telepathy* (Peepal Tree Press; Leeds, 1989).
*In a Boston Night* (TSAR Publications: Toronto, 2008).
*Lantana Strangling Ixora* (TSAR Publications: Toronto, 2013).
*Monsoons on the Fingers of Gid* (Mawanzi House: Toronto, 2018).
*The Ghost of Bellows Man* (Peepal Tree Press: Leeds, 1992).
*The Hungry Sailor* (TSAR Publications: Toronto, 2000).
*The Wintering Kundalini* (Peepal Tree Press; Leeds, 1989).
*Undisclosed Entrances* (Caribbean Press: Georgetown, 2013).

**PERSAUD, Seelall**

*Stepping Out of the Herd: My Life in the Guyana Police Force* (Selall Persaud: Georgetown, 2022).

**PERSAUD, Thakoor**

*Conflicts between Multinational Corporations and Less Developed Countries: The Case of Bauxite Mining in the Caribbean with special reference to Guyana* (Ayer Co. Pub.: Oxford, 1980).

**PERSAUD, Yesu**

*Reaching For The Stars: The Life of Yesu Persaud* (Caribbean Press: Georgetown, 2014).

**PERSAUD-EDWARDS, Parvati**

*Sacred Stones* (P. Persaud-Edwards: Georgetown, 1996).

**PERSICO, L.**

*For the Love of My Country* (Peepal Tree Press: Leeds, 2000).

**PETERMANN, A.**

*British Guiana* (Edinburgh and Dublin: London, 1850).

**PIERRE, Laureen; and Adrian Gomes**

*Amerindian Stories. Told in Makushi and English* (CBR Program and Red Thread Women's Press: Georgetown, 1994).
*Amerindian Stories. Told in Wapishana and English* (CBR Program and Red Thread Women's Press: Georgetown, 1994).

**PHILLANDER, A.S.**

*I like learning to read* (Toucan Publishing: Toronto, 2004).

**PHILLIPPE, E.**

*The Laughing Bird* (Wesley Press: London, 2000).

**PHILLIPS, Eric; and Jonathan O.P. Adams**

*The Guyana Reparations Story* [A Compilation of Four Books] (The Guyana Reparations Committee: Georgetown, 2016).
*Book 1 – In The Beginning; Book 2 – Africa Before Chattel Slavery; Book 3 – The African Guyanese Holocaust; Book 4 – The African Guyanese Reparations Claim.*

**____; Jonathan O.P.Adams; and Hazel Moses**

*The Guyana Reparations Story Playing With Words: A Fun Poetry Book for Children* (The Guyana Reparations Committee: Georgetown, 2013).

**PHILLIPS, Evan**

*A Voice from the Trees* (E. Phillips: Georgetown, 1974).

*Rhapsodies of Verse* (Jackson Fraser: Toronto, 1942).

*Survival: A Collection of Stories and Poems* (Brickman Publications: London,1959).

**PHILLIPS, Michael Angus (Mike)**

*Blood Rights* (St. Martin's: New York, 1989).

*London Crossings* (Continuum: London, 2001).

*The Late Candidate* (Michael Joseph: London, 1990).

**_____; and Trevor Phillips**

*Windrush: The Irresistible Rise of Multi-Racial Britain* (HarperCollins: London, 1998).

**PIERCE, Paulette**

*Non-capitalist Development: The Struggle to Nationalize the Guyanese Sugar Industry* (Rowman and Littlefield Publishers: London, 1984).

**PIERSON, R.H.; and J.O. Emmerson**

*Paddles over the Kamarang: The Story of the Davis Indians* (Pacific Press: Los Angeles, 1953).

**PINCKARD, George**

*Notes on the West Indies: Written During the Expedition under the Command of the Late General Sir Ralph Abercomby, Inclu. Observations on the Island of Barbadoes, and the Settlements Captured by the British Troops, upon the Coast of Guiana, Likewise Remarks Relating to the Creoles and Slaves of the Western Colonies, and the Indians of South America* (Hurst, Rees & Orme: London, 1806).

*Party Politics and Racial Division in Guyana* (University of Colorado Press: Denver, 1973).

**_______, ed.**

*Identity, Ethnicity and Culture in the Caribbean* (University of the West Indies: St. Augustine, 1997).

*Letters from Guiana 1796-7* (Daily Chronicle: Georgetown, 1942).

**PITMAN, F.**

*The Development of the British West Indies: 1700-1763* (Longman: London, 1967)

**PLEW, Mark, ed.**

*The Archaeology of Guyana* (University of Guyana: Turkeyen, 2005).

*Prehistoric Guiana* [written by Denis Williams] (Ian Randle Publishers: Kingston, 2004).

**_____; and Louisa Daggers**

*The Archaeology of Guyana,* 2nd Ed, (University of Guyana Press: Turkeyen, 2022).

**PLUNKETT, Shelagh**

*The Water Here is Never Blue: Intrigue and Lies From an Uncommon Childhood* (Penguin Books: Toronto, 2013).

**POLAK, A.M.**

*Major Timber Trees of Guyana: A Field Guide* (Tropenhos Foundation: Copenhagen, 1992).

**POLLARD, Duke**

*The Caribbean Court of Justice* (Ian Randle Publishers: Kingston, 2004).

**_______, ed.**

*The Caricom System: Basic Instruments* (Ian Randle Publishers, Kingston, 2003).

**POTTER, Gertrude**

*Road to Destiny* (Vantage Press: New York, 1959).

**POYNTING, Jeremy**

*East Indians in the Caribbean: A Bibliography of Imaginative Literature in English 1894-1984* (UWI Press; St. Augustine, 1984).

*The Second Shipwreck* (Peepal Tree Press: Leeds, 2008).

**PRASAD, Krishna**

*Born to Die: A Collection of Poems* (Krishna Prasad: Georgetown, 1977).

*Childhood Days: A Collection of Poems* (Krishna Prasad: Georgetown, 1976).

*Dawning Days: A Collection of Poems* (Krishna Prasad: Georgetown, 1976).

*Flames of Freedom: A Collection of Poems* (Krishna Prasad: Georgetown, 1978).

*Horizons of Life: A Collection of Poems* (Krishna Prasad: Georgetown, 1977).

*Life and Living: A Collection of Poems* (Krishna Prasad: Georgetown, 1980).

**PRASAD, Sarika**

*The Beast Within* (Sarika Prasad: Georgetown, 2017)

**PREMDAS, R.R.**

*Ethnic Conflict and Development: The Case of Guyana: Research on Ethnic Relations* (Avebury Publishing: Aldershot, 1995).

**PREMIUM, Barton**

*Eight Years in British Guiana, being the Journal of a Residence in that Province from 1840-48, Inclusive* (Longman: London, 1850).

**PRICE, Richard**

*The Guiana Maroons: Historical and Bibliographical Introduction* (Johns Hopkins University Press: Baltimore, 1978).

**PRICE, Sally**

*Co-Wives and Calabashes* - Women and Culture Series (University of Michigan Press: Ann Arbor, 1984).

**PRIMUS, Neil**

*Snatches of Life* (Xlibris: Bloomington, 2011).
*Rhythm of Life* (Xlibris: Bloomington, 2011).

**PROUD, Edward B.**

*The Postal History of British Guiana* (Proud Bailey: East Sussex, 2000).

**PUDDICOMBE, Ken**

*Down Independence Boulevard and Other Stories* (MiddleRoad Publishers: Toronto, 2017) [Winner of the 2022 Guyana Prize for Literature, Fiction].
*Junta: The Coup is On* (MiddleRoad Publishers: Toronto, 2014).
*Racing with the Rain* (Createspace: Vancouver, 2014).
*Unfathomable and Other Poems* (MiddleRoad Publishers: Toronto, 2020).

**_____; ed.,**

*Anthology: Twenty-six stories, Fiction and Non-Fiction* (MiddleRoad Publishers: Toronto, 2017).
*A Time to Love And a Time To Die* ((MiddleRoad Publishers: Toronto, 2020).
*Attitude* (MiddleRoad Publishers: Toronto, 2020).
*Dancing My Way to 80* (MiddleRoad Publishers: Toronto, 2019).
*Gabrielle* (MiddleRoad Publishers: Toronto, 2021).
*Generations* (MiddleRoad Publishers: Toronto, 2020).
*I Went To the End of the Rainbow* (MiddleRoad Publishers: Toronto, 2017).
*Love Has Two Moons* (MiddleRoad Publishers: Toronto, 2021).
*Meet Me at the Four Corners* (MiddleRoad Publishers: Toronto, 2021).
*People of Guyana* (MiddleRoad Publishers: Toronto, 2018.)
*Perfect Execution and Other Stories* (MiddleRoad Publishers: Toronto, 2017).
*Persons of Interest* (MiddleRoad Publishers: Toronto, 2019).

*Poems for Mary* ((MiddleRoad Publishers: Toronto, 2020).
*Ruthless Rhythms* (MiddleRoad Publishers: Toronto, 2022).
*Taste My Words* (MiddleRoad Publishers: Toronto, 2022).
*The Garden* (MiddleRoad Publishers: Toronto, 2021).
*Towards the Pebbled Shore* (MiddleRoad Publishers: Toronto, 2022).
*Wealth Through Real Estate Investing* (MiddleRoad Publishers: Toronto, 2021).
*Windward Legs* (MiddleRoad Publishers: Toronto, 2021).
*Witnesses and Other Stories* (MiddleRoad Publishers: Toronto, 2021).

**_____; et al**

*Scaling New Heights: 2022 Pakaraima Writers Anthology* (Middle Road Publishers: Toronto, 2022).

**PURCHAS, Samuel, ed.**

*Puchas: His Pilgrims* (S. Purchas: Glasgow, 1905).

# Q

**QUAMINA, L; and K. Larbi**

*East Indians in the Caribbean: A Select Bibliography* (University of the West Indies: St. Augustine, 1979).

**QUAMINA, Odida**

*All Things Considered: Can We Live Together?* (Exile Editions: Toronto, 1996).

*Cries from the Workplace: The Making of a Third World Working Class* (Zed Books: London, 1987).

*Mineworkers of Guyana: The Making of a Working Class* (Zed Books: London, 1987).

*Sometimes I Think About My Childhood* (O. Quamina: Georgetown, 1983).

**_____; et al, eds.**

*Growing Up in Pln. Mackenzie* (O. Quamina: Georgetown, 1979).

**QUAM, Glenn L.**

*Jonestown Massacre Occurs* (Brentwood University Press: New York, 1987).

**QUINN, D.B.**

*Raleigh and the British Empire* (Hodder and Stoughton: London, 1947).

# R

**R., J.**

*Chronology and Bibliography of Guiana* (James Thomson: Georgetown, 1885).

**RABE, Stephen G.**

*Eisenhower and Latin America: The Foreign Policy of Anti-Communism* (University of North Carolina Press: Chapel Hill, 1988).

*Most Dangerous Area in the World: John F. Kennedy Confronts Communist Revolution in Latin America* (University of North Carolina Press: Chapel Hill, 1999).

*U.S. Intervention in British Guiana: A Cold War Story* (University of North Carolina Press: Chapel Hill, 2005).

**RADOSH, Ronald**

*American Labour and the US Foreign Policy* (Random House: New York, 1969).

**RAGATZ, Lowell J.**

*A Guide for the Study of British Caribbean History, 1763-1834, including the Abolition and Emancipation Movements* (De Capo Press: New York, 1970).

*The Fall of the Planter Class in the British Caribbean 1763-1833* (GPO: Washington, D.C., 1928).

**RAGBEER, Mohan**

*India Under Siege, The Enemy Within* (Createspace: Vancouver, 2015).

*PGME: Stemming the Brain Drain from the Caribbean* (Createspace: Vancouver, 2017).

*The Indelible Red Stain: The Destruction of a Tropical Paradise – A Cold War Story,* 2vls. (CreateSpace: Vancouver, 2011).

**RAIN, Thomas**

*The Life and Labours of John Wray: Pioneer Missionary in British Guiana* (John Snow: London, 1892).

**RAJ, Basant**

*The Shadow of Dreams: Tears of the Diaspora* (E-Bookstore: Montgomery, 2008).

*Songs of Twilight* (E-Bookstore: Montgomery, 2009).

**RAJRUP, LATCHMAN**

*Goodbye Forever Vicky* (AuthorHouse: Bloomington, 2018).

**RALEGH, Sir Walter**

*The Discoverie of the Large, Rich, and Beauwtiful Empyre of Guiana (With a Relation of the Great and Golden Citie of Manoa (Which the Spanyards call El Dorado) and of the Provinces of Emeria, Arromaia, Amapaia, and Other Countries, with Their Riulers, Adjoyning* (Robert Robinson: London, 1596). Reprint. (Hakluyt: London, 1848). Reprint. (University of Manchester Press: Manchester, 1997). Reprint. (University of Oklahoma Press: Oklahoma City, 1998). Reprint. (Caribbean Press: Georgetown, 2013).

**RALPH, Michael Snr.**

*Engaging Guyana's Diaspora with the Fierce Urgency of Now* (Createspace: Vancouver, 2016).

*The Remarkable Ralphs of Guyanese Heritage: A Family Biography* (Createsapce: Vancouver, 2021).

**RAMAGE (Dabydeen), Sally**

*An Introduction to Intellectual Property* (iUniverse: Bloomington, 2004).

*Fraud - The Company Law Background* (iUniverse: Bloomington, 2006).

*Legal and Regulatory Framework: For Business in the UK* (iUniverse: Bloomington, 2004).

**RAMBAROSE, L.D.**

*Contemporary Poetry* (AuthorHouse: Bloomington, 2006).

**RAMBARRAN, Madeline**

*The Search For El Dorado Moves to England* (Enfield: Middlesex, 1978).

**RAMBIHAR, V.S.**

*A New Chaos Based Medicine Beyond 2000: A Response to Evidence.* Vol. 2 (Rambihar/Vashna Publications: Toronto, 2000).

*CHAOS 2000 From Cos to Cosmos: Making a New Medicine for a New Millennium* – 2-volume set (V.S. Rambihar/Vashna Publications: Toronto, 2000).

*CHAOS From Cos to Cosmos: A New Art, Science and Philosophy of Medicine, Health…and Everything Else.* Vol. 1 (Rambihar/Vashna Publications: Toronto, 2000).

*Heart and Now Global Heart: 25th Anniversary of Annual Valentine's Day for Heart Health Event* (VS Rambihar/Vashna Publications: Toronto, 2000).

*South Asian Heart: Preventing Heart Disease – from the heart to the edge of the diaspora* (VS Rambihar: Vashna Publications: Toronto, 1996).

*Tsunami Chaos Global Heart: Using Complexity Science to Rethink and Make a Better World* (VS Rambihar, SP Rambihar/VS Rambihar Jnr.,/Vashna Publications: Toronto, 2005). Available free online by searching title/key words/author or at: http://www.femmefractal.com/FinalwebTsunamiBK12207.pdf

**RAMCHAND, Ken**

*The West Indian Novel and Its Background* (Ian Randle Publishers: Kingston, 2004).

**RAMCHARITAR-LALLA, Charles Ebenezer Joseph**

*An Anthology of Local Indian Verse* (CEB Ramcharitar-Lalla: Georgetown, 1934).

**RAMCHARRAN, Bertie G.**

*The Guyana Court of Appeal: The Challenges of the Rule of Law in a Developing Country* (Ian Randle Publishers: Kingston, 2001).

**RAMDASS, A.I.**

*Goddess Thoughts: The Rest are Mere Details* (Lulu Press: Raleigh, 2005).

**RAMDEHOLL, Neville**

*The Pastures of Paradise* (Neville Ramdeholl: Georgetown, 2007).

**RAMDHAN, Vidya Devi**

*A Traveler's Tale: A Memoir* (Amazon Books: New York, 2015).

**RAMDIN, Hemchand**

*The Management Impact on University Research: The Case of the Research and Publications Fund* (Institute of Development Studies, University of Guyana: Turkeyen, 1977).

**RAMDIAL, Gowkarran**

*Shackles of Colonialism: A Long Poem* (R. Gowkarran: Georgetown, 1977).

**RAMHARACK, Baytoram**

*Against the Grain: Balram Singh Rai and the Politics of Guyana* (Chakra Publishing: San Juan, 2005).

*A Powerful Indian Voice, Alice Bhagwandai Singh: Reflections of her work in Guyana* (Xlibris: Bloomington, 2023).

*Centenary Celebration of the Arrival of Indians to British Guiana 1838-1938* (The British Guiana East Indian Association: Georgetown, 1938). Reprint. (Chakra Publishing: San Juan, 2001).

*Jung Bahadur Singh of Guyana (1886-1956): Politican, Ship Doctor: Labour Leader; and Protector of Indians* (Chakra Publishing: San Juan, 2019).

**_____; contr.**

'Remembering Alice Singh of Guyana: Notes from her Diary' in *180 Years of Indians in Guyana, 1838-2018* (Caribbean Hindu Network: San Juan, 2018).

**RAMHARACK, R.**

*Growing Up Guyanese* (R. Ramharack: New York, 1994).

**RAMJEET, Oscar**

*From Errand Boy to Solicitor-General: A Candid West Indian Story* (Caribbean Press: Georgetown, 2015).

**RAMJOHN, Sheer**

*Some Observations of the Humankind: A Memoir* (Friesen Press: Winnipeg, 2014).

**RAMKIRATH, Haimnauth**

*At Ease Like The Blooming Lotus* (LitFire Publishing: Atlanta, 2017).

*For A Troubled World* (LitFire Publishing: Atlanta, 2018).

*Rhythms of Ease and Wonder* (Archway Publishing: Bloomington, 2020).

*Stirrings of Hope & Other Poems* (New Book Authors Publishing: Madison, 2022).

*Unsung Verses* (New Book Authors Publishing: Madison, 2021).

**RAMNARINE, Devanand**

*The Political Economy of the US Caribbean Basin Recovery Act (1984)* (Queens University Press: Kingston, 1989).

*The Politics of the US Congressional approval in the passage of the Caribbean Basin Initiative* (Queens University Press: Kingston, 1989).

**_____, et al.**

*Toward a new Beginning: Report of the Four-Level Government Inquiry into the condition of Racial Minorities in Toronto* (Government of Ontario: Toronto, 1993).

**RAMNARINE, Mohabir**

*Beyond the Blackboard: A Memoir* (AuthorHouse: Bloomington, 2009).

**RAMNARINE, Tina**

*Creating Their Own Space: The Development of an Indian-Caribbean Musical Product* (University of the West Indies: Mona, 2000).

**RAMOS PEREZ, Demetrio**

*El mito del Dorado: Su génesis y proceso* (Academica National de la Historia: Caracas, 1973).

[Book in Spanish on El Dorado].

**RAMPERTAB, Maureen**

*Butterflies in Paradise* (Maureen Rampertab: New Amsterdam, 2013).

*Footprints from India : Stories of the Immigrants' Lives Celebrating Our History, Our Religion, Our Culture* (Maureen Rampertab: New Amsterdam, 2013).

*Story Time: A Collection of Children Stories* (Maureen Rampertab: New Amsterdam, 2013).

**RAMPHAL, Dwarka**

*Let us talk* (Vantage Press: New York, 1990).

**RAMPHAL, John Persaud**

*Let's Kiss and Dance* (Sugarcane Publishing: Markham, 2002).

*To Drink Your Kiss* (Sugarcane Publishing: Markham, 2003).

*V.S. Naipaul's Empty Chapel: His Background, Works, and Vision of the Third World* (Xlibris: New York, 2003).

**RAMPHAL, Kennard Deomitr**

*Dilchand Jons the Army* (KD Ramphal: Toronto, 2016).

*Escape to the Canadian Jungle* (KD Ramphal: Toronto, 2018).

*Seeram's Illusions* (KD Ramphal: Toronto, 2022).

*Slippery Ochro:* (KD Ramphal: Toronto, 2023).

*Teacher Ram's Fascination With Fire And Other Stories* (Roraima Publishers: Toronto, 2009).

*Imprints in Life's Journey* (Roraima Publishers: Toronto, 2013).

**RAMPHAL, Shridath Surendranath "Sonny"**

*Caribbean Challenges: Sir Shridath Ramphal's Collected Counsel* (Hansib Publications: Hertfordshire, 2013).

*Glimpses of a Global Life* (Hansib: Hertfordshire, 2014).

*Guyana in the World: The First of the First Fifty Years and the Predatory Challenge* (Hansib: Hertfordshire, 2017).

*Nkrumah and the Eighties* (The World Foundation: London, 1999).

*One World to Share: Selected Speeches of the Commonwealth Secretary-General, 1975-1979* (Hutchinson Benham: London, 1984).

*Our country the planet: Forging a Partnership for survival* (Island Press: London, 1992).

*The Commonwealth in World Affairs: The New Secretary General of the Commonwealth surveys its role* (Price Milburn for New Zealand Institute of International Affairs: Wellington, 1975).

*Time for Action: Report of the West Indian Commission* (University of the West Indies: Mona, 1992).

*Triumph for UNCLOS: The Guyana-Suriname Maritime Arbitration: A Compilation and Commentary* (Hansib: Hertfordshire, 2008).

_____; **and Ron Saunders, eds.**
*Inseparable Humanity: Anthology of Reflections* (Hansib Publications: Hertfordshire, 1988).

_____; **Willy Brandt; et al**
*North-South: A Program for Survival – The Report of the Independent Commission on International Development Issues Under the Chairmanship of Willy Brandt* (Pan Books Ltd.: London, 1980).

_____; **et al, eds.**
*Towards Sustainable Development: Fourteen Case-Studies prepared by African and Asian Journalists for the Nordic Conference on Environment and Development at Saltsjobaden, Stockholm, 8-10 May 1987* (Panos Institute: London, 1987).

_____; **Steven W. Sinding; and Nafis Sadik**
*Population Growth and Environmental Issues* (Praeger: New York, 1996).

**RAMRAJ, Robert**
*Guyana: Population, Environments, Economic Activities* (Battleground Printing & Publishing: Winston-Salem, 2003).
*Mental and Dictation and Other Stories* (Battleground Printing & Publishing: Winston-Salem, 2022).

**RAMRAJ, Victor and Daryl Dance, eds.**
*Fifty Caribbean Writers* (Greenwood Press: Westport, 1986).

**RAMRAYKA, Peter**
*Recycling a son of the British Raj* (Hansib: Hertfordshire, 2015).

**RAMSAHOYE, F.H.W.**
*The Development of Land Law in British Guiana* (Oceania Publications: New York, 1966).

**RAMSAHOYE, J.**
*A Mouldy Destiny: Visiting Guyana's Forbes Burnham* (Minerva Press: Milton Keynes, 1996).

**RAMSARAN, R.**
*Caribbean Survival and the Global Challenge* (Ian Randle Publishers: Kingston, 2002).

**RAMSAROOP, Peter**

*Hope for Nation* (Evolvent Technologies Inc.: Falls Church, 2004).

*Road to El Dorado* (Evolvent Technologies Inc: Falls Church, 2006).

*Securing Business Intelligence: Knowledge and Cyber Security in the Post 9/11 World* (Evolvent Technologies Inc: Falls Church, 2004).

*Surfing the Leadership Waves* (Evolvent Technologies Inc: Falls Church, 2003).

*Thriving in the Age of Terror* (Evolvent Technologies Inc: Falls Church, 2006).

**____; D. Beaulieu;; and M.J. Ball, eds.**

*Advancing Federal Sector Healthcare: A Model for Technology Transfer* (Springer Verlag: New York, 2001).

**RAMSAROOP, Yuvraj**

*Realizing the American Dream – the Personal Triumph of a Guyanese Immigrant* (Xlibris: Bloomington, 2010).

**RAMSARRAN, B.**

*Glossary of the Soul* (B. Ramsarran: Georgetown, 1938).

**RAMSON, Charles**

*In Pursuit of Justice* (Charles Ramson: Georgetown, 2012).

**RANDALL, Vicki**

*Women and Politics: An International Perspective* (Macmillan: London, 1987).

**RAPKIN, J.**

*British Guiana* (John Tallis & Co.: London, 1850).

**RASTOW, W.W.**

*The Stages of Economic Growth* (Cambridge University Press: Cambridge, 1960).

**RAUF, Mohammad, A.**

*Indian Village in Guyana: A Study of Cultural Change and Ethnic Identity* (E.J. Brill Academic Publishers: New York,1974).

**REID, Geary**

*A Productive Garden* (Geary Reid: Georgetown, 2020).

*Advancing God's Kingdom* (Geary Reid: Georgetown, 2020).

*Attracting and Retaining people to churches* (Geary Reid: Georgetown, 2022)

*Be Thankful* (Geary Reid: Georgetown, 2020).

*Becoming A Chief Executive Officer* (Geary Reid: Georgetown, 2020).

*Becoming a good candidate for promotion* (Geary Reid: Georgetown, 2022).

*Believers are called to be different* (Geary Reid: Georgetown, 2022).

*Budgeting and Performance Management for Organizations* (Geary Reid: Georgetown, 2022).
*Building Relationships and Avoiding Extra Marital Affairs* (Geary Reid: Georgetown, 2021).
*Building Sustainable Friendships* (Geary Reid: Georgetown, 2022).
*Can children ever repay their parents?* (Geary Reid: Georgetown, 2022).
*Care and Respect for the Elderly* (Geary Reid: Georgetown, 2021).
*CEO in Action* (Geary Reid: Georgetown, 2020).
*Children, Make Your Parents Proud* (Geary Reid: Georgetown, 2021).
*Conflict management through biblical principles* (Geary Reid: Georgetown, 2021).
*Cry no more, God is with you* (Geary Reid: Georgetown, 2022).
*Divorce and Remarriage* (Geary Reid: Georgetown, 2022).
*Dream big and live your dreams* (Geary Reid: Georgetown, 2022).
*Effective and Efficient Administrative Assistants* (Geary Reid: Georgetown, 2022).
*Effective Ministry for God's Kingdom* (Geary Reid: Georgetown, 2020).
*Embracing Corporate Governance: An Effective Board of Directors* (Geary Reid: Georgetown, 2021).
*Employees are Important* (Geary Reid: Georgetown, 2020).
*Enjoying Work* (Geary Reid: Georgetown, 2020).
*Enjoying Your Senior Years* (Geary Reid: Georgetown, 2021).
*Ethics and Professional Conducts for Believers* (Geary Reid: Georgetown, 2022).
*Everyone needs Forgiveness* (Geary Reid: Georgetown, 2021).
*Family and Business Analysis of Proverbs 31* (Geary Reid: Georgetown, 2022).
*Fathers are Important* (Geary Reid: Georgetown, 2021).
*Fear not, God is with you* (Geary Reid: Georgetown, 2022).
*Fellowship at the Family Table* (Geary Reid: Georgetown, 2021).
*Financial Management for Organizations* (Geary Reid: Georgetown, 2020).
*Finish Strong* (Geary Reid: Georgetown, 2020).
*From Singleness to Married Life* (Geary Reid: Georgetown, 2021).
*God delivers his children from Crisis* (Geary Reid: Georgetown, 2021).
*God outfoxed Great leaders and Satan* (Geary Reid: Georgetown, 2022).
*Going Hard after God* (Geary Reid: Georgetown, 2021).
*Growing an Organization through Marketing* (Geary Reid: Georgetown, 2020).

*Healing and Deliverance for God's people* (Geary Reid: Georgetown, 2021).
*I am Worshipping My Lord* (Geary Reid: Georgetown, 2020).
*Information Systems for Management* (Geary Reid: Georgetown, 2020).
*Invest in your children's development* (Geary Reid: Georgetown, 2022).
*Jesus' Birth, Death and Resurrection* (Geary Reid: Georgetown, 2022).
*Keep worshipping God in the storms* (Geary Reid: Georgetown, 2022).
*Leadership and Servanthood for Believers* (Geary Reid: Georgetown, 2020).
*Leadership: A Tough Call* (Geary Reid: Georgetown, 2020).
*Leading an Organization to Success* (Geary Reid: Georgetown, 2020).
*Let your faith arise* (Geary Reid: Georgetown, 2021).
*Lord, I am not ready to die* (Geary Reid: Georgetown, 2022).
*Make Learning Your Best Friend* (Geary Reid: Georgetown, 2020).
*Managing Your Organization* (Geary Reid: Georgetown, 2020).
*Metamorphosis: From Sinner to Saint* (Geary Reid: Georgetown, 2020).
*Modeling Kingdom Culture* (Geary Reid: Georgetown, 2021).
*Neighbors are Important* (Geary Reid: Georgetown, 2020).
*Parenting: Not an Easy Job* (Geary Reid: Georgetown, 2021).
*Preparing for Work* (Geary Reid: Georgetown, 2020).
*Preventing workplace burnout* (Geary Reid: Georgetown, 2021).
*Prosperity God's Way* (Geary Reid: Georgetown, 2020).
*Putting God First* (Geary Reid: Georgetown, 2022).
*Remaining Calm in Troubling times* (Geary Reid: Georgetown, 2020).
*Rescuing a Dying Organization* (Geary Reid: Georgetown, 2020).
*Restructuring an Organization* (Geary Reid: Georgetown, 2021).
*Shepherding God's Flock is Hard work* (Geary Reid: Georgetown, 2021).
*Simple Techniques for Managing Your Finances* (Geary Reid: Georgetown, 2020).
*Single Parenting: It Causes, Challenges and Continuity* (Geary Reid: Georgetown, 2022).
*Standing Up Against Domestic Violence* (Geary Reid: Georgetown, 2021).
*Starting a Business: From Idea to Profitability* (Geary Reid: Georgetown, 2020).
*Strategically establishing new churches* (Geary Reid: Georgetown, 2022).
*Success is Possible for Everyone* (Geary Reid: Georgetown, 2020).
*Teachers are the Key to the Future* (Geary Reid: Georgetown, 2020).

*The benefits of working* (Geary Reid: Georgetown, 2022).
*The Church's Impact in Society* (Geary Reid: Georgetown, 2020).
*The Importance of Motherhood* (Geary Reid: Georgetown, 2021).
*The roles of the Christian Husband* (Geary Reid: Georgetown, 2022).
*The roles of the husband* (Geary Reid: Georgetown, 2022).
*The simple keys to a happy relationship* (Geary Reid: Georgetown, 2022).
*Trading Poverty for Prosperity* (Geary Reid: Georgetown, 2020).
*Training Daughters to Become Responsible Mothers* (Geary Reid: Georgetown, 2021).
*Training Sons to Become Responsible Fathers* (Geary Reid: Georgetown, 2021).
*Treat Me well While I am Alive* (Geary Reid: Georgetown, 2021).
*Understanding and working with difficult bosses* (Geary Reid: Georgetown, 2022).
*Waiting on God* (Geary Reid: Georgetown, 2022).
*Way Maker, Miracle Worker* (Geary Reid: Georgetown, 2022).
*When Executives meet, What Happens?* (Geary Reid: Georgetown, 2020).
*Why attending Church is Important* (Geary Reid: Georgetown, 2020).
*Why Do Organizations Underperform?* (Geary Reid: Georgetown, 2020).
*Why People Choose to Marry* (Geary Reid: Georgetown, 2020).
*Winning Your Battle Against Satan's attacks* (Geary Reid: Georgetown, 2022).
*Winning Your Battle Against Suicide* (Geary Reid: Georgetown, 2020).
*Winning Your Next Interview* (Geary Reid: Georgetown, 2020).
*Working for the Lord* (Geary Reid: Georgetown, 2020).
*Your Prayers Matter* (Geary Reid: Georgetown, 2020).
*Your success will attract many followers* (Geary Reid: Georgetown, 2022)

**REID, Ptolemy**

*Our Agricultural Revolution* (Ministry of Agriculture: Georgetown, 1972).

**REITERMAN, T.; and John Jacobs**

*The Untold Story of the Rev. Jim Jones and His People* (E.P. Dutton: New York, 1982).

**RENO, Phillip**

*The Ordeal of British Guiana* (Monthly Review Press: New York, 1964).

**RENVILLE, Jason**

*Bring my Soul out of Prison* (Divine Intelligence Press: New York, 2008).

*Embracing Your Mark of Authenticity* (Divine Intelligence Press: New York, 2013).

**RESTON, James, Jr.**

*Our Father Who Art in Hell* (Times Books: New York, 1981).

**RICE, Robert**

*An American Bush Pilot in Guyana* (Proctor Publishing: Ann Arbor, 2002).

**RICH, Paul P.**

*Race and Empire in British Politics* (Cambridge University Press: Cambridge, 1986).

**RICHARDS, Jim**

*Gold Rush: How I Found, Lost, and Made a Fortune* (September Publishing: London, 2016).

**RICHARDS-GREAVES, Gillian**

*The Clucking Snake* (La Fleur Publishing: Conway, 2023).

*Eclectic Hair with Granny and Me* (La Fleur Publishing: Conway, 2021).

*Rediasporization: African Guyanese Kweh Kweh* (University of Mississippi: Oxford, 2020).

**RICHARDSON, G.**

*On the Diamond Trail in British Guiana* (Methuen & Co. Ltd: London, 1925).

**RICHMOND, Angus**

*The Open Prison* (Hansib Publications: Hertfordshire, 1988).

*A Kind of Living* (Casa de Las Americas: Havana, 1978). [Winner of the Casa de las Americas Literary prize, 1979].

**RICHMOND, James**

*Reflections of Today* (Habana Publishing: Havana, 1978).

*Where the Pomeroon Meets* (J. Richmond: New York, 1997).

*Out of My Skin* (J. Richmond: New York, 2006).

**RICKHEERAM, Harry**

*Across the Oceans: In Search for Loss Love* (Palm Tree Enterprises: New York, 2015).

**RICHMOND, James C.**

*On the Window of My Skin* (JC Richmond: New York, 2006).

**RICKFORD, John R.**

*African American Vernacular English: Features and Use, Evolution, Educational Implications* (Blackwell: London, 1999).

*Betty Shabbazz: A Life Before and After Malcolm X* (Sourcebooks: New York, 2003).
*Code Switching: Teaching Standard English in Urban Classrooms* (National Council of Teachers in English: Washington, D.C.: 2006).
*Dimensions of a Creole Continuum: History, Texts, and Linguistic Analysis of Guyanese Creole* (Stanford University Press: Palo Alto, 1988).
*Festival of Guyanese Words* (University of Guyana: Turkeyen, 1978).
*Ideas in Unexpected Places* (Northwestern University Press: Evanston, 2022).
*Language in the USA: Perspectives from the New Millenium* (Cambridge University Press: Cambridge, 2004).
*Speaking My Soul: Race, Life, and Language* (Routledge: New York, 2022).
*Spoken Soul: The Story of Black English* (Wiley: Hoboken, 2000). [Winner of American Book Award, 2001].
*The Routledge Companion to the Work of John R. Rickford* (Routledge: New York, 2019).

**_____; and Jeannette Allsopp**

*Language, Culture, and Caribbean Identity* (Canoe Press: Kingston, 2012)

**_____; and Penelope Eckert**

*Style and Sociolinguistic Variation* (Cambridge University Press: Cambridge, 2001).

**_____; and S. Romaine**

*Creole Genesis, Attitudes and Discourse* (Linguistic Society of America: New York, 2000).

**_____; et al**

*African American English: Structure, History and Use* (Routledge: London, 1998).
*African, American, Creole and Other English Vernaculars in Education* (Routledge: London, 2012).
*Analyzing Variation in English* (University of Guyana: Turkeyen, 1987).
*Language in the USA: Themes for the Twenty First Century* (Cambridge University Press: Cambridge, 2004).
*Raciolinguistics: How Language Shapes Our Ideas About Race* (Oxford University Press: Oxford, 2020).
*Variation, Versatility and change in Sociolinguistics and Creole Studies* (Cambridge University Press: Cambridge, 2021).
*Variation in Language* (Stanford University Press: Palo Alto, 1987).

*We Are An African People* (Oxford University Press: New York, 2016).

**RIDGEWELL, W.M.**

*The Forgotten Tribes of Guyana* (Tom Stacey: London, 1972).

**RIOS, Manuel Alberto Donis**

*Evolución Histórica de la Cartografía en Guayana y su Significación en Los Derechos Venezolanos sobre el Esequibo* (Academia Nacional de la Historia: Caracas, 1987).

**RIVER, Charles**

*Jim Jones and the Peoples Temple: The Most Notorious Cult and American History* (Createspace: New York, 2015).

**RIVIÈRE, Peter**

*Absent-Minded Imperialism: Britain and the Expansion of Empire in Nineteenth Century Brazil* (Tauris Academic Studies: New York, 1995).

*Individual and Society in Guiana* (Cambridge University Press: Cambridge, 1984).

**RIYASAT, Shyraz**

*A Self-Publishing Guide for Authors* (Shyraz Riyasat: Victoria, 2011).

**ROACH, Trenton**

*Thoughts, moods and feelings and wha dem se – a Glossary of Guyanese Proverbs* (T. Roach: Georgetown, 2008).

**ROBERTS, D.**

*Pure Love Passing Through* (AuthorHouse: Bloomington, 2006).

**ROBERTS, Pamela**

*Black Oxford: The Untold Stories of Oxford University's Black Scholars* (Signal Books: Oxford, 2013).

**ROBERTS, Terence**

*Homage: Stories* (Strategic Book Publishing: New York, 2015).

*New Writing Today From Guyana* (n.p.: n.p., n.d.).

**ROBINSON, G.**

*Martin Carter: University of Hunger, Collected Poems and Selected Prose* (Bloodaxe Books: Northumberland, 2006).

**ROCKMAN, Alexis**

*Guyanese* (Twin Palms: Santa Fe, 1996).

**RODNER, C.; M. Lentino; and R. Restall**

*A Checklist of the Birds of Northern South America: An Annotated Checklist of the Species and Subspecies of Ecuador, Colombia, Venezuela, Aruba, Curacao, Bonaire, Trinidad & Tobago, Guyana, Suriname, and French Guiana* (Yale University Press: New Haven, 2000).

**RODNEY, Patricia** [wife of the late Dr. Walter Rodney]
*Caribbean State, Health Care, and Women: An Analysis of Barbados and Grenada during 1979-1983* (Africa World Press: Trenton, 1986).

**RODNEY, Walter**
*A History of the Guyanese Working People, Vol 1, 1881-1905* (Johns Hopkins University Press: Baltimore, 1981).
*Groundings with my brothers* (Bogle-L'Ouverture Publications: London, 1969).
*Guyanese Sugar Plantations in the Late Nineteenth Century: A Contemporary Description from the "Argosy"* (Release Publishers: Georgetown, 1979).
*History of the Upper Guinea Coast* (Oxford University Press: Oxford,1970).
*How Europe underdeveloped Africa* (Howard University Press: Washington D. C., 1974).
*Kofi Baado, Out of Africa* (SN: Georgetown, 1980). Reprint. (Guyana Book Foundation: Georgetown, 2004).
*Peoples Power, No Dictator* (Working Peoples Alliance: Georgetown, 1979).
*West Africa and the Atlantic Slave Trade* (East African Publishing House, Nairobi, 1969).
*World War II and the Tanzanian Economy* (East African Publishing House: Nairobi, 1976).

**_____, ed.**
*Guyanese Sugar Plantations in the late Nineteenth Century* (Release Publishers: Georgetown, 1980).

**_____; Andaiye; and Nigel Westmaas, eds.**
*Lakshmi out of India* (Guyana Book Heritage: Georgetown, 2000).

**RODRIGUES, Basil**
*An Arawak Biography* (Basil Rodrigues: Georgetown, 1994).

**RODRIGUES, James C.**
*Poems on Guyana: Verse in Reverie* (Forum Printery: Georgetown, 1965).

**RODRIGUES, Waveney**
*Life's Scrapbook* (Ilfracombe, Devon: Stockwell, 1974).
*Reflections* (n.p: n.p., 1962).

**RODRIGUEZ, Junius P.**
*Encyclopedia of Slave Resistance and Rebellion,* 2 vols. (Greenwood Publishing: Westport, 2006).

**RODWAY, Cecily**

*Facing the Wind: Women Who Laughed at the Wind* (Africa World Press: Trenton, 2007).

*Sunstreams and Shadows* (Africa World Press: Trenton, 2001).

**RODWAY, James**

*Annals of British Guiana* (Hodder & Stoughton: London, 1912).

*Chronological History of the Discovery and Settlement of Guiana, 1493-1668,* 4 vols. (J. Thomson: Georgetown, 1888-1894).

*Forest and Stream* (Hodder & Stoughton: London, 1910).

*Guiana: British, Dutch, and French* (T. Fisher Unwin: London, 1912).

*Handbook of British Guiana* (Royal Agricultural and Commercial Society: London, 1893).

*History of British Guiana from 1668,* 3 vols. (J. Thomson: Georgetown, 1891-4).

*In Guiana Wilds: A Study of Two Women* (T. Fisher Unwin: London, 1899).

*In the Guiana Forest: Studies of Nature in Relation to the Struggle for life* (n.p.: London, 1894). Reprint. (Negro Universities Press: New York, 1969).

*Our Native Orchids* (J. Thomson: Georgetown, 1885).

*Story of Georgetown* (Argosy Co.: Georgetown, 1920). Reprint. (Guyana Heritage Society: Georgetown, 1997).

*The West Indies and the Spanish Main* (T. Fisher Unwin: London, 1896).

*The Story of Forest and Stream* (Newnes: London, 1897).

**_____; and James H. Stark**

*Stark's Guide Book and History of British Guiana* (James H. Stark: Boston, 1898).

**_____; and Thomas Watt**

*Chronological History of the Discovery and Settlement of Guiana, 1493-1668*. 4 vols. (Royal Gazette Office: Georgetown, 1888-1894).

**ROHLEHR, Gordon**

*A Scuffling Islands: Essays on Calypso* (Lexicon: Port of Spain, 1988).

*An Anthology of Oral and Related Poetry from the Caribbean* (Longman: London, 1994).

*Calypso and Society in Pre-Independence Trinidad* (Lexicon: Port of Spain, 1989).

*Is Massa Dad Dead? Black Moods in the Caribbean* (Anchor Books: New York, 1974).

*Musings, Mazes, Muses, Margins* (Peepal Tree Press: Leeds, 2018).

*My Strangled City* (Peepal Tree Press: Leeds, 2019).

*My Whole Life is Calypso: Essays on Sparrow* (University of the West Indies: St. Augustine, 2015).
*Perfected Fables Now: Essays on the Closure of a Cycle* (Peepal Tree Press: Leeds, 2019).
*The Shape of That Hurt and Other Stories* (Peepal Tree Press: Leeds, 2021).

**_____; and Victor D. Questel**

*Collected Poems: With Gordon Rohlehr* (Peepal Tree Press: Leeds, 2016).

**ROHEE, Clement J.**

*Clement James Rohee: Selected Parliamentary speeches: 1994-1996* (Ministry of Foreign Affairs: Georgetown, 1996).
*Guyana's Foreign Policy Towards the Twenty-First Century: Selected Speeches 1996-1999* (Ministry of Foreign Affairs: Georgetown, 2011).
*My Story My Song* (Outskirts Press: Denver, 2021).
*Securing Our Nation: A Compilation of Speeches made by the Minister of Home Affairs since assuming office in 2006* (Ministry of Home Affairs: Georgetown, 2011).
*Our Public Security Legislative Agenda: Bills, Motions and Debates* (Ministry of Home Affairs: Georgetown, 2012).
*Those Days* (Peoples Progressive Party: Georgetown, 2011).
*Facing the Challenges, Reform of the European Union – Sugar Regime* (Peoples Progressive Party: Georgetown, 2012).

**_____; and Dr. Cheddi Jagan**

*Guyana: A Bed of Thorns* (Peoples Progressive Party: Georgetown, 1984).

**ROHEE, Dave**

*Bush Flying: A Pilot's Nightmare* (Mulberry Books: Qualicum Beach, 2020).

**ROMUALDI, Serafino**

*Presidents and Peons: Recollections of a Labour Ambassador in Latin America* (Funk and Wagnalls: New York, 1967).

**ROONEY, L.F.**

*A Voyage to Demerara* (Society for Propagation of the Gospel in Foreign parts: London, 1953).

**ROOPNARAINE, Lomarsh**

*Indentured Muslims in the Diaspora: Identity and Belonging of Minority Groups in Plural Societies* (Manohar Publishing: New Delhi, 2016).

*Indian Indenture in the Danish West Indies* (Palgrave-Macmillan: London, 2016).

*The Indian Caribbean: Migration and Identity in the Diaspora* (University Press of Mississippi: Jackson, 2018). [2018 Gordon K & Sybil Lewis Book Award]

*Thought-Provoking Newspaper Articles 2015-2017* (Lambert Academic Publishing: London, 2017).

**ROOPNARAINE, Rupert**

*Primacy of the Eye: The Art of Stanley Greaves* (Peepal Tree Press: Leeds, 2003).

*Suite for Supriya* (Peepal Tree Press: Leeds, 1993).

*The Web of October: Rereading Martin Carter* (Peepal Tree Press: Leeds, 1986).

*The Sky's Wild Noise: Selected Essays* (Peepal Tree Press: Leeds, 2012).

**ROSILA, I.**

*The Shadow Behind My Rainbows* (AuthorHouse: Bloomington, 2005).

**ROSS, Ivan A**

*The Cultural and Political History of Guyana: President John F. Kennedy's Interference in the Country's Democracy* (Archway Publishing: New York, 2021).

**ROTARACT Club**

*The Indigenous People of Guyana* (Rotaract Club of Georgetown: Georgetown, 1995).

**ROTH, Vincent** [Walter Roth's son]

*A Life in Guyana, Volume 1: A Young Man's Journey 1889-1923* (Peepal Tree Press: Leeds, 2003).

*A Life in Guyana, Volume 2: the Later Years 1924-35* (Peepal Tree Press: Leeds, 2003).

*Bibliography of British Guiana: Compiled Under the Aegis of the British Guiana Bibliography Committee* (Colonial Government: Georgetown, 1948).

*Fish Life in British Guiana* (Daily Chronicle: Georgetown, 1943).

*Handbook of Natural Resources of British Guiana* (Interior Development Committee: Georgetown, 1945).

*Notes and Observations on Fish Life in British Guiana. A Popular Guide to Colonial Fishes. With an Appendix comprising "The Fisheries of British Guiana" by Professor H H Brown.* (Colonial Government: Georgetown, 1943).

*Notes on Animal Life in British Guiana* (Colonial Government: Georgetown, 1945).
*Pathfinding on the Mazaruni 1922-1924* (n.p.: Georgetown, 1949).
*Roth's Pepper-pot* (Daily Chronicle: Georgetown, 1958).
*Tales of the Trails* (Daily Chronicle: Georgetown, 1960).

**ROTH, Walter, E.**

*Additional Studies of the Arts, Crafts, and customs of the Guiana Indians, with special reference to those of southern British Guiana* (US GPO: Washington D.C., 1929).
*An Enquiry into the Animism and Folklore of the Guiana Indians* (Smithsonian Institution: Washington D.C., 1915).
*An Introductory Study of the Arts, Crafts, and Customs of the Guiana Indians* (US GPO: Washington D.C., 1924).

**______., ed. and trans.**

*Robert Hermann Schomburgk's Travels in Guiana and on the Orinoco during the years 1835-39. According to his reports and Communications to the Geographical Society of London* (n.p.: Georgetown, 1931).
*Travels in British Guiana during the years 1840-44,* 2 vols. (Daily Chronicle: Georgetown, 1922/23).

**______., trans.**

*Koch-Grunberg, T. From Roraima to the Orinoco: Results of a Journey in North Brazil and Venezuela in the Years 1911-13.* Vol.3 (Chronicle: Georgetown, 1917).

**ROUT, Leslie B.**

*Which way out? An Analysis of the Venezuela/Guyana Border Dispute* (Michigan State University Press: East Lansing, 1971).

**RUHOMAN, Joseph**

*India: The Progress of her People at Home and Abroad and How Those in British Guiana may improve Themselves* (n.p.: n.p., 1894).
*The Triple Crown* (Daily Chronicle: Georgetown, 1930).

**RUHOMAN, Peter**

*A Centenary History of the East Indians in British Guiana 1838-1938* (Daily Chronicle: Georgetown, 1947). Reprint. (East Indians 150th Anniversary Committee: Georgetown, 1988).

**RUIA, Jelena**

*La Busqueda de El Dorado Por Guayana* (School of Spanish American Studies: Seville, 1959).

**RUPNARAIN, Richard**

*A Day in the Life of Satan: And Why It Matters to Us* (Christian Book Publishers: Toronto, 2021).

*After God's Heart: Devotionals Inspired by King David* (Christian Book Publishers: Toronto, 2018).
*Aliens, UFOs, Mars Rush: Gearing Up for Cosmic War* (Christian Book Publishers: Toronto, 2021).
*Antichrist: Studies in Daniel 7-12* (Christian Book Publishers: Toronto, 2018).
*Apostasy: Avoid the Great Falling Away* (Christian Book Publishers: Toronto, 2019).
*Barabbas or Jesus: Which Son Will Save Us?* (Christian Book Publishers: Toronto, 2021).
*Bartica* (Richard Rupnarain: Toronto, 2008).
*Bartica: Tales from the Diaspora, Vol.2* (Christian Book Publishers: Toronto, 2021).
*Beauty for Ashes: The Great Exchange* (Christian Book Publishers: Toronto, 2020).
*Beyond a Curse: Living Without Fear* (Christian Book Publishers: Toronto, 2019).
*Beyond the Leaves: In Pursuit of the Fruitful Life* (Christian Book Publishers: Toronto, 2015).
*Biblical Mysteries* (Christian Book Publishers: Toronto, 2017).
*Bramdeo and Juliet: An Interracial Love Story Set in 1963 British Guiana* (Christian Book Publishers: Toronto, 2015).
*Breaking Siege: Avoid Spiritual Lockdown* (Christian Book Publishers: Toronto, 2020).
*Built for Goodness: Revisiting Genesis for Answers to Divisive Issues* (Christian Book Publishers: Toronto, 2020).
*Chalkdust in My Eyes: Tales from the Diaspora, Vol.6* (Christian Book Publishers: Toronto, 2015).
*Choke and Rob: Tales from the Diaspora, Vol.5* (Christian Book Publishers: Toronto, 2015).
*Complete in Christ* (Christian Book Publishers: Toronto, 2016).
*Conquering Shame* (Christian Book Publishers: Toronto, 2017).
*Cool Shade: Tales from the Diaspora, Vol.1* (Christian Book Publishers: Toronto, 2014).
*Cosmic Conversations: Interviews with God and the Devil* (Christian Book Publishers: Toronto, 2004).
*Demon in the House: Detect and Defeat Satan* (Christian Book Publishers: Toronto, 2015).
*Devices of the Devil: Satanic Strategies to Defeat Believers* (Christian Book Publishers: Toronto, 2020).

*Dig Deeper: Revisiting the Miracles of Elisha, Vol.1* (Christian Book Publishers: Toronto, 2019).
*End of Days: From Rapture to New Heavens and Earth* (Christian Book Publishers: Toronto, 2016).
*Fight for Your Destiny* (Christian Book Publishers: Toronto, 2017).
*Gruesome to Glorious: The Gore and Glory of Easter* (Christian Book Publishers: Toronto, 2016).
*Guyanese Nights: Tales from the Diaspora, Vol.3* (Christian Book Publishers: Toronto, 2014).
*Guyanese Nights: Tales from the Diaspora. 3 Vols.* (Evalis: Brampton, 2020).
*Handwriting on the Wall: Studies in Daniel 1-6* (Christian Book Publishers: Toronto, 2018).
*Hard After God: Laying Hold of the God who Laid Hold of Me* (Christian Book Publishers: Toronto, 2018).
*Humans 2.0: Avoid Irrelevance in the Age of Artificial Intelligence* (Christian Book Publishers: Toronto, 2021).
*I Thank My God I Speak with Tongues: On the Benefits of Spirit Baptism* (Christian Book Publishers: Toronto, 2015).
*Ichabod: The Glory Has Departed* (Christian Book Publishers: Toronto, 2017).
*Introduction to Christology* (Christian Book Publishers: Toronto, 2014).
*Jacob's Ladder: Shadows of Elemental Christology* (Christian Book Publishers: Toronto, 2014).
*Jesus Christ, a Necessary Idea* (Christian Book Publishers: Toronto, 2021).
*Keys to Breakthrough Prayers* (Christian Book Publishers: Toronto, 2022).
*Knowing God: The Essence of Eternal Life* (Christian Book Publishers: Toronto, 2022).
*Life According to Ivy: Lessons from a Dog* (Christian Book Publishers: Toronto, 2017).
*Life in the Secret Place: Power and Blessing of Intimacy with God* (Christian Book Publishers: Toronto, 2015).
*Live with Precision: Walking in Step with God's Plan for Your Life* (Christian Book Publishers: Toronto, 2015).
*Magnificent Obsession: Pursuing the Love that Pursues Us* (Christian Book Publishers: Toronto, 2015).
*Maintaining the Glow: Burning for God without Burnout* (Christian Book Publishers: Toronto, 2016).

*Making Church Fun Again: A Call for a Return to Pentecost* (Christian Book Publishers: Toronto, 2016).
*Ministry Made Easy: Strategies to Prevent Burnout* (Christian Book Publishers: Toronto, 2022).
*No Greater Name, No Higher Purpose* (Christian Book Publishers: Toronto, 2014).
*No More Temple: Revisiting the Doctrines of the Church & Israel* (Christian Book Publishers: Toronto, 2018).
*Pray and Push: On Faith and Perseverance* (Christian Book Publishers: Toronto, 2021).
*Pray This Way: A Radical Take on the Lord's Prayer* (Christian Book Publishers: Toronto, 2017).
*Preaching Doom in a Culture of Censorship: Timely Messages from the Book of Jonah* (Christian Book Publishers: Toronto, 2017).
*Road to Armageddon* (Christian Book Publishers: Toronto, 2021).
*Secure the Upper Springs: Key to Abundant Life* (Christian Book Publishers: Toronto, 2019).
*Settled on Dregs: The Evil of Laziness* (Christian Book Publishers: Toronto, 2021).
*Shift the Atmosphere: Sermons on Spiritual Warfare from Joshua* (Christian Book Publishers: Toronto, 2019).
*Shine Like the Stars: Sharing Jesus in a Post-Christian World* (Christian Book Publishers: Toronto, 2020).
*Sigh and Cry, or Die: A Call to the Church for Prayer* (Christian Book Publishers: Toronto, 2016).
*Social Distancing and the Power of Isolation* (Christian Book Publishers: Toronto, 2016).
*Surviving the Storm: Encouragement for Tough Times in Ministry* (Christian Book Publishers: Toronto, 2019).
*Susanna: Unsung Heroine of the 1823 Demerara Slave Rebellion* (Christian Book Publishers: Toronto, 2020).
*The Diabolical Mind: Getting Inside Satan's Head* (Christian Book Publishers: Toronto, 2018).
*The Dissolution of Heaven and Earth: Planet Earth's Last Days* (Christian Book Publishers: Toronto, 2019).
*The Face of God: The Saints' Ultimate Quest* (Christian Book Publishers: Toronto, 2016).
*The Great Reset: Positioning for the New World Order* (Christian Book Publishers: Toronto, 2021).
*The Greatest: On The Incomparable Christ* (Christian Book Publishers: Toronto, 2019).

*The Heaven Jesus Gained for Me: A Walk with Jesus on the Bright Side of Redemption* (Christian Book Publishers: Toronto, 2022).
*The Hell Jesus Went Through for Me: A Walk with Jesus on the Dark Side of Redemption* (Christian Book Publishers: Toronto, 2022).
*The Mystery of God: Demystifying the Triune Godhead* (Christian Book Publishers: Toronto, 2016).
*The Pentecostal Show: Funny Stories with a Moral Underlining* (Christian Book Publishers: Toronto, 2020).
*The Pursuit of Excellence: Meditations on the Power of Righteousness* (Christian Book Publishers: Toronto, 2019).
*The Spirits of Le Ressouvenir: Tales from the Diaspora, Vol.4* (Christian Book Publishers: Toronto, 2014).
*The West Indian Bible: Proverbs of the Caribbean* (Christian Book Publishers: Toronto, 2014).
*Thy Kingdom Come: Discussions on the Kingdom of God* (Christian Book Publishers: Toronto, 2016).
*Transfigured for Transformation* (Christian Book Publishers: Toronto, 2017).
*Treasures and Hidden Riches* (Christian Book Publishers: Toronto, 2018).
*Two Israels, One Jew: Deconstructing NT Theology on Israel and Jewishness* (Christian Book Publishers: Toronto, 2019).
*Waiting on Sons: Answering Climate Change, Terrorism, and Moral Decay* (Christian Book Publishers: Toronto, 2016).
*When the Music Fades: Perspectives on Ministry* (Christian Book Publishers: Toronto, 2019).
*Where is the Babylon I Built? And Other Soul-Searching Questions* (Christian Book Publishers: Toronto, 2020).
*Women to Remember* (Christian Book Publishers: Toronto, 2014).

**RUSSEL, Jesse; and Ronald Cohn**
*Bharrat Jagdeo* (Books on Demand: Miami, 2013).
*Robert Corbin* (Books on Demand: Miami, 2013).

**RUTHERFORD, Anna; and Donald Hannah, eds.**
*Commonwealth Short Stories* (Edward Arnold: London, 1971).

**RUTHERFORD, K.G.; and T.L. Hills**
*Soils of the Rupununi Savanna/Forest Ecotone-Southern Guiana* (McGill University: Montreal, 1979).

# S

**SADEEK, Sheik**

*Across the Green Fields and Five Other Stories* (Sheik Sadeek: Georgetown, 1974).

*Black Bush* (Sheik Sadeek: Georgetown, 1974).

*Bound Coolie: Or the Immigrant* (Sheik Sadeek: Georgetown, 1958).

*Bundarie Boy* (Sheik Sadeek: Georgetown, 1974). [Winning novel of the 1961 National Gold Medal].

*Dreams and Reflections* (Sheik Sadeek: Georgetown, 1969).

*No Greater Day and Four More Adult Stories. A Short Story Collection* (Sheik Sadeek: Georgetown, 1974).

*Fish Koker* (Sheik Sadeek: Georgetown, 1958). [Winner of the 1958 Cheddi Jagan Gold Medal].

*Savannah's Edge* (Sheik Sadeek: Georgetown, 1968).

*Song of the Sugarcanes* (Sheik Sadeek: Georgetown, 1975). [Wining novel of the 1959 National Gold Medal. The book was made into a film in 1980].

*The Diamond Thieves and Four More Stories* (Sheik Sadeek: Georgetown, 1974).

*The Malali Makers* (Sheik Sadeek: Georgetown, 1979).

*The Pork Knockers and Four Other Stories* (Sheik Sadeek: Georgetown, 1974).

*Windswept and 3 Other Stories* (Sheik Sadeek: Georgetown, 1968).

*Windswept and Other Stories* (Sheik Sadeek: Georgetown, 1969).

*Windswept: Selected Dozen Short Stories* (Sheik Sadeek: Georgetown, 1980).

**SAHADEO, Ramnarine**

*Mohandas K. Gandhi: Thoughts, Words, Deeds: His Source of Inspiration: Bhagavad-Gita* (Xlibris: Bloomington, 2011).

**_____; ed.**

*The Bhagavad-Gita in English with Quotes. Comments by Gandhi* (Xlibris: Bloomington, 2021).

**SAHOYE-SINGH, Jeanette**

*Legends, Lines, Love and Loss* (J. Sahoye-Singh: Toronto, 2006).

**SALKEY, Andrew, ed.**

*Breaklight: An Anthology of Caribbean Poetry* (Hamish Hamilton: London, 1971).

*Caribbean Essays: An Anthology* (Evans Brothers: London, 1972).
*Caribbean Folk Tales and Legends* (Bogle L'Ouverture: London, 1980).
*Georgetown Journal: A Caribbean Writer's Journey from London via Port of Spain to Georgetown, Guyana* (New Beacon Books: Surrey, 1972).
*West Indian Stories* (Fabian and Fabian: London, 1960).

**SALLAHUDEEN**

*Georgetown Journal* (New Beacon Books: London, 1972).
*Guyana: The Struggle for Liberation 1945-92* (Sallahudeen: Georgetown, 1992).
*Labour at the Crossroads* (New Guyana Company Ltd.: Georgetown, 1992).

**SAM, Yvonne**

*Life's many Faces* (Xlibris: Bloomington, 2013).

**SAMAD, Daizal**

*Land Beneath the Wind: New Writing from America, Pacific, and Asia* (University of Hawaii Press: Honolulu, 1999).
*The Mirror That tells Its Tales* (Page Publishing: New York, 2019).

**____; and Ashwannie Harripersaud**

*Rivers Whisper Stars: Poems* (Maygen Publications: Kuala Lumpur, 2000).
*Wholeness and Home in West Indian Literature* (University of Guyana: Georgetown, 2022).

**SAMAROO, Jean Janki**

*A Gift of Love, Robert Janki: Poems* (J.J. Samaroo: Toronto, 2023).
*Late Blooms: Inspiration for Seniors* (J.J. Samaroo: Toronto, 2020).
*Making New Friends* (J.J. Samaroo: Toronto, 2020).
*Strong Women Make History* (Kindle, e-book: Toronto, 2021).

**SAMAROO, Shaun Michael**

*Be the Perfect You* (Kind Media Ministry: Toronto, 2005).
*Being the Voice of Good Conscience* (Kind Media Ministry: Toronto, 2003).
*My Thoughts on Life* (Kind Media Ministry: Toronto, 2004).
*Nightmares of Knowledge* (Kind Media Ministry, Toronto, 2001).
*Reflections* (Kind Media Ministry: Toronto, 2002).

**SAMPATH, Nelson Emmanuel, ed.**

*The Literature of the Indian Diaspora* (Greenwood Press: New Haven, 1992).

**SAMUEL, Raphael, ed.**

*Village Life and Labour* (Routledge & Kegan Paul: London, 1975).

**SANAHI, Shari**

*Burned Bridges Lead to Better Roads* (Marcon Press: New York, 2021).

**SANCHO, Thomas Anson**

*Guyana/Venezuela Border Dispute* (Ministry of Foreign Affairs: Georgetown, 1966).

*Highlights of Guyana's History: An Independence Publication* (National History and Arts Council: Georgetown, 1966).

*Lines and Rhymes: A Collection of Verse* (Labour Advocate Printing Department: Georgetown, 1962).

*Octave* (T. Anson Sancho: Georgetown, 1971).

*To England and Back* (T. Anson Sancho: Georgetown, 1969).

*The Ballad of 1763: The Story of Cuffy's Rebellion Narrated in Verse* (Government of Guyana: Georgetown, 1970).

*The Green Way: A Biography of Hamilton Green* (T. Anson Sancho: Georgetown, 1996).

**SANDERS, Andrew**

*The Powerless People: An Analysis of the Amerindians of the Corentyne River* (Macmillan: London, 1987).

**SANDERS, Douglas**

*Amerindian Peoples in Guyana* (University of British Columbia: Vancouver, 1995).

**SANDERS, Sir Ronald**

*A Commonwealth of the People: Time for Urgent Reform* (Commonwealth Secretariat: London, 2011).

*Antigua and Barbuda: A Little Bit of Paradise: A historical and contemporary guide to Antigua and Barbuda* (Hansib Publications: Hertfordshire, 1994).

*Broadcasting in Guyana: Case Studies on Broadcasting Systems* (Routledge & Kegan Paul: London, 1978).

*Crumbled Small: The Commonwealth Caribbean in World Politics* (Hansib Publications: Hertfordshire, 2005).

*Dyslexia From a Cultural Perspective* (Hansib Publications: Hertfordshire, 2007).

*Reflections from the Frontline: Developing Country negotiations in the WTO* (The Academic Foundation: London, 2012).

*Shridath Ramphal: The Commonwealth and the World* (Hansib Publications: Hertfordshire, 2008).

*A Commonwealth of the People: Time for Urgent Reform* (Commonwealth Secretariat: London, 2011).

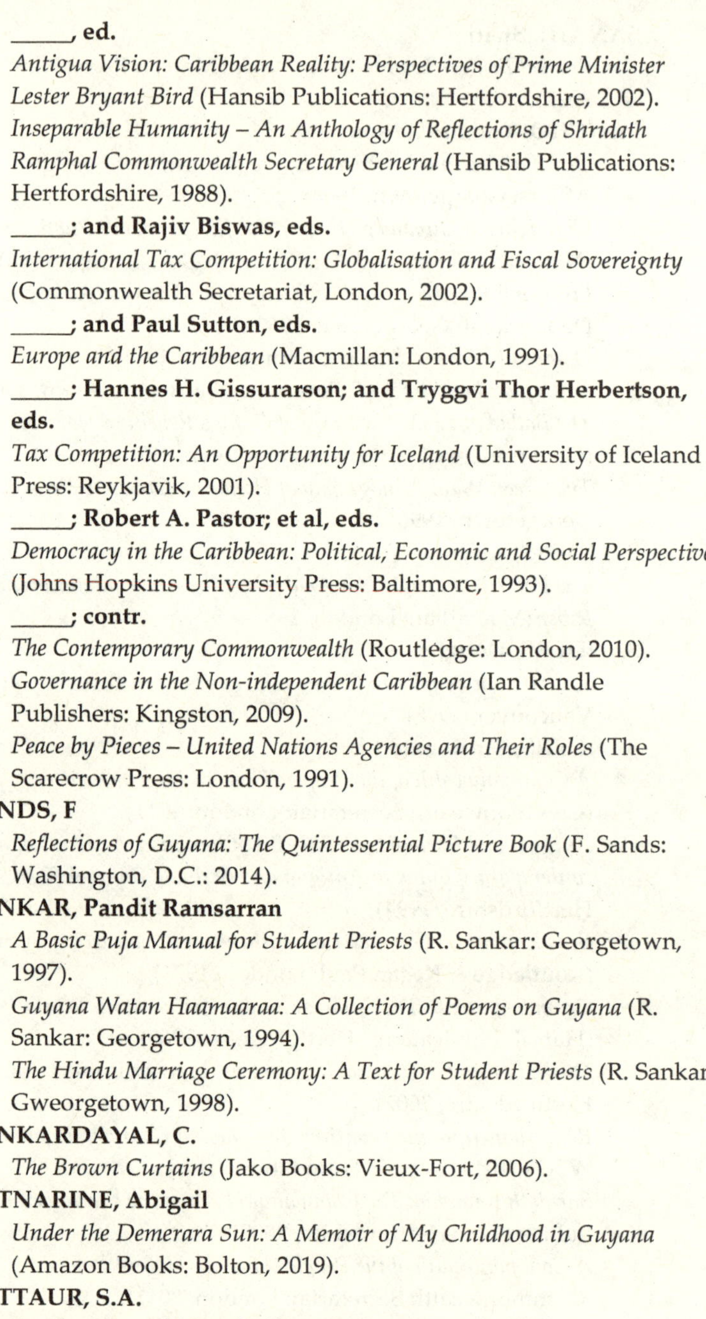

**_____, ed.**

*Antigua Vision: Caribbean Reality: Perspectives of Prime Minister Lester Bryant Bird* (Hansib Publications: Hertfordshire, 2002).

*Inseparable Humanity – An Anthology of Reflections of Shridath Ramphal Commonwealth Secretary General* (Hansib Publications: Hertfordshire, 1988).

**_____; and Rajiv Biswas, eds.**

*International Tax Competition: Globalisation and Fiscal Sovereignty* (Commonwealth Secretariat, London, 2002).

**_____; and Paul Sutton, eds.**

*Europe and the Caribbean* (Macmillan: London, 1991).

**_____; Hannes H. Gissurarson; and Tryggvi Thor Herbertson, eds.**

*Tax Competition: An Opportunity for Iceland* (University of Iceland Press: Reykjavik, 2001).

**_____; Robert A. Pastor; et al, eds.**

*Democracy in the Caribbean: Political, Economic and Social Perspectives* (Johns Hopkins University Press: Baltimore, 1993).

**_____; contr.**

*The Contemporary Commonwealth* (Routledge: London, 2010).

*Governance in the Non-independent Caribbean* (Ian Randle Publishers: Kingston, 2009).

*Peace by Pieces – United Nations Agencies and Their Roles* (The Scarecrow Press: London, 1991).

**SANDS, F**

*Reflections of Guyana: The Quintessential Picture Book* (F. Sands: Washington, D.C.: 2014).

**SANKAR, Pandit Ramsarran**

*A Basic Puja Manual for Student Priests* (R. Sankar: Georgetown, 1997).

*Guyana Watan Haamaaraa: A Collection of Poems on Guyana* (R. Sankar: Georgetown, 1994).

*The Hindu Marriage Ceremony: A Text for Student Priests* (R. Sankar: Gweorgetown, 1998).

**SANKARDAYAL, C.**

*The Brown Curtains* (Jako Books: Vieux-Fort, 2006).

**SATNARINE, Abigail**

*Under the Demerara Sun: A Memoir of My Childhood in Guyana* (Amazon Books: Bolton, 2019).

**SATTAUR, S.A.**

*For the Glory of Islam* (S. Sattaur: Georgetown, 1941).

**SAUL, S.B.**

*Studies in British Overseas Trade 1870-1914* (n.p.: Liverpool, 1960).

**SAWH, Balram Terry**

*Immigrating to Canada: A Realistic Path to Success for New Canadians, Immigrants, Business and Government* (T. Sawh: Toronto, 2011).

**SAWH, Ramcharran**

*The Hidden Treasure and Other Stories* (R. Sawh: Georgetown, 1980).

*Waterloo and Other Stories* (R. Sawh: Georgetown, 1982).

**SAWH, Roy**

*From Where I Stand* (Hansib Publications: Hertfordshire, 1987).

**SCHEERES, Julia**

*A Thousand Lives: The Untold Story of Hope, Deception and Survival at Jonestown* (Free Press: New York, 2011).

**SCHLESINGER Jr., Arthur A.**

*A Thousand Days: John F. Kennedy in the White House* (Houghton Mifflin: New York, 1965).

**SCHOMBURGK, O.A.**

*Robert Hermann Schomburgk's Reisen in Guiana und am Orinoko, wahrend der Jahre 1835-1839* (JJ Webber: Leipzig, 1841).
[Book in German of Schomburgk's travels in British Guiana].

**SCHOMBURGK, Richard Moritz**

*Travels in British Guiana during the years 1840-44,* 2 vols., (George Wigand: Leipzig, 1848).

**SCHOMBURGK, Sir Robert Herman**

*A Description of British Guiana, Geographical and Statistical* (Frank Cass: London, 1949).

*A Description of British Guiana, Geographical and Statistical: Exhibiting its Resources and Capabilities, Together with the Present and Future Condition and Prospects of the Colony* (Simpkin, Marshal & Co: London, 1840).

*Comparative Vocabulary of Eighteen Languages and Dialects of Melian Tribes Inhabiting Guiana* (Simpkin, Marshal & Co.: London, 1848).

*Ichthyology: Fishes of British Guiana,* 2 vols. (Simpkin, Marshal & Co.: London, 1843).

*The History of Barbados* (Longman, Brown, Green, and Longmans: London, 1848).

*The Natural History of the Fishes of Guiana,* 2 vols. (W.H. Lizar: Edinburgh, 1841-43).

*Travels in Guiana and on the Orinoco During the Years 1835-1839* (George Wigand: Leipzig, 1841).

*Twelve Views in the Interior of Guiana* (Ackerman: London, 1841).

**_____, ed.**

*The Discoverie of the Large, Rich, and Beauwtiful Empyre of Guiana (With a Relation of the Great and Golden Citie of Manoa (Which the Spanyards call El Dorado) and of the Provinces of Emeria, Arromaia, Amapaia, and Other Countries, with Their Riulers, Adjoyning* (Hakluyt: London, 1848).

**SCOBIE, John**

*Black Britannia: A History of Blacks in Britain* (Johnson Publishers: Chicago, 1972).

**SCOBLE, John**

*Hill Coolies: A Brief Exposure of the Deplorable Conditions of the Hill Coolies in British Guiana and Mauritius* (Harvey & Darton: London, 1839).

**SCOLES, Rev. Ignatius**

*Sketches of African and Indian Life in British Guiana* (Jesuit Missions: London, 1885).

**SEAFORTH, Compton Eustace**

*Folk Healing Plants Used in the Caribbean* (Al Falaah Publications: Port of Spain, 1998).

**SEALES, Ronald S.**

*Cry of the Black Bird* (AuthorHouse: Bloomington, 2006).

*Return of the Arawak* (AuthorHouse: Bloomington, 2008).

*The OMAI File* (AuthorHouse: Bloomington, 2008).

**SEALY, Theodore**

*Sealy's Caribbean Leaders: A Personal Perspective on Major Caribbean Leaders, Pre and Post Independence* (LMH Publishing: Kingston, 2004).

**SEARWAR, L, ed.**

*Cooperative Republic, Guyana, 1970: A Study of Aspects of Our Way of Life* (Ministry of Education: Georgetown, 1970).

**_____, ed.**

*Guyana and the World: Selected Editorials* (2008).

**_____; and Ian McDonald, eds.**

*They Came in Ships: An Anthology of Indo-Guyanese Prose and Poetry* (Peepal Tree Press: Leeds, 1998).

**SEECHARAN, Clem**

*Bechu: Bound Coolie Radical in British Guiana, 1894-1901* (University of the West Indies Press: Mona, 1999).

*Cheddi Jagan and the Cold War, 1946-1991* (Ian Randle Publishers: Kingston, 2023).

*Cricket and Indian Identity in Colonial Guyana 1890s-1960s: Encyclopaedia of National Cultures* (Macmillan: New York, 2000).
*Encyclopaedia of the Indian Diaspora* (National University of Singapore: Singapore, 2006).
*Finding Myself: Essays in Race Politics and Culture* (Peepal Tree Press: Leeds, 2015).
*From Ranji to Rohan* (Hansib Publications: Hertfordshire, 2009).
*Hand in Hand History of Cricket in Guyana 1865-1897 Vol. 1 – The Foundation* (Hansib Publications: Hertfordshire, 2016).
*Hand in Hand History of Cricket in Guyana 1898-1914, Vol. 2 – A Stubborn Mediocrity* (Hansib Publications: Hertfordshire, 2018).
*Hand in Hand History of Cricket in Guyana 19151-31, Vol. III: A Difficult Consolidation* (Soon to be Published).
*India and the Progress of her People at Home and Abroad* (University of the West Indies Press: Mona, 2001).
*India and the Shaping of the Indo-Guyanese Imagination 1890-1920* (Peepal Tree Press: Leeds, 1993).
*Indians in British Guiana* 1919-29 (Macmillan: London, 1999).
*Joseph Ruhoman's India: The Progress of her people at home and abroad and how those in the West Indies and British Guiana may improve themselves* (UWI Press: St. Augustine, 2001).
*Mother India's Shadow Over El Dorado: Indo-Guyanese Politics and Identity 1890s-1930s* (Ian Randle Publishers: Kingston, 2011).
*Muscular Learning: Cricket and Education in the Making of the British West Indies at the End of the Nineteenth Century* (Ian Randle Publishers: Kingston, 2006).
*Sweetening Bitter Sugar: Jock Campbell's British Guiana 1934-1966* (University Press of the West Indies: Kingston, 2003).
*The Anatomy of Indian Achievement in British Guiana, 1919-1929* (Macmillan: London, 1997).
*Tiger in the Stars: The Anatomy of Indian Achievement in British Guiana 1919-1929* (Macmillan: London, 1997).

**_____; and Frank Birbalsingh**

*Indo-West Indian Cricket* (Hansib Publications: Hertfordshire, 1988).

**_____; and Ian McDonald**

*An Abounding Joy: Essays on Sports* (Hansib Publications: Hertfordshire, 2019).
*Joe Solomon and the Spirit of Port Mourant: The Making of the Guyana and West Indies Cricketer and Its Context, 1930s-60s* (Hansib Publications: Hertfordshire, 2022).

**SEECOMAR, Judaman**

*Contributions Towards the Resolution of Conflict in Guyana* (Peepal Tree Press: Leeds, 2002).

*Democratic Advance and Conflict Resolution in Post-Colonial Guyana* (Peepal Tree Press: Leeds, 2007).

**SEEPERSAUD, Ramdyal**

*A Select Bibliography of the Works of Guyanese and on Guyana on the Occasion of Guyana Week Feb 19-25 1967* (Government Printery: Georgetown, 1967).

**SEGAL, R.**

*The Black Diaspora* (Faber and Faber: London, 1995).

**SEMPLE, Berkley**

*Flight and Other Poems* (Word Limit Solutions: New York, 2021).

*Lamplight Teller* (WD Books: San Gabriel, 2004).

*The Draught Players* (WD Books: San Gabriel, 2007).

*The Limers* (WD Books: San Gabriel, 2005).

*The Solo Flyer and Other Poems* (WD Books: San Gabriel, 2005).

**SENAUTH, Frank**

*The Last Call: Curse of the Bhutto's Name* (AuthorHouse: Bloomington, 2008).

*The Making of Guyana: From a Wilderness to a Nation* (AuthorHouse: Bloomington, 2009).

**SERRAO, Desmond**

*The Other Side of the Medical Coin* (Xlibris: Bloomington, 2012).

**SEWEL, W.G.**

*The Ordeal of Free Labour in the British West Indies* (n.p.: London, 1861).

**SEYMOUR, A.J.**

*A Bethlehem Alleluia* (A.J. Seymour: Georgetown, 1974).

*A Survey of West Indian Literature* (A.J. Seymour: Georgetown, 1976).

*A Treasury of Guyanese Poetry* (Guyana National Lithographic: Georgetown, 1980).

*An Anthology of Guianese Poetry* (A.J. Seymour: Georgetown, 1954).

*Autobiography* (Labour Advocate Printery: Georgetown, 1976).

*Black Song* (Labour Advocate: Georgetown, 1971).

*Caribbean Literature* (Argosy Company Ltd.: Georgetown, 1951).
*Collected Poems, 1937-1989* (Blue Parrot Press: New York, 2000).
*Dictionary of Guyanese Folklore* (National History and Arts Council: Georgetown, 1975).
*Edgar Mittelholzer: The Man and His Work* (Labour Advocate Printery: Georgetown, 1968).
*Fourteen Guianese Poems for Children* (Master Printery: Georgetown, 1953).
*Growing Up in Guyana* (Labour Advocate Printery: Georgetown, 1976).
*Guiana Book* (Argosy: Georgetown, 1948).
*I Live in Georgetown* (Labour Advocate Printery: Georgetown, 1974).
*Images of Majority* (Labour Advocate Printery: Georgetown, 1978).
*Independence Ten: Guyanese Writing, 1966-76* (Government of Guyana: Georgetown, 1978).
*Introduction to Guyanese Writing* (National History and Arts Council: Georgetown, 1971).
*Italic* (Labour Advocate Printery: Georgetown, 1974).
*Leaves from the tree* (Master Printery: Georgetown, 1951).
*Love Song* (Labour Advocate Printery: Georgetown, 1975).
*More Poems* (Daily Chronicle: Georgetown, 1940).
*New Writing in the Caribbean* (The Guyana Lithographic Company Ltd: Georgetown, 1972).
*Over Guiana, Clouds* (Demerara Standard Establishment: Georgetown, 1944).
*Passport* (Labour Advocate Job Printing Dept: Georgetown, 1972).
*Patterns* (A.J. Seymour: Georgetown, 1970).
*Pilgrim Memories* (Labour Advocate Printers: Georgetown, 1978).
*Selected Poems* (British Guiana Lithographic Co., Ltd.: Georgetown, 1965). Reprint (Labour Advocate Job Printing Dept.: Georgetown, 1983).
*Song to Man* (Labour Advocate: Georgetown, 1973).
*Studies in West Indian Poetry* (Labour Advocate Printery: Georgetown, 1974).
*Studies of Ten Guyanese Poems* (Ministry of Education: Georgetown, 1980).
*Sun's in my blood* (Demerara Standard Establishment: Georgetown, 1945).
*The Kykoveral Anthology of Guianese Poetry* (British Guiana Lithographic: Georgetown, 1954).

*The Making of Guyanese Literature* (A.J. Seymour: Georgetown, 1978, 1980).
*The Years in Puerto Rico and Mackenzie* (A.J. Seymour: Georgetown, 1983).
*Themes of Song* (A.J. Seymour: Georgetown, 1961).
*Verse* (Daily Chronicle: Georgetown, 1937).
*West Indian Poetry* (A.J. Seymour: Georgetown, 1981).
**_____.; and Elma Seymour, eds.**
*Dictionary of Guyanese Biography* (A.J. Seymour: Georgetown, 1984).
*My Lovely Native Land: An Anthology of Guyana* (Longman: London, 1971).

**SEYMOUR, Elma Editha [AJ Seymour's wife].**
*Early Childhood Education in Guyana* (E.E. Seymour: Georgetown, 1982).
*Sun is a Shapely Fire* (Labour Advocate: Georgetown, 1973).

**SEYMOUR, Rudy**
*The Burnham Story* (People's National Congress: Georgetown, 1968).
*The Preacher Meets Big Mama* (Rudy Seymour: Georgetown, 1968).
*Peter Palaver* (Rudy Seymour: Georgetown, 1969).

**SHAH, Ryhaan**
*A Death in the Family* (Cutting Edge Press: London, 2014).
*A Silent Life* (Peepal Tree Press: Leeds, 2005).
*Weaving Water* (Cutting Edge Press: London, 2013).

**SHAH ROATH, Seeta Terry**
*Performance Poetry: Guyana, Now and Then* (Roath Publishing: Montana, 2020).
*The Return of Latchmini: A Historical Novel Set in 1894* (Roath Publishing: Montana, 2022).
*Under the Calabash Tree* (Roath Publishing: Montana, 2020).
*Wanderlust: A Collection of Short Stories: Guyana to Montana 1983-2021* (Roath Publishing: Montana, 2022).

**SHAHABUDDEEN, Dr. Mohamed**
*Constitutional Development in Guyana 1621-1978* (Guyana Printers Ltd.: Georgetown, 1978).

*From Plantocracy to Nationalisation* (University of Guyana: Turkeyen, 1983).

*International Criminal Justice at the Yugoslav Tribunal: A Judge's Recollection* (Oxford University Press: Oxford, 2012).

*Nationalisation of Guyana Bauxite: The Case of Alcan* (Guyana National Printers Ltd.: Georgetown, 1981).

*Precedent in the World Court* (Cambridge University Press: Cambridge, 1996).

*The Conquest of Grenada: Sovereignty in the Periphery* (University of Guyana: Turkeyen, 1986).

*The Legal System in Guyana* (Guyana Printers Ltd.: Georgetown, 1973).

**SHAHABUDDEEN, Sieyf** (son of Dr. Mohamed Shahabuddeen)

*Judge Mohamed Shahabuddeen: A Pictorial Biography* (Amazon Books: Bolton, 2022).

**SHAJAD, Simon**

*The Guyanese Princess* (Trafford Publishing: London, 2021).

**SHAMANE**

*Faith and Love* (AuthorHouse: Bloomington, 2012).

**SHARMA, P.D.**

*New Caribbean Man* (Hayward Carib House: London, 1981).

**SHAW-BARRINGTON, Grace**

*Most Popular Guyanese Recipes: A Cookbook of Essential Food and Recipes Direct From Guyana* (Createspace: Scotts Valley, 2022).

**SHEIK HASSAN PRODUCTIONS**

*Historical Georgetown, Guyana, South America* (Sheik Hassan Productions, Georgetown, 2000).

**SHEOGOBIND, Stanton**

*A Boy, A Man, and A Game* (Xlibris: Bloomington, 2019).

**SHEPHERD, K.**

*On Your Mark: The Message of Mark* (AuthorHouse: Bloomington, 2006).

**SHEPHERD, Phyllis, ed.**

*Bibliography of Guyanese Plays* (National Library of Guyana: Georgetown, 1967).

**SHEPHERD, Robert**

*Iain Macleod* (Hutchinson: London, 1984).

**SHEPHERD, Verene A., ed.**

*Maharani's Misery: Narratives of a Passage from India to the Caribbean* (UWI Press: Mona, 2002).

*Women in Caribbean History: An Introductory Text for Secondary Schools* (Ian Randle Publishers: Kingston, 2000).

**SHERIDAN, Richard**

*Doctors and Slaves: A Medical and Demographic History of Slavery in the British West Indies 1680-1834* (Cambridge University Press: Cambridge, 1985).

**SHERRETT-GONZALEZ, Patricia**

*Where does purpose gather us* (Word Alive Press: Toronto, 2013).

**SHEWCHARAN, Narmala**

*Beauty Lies Within* (N. Shewcharan: Georgetown, 1979).
*Tomorrow is Another Day* (Peepal Tree Press: Leeds, 1994).
*The Dream of Every Heart* (Peepal Tree Press: Leeds, 2006).

**SHINEBOURNE, Jan Lowe**

*Chinese Women* (Peepal Tree: Leeds, 2010).
*The Godmother and Other Stories* (Peepal Tree Press: Leeds, 2003).
*The Last English Plantation* (Peepal Tree Press: Leeds, 1988).
*The Last Ship* (Peepal Tree Press: Leeds, 2015).
*Timepiece* (Peepal Tree Press: Leeds, 2003).

**SHIW PARSAD, Basmat**

*Domestic Violence: A Study of Wife Abuse Among East Indians of Guyana* (Caribbean Studies Association: Georgetown, 1988).

**SHIWNANDAN, Ravindra**

*A Quick Guide for Altar Workers: Reaping a Great Harvest of Souls* (R. Shiwnandan: Georgetown, 2019).
*Advancing Kingdom Citizenship* (R. Shiwnandan: Georgetown, 2021).
*Called to the 5-FLD Ministry* (R. Shiwnandan: Georgetown, 2022).
*Overcoming the Strongman: A Handbook of Spiritual Warfare* (R. Shiwnandan: Georgetown, 2019).
*Rebounding: A Christian Doctor's Guide to Understand Suffering and Recovery From Life's Difficult Moments* (R. Shiwnandan: Georgetown, 2019).
*The Dynamics of Freedom* (R. Shiwnandan: Georgetown, 2019).
*The Principles of Stabilizing Leadership* (R. Shiwnandan: Georgetown, 2021).
*Understanding God's End-Time Schedule* (R. Shiwnandan: Georgetown, 2022).

**SIFONTES, Horacio Cabrera**

*La Verdad Sobre Nuestra Guyayan Esequiba* (Monte Avila: Caracas, n.d.).

[Book in Spanish on Venezuela's claim over Essequibo].

**SILVERMAN, M.**

*Rich People and Rice: Factional Politics in Rural Guyana* (Brill Academic Publishers: New York, 1994).

**SIMEY, T.S.**

*Welfare and Planning in the West Indies* (Oxford University Press: Oxford, 1946).

**SIMMS, Peter**

*Trouble in Guyana: An account of people, personalities and politics as they were in British Guiana* (George Allen & Unwin: London, 1966).

**SIMON, Koreen A.**

*Thrive Like a Dandelion: A Self-Empowerment Journey of Fifty-Two Steps* (Virtual Bookworm: College Station, 2009).

**SINCLAIR, Donald**

*Rejoyce: A Memorial Celebration of the Life of Joyce E. Sinclair* (Donald Sinclair: Georgetown, 2021).

**SINCLAIR, Joyce.**

*Courtesy Tips for Children* (Joyce Sinclair: Georgetown, 2008).

*High Quality Customer Care for Polishing Your Telephone Manners* (Joyce Sinclair: Georgetown, 2009).

*Receptive Courtesies* (Joyce Sinclair: Georgetown, 2008).

**SINCLAIR, Maja**

*A Guyanese Jaguar Soil* (Maja Sinclair: Georgetown, 2020).

**SINGH, Bahadur I**

*Indians in the Caribbean* (Omnetel Press: London, 1983).

**SINGH, Barney**

*Tales in the Guyanese Vernacular* (Createspace: Vancouver, 2012).

**SINGH, Pandit Birbal**

*Petals from my Rose Garden* (Birbal Singh: Toronto, 2007).

**SINGH, Chaitram**

*Guyana: Politics in a Plantation Society* (Praeger Publishing: New York, 1988).

*The February 23rd Coup* (iUniverse Inc.: Bloomington, 2011).

*The Flour Convoy* (iUniverse Inc.: Bloomington, 2011).

**SINGH, David**

*A Passion to Succeed* (ECW Press: Toronto, 2006).

*Health, Wealth Happiness: You Can Control Your Destiny* (ECW Press: Toronto, 2003).

*Retire Early and Wealthy: 7 Steps to Wisdom and Financial Freedom* (ECW Press: Toronto, 2004).

*The Making of Fortune: The Story of Building Fortune Financial With Advice You Can Use to Build Your Own Fortune* (Stoddart Publishing: Toronto, 1996).

**SINGH, Devi Lolita**

*Affirmation Stories from the Magic Window: I am Positively Grand* (Amazon Books: Bolton, 2022).

**SINGH, Doodnauth**

*Hunted: A Collection of Poems* (D. Singh: Georgetown, 1990).

*Showers of Betrayal* (D. Singh: Georgetown, 1991).

**SINGH, I.J. Bahadur, ed.**

*Indians in the Caribbean* (Sterling Publishers: New Delhi, 1987).

**SINGH, Jai Narine**

*Guyana: Democracy Betrayed* (Kingston Publishers: Jamaica, 1996).

**SINGH, Jagdish R.**

*Adventures of the Homeless* (Llumina Press: Tamarac, 2008).

*Earthly Tribulations* (Writers Club Press: Denver, 2003).

*Pandora's Heartaches* (Writers Club Press: Denver, 2005).

*Strange Misfortunes* (Llumina Press: Tamarac, 2009).

*The Tolerance of Hinduism* (Writers Club Press: Denver, 2007).

*The True Self* (Writers Club Press: Denver, 2002).

**SINGH, Dr. Jang B.**

*Sustainability: The Influence of Leadership and Culture* (Friesen Press: Winnipeg, 2021).

**SINGH, Major General (r'td), Joseph G.**

*Growing up in British Guiana: 1945-1964* (JG Singh: Georgetown, 2011).

**_____, ed.**

*Guyana: The Lost El Dorado: My Fifty Years in the Guyanese Wilds: Matthew French Young's Memoirs* (Peepal Tree Press: Leeds, 1998).

*The Mataruki Trail: The Story of the British Guiana Boundary Commission 1929-1939. From the Manuscript of C. Arthur Hudson* (Sheik Hassan Productions: Georgetown, 2004).

*Caesar De Freitas's "On the Frontier of Guyana and Brazil"* (Sheik Hassan Productions: Georgetown: 2010).

**SINGH, Jotis**

*Selected aspects of Guyanese fertility: Education, Mating and Race* (Australian National University: Canberra, 1980).

**SINGH, Karna Bahadur**

*Kali's Feast: The Goddess of Indo-Caribbean Ritual and Fiction* (Release Publishers: Georgetown, 1994).

*Temples and Mosques: An Illustrated Study of East Indian Modes of Worship in Guyana* (Release Publishers: Georgetown, 1980).

*The Feast and Festivities of Mother Kali* (Release Publishers: Georgetown, 1995).

**SINGH, Leela**

*Random Rhythmic Tipples* (L. Singh: Georgetown, 1972).

**SINGH, Naresh**

*Sustainable Livelihoods* (Kumarian Press: Bloomfield, 2001).

**SINGH, Paul**

*Guyana: Socialism in a Plural Society* (University of Guyana: Turkeyen, 1971).

*The Guyana Experience and Local Democracy in the Commonwealth Caribbean: A Study of Adaptation and Growth* (Longman Caribbean: London, 1972).

**SINGH, P.**

*Fireflies: A Collection of Poems* (n.p.: n.p., n.d.).

*Woman of the Mahabharat* (n.p.: New York, 2001).

**SINGH, Rajkumari**

*A Collection of Poems* (R. Singh: Georgetown, 1971).

*Children Stories of Guyana: A Compilation* (R. Singh: Georgetown, 1972).

*Days of the Sahib* (R. Singh: Georgetown, 1971).

*Garland of Stories* (Arthur Stockwell: Devon, 1960).

**_____; Sheila King; et al**

*Stories from Guyana* (R. Singh.: Georgetown, 1972).

**SINGH, Ronald**

*Fragrance of a Desert Rose: A Book of Poems* (International Development Consultants: n.p., 1997).

**SINGH, Roopnandan**

*Crab-man: An Anthology of Short Stories and Poems* (Roopnandan Singh Publications: Georgetown, 2003).

*Death is a Friend* (Roopnandan Singh: Georgetown, 2008).

*Dimensions of Life: A Collection of Poems* (Roopnanadan Singh Publications: Georgetown, 1993).

*Eternal Quest: A Selection of Poems by Guyanese Writers* (Association of Guyanese Writers & Artists: Georgetown, 2000).

*Eve* (Association of Guyanese Writers & Artists: Georgetown, 1995).

*Introspection: A Collection of Poems* (Roopnandan Singh Publications: Georgetown, 1994).
*Just a Number* (Association of Guyanese Writers & Artists: Georgetown, 2001).
*Roll Play* (Association of Guyanese Writers & Artists: Georgetown, 1998).
*Shadow in the Dark* (Association of Guyanese Writers & Artists: Georgetown, 2000).
*Sky Dance* (Association of Guyanese Writers & Artists: Georgetown, 1997).
*Talking with Myself: A Collection of Poems* (Roopnandan Singh Publications: Georgetown, 1993).
*The Thorn in the Rose* (Roopnandan Singh: Georgetown, 1994).

**SINGH, R. Lal**

*A Collection of Poems Celebrating the Richness of Life* (Gwen Singh: New York, 1971).
*Gift of the Forest* (Longmans: London, 1952).
*Gwendolyn and Me, The Boughs of Love* (Gwen Singh: New York, 1971).

**SINGH, Samuel**

*My Voice* (AuthorHouse: Bloomington, 2008).

**SINGH, Seopaul**

*Anatomy of Race Politics: Economics and Violence Against Diaspora Indians* (Createspace: Scotts Valley, 2017).
*Changing Moods: A Collection of Poems* (S. Singh: New York, 2002).
*Libert of Conscience* (S. Singh: New York, 2019).
*My Voice of Conscience: Of Gods and Demi-Gods* (Createspace: Scotts Valley, 2019).

**SINGH, Soshinie**

*The Phoenix Letters Return: Letters to My Younger Self* (Amazon Books: Bolton, 2017).

**SINGH, Subraj**

*Rebelle and Other Stories* (Amazon Books: Bolton, 2015). [Winner of the 2015 Guyana Prize for Literature, Fiction].

**SINGH, Thomas B.**

*Study of the Socio-Economic Impact of the Closure of GuySuCo Sugar Estates on Sugar Workers in Guyana* (International Labour Organization: Geneva, 2021).

**SINGH, Dr. Tulsi Dayal**

*Accolades to Berbice High School on its Centenary Anniversary* (Guyenterprise: Georgetown, 2016).

**SINGH, Valerie**

*For The Love of Grandma* (Amazon Books: Bolton, 2009).

**SINGH, W.G.; and Wagner, A.R.**

*Assassination Cry of a Failed Revolution: The Truth about Dr. Walter Rodney's Assassination* (Xlibris: Bloomington, 2006).

**SINGHROY, Dr. Vernon**

*Advances in Remote Sensing for Infrastructure Monitoring* (Springer Publishing: Cham, 2021).

*Encyclopaedia of Remote Sensing* (Springer Publishing: Cham, 2014).

*New Technology of Geosciences* (CRC Press: London, 1997).

*Remote Sensing and GIS for Site Characterization: Applications and Standards* (ASTM International: Philadelphia, 1996).

*Remote Sensing: Invesrion Problems and Natural Hazards* (Pergamon Press: London, 1998).

*Sand Gravel Resources and Quaternary Geology of the Pas Region* (Manitoba Energy and Mines: Winnipeg, 1980).

*Spatial Methids for Solution of Environmental and Hydrologic Problems: Science Policy and Standardization* (ASTM International: Philadelphia, 2003).

**_____; contr.**

"Advanced radar images for monitoring Transportation, Energy, Mining and Coastal Infrastructure," in *Advanced Remote Sensing for Infrastructure Monitoring* (Springer Publishing: Cham, 2020).

"Geological Mapping using Earth Magnetic Field," in *Encyclopedia of Remote Sensing* (Springer Publishing: Cham, 2014).

"Interpretation of SAR Images for Coastal Zone Mapping in Guyana," in *Land use Land Degradation and Land Management in Guyana* (McGill University Press: Montreal, 1997).
"Landslides," in *Encyclopedia of Remote Sensing* (Springer Publishing: Cham, 2014).
"Monitoring and Mapping areas affected by Water control projects in Coastal Guyana," in *Hydrology in the Humid Tropic Environment* (IAHS: New York, 1997).
"Operational Applications of Radar Images in *Handbook of Satellite Applications*," (Springer Publishing: Cham, 2013).
"Remote Sensing and Geologic Structure," in *Encyclopedia of Remote Sensing* (Springer Publishing: Cham, 2014).
"Remote Sensing for Landslide Assessment," in *Landslides Hazard and Risk* (Wiley: Hoboken, 2005).
"Remote Sensing Techniques for Geological Mapping and Exploration," in *Geoinfomatics for Natural Resource Management* (Nova Science Publishers: New York, 2009).
"Satellite and Airborne Sensing to Characterize Mining Areas-Selected Sites in Canada," in *Remote Sensing for Site Characterization* (Springer Verlag: New York, 1997).
"Satellite remote sensing applications for landslide detection and monitoring," in *Landslide Disaster Risk Reduction* (Springer Publishing: Cham, 2008).

**SIRVAITIS, Kasli**

*Guyana in Pictures* (Twenty-first Century Books: New York, 2009).

**SISCO, G.C.**

*Guyana's Economic Recovery: Leadership, Will-power and Vision: Selected Speeches of H.D. Hoyte* (Free Press: Georgetown, 1997).

**SIZER, N.**

*Profit Without Plunder: Reaping Revenue from Guyana's Tropical Forest Without Destroying Them* (World Resources Institute: London, 1997).

**SLOWE, Lloyd**

*Twelve Essentials for a Successful Marriage* (AuthorHouse: Bloomington, 2008).

**SMARTT, Jacqueline,**

*Navigators Travel to Guyana: Based on an Idea by Howard Liverpool* (Createspace: Scotts Valley, 2015).

**SMITH, Anthony**

*Explorers of the Amazon* (Viking: New York, 1990).

**SMITH, Dorcia, et al; eds.**
*Caribbean Without Borders: Literature, Language and Culture* (Cambridge Scholars Publishing: Cambridge, 2008).

**SMITH, Gregory and Anne R. Wagner**
*Assassination Cry of a Failed Revolution – The Truth About Dr. Walter Rodney's Death* (Xlibris: Bloomington, 2007).

**SMITH, Joseph Burkholder**
*Portrait of a Cold Warrior* (G.P. Putnam's Sons: New York, 1976).

**SMITH, M.G.**
*The Plural Society in the British West Indies* (n.p.: Los Angeles, 1965).

**SMITH, R.T.**
*British Guiana* (Oxford University Press: Oxford, 1962).
*Kinship and Class in the West Indies: A Genealogical Study of Jamaica and Guyana* (Cambridge University Press: Cambridge, 1988).
*The Negro Family in British Guiana: Family Structures and Social Status in the Villages* (Routledge and Kegan Paul: London, 1956).

**SMOCK, Kirk**
*Guyana*, 2nd ed. (Bradt Travel Guides: London, 2013).
*Annals of British Guiana* (Hodder & Stoughton: London, 1912).

**SNYDER, D.E.**
*The Birds of Guyana* (Peabody Museum: Massachusetts, 1966).

**SODERBERG, D.**
*A Time for Choosing* (AuthorHouse: Bloomington, 2005).
*Mr. Protestant* (AuthorHouse: Bloomington, 2005).
*The Amsterdam Connection* (AuthorHouse: Bloomington, 2006).
*The Winds of Change* (AuthorHouse: Bloomington, 2006).

**SOLOMON, Jay**
*Taste of the Tropics: Traditional and Innovative Cooking from the Pacific and Caribbean* (n.p.: n.p., n.d.).

**SOMDAT, M; and R. Gampat, eds.**
*180 Years of Indians in Guyana, 1838-2018* (Caribbean Hindu Network: Georgetown, 2018).

**SOOKHDEO, Jaikissoon**
*Let not the great* (Arthur Stockwell: Devon, 1964).

**SOOKRAM, Narine Dat**
*The Teenage Years: A Collection of Love Poems* (N.D. Sookram: Georgetown, 2013).

**SOUTH RUPUNUNI CONSERVATION SOCIETY (SRCS)**
*Basic Guide to Amphibians and Reptiles* (SRCS: Lethem, 2023).
*Mammals of the Rupununi* (SRCS: Lethem, 2021).
*Mawuusa and the Giant Anteater* (SRCS: Lethem, 2023).

**SPEIRS, Rev. James**

*The Proverbs of British Guiana with an Index of Principal Words, an Index of Subjects, and a Glossary* (Argosy: Georgetown, 1902).

**SPENCER, Stephen**

*A Dream Deferred: Guyanese Identity and the Shadow of Colonialism* (Hansib Publications: Hertford, 2007).

**SPINNER, Thomas J., Jr.**

*A Political and Social History of Guyana 1945-1983* (Westview Press: Boulder, 1984).

**ST. AUBIN DE TERAN, Lisa** [Jan Carew's daughter]

*A Valley in Italy* (Penguin Books: New York, 1995).

*Black Idol* (Jonathan Cape: London, 1987).

*Joanna* (Virago Press: London, 1990).

*Keepers of the House* (Jonathan Cape: London, 1982).

*The Bay of Silence* (Jonathan Cape: London, 1986).

*The High Place* (Jonathan Cape: London, 1985).

*The Long Way Home* (Harper and Row: New York, 1982).

*The Marble Mountain: And Other Stories* (Jonathan Cape: London, 1989).

*The Slow Train to Milan* (Harper and Row: New York, 1983).

*The Tiger* (Franklin Watts: New York, 1985).

**ST. AUBYN, Dorothy**

*Amerindian Folk Tales from the Caribbean* (Demerara Mutual Life: Georgetown, 2007).

**ST. CLAIR, T.S.A.**

*A Residence in the West Indies* (n.p.: n.p., n.d.).

*A Soldier's Sojourn in British Guiana 1806-08* (Chronicle: Georgetown, 1947).

**ST. PIERRE, M.**

*Anatomy of Resistance: Anti-colonialism in Guyana 1823-1966* (Macmillan-Caribbean: London, 1999).

**STANDING, G.; and R. Szal**

*Cultural Policy in Guyana* (UNESCO: Paris, n.d.).

*Poverty and Basic Needs: Evidence from Guyana and the Philippines* (UNIRIB: New York, 1979).

**STEDMAN, John Gabriel**

*Narrative of a Five-Year Expedition Against the Revolted Negroes of Suriname, in Guiana, on the Wild Coast of South America; from the Year 1772 to 1777; Elucidating the History of That Country and Describing its Productions with an Account of the Indians of Guiana, and Negroes of Guinea*. 2 vols. (J. Johnson: London, 1806). Reprint. (The Imprint Society: Boston, 1971).

**STEPHENSON, Carlton**

*Business as usual* (Longrass Publishing: New York, 2009).

**STEWARD, J.H.; and L. Faron**

*Native Peoples of South America* (McGraw-Hill: New York, 1959).

**_____; eds.**

*Handbook of South American Indians: The Comparative Ethnology of South American Indians* (US Government Printing: Washington D.C., 1949).

**STOBY, E.S.**

*British Guiana Centenary Year Book 1831-1931* (n.p.: Georgetown, 1931).

**STOLL, Allyson; Erin Lierl; and Leon Saul**

*Lessons in Guyanese History from Abolition to Rastafari* (Guyana Institute of Historical Research: Georgetown, 2018).

**STUART, Andrea**

*Sugar in the Blood: A Family Story of Slavery and Empire* (Alfred A. Knopf: New York, 2013).

**SUBHAN, Neaz**

*Coming Back: An Escape From Suicide* (Neaz Subhan: Georgetown, 2020).

**SUBRYAN, Carmen Barclay**

*Black-Water People: A Novel about the Allicocks of the Upper Demerara Area, Guyana, South America* (Demerara Press: Beltsville, 2003).

*Rachel's Tears* (Demerara Press: Baltimore, 2000).

**SUE-A-QUAN, Goomatie**

*3 Dynamic Rabbits: Rabbit Family Relationship* (Xlibris Corporation: Bloomington 2007).

*A Seal Fascination at Sea* (Xlibris Corporation: Bloomington 2008).

*Just Like My Mom on Mother's Day* (Xlibris Corporation: Bloomington 2007).

*Just Like My Dad on Father's Day* (Xlibris Corporation: Bloomington 2007).

*Naughty Hawk and the Squirrel* (Xlibris Corporation: Bloomington 2007).

**SUE-A-QUAN, Trevor**

*Cane Reapers: Chinese Indentured Immigration to Guyana* (Riftswood Publishers, Vancouver, 1999).

*Cane Ripples* (Cane Press: Vancouver, 2003).

*Cane Rovers: Stories of the Chinese Guyanese Diaspora* (Riftswood Publishing: Parksville, 2012).

**SUKHDEO, Frederick**

*The Impact of Emigration on Manpower Resources in Guyana* (University of Guyana: Turkeyen, 1972).

*The Working Class Struggle for Freedom and Socialism* (Ministry of National Development: Georgetown, 1975).

**SUKHDEO, Gokarran**

*Poems of Love and Liberty* (Gokarran Sukhdeo: New York, 1998).

*The Silver Lining* (Gokarran Sukhdeo: New York, 1998). [Winner of the Guyana Prize, 1998]

**SUKHRAM, Barry L.**

*Divide and Conquer: The Split in the People's Progressive Party of British Guiana and the Cold War* (Hansib Publications: Hertfordshire, 2013).

**SUKHU, Leela**

*Scattered Leaves* (Sheik Sadeek: Georgetown, 1968).

**SUTCLIFFE, Katherine**

*Shadow Play* (Avon Books: Miami, 1991)

**SUTHERLAND, Fraser**

*Jonestown: A Poem* (McClelland & Stewart: Toronto, 1996).

**SUTTON, P.; A.M. Bissessar; P. Osei; and M. Scott**

*Modernizing the State* (Ian Randle Publishers: Kingston, 2006).

**SWAIN, Danielle**

*The Guyana Annual Magazine: Folklore Edition* (Guyenterprise: Georgetown, 2020).

**SWAN, M.**

*British Guiana: Land of Six Peoples* (Penguin: London, 1967).

*Marches of El Dorado: British Guiana, Brazil and Venezuela* (Jonathan Cape: London, 1958).

**SWAN, Bernadette N.**

*Tribute to Frederick Gordon Sadool* (Bernadette N. Swan Social Care Foundation: Edmonton, 2009).

**SWAN, Carlington Roy**

*Footprints Along The Way: Malgre Tout Roman Catholic Church – A Collection of Facts, Issues, and Events of Earlier Days* (LBA Publications: Toronto, 2004).

**SYLVESTER, CRAIG**

*Bringing Guyana Into The 21st Century* (Georgetown Consulting Group: Georgetown, 2017).

**SZULC, Tad**

*The US and the Caribbean* (Prentice Hall: New York, 1971).

# T

**T., H.**

*Stray Thoughts* (The Argosy Co. Ltd: Georgetown, 1889).

**TAHARALLY, K,**

*Anthrophanies 1 to 4* (S. Prakash: New Delhi, 1983).

**TALBURT, Tony**

*Rum, Rivalry & Resistance: Fighting for the Caribbean Spirit* (Hansib Publications: Hertfordshire, 2010).

**TAMAYO, Isbelia Sequera; et al**

*Guayana Esequiba: Espacio Geopolitico* (Academia Naciónal de Ciencias Económicas: Caracas, 1992).
[Book in Spanish on the Essequibo].

**TANG NAON, Gemm; and Bailiry Barbara, eds.**

*Gender Equality in the Caribbean* (Ian Randle Publishers: Kingston, 2002).

**TAYLOR, Conrad**

*Path to Freedom: My Story of Perseverance* (TCF Business Group: Ocoee, 2011).

**TAYLOR, Douglas**

*Languages of the West Indies* (Johns Hopkins University Press: Baltimore, 1977).

**TAYLOR, Michael**

*The Interest: How the British Establishment Resisted the Abolition of Slavery* (Bodley House: London, 2020).

**TEE-VAN, Helen Damrosch**

*Red Howling Monkey: The Tale of a South American Indian Boy* (Macmillan: New York, 1926).

**TEMPLE, Bob; and J.D. Henderson**

*Guyana: Discovering South America* (Mason Crest Publishers: London, 1988).

**TENNANT, R.**

*British Guiana and its Resources* (n.p.: London, 1895).

**TENNASSEE, Paul**

*Guyana: A Case for Free & Fair Elections* (ISDG: Port-of-Spain, 1989).
*Guyana: A Nation in Ruins* (GRRS: Toronto, 1982).
*Guyana: A Nation-State too Young to Die* (Carisform: Curacao, 1987).
*The DLM: Origin-Diagnosis-Ideology-Objective-Structure-Programme* (DLM Publications: Georgetown, 1989).

*DLM and the Guyana of Tomorrow: Free & Fair Elections Now: Towards a New Guyana* (ISDG: Port-of-Spain, 1990).

**_____; et al**

*Caribbean Integration & The Labour Movement,* Parts 1 and 2 (Carisform: Curacao, 1988).

*Caribbean Workers' Struggle for Real Democracy* (FLACP: Caracas, 1987).

*Emergence of the Caribbean Labour Movement* (Caribbean Labour Series: Port-of-Spain, 1987).

*Europe 1992 and its impact on Caribbean and Latin American Working Class* (n.p.: n.p., n.d.).

*Perspectiva sobre la Integracion en el Caribe y America Latina, publicado en el documento sobre 1er Ecuentro Latino Americano de Trabajadores, Republica Dominicana* (n.p.: n.p., 1992).

*State Capitalism and Ideological Opportunism: Bauxite and Sugar Workers Struggle* 1970-80 (Carisform: Curacao, 1989).

*The oil industry and nationalization: Who benefits?* (Caribbean Labour Series: Port-of-Spain, 1986).

*Venezuela. Los obreros petroleros y la lucha por la democracia* (CEIP: Caracas, 1979).

**TERAN, Iseult** [Jan Carew's granddaughter]

*Dolce Vita* (Flamingo-Harper Press: London, 1999).

**THAKUR, P.S.**

*Guyana: Political and Social Satire* (Cowhood Inc.: Toronto, 1987).

**THIONGO, Nguigi Wa**

*Homecoming: Essays on African and Caribbean Literature, Culture and Politics* (Heinemann: London, 1972).

**THOMAS, Clive Y.**

*Dependence and Transformation: The Economics of the Transition to Socialism* (Monthly Review Press: New York, 1974).

*Guyana: The Political Economy of Cooperative Socialism* (University of Guyana: Georgetown, 1982).

*Plantations, Peasants, and State: A Study of the Mode of Sugar Production in Guyana,* vol. 5 (Center for Afro-American Culture and Society: Los Angeles, 1984).

*The Poor and the Powerless* (Monthly Review Press: New York, 1988).

*The Rise of the Authoritarian State in Peripheral Societies* (Monthly Review Press: New York, 1984).

*The Structure, Performance, and Projects of Central Banking in the Caribbean* (University of the West Indies: Kingston, 1972).

**_____., ed.**

*Politics and Public Policy in the Contemporary American West* (University of New Mexico: Albuquerque, 1991).

**_____.; and Havelock Brewster**

*The Dynamics of West Indian Economic Integration* (University of the West Indies: Kingston, 1967).

**_____.; et al.**

*Economic Theory and Development Options for the Caribbean* (Ian Randle Publishers: Kingston, 2006).

**THOMAS, Desmond**

*Electoral System Reform for a Diverse Nation: The Case of Guyana* (D. Thomas: Georgetown, 2020).

**THOMAS, Elon M.**

*Poems from the Light to the Darkness and Back to Life, The Power of Word: The Eldincal Chonicles Book* (AuthorHouse: Bloomington, 2008).

**THOMAS, Erwin K.**

*A Life of Prayer, Devotion, and Pandemic* (Createspace: Scotts Valley, 2021).

*A Weekly Encounter: Fifty-Two Meditations of Home* (Createspace: Scotts Valley, 2015).

*Devotions and Ailment: Physical and National Ills* (Createspace: Scotts Valley, 2022).

*Dfurstane's Spiritual Beliefs* (Createspace: Scotts Valley, 2020).

*Gifts of God: Reflections and Affirmations* (Createspace: Scotts Valley, 2017).

*Guyana's Seawall Girl* (Createspace: Scotts Valley, 2018).

*Heaven Bound: Bread of Life* (Createspace: Scotts Valley, 2019).

*Keys of Faith: Fifty-Two Meditations for Living* (Createspace: Scotts Valley, 2016).

*Life's Passages: From Guyana to America* (Createspace: Scotts Valley, 2018).

*Sunlit Stream of Water: Devotions for Religious Naturalists* (Createspace: Scotts Valley, 2020).

**_____; and Brown H. Carpenter**

*Mass Media in 2025: Industries, Organizations, People, and Nations* (Greenwood Press: Hartford, 2001).

**THOMAS, Mary**

*Guyana: A Bibliography on National Development, 1966-1976* (Council on Planning Librarians: Monticello, 1977).

**THOMASSON, Frank**

*A History of Theatre in Guyana: 1800-2000* (Hansib Publications: Hertfordshire, 2009).

**THOMPSON, Alvin O.**

*A Documentary History of Slavery in Berbice* (Free Press: Georgetown, 2002).

*Brethren of the Bush: A Study of Runaways and Bush Negroes in Guyana* (University of the West Indies: Cave Hill, 1975).

*Colonialism and Underdevelopment in Guyana 1580-1803* (Caribbean Research and Publications: Kingston, 1987).

*Haunting Past: Politics, Economics and Race in Caribbean Life* (M.E. Sharpe Inc.: New York,1997).

*Maroons of Guyana: Some Problems of Slave 1750-1814* (Free Press: Georgetown, 2000).

*The Berbice Revolt, 1763-64* (Free Press: Georgetown, 1999).

*The Haunting Past: Politics, Economics and Race in Caribbean Life* (Ian Randle Publishers: Kingston, 2002).

*Unprofitable Servants: Crown Slaves in Berbice, Guyana 1803-31* (University of Oklahoma Press: Oklahoma City, 2002).

**_____., ed.**

*In The Shadow of the Plantation: Caribbean History and Legacy* (Ian Randle Publishers: Kingston, 2002).

*Unprofitable Servants* (University Press of the West Indies: Kingston, 2002).

**THOMPSON, Gary**

*Inspire the Child* (Corporate Advocates Inc.: Georgetown, 2009).

*Strategic Communication* (Corporate Advocates Inc.: Georgetown, 2011).

**THORNBURN, C.C.**

*No Messing: The Story of an Essex Man: The Autobiography of John Castelfranc Cheveley I, 1795-1870* (Crosswave Publishing: Chichester, 2012).

**THORP, Rosemary, ed.**

*Latin America in the 1930s* (Macmillan: London, 1984).

**TING-A-KEE, Scott**

*Red Hibiscus* (Way Wivz Publishing: London, 2018).

**TINKER, Hugh**

*A New System of Slavery: The Export of Indian Labour Overseas 1830-1920* (Hansib Publications: Hertfordshire, 1990).

*Separate and Unequal: India and the Indians in the British Commonwealth, 1920-1950* (C. Hurst: London, 1976).

*The Banyan Tree: Overseas Emigrants from India, Pakistan and Bangladesh* (Oxford University Press: Oxford, 1977).

**TIWARI, Maya**

*Ayurvedic: A Life of Balance – The Complete Guide to Ayurvedic Nutrition and Body Types with Recipes* (Ballantine: New York, 1994).

*The Path of Practice: A Woman's Book of Healing with Food, Breath and Sound* (Ballantine: New York, 2000).

*Women's Power to Heal Through Inner Medicine* (Ballantine: New York, 2012).

**TODD, W.D.; and D.H. Shayt**

*Stabroek Market and The Public Clocks of the Cooperative Republic of Guyana* (Smithsonian Institution: Washington, D.C., 1991).

**TOWNSEND, W.A.**

*The Postage Stamps and Postal History of British Guiana* (Royal Philatelic Society: London, 1970).

**TRACY, Frances V.**

*Wapishana-English and Engish-Wapishana Dictionary* (SIL Publications: Oklahoma City, 1972).

**TROLLOPE, A.**

*The West Indies and the Spanish Main* (n.p: London, 1867).

**TROSS, O.C.**

*Another Thought* (AuthorHouse: Bloomington, 2006).

**TROTMAN, Donald A.R.**

*Forest Leaves* (Ashgrove Publishers: Georgetown, 2010).

*Poems of My People: British Guiana* (DAR Trotman: Guyana, 1965).

*Voices of Guyana: An Anthology* (International P.E.N., Guyana Centre Publication: Georgetown, 1968).

*Waiting for Justice* (Ashgrove Publishers: Georgetown, 2008).

**TROTMAN Joyce; James Speirs**

*The Proverbs of Guyana Explained* (Bogle-L'Ouverture Press: London, 2006).

**TROTMAN, Raphael**

"Life & Death" in *Fletcher Perspectives*, Spring 2002.

*International Dispute Resolution: The Guyana/Suriname Boundary Dispute Revisited* (Fletcher School of Law and Diplomacy: Medford, 2002).

*The 'Wars of the West Indies' and the Threat of State Disintegration in Guyana, Trinidad & Tobago, and Jamaica,* Master's Thesis (Fletcher School of Law and Diplomacy, Medford, 2002).

*Parliament in the Republic of Guyana* (Isaiah Publications: Georgetown, 2014).

**_____; contr.**

*Change: Selected Writings and Speeches Of My Journey For Change* (Isaiah Publications: Georgetown, 2011).

**TROTMAN, Robert D.**

*Stories from El Dorado: Stories of Boys and Girls in Guyana* (Nazarene Publishing House: Kansas City, 1978).

**TROTZ, Alissa, ed.**

*The Point is to Change the World : Selected Writings of Andaiye* (Pluto Press : London, 2020).

**_____; and Linda Peake**

*Gender, Ethnicity and Place : Women and Identity in Guyana* (Ian Randle Publishers : Kingston, 2014).

**______; and Arif Bulkan**

*Unmasking the State: Politics, Society and Economy in Guyana, 1992-2015* (Ian Randle Publishers: Kingston: 2019).

**TROTZ, Clarence I.**

*A History of the Queen's College of Guyana (1940-2010), Vol.1 : The beginning of change and innovation at Queen's College* (QC Alumni Association: Toronto, 2023).

**_____; and A. Farly**

*CXC Physics* (Macmillan: London, 2007).

**TROTZ, Eunice**

*Evaluation of the Bachelor Education programme* (University of Guyana: Turkeyen, 1987).

**TSANG, M.C.; et al.**

*Access, Equity and Performance: Education in Barbados, Guyana, Jamaica and Trinidad and Tobago* (IADB: Washington D.C., 2002).

**TURCOTTE, Elise**

*Guyana* (Coach Books: London, 2014).

**TURNER, Harry Everard; and Terence McCann, eds.**

*The Rupununi Development Company: The Early History,* (Turner: Georgetown, 1966). Republished by the Guyana Heritage Society in 2022.

# U

**UK PARLIAMENTARY HUMAN RIGHTS GROUP**

*Something to Remember, Guyana 1980 Elections* (UK Parliament: London, 1981).

**UNITED FORCE**

*Highways to Happiness* (United Force: Georgetown, 1964).

**UNITED REPUBLICAN PARTY**

*The New Beginning* (United Republican Party: Georgetown, 1987).

**UNIVERSITY OF GUYANA**

*Contemporary Issues in Policing the Guyanese State* (University of Guyana Library: Turkeyen, 2012).

*Criminality, Human and Social Development and Global Economic Crises: Contemporary and Theoretical Concerns* (University of Guyana: Turkeyen, 2013).

*Dr Jay Sobhraj: An Impactful life shaped by Passion, Family, and Discipline* (Office of the Vice-Chancellor, University of Guyana Press (Guyanese Exemplar Series): Turkeyen, 2022).

*Dr Yesu Persaud: Iconic Leader in Business Innovation* (Office of the Vice-Chancellor, University of Guyana Press (Guyanese Exemplar Series): Turkeyen, 2021).

*Elections and Unrest In Guyana* (University of Guyana: Turkeyen, 2004).

*Exploring Values for The Remaking Of Public Institutions* (University of Guyana: Turkeyen, 2001).

*Globalisation, Ethics and Human Development* (University of Guyana: Turkeyen, 2002).

*Guyana's Public Policy and Post-Colonial Transformation in Perspective: The Politics of Radical Nationalism: The Sugar and Bauxite Industries* (University of Guyana: Turkeyen, n.d.).

*Implementing Children's Rights in Guyana: Institutional Support And Issues In The Situation of Children's Rights* (University of Guyana: Turkeyen, 2001).

*Power, Transnational Terrorism and the Diffusion Of Insecurity: Conclusions From An American Tragedy* (University of Guyana: Turkeyen, 2004).

*Public Service Management in Small States: Minority Government and Experiences in Parliamentary Accountability in Guyana* (Paper presented at International Research Society for Public Management (IRSPM) Regional Conference, UWI: Mona, 2015).

*The 'Ends' of Public Sector Reform* (Paper presented at International Research Society for Public Management (IRSPM) Regional Conference, UWI: Mona, 2015).

*The Community Development Agenda and Governance in Guyana: Missing Dimensions and Prospects* (University of Guyana Library: Turkeyen, 2012).

*The Material Culture of the Wapishana of the South Rupununi Savannahs in 1989* (Amerindian Research Unit, University of Guyana: Turkeyen, 1992).

*The Sociology of Race in Guyana 2016 and Beyond: Social Cohesion and Contending Solidarities* (University of Guyana: Turkeyen, 2016).

*University of Guyana: Heartbeat of a Nation. Proud Legacy, Bold Destiny* (University of Guyana 50th Anniversary Committee: Turkeyen, 2015).

**US ARMY COMMAND**

*US Military Interventions in the Caribbean from 1898 to 1998: Lessons for Caribbbean Leaders* (Createspace: Scotts Valley, 2014).

**US GOVERNMENT**

*Guyana and Belize - Country Studies* (Department of the Army, US Government: Washington, D.C., 2000).

*The Assassination of Representative Leo J. Ryan and the Jonestown Guyana Tragedy: Report of a Staff Investigative Group to the Committee on Foreign Affairs* (US House of Representatives, Government Printing Office: Washington, D.C., 1979).

**UNIVERSITY OF IFE,**

*And Finally They Killed Him: Speeches and Poems at a Memorial for Walter Rodney* (University of Ife: Osun, 1980).

**UWI-CARICOM**

*Caricom Single Market and Economy: Genesis and Prognosis* (Ian Randle Publishers: Kingston, 2006).

*Caricom Single Market: Challenges, Benefits, Projects and The Integrationist* (Ian Randle Publishers: Kingston, 2006).

*Confronting Challenges, Maximising Opportunities* (Ian Randle Publishers: Kingston, 2006).

# V

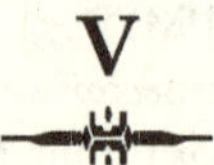

**VAN BERKEL, Adriaan**

*Travels in South America Between the Berbice and Essequibo Rivers, and in Surinam 1670-1689* (Daily Chronicle: Georgetown, 1941). [English edition translated and edited 1925 by Walter E Roth. Originally published in Dutch in Amsterdam in 1695].

**VAN HEUVEL, J.A.**

*El Dorado: Being a Narrative of the circumstances which gave rise to reports, in the sixteenth century…* (J. Winchester, New World Press: New York, 1844).

**Van SERTIMA, Ivan**

*Among the Common People of British Guiana* (C.K. Jardine: Georgetown, 1897).

*Scenes and Sketches: Georgetown 1899* (The Argosy Press: Georgetown, 1899).

*Scenes and Sketches of Demerara Life* (The Argosy Press: Georgetown, 1899).

*The Creole Tongue of British Guiana* (n.p.: New Amsterdam, 1905).

**VAN SERTIMA, Ivan** [No relation to the above. This author was born in Bartica]

*Early America Revisited* (Transaction Books: Somerset, 2002).

*Golden Age of the Moor* (Transaction Publishers: Piscataway, 1996).

*Great African Thinkers,* Vol. 1: *Cheikh Anta Deip* (Transaction Books: Somerset, 1986).

*They Came Before Columbus: The African Presence in Ancient America* (Random House: New York, 1976).

**_____, ed.**

*African Presence in Early Asia* (Transaction Books: Somerset, 1995).

*African Presence in Early Europe* (Transaction Books: Somerset, 1986).

*Black Women in Antiquity* (Transaction Books: Somerset, 1990).

*Blacks in Science: Ancient and Modern* (Transaction Books: Somerset, 1984).

*Egypt Revisited* (Transaction Books: Somerset, 1990).

*Egypt: Child of Africa* (Transaction Books: Somerset, 2002).

*Great Black Leaders: Ancient and Modern* (Transaction Books: Somerset, 1988).

*Nile Valley Civilization* (Transaction Books: Somerset, 1989).
*The Golden Age of the Moor* (Transaction Books: Somerset, 1991).
**_____; et al**
*Caribbean Writers: Critical Essays* (New Beacon: London, 1968).

**VATUK, Ved Prakash**
*British Guiana* (Monthly Review Press: New York, 1963).

**VAUGRANTE, Claire Allsopp**
*Born in Adventure: A Glimpse at the Life and Works of O'Donna Allsopp: Guyanese Landscape Artist* (C.A. Vaugrante: Georgetown, 2022).

**VEECOCK, Inge**
*Glimpses of Victorian British Guiana* (Inge Veecock: London, 2007).

**VENESS, Rev. W.T.**
*El Dorado: British Guiana as a Field for Colonisation* (Cassell, Petter, and Galpin: London, 1867).
*Ten years of Mission Life in British Guiana: An Account of the Memoirs of Rev. Thomas Youd* (SPCK: London, 1838).

**VENEZUELAN GOVERNMENT**
*Documents Relating to the Boundary Between Venezuela and British Guiana,* Vol. III (Wentworth Press: London, 2019).

**VENNER, K.D.**
*A Development Agenda for the Caribbean* (Ian Randle Publishers: Kingston, 2007).

**VERASAMI, Barbra; Dwarka Ramphal; and Kennard Ramphal**
*Imprints in Life's Journeys* (Roraima Publishers: Toronto, 2013).

**VERRILL, A. Hyatt**
*The Boy Adventurers in the Land of El Dorado* (G.P. Putnam's Sons: London, 1923).

**VESEY, Eugene**
*The Spanish Girl* (Clink Street Publishing: Manchester, 2022).

**VIRAPEN, John**
*Side Effects: Death – Confessions of a Pharma Insider* (Virtual Bookworm: College Station, 2013).
*Medicine Cult: A Prescription for Side Effects and Death* (Virtual Bookworm: College Station, 2011).

**VON HAGEN, Victor Wolfgang**
*The Gold of El Dorado: The Quest for the Gilded Man* (Granada Publishing: London, 1974).

# W

**WADE, Adrian A.**

*Lichfield 12: A Book of Short Stories and Poems* (Createspace: Scotts Valley, 2016).

**WALCOTT, Michael**

*A Cathedral Inside: Odyssey of a Guyanese Family* (Booksurge Publishing: Charleston, 2005).

**WALDRON, Victor**

*The Undiminished Link: Forty Years and Beyond* (Hansib Publications: Hertfordshire, 2007).

**WALLACE, E.**

*The British Caribbean: From the Decline of Colonialism to the End of Federation* (University of Toronto Press: Toronto, 1977).

**WALROND, Eric**

*A Cathedral Inside: Odyssey of a Guyanese Family* (Booksurge Publishing: Charleston, 2005).

**WALKER, James**

*Letters on the West Indies* (Hard Press Publishing: New York, 2020).

**WALLBRIDGE, Rev. Edwin A.**

*The Demerara Martyr: Memoirs of the Reverend John Smith, Missionary of Demerara* (Daily Chronicle: Georgetown, 1943).

[Originally published in 1848 as *Memoirs of Rev. John Smith*].

**WALMSLEY, Anne**

*Guyana Dreaming: The Art of Aubrey Williams* (Dangaroo Press: London, 1990).

*The Caribbean Artists Movement 1966-72* (New Beacon Books: London, 1994).

**_____; and Stanley Greaves**

*Art in the Caribbean* (New Beacon Books: London, 2010).

**WALNE, Peter**

*A Guide to Manuscript Resources for the History of Latin America and the Caribbean in the British Isles* (Oxford University Press: Oxford, 1973).

**WALROND, Eric**

*In Search of Asylum: The Later Writings of Eric Walrond* (University Press of America: Miami, 2017).

*Tropic Death* (Collier Books: New York, 1972).

**WALTERS, Pam** (née Winter)
*Demerara Sugar: Childhood on a Sugar Plantation* (Rock's Mills Press: Oakville, 2020).

**WANG, Sing-wu**
*The Organization of Chinese Emigration 1846-1888* (Chinese Materials Center Inc.: San Francisco, 1978).

**WAPISHANA LANGUAGE PROJECT (WLP)**
*Apostlenao Dauõaõo* (WLP: Lethem, 1986).
*Daonaioranao Madaowukaõ Azookaõo Gold Ati Naõiki and Jonah Kidoopan Dauõaõo (The Men Who Did Not Want to Worship Gold and How Jonah Was getting Away)* (WLP: Lethem, 1990).
*David Naõiki Goliath Dauõaõo* (WLP: Lethem, 1987).
*Irodaadab Naõapain Odiniz Bai* (WLP: Lethem, 1996).
*Jesus Kadishitan Dauõaõo* (WLP: Lethem, 1989).
*Jesus Shakatan Dauõaõo* (WLP: Lethem, 1988).
*Kadorari Dauõaõo* (WLP: Lethem, 1996).
*Kainaõa Idikinaudaõu Bakanuõiti Kotuõainaonao* (WLP: Lethem, 1996).
*Matada Dauõaõo* (WLP: Lethem, 1996).
*Paul Saadanii Kida Karita Thessalonica Sannao Ati* (Paul's Letters to the Thessalonians) (WLP: Lethem, 1992).
*Sakadii Kizai 37-50 Joseph Dauõaõo* (WLP: Lethem, 1989).
*Sakatadin Kizai Kiõa* (WLP: Lethem, 1980).
*Sakatdin Kizai Kiõ* (WLP: Lethem, 1976).
*Scholar's Dictionary and Grammar of the Wapishana Language* (WLP: Lethem, 2000).
*Songs in Wapishana* (WLP: Lethem, 1990).
*Taawab Naõapain Anowan Dauõaõo* (WLP: Lethem, 1996).
*Wapishana Primer* (WLP: Lethem, 1986).
*Zuna Dani Kotuõainaonao Dauõaõo* (WLP: Lethem, 1996).

**WARD, Abigail; et al**
*Representations on Slavery* (University of Manchester: Manchester, 2011).

**WARNER, G.F., ed.**
*The Voyage of Robert Dudley to the West Indies* (Hakluyt Society Publications: London, 1899).

**WARNER, Keith Q.**
*On Location : Cinema and Film in the Anglophone Caribbean* (Macmillan: London, 2000).

**WARNER-LEWIS, Maureen**
*Central Africa in the Caribbean; Transending Time, Transforming Cultures* (UWI Press: Mona, 2003).

**WARREN, Adrian**
*Roraima: Report of the 1971 British Expedition to Mount Roraima in Guyana, South America* (Seacourt Press: London, 1971).

**WATERTON, Charles**
*Wanderings in South America* (J. Mawman: London, 1825).
*Wanderings in South America, the North-west of the United States and the Antilles in the Years 1812, 1816, 1820 and 1824.* (Hutchinson & Co.: London, 1906). Reprint. (Sturgis & Walton: New York, 1925).

**WATKINS, Graham; with Pete Oxford and Reneé Bish,**
*Rupununi: Rediscovering a Lost World* (Earth in Focus: Arlington, 2011).

**WATSON, Dennis; and Christine Craig, eds.**
*Guyana at the Crossroads; North-South Centre* (Transaction Publishers: New Brunswick-New Jersey, 1992).

**WATSON, Ivan**
*To Gain a Land: A Collection of Poems* (Ivan Watson: Georgetown, 1972).

**WATSON, J.A.**
*A Hundred Years of Sugar Refining: The Story of Love Lane Refinery 1872-1972* (Tate & Lyle: Liverpool, 1973).

**WATSON, Myrtle**
*Kite Flying in the Village: A Guyanese Girl`s Story* (AuthorHouse: Bloomington, 2011).

**WATTS, David**
*The West Indies: Patterns of Development, Culture and Environmental Change Since 1492* (Cambridge University Press: Cambridge, 1987).

**WAUGH, Alec**
*A Family of Islands: A History of the West Indies* (Weidenfeld and Nicolson: London, 1964).

**WAUGH, Evelyn**
*Ninety-Two Days: The Account of a Tropical Journey Through British Guiana and Part of Brazil* (Methuen: London, 1933).

**WAVELL, Stewart; Audrey Butt; and Nina Epton, eds.**
*Trances* (George Allen and Unwin: London, 1966).

**WEBBER, A.R.F.**

*A Centenary History and Handbook of British Guiana* (The Argosy Co. Ltd: Georgetown, 1931).

*An Innocent Abroad* (n.p.: n.p., n.d.).

*British Guiana, the Essequibo and Potaro Rivers with an Account of a Visit to the Recently-Discovered Kaiteur Falls… and Descriptive Notes on the Geology of Guiana* (Edward Stanford: London, 1873).

*Glints from an Anvil* (n.p.: n.p., n.d.).

*Life in New York* (n.p.: n.p., n.d.).

*Those that be in bondage: A Tale of Indian Indentures and Sunlit Western Waters* (Daily Chronicle: Georgetown, 1917). Reprint. (Calaloux Publications: Wellesley, 1988).

**WEBBER, E.J.**

*British Guiana, the Essequibo and Potaro Rivers with an Account of a visit to the recently-discovered Kaieteur Fall* (Stanford: London, 1873).

**WELSH, Sarah Lawson; and Alison Donnell, eds.**

*The Routledge Reader in Caribbean Literature* (Routledge: Oxford, 1996).

**WESTALL, Claire**

*The Rites of Cricket and Caribbean Literature* (Springer International Publishing: New York, 2021).

**WESTMAAS, Nigel**

*A Political Glossary of Guyana* (Edwin Mellen Press: New York, 2021).

"A Martin Carter Prose Bibliography," in *Martin Carter: Selected Poems* (Red Thread Women's Press: Georgetown, 1997).

"An Organic Pan-Africanist: Eusi Kwayana, Guyana and Global Pan-Africanism" in *Black Power in the Post-Independence Anglophone Caribbean* (University Press of Florida: Miami, 2014).

"Firebrands, Trade Unionists and Marxists: The Shadow of the Russian Revolution, the Colonial state, and the Emergence of the Left in Guyana, 1917- 1956," in *The Red and the Black: The Russian Revolution and the Black Atlantic.* Vol 1 (Manchester University Press: Manchester, 2021).

"Musings on Walter Rodney, the Black Power Movement and Race and Class in Guyana," in *The Fire that Time: Transnational Black Radicalism and the Sir George Williams Occupation* (Black Rose Books: Montreal, 2022).

"The Slave Woman: Her Condition and Beliefs," _in *An Introductory Reader for Women's Studies in Guyana* (Red Thread Women's Press: Georgetown, 2000).

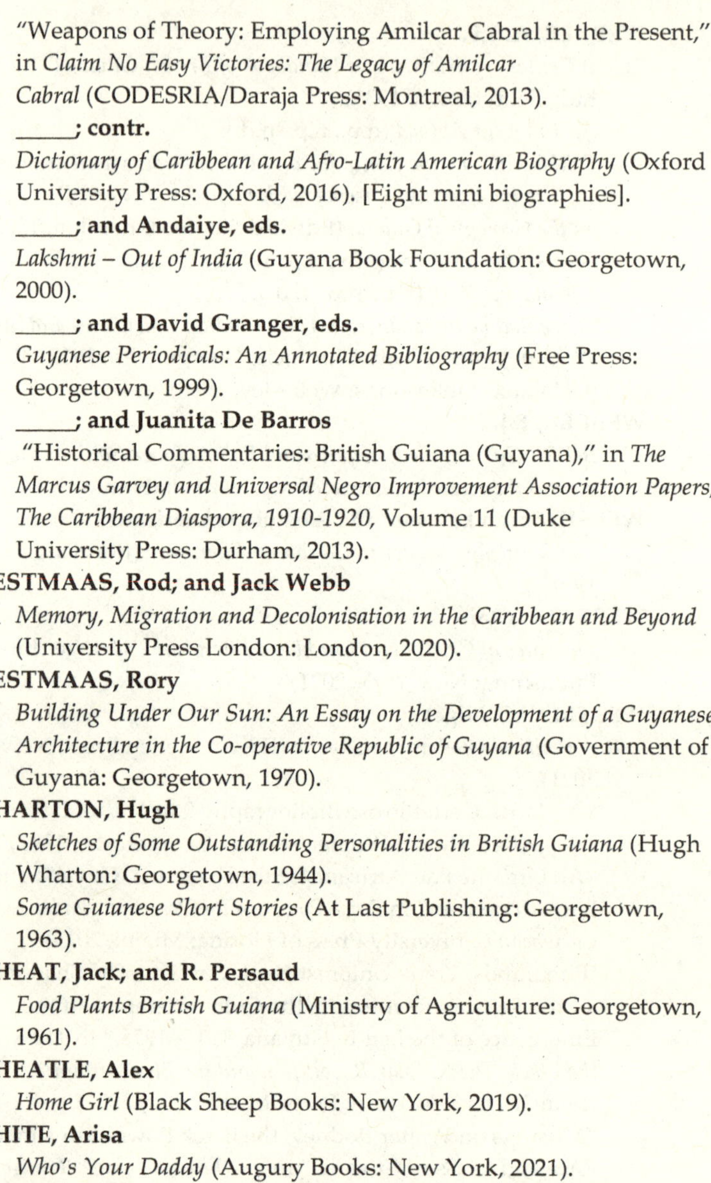

"Weapons of Theory: Employing Amilcar Cabral in the Present," in *Claim No Easy Victories: The Legacy of Amilcar Cabral* (CODESRIA/Daraja Press: Montreal, 2013).

**_____; contr.**

*Dictionary of Caribbean and Afro-Latin American Biography* (Oxford University Press: Oxford, 2016). [Eight mini biographies].

**_____; and Andaiye, eds.**

*Lakshmi – Out of India* (Guyana Book Foundation: Georgetown, 2000).

**_____; and David Granger, eds.**

*Guyanese Periodicals: An Annotated Bibliography* (Free Press: Georgetown, 1999).

**_____; and Juanita De Barros**

"Historical Commentaries: British Guiana (Guyana)," in *The Marcus Garvey and Universal Negro Improvement Association Papers, The Caribbean Diaspora, 1910-1920,* Volume 11 (Duke University Press: Durham, 2013).

**WESTMAAS, Rod; and Jack Webb**

*Memory, Migration and Decolonisation in the Caribbean and Beyond* (University Press London: London, 2020).

**WESTMAAS, Rory**

*Building Under Our Sun: An Essay on the Development of a Guyanese Architecture in the Co-operative Republic of Guyana* (Government of Guyana: Georgetown, 1970).

**WHARTON, Hugh**

*Sketches of Some Outstanding Personalities in British Guiana* (Hugh Wharton: Georgetown, 1944).

*Some Guianese Short Stories* (At Last Publishing: Georgetown, 1963).

**WHEAT, Jack; and R. Persaud**

*Food Plants British Guiana* (Ministry of Agriculture: Georgetown, 1961).

**WHEATLE, Alex**

*Home Girl* (Black Sheep Books: New York, 2019).

**WHITE, Arisa**

*Who's Your Daddy* (Augury Books: New York, 2021).

**WHITE, R.J.**

*Six years in Hammock Land. A Historical Sketch of the Lutheran Church in British Guiana. With Observation and Experiences* (United Lutheran: Philadelphia, 1922).

**WHITE, Rev. Walter G., trans.**

*At Home with the Makuchis* (Harrison: Ipswich, 1922).

*Wakumaim Johanes Thawere* (British and Foreign Bible Society: London, 1923). [St John's Gospel in Makuchi].

**WHITFIELD, R.**

*Hints on Villages, Villagers; on Drainage, Cultivation, Roads, Taxation* (n.p.: Georgetown, 1873).

**WHITEHEAD, Neil**

*Beyond the Visible and the Material: The Amerindianization of Society in the Work of Peter Riviere* (Oxford University Press: Oxford, 2001).

*Dark Shamans: Kanaima and the Poetics of Violent Death* (Duke University Press: Durham, 2002).

*Histories and Historicities of Amazonia* (University of Nebraska Press: Omaha, 2003).

*Lords of the Tiger Spirit: A History of the Caribs in Colonial Venezuela, 1498-1820* (Foris: Dordrecht, 1988).

**_____, ed.**

*The Discoverie of the Large, Rich, and Beauwtiful Empyre of Guiana (With a Relation of the Great and Golden Citie of Manoa (Which the Spanyards call El Dorado) and of the Provinces of Emeria, Arromaia, Amapaia, and Other Countries, with Their Riulers, Adjoyning* (University of Oklahoma Press: Oklahoma City, 1998).

*The Patamona of Paramakatoi and the Yawong Valley: An Oral History* (Walter Roth Museum of Anthropology: Georgetown, 1996).

**_____; and Stephanie W. Alen**

*Anthropologies of Guayana: Cultural Spaces in Northeastern Amazonia* (University of Arizona Press: Tucson, 2009).

**_____; and Peter Hulme, eds.**

*Wild Majesty: Encounters with Caribs from Columbus to the Present Day: An Anthology* (Oxford University Press: Oxford, 1992).

**WHITFIELD, D.**

*Caribbean Breeze* (Ian Randle Publishers: Kingston, 1993).

**WHITNEY, Alex**

*Voices in the Wind: Central and South American Legends* (D. McKay Co.: New York, 1976).

**WICKENDEN, J.**

*Beyond the High Savannahs* (Longmans: London, 1956).

**WIGHT, Martin**

*The Development of the Legislative Council 1606-1945* (n.p.: London, 1946).

**WILBERT, J.**

*Folk Literature of the Warrao Indians* (University of California: Los Angeles, 1970).

**WILL, H.A.**

*Constitutional Change in the BWI 1880-1903 with special reference to Jamaica, British Guiana, and Trinidad* (Clarendon: Oxford, 1971).

**WILLIAM, Evelyn A.**

*The Art of Denis Williams* (Peepal Tree Press: Leeds, 2012).

**WILLIAMS, Brackette F.**

*Dutchman Ghosts and the History Mystery. Virtual Colonizer and Colonised Interpretations of the 1763 Slave Rebellion* (Academic Journal Offprint: Durham., 1990).

*Stains on my name, war in my veins: Guyana and the politics of cultural struggle* (Duke University Press: Durham, 1991).

**WILLIAMS, Charlotte**

*Sugar & Slate* (Planet Press: Bangor, 2002).

*Denis Williams: A Life in Works: New and Collected Essays* (Rodopi: Amsterdam, 2013).

**WILLIAMS, Denis**

*Ancient Guyana* (Department of Culture: Georgetown, 1985).

*Contemporary Art in Guyana* (Bovell Printery: Georgetown, 1976).

*Giglioli in Guyana 1922-72* (National History and Arts Council: Georgetown, 1973).

*Guyana: Colonial Art in Revolutionary Art, 1966-1976* (Guyana National Service: Georgetown, 1976).

*Icon and Image: A study of sacred and secular forms of African classical art* (Allen Lane: London, 1974).

*Other Leopards* (New Authors Limited: London, 1963).

*Pages in Guyanese Pre-History* (Walter Roth Museum of Anthropology: Georgetown, 1995).

*Prehistoric Guiana,* ed. Mark Plew (Ian Randle Publishers; Kingston, 2004).

*The Archaic of North-Western Guyana* (University of Guyana History Society: Turkeyen, 1969).

*The Other Temptation: A. Novel* (Calder and Boyars: London, 1968).

*The Third Temptation: A Novel* (Calder and Boyars: London, 1968). Reprinted by Peepal Tree: Leeds, 2010).

**WILLIAMS, E.; et al**

*Geological Survey of Guyana* (Geological Surveys Department: Georgetown, 1967).

*Records* (E. Williams: Georgetown, 1967).

**WILLIAMS, Emily**

*Poetic Negotiations of Identity in the Works of Kamau Braithwaite, Wilson Harris, Olive Senior, David Dabydeen* (Edwin Muller Press: New York, 2000).

**WILLIAMS, Eric**

*Britain and the West Indies* (Longmans: London, 1969).

*Capitalism and Slavery* (University of North Carolina Press: Chapel Hill, 1994).

*Documents of West Indian History 1492-1655* (PNM Pub Co: Port-of-Spain, 1963).

*Documents on British West Indian History 1807-33* (PNM Pub Co: Port-of-Spain, 1952).

**WILLIAMS, Evelyn A.**

*The Art of Denis Williams* (Peepal Tree Press; Leeds, 2012).

**WILLIAMS, Rev. James**

*Grammar Notes & Vocabulary of the Language of the Makuchi Indians of Guiana* (St. Gabriel-Mödling: Vienna, 1932).

**WILLIAMS, Milton Vishno**

*Pray for Rain* (M. Williams: Georgetown, 1958).

*Sources of Agony* (M. Williams: Georgetown, 1979).

*Years of fighting Exile – Collected Poems 1955-85* (Peepal Tree Press, Leeds, 1986).

**WILLIAMS, Mona**

*Bishops: My Turbulent Colonial Youth* (Mallinson Rendel: Wellington, 1995).

**WILLIAMS, N.D.**

*Ikael Torass* (n.p: n.p., 1976).

*Julie Mango* (Peepal Tree Press: Leeds, 2003).

*Prash and Ras* (Peepal Tree Press: Leeds, 1997).

*The Crying of Rainbirds* (Peepal Tree Press: Leeds, 1991).

*The Friendship Shoes* (Xilibris Corp.: Denver, 2006).

*The Silence of Islands* (Peepal Tree Press: Leeds, 1994).

*When the Mark Buss* (Peepal Tree Press: Leeds, 2001).

**WILLIAMS, Oneeka**

*5 Habits of Positivity – To Cope, Hope, and Be Well in Tough Times* (Mascot Books: Hernden, 2021).

*Dr. Dee Dee Dynamo's Mars to Pluto* (Mascot Books: Hernden, 2013).

*Dr. Dee Dee Dynamo Beemee Breakthru* (Mascot Books: Hernden, 2017).

*Dr. Dee Dee Dynamo's Saturn Superman* (Mascot Books:

Hernden, 2015).

*Dr. Dee Dee Dynamo's Mission to Pluto* (Mascot Books: Herndon, 2013).

**WILLIAMS, P.E.; J.T. Parry; and M.J. Eden**

*Land Use, Land Degradation and Land Management in Guyana* (Commonwealth Geographical Bureau: London, 1997).

**WILLIAMS, W.**

*We Live in Guyana* (Bucks: London, 1986).

**WILLIAMSON, James A.**

*English Colonies in Guiana and on the Amazon 1604-1668* (The Clarendon Press: Oxford, 1923).

**WILLS, Fred**

*A Time for Action: To Create a New International System* (Ministry of Foreign Affairs: Georgetown, 1976).

**WILSON, Donald G., ed.**

*New Ships. An Anthology of West Indian Poems for Secondary Schools* (Savacou Publications: Georgetown, 1971).

**WILSON, Eward**

*Eusi Kwayana* (Amazon Books: Bolton, 2022).

**WILSON, Fr. J.B.**

*History of the British Guiana Teachers' Association* (n.p.: Georgetown, 1944).

**WILSON, Gar**

*Terror in Guyana - Phoenix Force No. 47* (Harlequin Books: New York, 1990).

**WILSON, Harold**

*A Personal Record: The Labour Government, 1964-1970* (Little Brown: Boston, 1971).

**WILSON-TAGOE, Nana**

*Historical Thought and Literary Representation in West Indian Literature* (University Press of Florida: Miami, 1998).

**WINTER, Alexander**

*Indian Pictured Rocks in British Guiana* (Judd and Co.: London, 1887).

*Indian Pictured Rocks of Guiana* (Funds of the Potaro Mission: New Amsterdam, 1881).

**WINTER, Phil H.**

*Earth Has No Place* (A Stockwell, Ilfracombe: Devon, 1970).

**WISE, David; and Thomas B. Ross**

*The Invisible Government* (Random House: New York, 1964).

**WISHART-EUDOXIE, Ann**

*A Guyanese Story – Steps in My Journey* (Guardian Books: Toronto, 2003).

**WISHART, Jennifer**

*The Prehistoric Arawak of Guyana* (Walter Roth Museum of Anthropology: Georgetown, 1995).

*The Prehistoric Warau of Guyana* (Walter Roth Museum of Anthropology: Georgetown, 1994).

**WOMEN'S STUDIES GROUP, University of Guyana**

*Women in Guyana: Facts and Figures* (Caricom: Georgetown, 1988).

**WONG, Dwayne (Omowale)**

*Black Man of Guyana: The Political Biography of Eusi Kwayana* (Createspace: Scotts Valley, 2020).

*In Search of African History and Liberation* (Createspace: Scotts Valley, 2012).

**WOOD, C.**

*Safari South America: The Saki Monkeys of Guyana and Other Wildlife* (Taplinger: New York, 1973).

**WOODEN, Kenneth, ed.**

*The Children of Jonestown* (McGraw-Hill: New York, 1980).

**WOODS, C.A.**

*Biography of the West Indies: Past, Present and Future* (Sandhill Cave Press, Inc.: Gainesville, 1989).

**WOOLFORD, Hazel M.**

*A Guide to the Sources on the Public Life of H.D. Hoyte* (Guyana Institute of Historical Research: Georgetown, 2001).

*Guyanese Women Leaders* (Guyana Institute of Historical Research: Georgetown, 2015).

*Kids History African-Guyanese Colouring Book of Guyana* (Guyana Institute of Historical Research: Georgetown, 2017).

*Kids History Illustrated of First Ladies of Guyana* (Guyana Institute of Historical Research: Georgetown, 2017).

*Kids History Illustrated of Presidents of Guyana* (Guyana Institute of Historical Research: Georgetown, 2021).

*Kids History Illustrated of Prime Ministers of Guyana* (Guyana Institute of Historical Research: Georgetown, 2015).

**WRAY, Godfrey**

*Beyond Revenge* (Peepal Tree Press: Leeds, 2008).

**WRIGHT, Mark**

*Healing Our Community One Recipe at a Time: A Prescription for Health Healing and Longevity* (Amazon Books: 2020).

**WYMAN, Russell A**

*Recollections 2: The Untravelled World* (Nine Pines Publishing: Mantivck, 1994).

# Y

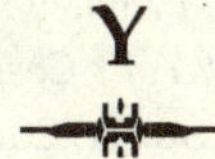

**YANSEN, C.A.**

*Random Remarks on Creolese* (CA Yansen: London, 1979).

**YARDAN, S.**

*The Listening of Eyes* (National History and Arts Council: Georgetown, 1976).

**YASSIN, Mohamed Fazloor**

*Black and Muddy Water: Two Short Stories* (M.F. Yassin: Georgetown, 1992).

*Burnt Sugar Cane Remarks* (M.F. Yassin: Georgetown, 1992).

*Lost on Iguana Island* (a novella) (M.F. Yassin: Georgetown, 1993).

**YAW, Fitzgerald, contr.**

*On Black Revolutionaries: In Tribute to a Scholar: Appreciating C.L.R. James* (University of the West Indies: Mona, 1990).

**YDE, Jens**

*Material Culture of the Waiwái* (National Museum of Denmark: Copenhagen, 1965).

**YEE, Min S.; et al**

*In My father's House: The Story of the Layton Family and Jim Jones* (Berkeley Books: New York, 1982).

**YHIP, Terence M.**

*From Rags to Riches: Is Guyana Ready for the Oil Bonanza* (Amazon Books: Bolton, 2021).

*The Caribbean Economies at a Crossroads – Tough Choices and Practical Solutions* (Palgrave-Macmillan: London, 2023).

**_____; and Bijan M.D. Alagheband**

*The Practice of Lending: A Guide to Credit Analysis and Credit Risk* (Amazon Books: Bolton, 2020).

**YOUNG, Allan**

*The Approaches to Local Self-Government in British Guiana* (Longmans, Green & Co. Ltd.: London, 1958).

**YOUNG, M.; and P. Wilmott**

*Family and Kinship in East London* (Routledge and Kegan Paul: London, 1957).

**YOUNG, Mark Geoffrey**

*The Best Ever Book of Guyanese Jokes: Lots and Lots of Jokes Specially repurposed For You-Know-Who* (Createspace: Vancouver, 2012).

*The Best Ever Book on Money Saving Tips for Guyanese Citizens: Creative ways to Cut Your Costs, Conserve Capital and Keep Your Cash* (Createspace: Vancouver, 2013).

**_____; and Dick Debartolo**

*The Best Ever Guide to Demotivation for Guyanese: How To Dismay, Dishearten, and Disappoint Friends, Family and Staff* (Createspace: Vancouver, 2013).

**YOUNG, Matthew French**

*Guyana: The Lost El Dorado; My Fifty Years in the Guyanese Wilds* (Peepal Tree Press: Leeds, 1998).

# Z

**ZAHL, Paul A.**

*To the Lost World* (Travel Book Club: London, 1948).

**ZAMBRANO VELASCO, José Alberto**

*The Essequibo: Our Historic Claim* (Ministry of Foreign Relations: Caracas, 1982).

**ZHENG, Alan, trans.**

*The Chinese in British Guiana,* abridged ed. in Mandarin (Caribbean Press: Georgetown, 2013).

**ZHINGOORA BOOKS**

*Guyana* (Createspace: Scotts Valley, 2012).

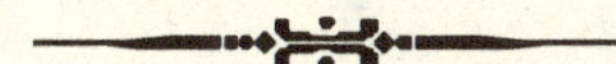

## INDEX BY TITLE

# APPENDIX A

## CLASSIFICATION BY CATEGORY

### AFRO-GUYANESE

*A Documentary History of Slavery…*
*A Choice of Straws…*
*A Kind of Homecoming*
*A Man Called Garvey…*
*Africa Before Chattel…*
*Africa's Challenge To…*
*African American Contributions…*
*African Diasporic…*
*African Extremism…*
*African Literature*
*African Saga in Drama*
*African Slavery in Latin America…*
*African Voices of the Atlantic Trade…*
*After Africa…*
*Arise Africa…*
*Betty Shabbazz…*
*Black America: The Street and Campus…*
*Black Britannia…*
*Black Edwardians…*
*Black Oxford…*
*Black Routes: Legacy of African Diaspora…*
*Blackness & the Dreaming Soil…*
*Berbician Griot…*
*Bibliography of the Africans in Guyana…*
*Black Guyanese Immigrant…*
*Black Talk…*
*Black Teacher…*
*Black Water People…*
*Black-Water People: About the Allicocks…*
*Black Watuh Tales*
*Brethren of the Bush…*
*Buxton Rising…*
*Claim No Easy Victories…*
*Comfa Religion and Creole Language*
*Crime Without Punishment…*
*Defining Moments*
*Doctors and Slaves…*
*Domestic Violence…*
*Don't Give Up on Us*
*Elijah…*
*Emancipation…*
*Encounters…*
*Encyclopedia of Slave Resistance and Rebellion*
*Freedom Won…*
*From Slavery to the Present…*
*Gang Gang*
*Ghosts in our blood…*
*Global Circuits…*
*Guyana Dreaming: The Art of Aubrey Williams…*
*Guyanese Komfa…*
*Hearing Slaves Speak…*
*Honorary White…*
*International Afro Mass Media…*

*Folk Tales and Legends of Some Guyana...*
*Fr Cary-Elwes S.J. and the Alleluia Indians*
*Guiana Legends*
*Guyana Legends: Folktales of Indigeneous...*
*Handbook of South American Indians*
*Histories & Historicities of Amazonia…*
*Image of the New World*
*Indian Missions in Guiana*
*Indian Tribes of Guiana: Legends and Myths*
*Indios de Roraima*
*Legends and Myths of the Aboriginal…*
*Lords of the Tiger Spirit: A History of the Caribs*
*Makushi Lifestyles and Biodiversity Use*
*Material Culture of the Waiwai*
*Mission Work Among the Indian Tribes*
*Native Peoples of South America*
*Of Passionate Curves…*
*Paddles over the Kamarang: Riptide…*
*Robberroadsters…*
*ShadowWalkers…*
*The Story of the Davis Indians*
*Red Gold: Conquest of the Brazilian Indians*
*Return of the Arawak*
*Rural and Interior Development Policy...*
*Sketches of Amerindian Tribes*
*The Akawaio, the Upper Mazaruni*
*The Amerindian Way…*
*The Amerindians and the Europeans*
*The Amerindians of British Guiana 1803-1873*
*The Apple Experiment…*
*The Barama River Caribs*
*The Central Arawaks*
*The Central Caribs*
*The Flying Priest: A Journal*
*The Forgotten Tribes of Guyana*
*The Gentle People*
*The Indian Tribes of Guiana: Their Condition…*
*The Indigenous Condition in Guyana*
*The Indigenous People of Guyana*
*The Life Cycle…*
*The Lowland Indians of Amazonia*
*The Material Culture of the Wapishana*
*The Patamona of Paramakatoi*
*The Populations of Guyanese Amerindian...*
*The Powerless People: An Analysis...*
*The Rupununi Savannas: A Visual Journey*
*The Situation of the Indian in South America*
*The Survival of Indigenous…*
*The Wings of Iere: Amerindian Legends*

*Thinking About Amerindians*
*Twice Upon a Time…*
*Twice Upon 2*
*Voices in the Wind: Central and South...*
*Wai Wai: Religion and Society...*
*Wai Wai: Through the Forests North...*
*Wapishan Ethnoecology…*
*Waramadong: A case Study for Amerindian*
*William Hilhouse's Indian Notices 1825*

**AMERINDIAN LANGUAGES**

*A Brief Introduction of Some Aspects of the…*
*A Short Dictionary f the Warau Language*
*A Short Grammar and Dictionary*
*Aknoro Kaan Nakihtotho*
*An Arawak-English Dictionary*
*Apostlenao Dauõaão*
*Comparative Vocabulary of Eighteen Languages*
*Daonaioranao Madaowukaõ Azookaão Gold*
*David Naõiki Goliath Dauõaão*
*Grammar Notes & Vocabulary of the…*
*Handbook of Amazonian Languages*
*Irodaadab Naõapain Odiniz Bai*
*Iwokramî pantoni: Stories about Iwokrama*
*Jesus Kadishitan Dauõaão…*
*Jesus Shakatan Dauõaão…*
*Kabelhechino…*
*Kadorari Dauõaão…*
*Kainaõa Idikinaudaõu Bakanuõiti…*
*Languages of the Guianas*
*Matada Dauõaão…*
*Paul Saadanii Kida Karita Thessalonica…*
*Sakadii Kizai 37-50 Joseph Dauõaão…*
*Sakatadin Kizai Kiõa…*
*Sakatdin Kizai Kiõ…*
*Scholar's Dictionary and Grammar of…*
*Songs in Wapishana…*
*Taawab Naõapain Anowan Dauõaão…*
*The Arawack Language of Guiana…*
*The Arawak Language in Guyanese Culture*
*The Arawak Language of Guiana*
*Twenty-eight Lessons in Loko (Arawak)*
*Wakumaim Johanes Thawere…*
*Wapishana Primer…*
*Wapishana-English Dictionary*
*Wild Majesty…*
*Zuna Dani Kotuõainaonao Dauõaão…*

**ARCHAEOLOGY**

*African Presence in Early Asia*
*African Presence in Early Europe*
*Ancient Guyana*
*Archaeological Investigations*
*Egypt: Child of Africa*
*Excavations in the Cuenca Region*
*Indian Pictures Rocks in British Guiana*
*Indian Pictures Rocks of Guiana*
*Nile Valley Civilization*
*Pages in Guyanese Pre-History*
*Prehistoric America*
*Prehistoric Guiana*
*The Prehistoric Arawak of Guyana*
*The Prehistoric Warau of Guyana*
*They Came Before Columbus*

**ARCHITECTURE**

*Building Under the Sun…*
*City of Wooden Houses…*
*Historical and Present Day Views of…*

**ARTS AND THEATRE**

*A History of Theatre in Guyana*
*Art in the Caribbean*
*Aubrey Williams…*
*Contemporary Art in Guyana…*
*Guyana Dreaming:Art of Aubrey Williams*
*Guyana: Colonial Art…*
*Icon and Image: A Study of…*
*Poulbet of Montmartre*
*Sculptures, Paintings and Drawings*
*The Art of Denis Williams*
*The Arts of Guyana…*
*The Arts of Stanley Greaves…*
*Theatre in the Caribbean…,*

**BIBLIOGRAPHY**

*A Bibliography of Guyana Anthropology*
*A Bibliography of Neo-*
*A-Z of Guyanese Words…*
*A.J. Seymour: A Bibliography*
*African Literature*
*A Passion to Succeed*
*A Select Bibliography of the Works of Guyanese*
*Bauxite, Sugar, and Mud*
*Bibliography of British Guiana*
*Bibliography of Guyana and Guyanese Writers*
*Bibliography of Guyanese Plays…*
*Bibliography of Literature from Guyana*
*Bibliography of the Mazaruni Area, Guyana*
*Bibliography of the West Indies...*
*Bibliography of West Indian Church History*
*Bibliography of Women Writers…*

*Chronology and Bibliography of Guiana*
*Critical Writings on Commonwealth Literatures*
*Critics on West Indian Literature*
*East Indians in the Caribbean: A Bibliography*
*Dictionary of Caribbean…*
*Forests and Forestry…*
*Guide to the published works…*
*Guyana Periodicals*
*Guyana: A Bibliography…*
*Guyanese Literature*
*Guyanese Writers*
*Independence Ten…*
*National Bibliography of Guyana…*
*Race and Ethnic…*
*Sir Walter Ralegh: An Annotated Bibliography*
*The 3rd World: Colombia, Venezuela, Guyana*
*The Proverbs of British Guiana*
*V.S. Naipaul's Empty Chapel*
*Wilson Harris*
*Women in the Caribbean…*

**BIOGRAPHY AND AUTOBIOGRAPHY**

*A Biographical Overview…*
*A Dynasty Created*
*A Guyanese Alphabet*
*A Guyanese Story – Steps in My Journey*
*A Life in Guyana, Vol. 1*
*A Life in Guyana, Vol. 2*
*A Life of Blessings…*
*A Passion to Succeed*
*A Patriot of Paternalism*
*A Proud Product…*
*A snake in my shoe…*
*A woman of her time*
*AJS at 70…*
*An Accidental Life…*
*An Arawak Biography*
*Arthur Small…*
*Ashton Chase: The Bengal Tiger…*
*Autobiography: AJ Seymour*
*Beyond The Breaks…*
*Bharrat Jagdeo*
*Biographical Dictionary of Guyana*
*Biographical Portraits*
*Biography of the West Indies*
*Blacks in Science*
*Born Between the Lines…*
*Born in Adventure…*
*C.D. Christie's Autobiography – My Life*
*Canadians of Guyanese Descent*
*Caribbean Publishing in Britain: Arif Ali*
*Caryl's Closet…*
*David Leslie Lorain Melville…*
*Dr. Jay Sobhraj*
*Dr. Yesu Persaud…*
*Episodes of My Life…*
*Guyanese Achievers USA & Canada*
*Charles Waterton, 1782-1865*
*Cheddi Jagan – My Fight for Guyana's Freedom*
*Critchlow: His Main…*
*Denis Williams: A Life in Works...*

*Dictionary of Guyanese Biography*
*Dictionary of Latin American…*
*Doodnauth and Charran…*
*Edgar Mittelholzer: The Man and His Works*
*Eusi Kwayana…*
*Footprints of a farmer…*
*Frank Worrell…*
*From Errand Boy…*
*From Guyana to America…*
*From Legall to Legal…*
*Fulfilling of a Vision…*
*Giglioni in Guyana 1922-72*
*Grass Roots of Guyana*
*Great African Thinkers*
*Great Black Leaders*
*Guyana Man…*
*Guyanese People by Occupation*
*Guyanese Politicians*
*Heroes…*
*Heroes of Our Nation…*
*Historical and Biographical Essays…*
*Judge Mohamed Shahabuddeen…*
*JW Chinapen, Educator and Poet*
*Kayman Sankar: The Ultimate Rice Magnate*
*Legends, Lines, Love…*
*Life and Times of Dr. Cheddi Bharrat Jagan*
*Life and Works of Bill Rogers*
*Life of Gladstone…*
*Living My Dreams…*
*Marcus Garvey…*
*Mama Lou Tales…*
*Memoirs of a Governor: A Man for the People*
*Mittelholzer, Edgar Austin*
*My Brother Mac*
*My Father's House*
*My Tenure as Guyana's…*
*No Messing: The Story of an Essex Man…*
*Norman Cameron…*
*Old Square-Toes*
*Overcoming the Odds: Reds*
*Passaic: The True Story…*
*Perreira's Bio...*
*Path to Freedom: My Story of Perseverance*
*Paul Robeson*
*Peasant Farmer…*
*Poetic Negotiations…*
*Portrait of a Cold Warrior*
*Post Colonialism…*
*Quintin Hogg: A Biography*
*Reaching for the Stars…*
*Recycling A Son…*
*Rise of the Phoenix*
*Robert Corbin*
*Rupununi Mission: The Story of Fr. Cuthbert…*
*Sir Lionel*
*Sketches of Some…*
*Smith of Demerara*
*Some Black Women*
*Son of Guyana*
*Speaking My Soul…*
*Sugar in the Blood…*
*The Achievements of Stephen Campbell*
*The Apostle of the Indians of Guiana*
*The Art of David Dabydeen*
*The Demerara Martyr: Memoirs*

*Our Native Orchids…*
*Plant Diversity of the Iwokrama Forest*
*Preliminary Checklist of the Plants of…*
*Principal Timbers of British Guiana*
*Smithsonian Plant Collections, Guyana*
*The Ferns and Fern Allies…*
*The New Conquistadors…*
*Trees of Guyana: A Seedling Identification Guide*
*Wild Flowers of Georgetown…*

**BUSINESS and ACCOUNTING**

*A Definitional Study…*
*A Golden Eagle: How I Soared to Millions...*
*A Hundred Years of Sugar Refining*
*A Passion to Succeed*
*A Practical Guide to Auditing...*
*Accountants & Related Professionals*
*Accounting, Auditing, Finance, & Related …*
*An Introduction to Computers and the Internet*
*An Introduction to Intellectual Property*
*An Introduction to Windows*
*Banking and the Foreign…*
*Becoming a CEO…*
*Becoming a good candidate…*
*British African Entrepreneurship…*
*British Caribbean Enterprises…*
*Budgeting and Performance…*
*CEO in Action…*
*Cutting Edge Internal Auditing…*
*Dictionary of Risk, Governance, & Control…*
*Directory of Global Professional Accounting...*
*Directory of International Professional*
*Effective and Efficient Admin. Assts….*
*Embracing Corporate Governance...*
*Employees are important…*
*Enjoying work…*
*Financial Management for…*
*Fraud – the Company Law background*
*Fundamentals of Financial Management*
*Gold Rush…*
*Growing an organization…*
*Guyana Business Law…*
*Guyana Information Strategy…*
*Guyana: Doing Business*
*Handbook of Global Professional Accounting*
*Handbook of Global Professional Business*
*Health, Wealth Happiness*
*Information Systems…*
*International Tax Competition*
*Leading an Organization…*

**CARIBBEAN ISSUES**

*The Commonwealth Caribbean*
*The Conquest of Grenada…*
*The Contemporary Caribbean…*
*The Culture of Gender…*
*The Dynamics of West Indian*
*The Evolution of the Peasantry in the...*
*The Guyana Experience…*
*The Last Caribbean Frontier…*
*The Making Of The Caribbean...*
*Sir Arthur Lewis Nobel Laureate: A Biog...*
*The New Caribbean*
*The New Cuban Presence in the Caribbean*
*The Political Economy…*
*The Political History of the Caribbean*
*The Political History of Caricom…*
*The Politics of Integration…*
*The Politics of Labour…*
*The Politics of the Caribbean…*
*The Practice of Public Relations…*
*The Quest for Security…*
*The Red Book of the West Indies*
*The Routledge Reader…*
*The USA in South America*
*The Wars of the West Indies…*
*The West Indies with British Guiana and...*
*Understanding the Contemporary Caribbean…*
*West Indian Nationhood…*
*Wholeness and Home in…*

**CATTLE RANCHING**

*Encyclopaedia of the Guyanese Amerindians…*
*History of the Rupununi Development Company…*
*Jungle Cowboy…*
*Raiders of the Rupununi*
*The Rupununi: A Visual Journey…*
*The Rupununi Development Company….*

**CHEDDI JAGAN**

*Address by Cheddi Jagan…*
*British Guiana: A Challenge to Labour*
*Caribbean Revolution*
*Cheddi Jagan: National Assembly Speeches…*
*Cheddi Jagan – My Fight For Guyana's Freedom*
*Cheddi Jagan and the Cold War…*
*Cheddi Jagan and the Politics of Power – British Guiana's Struggle for Independence*
*Cheddi Jagan: Reflections on My Father*
*Cheddi Jagan: Selected Correspondences*
*Cheddi Jagan: Selected Speeches*
*Communication, Power and Change...*
*Forbidden Freedom*

**CHILDREN**

*Laura in the Linchkit…*
*Lia and Ellie…*
*Lend me your wings*
*Letters for Lettie, and Other Stories*
*Life Doesn't Frighten Me at All*
*Limbo Dancer in Dark Glasses*
*Livingroom*
*Long Live Brer Anansi…*
*Loveliness for a Goat-Born Lady*
*Myrtle Turtle…*
*Oreo: The Token Black Kid…*
*Man to Pan*
*Marlee the Manatee*
*Mysterious Association and the Virtu Gems*
*Naughty Hawk and the Squirrel*
*No, Baby, No…*
*Oriki and the Monster Who Hated Balloons*
*Ovid the Octopus…*
*Patricia the Baby Manatee and Other Stories*
*Points of View with Professor Peekabo*
*Praise of Love and Children*
*Pumpkin, Grumpkin…*
*Race and Guyana: Gulliver's Tales*
*Six Magic Cans…*
*Startling the Flying Fish…*
*Stories from El Dorado*
*Stories from India for Children*
*Story Time: A Collection of Children Stories*
*Sun Time Snow Time…*
*Tales of Makonaima's Children*
*Teddy the Toucan*
*The Adventures of Marlee…*
*The Adventures of Brer Anansi…*
*The Alligator and the Sun…*
*The Alligator Ferry Service…*
*The Bear with a Crinkled Ear*
*The Best of Brer Anansi…*
*The Children of Berlin…*
*The Dog who Loved Flowers*
*The Emperor's Dan-dan*
*The Granny JJ…*
*The Great Snakeskin*
*The Lure of the Mermaid and…*
*The Mighty Itanami…*
*The Monster Who Loved Cameras*
*The Monster Who Loved Telephones*
*The Monster Who Loved Toothbrushes*
*The Mysterious Association…*
*The Princess of the Forest…*
*The Rainbow's End…*
*The Rescue of Baby Meek…*
*The Riddle…*
*The Secret of El Dorado…*
*The Story of a Great Warrior…*
*The Third Gift*
*The Three Princes…*
*The Young Inferno…*
*The Zoo…*
*Tiger's Birthday Party…*
*This is the Rupununi: A Simple Story Book*

*Thumbelina and the Yarrow*
*Toco the Terrible: How Toco Got a New name and a New Tail*
*Unique Story Book…*
*Wanda, the White Jaguar…*
*We animals would like a word with you*
*We couldn't provide…*
*When Grandpa Cheddi was a boy*
*Whoa, Baby, Whoa…*
*Why is the Sky*

**CHINESE-GUYANESE**
*Cane Reapers: Chinese Indentured…*
*Cane Ripples*
*Cane Rovers: Stories of the Chinese Guyanese Diaspora*
*Chinese Women*
*From the Middle Kingdom*
*Indentured Labour…*
*Reading Mr. Chin…*
*Scenes from the History of the Chinese*
*The Chinese in British Guiana*
*The Chinese in British Guiana,* abridged ed. in Mandarin
The Chinese in Guyana…

**CHURCH HISTORY**
*A Historical Survey of Christ Church*
*A History of All Saints' Parish*
*A History of the Anglican Church in Guyana*
*A History of the Lutheran Church in Guyana*
*A Short History of St. George's…*
*A Short History of the Guyana Presbyterian Church*
*A History of the Versailles Hindu Temple...*
*Called to be more: Windows on the work and witness*
*Diocesan Pot-Pourri*
*Footprints Along the Way (Malgre Tout Catholic Church)*
*Fr Cary-Elwes S.J. and the Alleluia Indians*
*From Ashes to Ferro-Concrete*
*History of Religions in the Caribbean*
*Indian Missions in Guiana*
*Men of Faith*
*More Ramblings of a Parish Priest*
*Notes of the History of the Church in Guiana*
*Old-Style Missionary*
*Paddles over the Kamarang: The Story of the Davis Indians*
*Pages from the History of the Scottish Kirk…*
*Six Years in Hammock land: A Historical Sketch of the Lutheran Church*
*Tales of Inns and Temples*
*Ten Years of Mission Life in British Guiana*
*The Good News on the Wild Coast*

*The Ramblings of a Parish Priest*
*The Words and Works of Alan John Knight*

**CONSERVATION**
*Biodiversity Assessment of the Eastern Kanuku*
*Forests For Sale*
*Land Use, Land Degradation Situation Analysis*
*Indigenous Use of the Forest*
*The Iwokrama Forest…*

**COOKING**
*An Adventure in Caribbean Cuisine*
*Black Cake Mix*
*Caribbean Cuisine*
*Classic Caribbean Cooking*
*Cooking Book Guyana…*
*Guyana's Tasting Exotic…*
*Guyanese Easy to Follow…*
*Guyanese Seed of Soul*
*Guyanese Seed of Soul: How to Prepare West Indian Food*
*Guyanese Seed of Vegetables, Seafood, and Desserts...*
*Guyanese Style Cooking*
*In Nirmala's Kitchen*
*Just Eat…*
*Leela's Guyanese Anglo-Indian…*
*Most Popular Guyanese…*
*Passion: Healthy Recipes with Passion Fruit*
*Roth's Pepper-pot*
*Taste of Carifesta*
*Taste of the Tropics*
*The Complete Caribbean Cookbook*
*The Sugar Reef Caribbean Cookbook*

**COUNTRY PROFILE**
*A Description of British Guiana…*
*A Portrait of Guyana…*
*Anguilla…*
*Antigua & Barbuda…*
*Area Handbook for Guyana…*
*Barbados…*
*British Guiana*
*Colombia and Venezuela and the Guianas*
*Dominica…*
*Economy of Guyana…*
*Forest and Stream*
*Grenada…*
*Guyana*
*Guyana and Belize*
*Guyana at 50…*
*Guyana in Pictures*
*Guyana: Discovering South America…*
*Guyanese Travel Talks…*
*Handbook of British Guiana*
*Handbook of Natural Resources*
*India…*
*Jamaica…*
*Mapping in Guyana…*
*Panorama…*
*Reflections of Guyana…*
*Reflections on our Homeland…*
*Saint Lucia…*
*Search and Find…*
*Tobago…*
*Trinidad & Tobago…*

*Twelve Views in the Interior of Guiana*
*Venezuela, Guyana, French Guiana…*

**CULTURAL ISSUES**
*Adventures in the Field of Culture*
*Cultural Identity and Creolisation in National Unity*
*Cultural Policy in Guyana*
*Identity, Ethnicity and Culture in the Caribbean*
*Language, Cultural and Caribbean Identity*
*Dictionary of Guyanese Folklore…*
*Metegee: The History and Culture of…*
*On Location: Cinema and Film…*
*Origins and Development…*
*Temples and Mosques…*
*The Guyanese Culture…*
*The Guyanese Slang Alphabet…*

**ECONOMIC DEVELOPMENT**
*An Econometric Model of the Guyanese*
*Bright Road to El Dorado…*
*Conflicts between Multinational Corporations*
*Criminality, Human and Social…*
*Development Challenges and Cooperation*
*Economic and Social Progress in Latin America*
*Economic Development of Guyana 1953-64*
*Economic Development of Latin America*
*Economic Recovery Programme*
*Economics of Adoption*
*Economics of Labour*
*Empowering a Peasantry in a Caribbean Context*
*Essays…*
*Facing the Challenges, Reform of the European Union – Sugar Regime*
*From Rags to Riches…*
*Globalisation, Ethics…*
*Guyana Emergent: The Post Independence Struggle*
*Guyana: Economic Recovery and Beyond*
*Guyana: From State Control to Free Market*
*Guyana: Microcosm of Sustainable*
*Guyana's Coinage, 1808-2008*
*Guyana's Economic Recovery…*
*Guyana's Golden Age…*
*Guyana's Great Economic…*
*International Development Issues*
*Issues in Guyana's Development…*
*Labour in the West Indies*
*Nationalisation of Guyana's Bauxite*
*Noncapitalist Development: Struggle to Nationalize the Guyanese Sugar Industry*

*Plantation Economy: Population and…*
*Problems of Development in beautiful countries*
*Profit Without Plunder*
*Resource Sustainability and…*
*Rural Development…*
*Small Enterprise…*
*South American Economic Handbook*
*Studies in British Overseas Trade*
*Structural Adjustment*
*Study of the Socio-…*
*Sugar in British Guiana*
*Sustainable Development…*
*Ten Years of Caricom*
*The Akawaio, the Upper Mazaruni…*
*The American Takeover: Industrial Emergence*
*The Economic Development of Guyana, 1953-1964*
*The Political Economy of the US Caribbean Basin*
*The Post-War Planning Experience in Guyana*
*The Stages of Economic Growth*
*The Structure, Performance, and Projects of*
*Theory of Economic Growth*
*To Survive Sensibly…*
*Wealth Through Real Estate…*

**ECOSYSTEM**

*In the Guiana Forest: Studies of Nature in…*
*Soils of the Rupununi Savanna*
*The Savanna Ecosystem of Northern Rupununi*
*The Story of Forest and Stream*

**EDUCATION**

*150 Years of Education in Guyana*
*A Century of West Indian Education*
*A History of the Queen's College*
*A Matter…*
*A Matter of State…*
*A Study of the Dip.Ed…*
*Access, Equity and Performance*
*Accolades to Berbice High…*
*An Educational Journey*
*Born to Succeed…*
*African American English…*
*African American Vernacular…*
*African American, Creole…*
*Analyzing Variation in…*
*Citizenship Education for Small States: Guyana*
*Code Switching…*
*Creole Genesis…*
*Creole Indigeneity…*
*CXC Physics*

**EL DORADO**

*Marches of El Dorado*
*Oil Dorado…*
*Passage from India to El Dorado*
*Road to El Dorado*
*School Edition…*
*Searching for El Dorado*
*Stories from El Dorado*
*The Boy Adventurers…*
*The Creature in the Map…*
*The Discoverie of the Large. Rich, and…*
*The Elusive El Dorado*
*The Gold of El Dorado*
*The Language of El Dorado*
*The Loss of El Dorado*
*The Search for El Dorado*
*The Unmuffled Voices of El Dorado*

**ENVIRONMENT**
*Forests for Sale*
*Guyana: Population, Environments…*
*Guyana: Fragile Frontier*
*North-South: A Program for Survival*
*Our Country the Planet*
*Population Growth and Environmental Issues*
*The West Indies: Patterns of Development*

**ESPIONAGE**
*A Covert Life: Jay Lovestone, Communist...*
*A Look Over My Shoulder: A Life in the Central Intelligence Agency*
*CIA and American Labour: The Subversion of the AFL-CIO's Foreign Policy*
*From Cubana…*
*Georgetown Spies…*
*Inside the Company: CIA Diary*
*The Bear in the Backyard: Moscow's…*
*The CIA and the Cult of Intelligence*
*The CIA: A Forgotten History: US Global Interventions...*
*Undercover: Memoirs of an American Secret Agent*

**FAMILY LIFE**
*Clarise Cumberbatch Wants to go Home*
*Guyana Farewell: A Recollection of…*
*Immigrant #99840 and Canecutter #7074…*
*Legend of the Swan Children*
*Schooldays in the Colony*
*The Matrifocal Family…*
*The Negro Family in British Guiana*
*Through Faith & Luck…*

**FOLK TALES**
*A Plate-a-Guyana Cook-Up: A Collection of Guyanese Proverbs*
*Calabash in my hand*
*Calabash Parkway*
*Fables and Tales of Guyana*
*Folk Literature of the Warrao Indians*

*Folk Tales and Legends of Some Guyana Amerindians*
*Something Buried in the Yard…*
*Going Home and Other Tales from Guyana*
*Guiana Legends…*
*Legends and Myths of the Aboriginal Peoples*
*Legends of the Emperor's Ring*
*Makonaima and Pia*
*Scattered Jewels*
*Short & Sweet: A Collection of Guyanese Stories and Fables*
*Stories from Guyana*
*Tales of the Spirits*
*Tales in the Guyanese Vernacular*
*Tales of Makonaima's Children*
*Tales Strange But True*
*Teacher Ram's Fascination with Fire And Other Stories*
*Terror Island*
*The Best Ever Book of Guyanese Jokes: Lots and Lots of Jokes...*
*The Proverbs of Guyana Explained*
*Thoughts, moods and feelings and wha dem se – a Glossary of Guyanese Proverbs*
*True-True Stories*

**FOREIGN INTERFERENCE**

*A Personal Record: The Labour Government, 1964-1970*
*A Thousand Days: John F. Kennedy in the White House*
*Ambivalent Anti-Colonialism: the United States and the...*
*America Foreign Relations Since 1600: A Guide to the Literature*
*American Foreign Policy…*
*American Labour and the US Foreign Policy*
*An Unfinished Life: John F. Kennedy, 1961-1963*
*British Exploits in South America*
*Brother's Keepers…*
*Counter Hegemony*
*Eisenhower and Latin America: The Foreign Policy of Anti-Communism*
*Harold Macmillan, Vol. 2, 1957-1986*
*Harold Macmillan: A Biography*
*How Leaders Reason…*
*Iain Macleod*
*Ideology and US Foreign Policy*
*Inside the Company; CIA Diary*
*John F. Kennedy: The Great Crises*
*Kennedy, Macmillan and the Cold War: The Irony of Independence*
*Most Dangerous Area in the World: John F. Kennedy Confronts Communist...*
*Presidents and Peons: Recollections of a Labour*

*Ambassador in Latin America*
*Robert Kennedy in His Own Words: The Unpublished Recollections...*
*Short History of US…*
*The American Takeover: Industrial Emergence*
*The Caribbean, Whose Backyard*
*The CIA and the Cult of Intelligence*
*The Cold War and Decolonization in British Guiana...*
*The Cultural and Political History…*
*The Democracy Perspective in the Americas*
*The Invisible Government*
*The United States in the Caribbean*
*The USA and the Caribbean*
*The USA in South America*
*US Intervention in British Guiana*
*US Intervention in Central America…*
*Waging Peace: How Eisenhower Shaped an Enduring Cold War Strategy*
*US Military Interventions…*
*We Now Know: Rethinking Cold War History*

**FOREIGN RELATIONS**

*Changing State/Society…*
*The ACP Ambassadorial Group*
*The OAS and Regional Planning…*
*Counter Hegemony…*
*Developing with Foreign…*
*Guyana Brazil Relations…*
*New Directions…*
*The Shifting Foreign Policy…*

**GENERAL**

*5 Habits of Positivity…*
*5 one-act plays…*
*360 Pieces of Diamond*
*A Boy, A Man…*
*A Chapbook*
*A Cloud of Witnesses*
*A Guyanese Jaguar Soil…*
*A Few Things Our Sons…*
*A History of Film*
*A Guide to Better Sex…*
*A Guide to Manuscript Resources…*
*A Hot Country…*
*A Kind of Living*
*A Kind of Living*
*A Piling of Clouds…*
*A Season of Sometime*
*A Self-Publishing Guide…*
*A Splendid Dozen*
*A Tapestry of Life*
*A Traveler's Tale…*
*A Visitor from Home…*
*A Voice Crying…*
*Adventures of the Homeless*
*Adversity is temporary…*
*All Decent Animals*
*All sorts to make a world…*
*All Things Considered…*
*America in Crisis…*
*An Anthology of Shivers…*
*An Introduction to Guyanese…*

*Fifty Caribbean Writers…*
*Fifty Years of Flying*
*For the Millions*
*Freedom from Fear…*
*From Utopia to Paradise…*
*From Where I Stand*
*From Word to Word…*
*Generational Curse…*
*Geomorphology of Guyana*
*Glimpses of Victorian BG…*
*Globalization…*
*Glossary of the Soul…*
*Goddess Thoughts…*
*God's Spider…*
*Groovy Grammar…*
*Guyana and the World…*
*Guyana and Trinidad…*
*Guyana Classics…*
*Guyana: A Composite Monograph*
*Guyana In Depth…*
*Guyana Redux…*
*Guyana's Seawall Girl…*
*Guyanese Achievers in the UK*
*Haiku*
*Happiness: Naked Truths*
*Heads and Tails…*
*Hero The Warrior…*
*HerSTory: A Ganificent Tale*
*High Impact Set B Plays…*
*High Quality Customer Care…*
*Hope for Nation…*
*House of Waiting*
*How to adopt your school…*
*How to Get Better…*
*Human (In) Security…*
*I am a Guyanese…*
*I is a BV Man…*
*I went to the end…*

*Icon and Image…*
*If Wishes Were Horses…*
*Illustrious Exile*
*Images of Majority*
*Imagining the world*
*In a Boston Night*
*In Pursuit of Betterment…*
*In Search of Asylum…*
*In So Many Words…*
*In the Key…*
*India, Under Siege…*
*Innovation and Transformation…*
*International Dispute Resolution…*
*Italic*
*Japan*
*Just Deserts…*
*Kal Aaj aur Kal…*
*Killing, Eating, and …*
*Kind of Living…*
*Kiskadee…*
*Labaria Puraan*
*Labour at the…*
*Land beneath the wind…*
*Late Blooms…*
*Leaves of Life…*
*Leaves in the Wind…*
*Leemo: A True Story of a*
*Liberty of Conscience…*
*Life and Death…*
*Little Sand Key…*
*Living with intention…*
*Location of the Painted…*
*Love and Gold…*
*Love has two moons…*
*Luminous Ink…*
*Let not the great…*
*Let us talk*
*Letters of Thanks…*
*Letters to America…*

*Life in New York*
*Life's many…*
*Life's Scrapbook…*
*Light Transports…*
*Like Father…Like Son…*
*Like Heaven...*
*Limbolands*
*Little Savings Grow…*
*Living My Dreams*
*London Crossings…*
*Loss on Iguana Island…*
*Lyrical Hues*
*Ma Mae's Legacy…*
*Made in Guyana…*
*Making new friends…*
*Mammals of the Rupununi…*
*Man`s Friendship...*
*Marriage, Sex, and the…*
*Marriage is God's Gift…*
*Mawuusa and the…*
*Meditations…*
*Meet me at the four…*
*Making a Difference…*
*Manual Rating in*
*Georgetown…*
*Me…*
*Midnight Robber…*
*Milestones in Village…*
*Modern Western Fiction and*
*Sanskrit Aesthetics...*
*Moments of Leisure*
*More About Leemo...*
*Morning Meditations…*
*Morse The End f the Road…*
*Mudheads…*
*My Strangled City…*
*My Thoughts on Life*
*My Voice*
*My Voice of…*
*Navel String…*
*Negative Ecstasy…*
*Nelson's West Indian*
*Readers*
*New Guyanese*
*Publications…*
*New Overseer's Manual…*
*New People…*
*New Shoes…*
*New Writing Today…*
*Nightmares of Knowledge*
*No Entry*
*No Land, No Mother…*
*No More Drama…*
*No More Pets…*
*No Word in Guyanese…*
*Nostalgias*
*Octave…*
*One Leper's Heart*
*Organised Labour…*
*Other Leopards…*
*Our Country, The Planet…*
*Out of My Skin*
*Outings for Everyone…*
*Overcoming the Void*
*Overseer's Manual*
*PGME: Stemming the Brain*
*Drain…*
*Passport to Here and there…*
*Pepper Seed…*
*Perfected Fables…*
*Perseverance and Dignity*
*Persons of Interest…*
*Pictures for Georgetown…*
*Pilgrim memories*
*Possibilities…*
*Preparing a Dramatic…*
*Primacy of the Eye*
*Princess Marie Minnehaha of*
*Manoa*
*Proverbial Wisdom from*
*Guyana*
*Pure Love Passing Through*

*The Garden…*
*The Ghost of Memory…*
*The Gift of Scream*
*The Girl Who Hated Maths…*
*The Golden Arrowhead*
*The Great Collection…*
*The Greats…*
*The Guyana Annual…*
*The Guyana Mosaic*
*The Guyaspora in Canada…*
*The Hangman`s Game*
*The Hinterlands…*
*The Jewish Nation…*
*The Language of El Dorado*
*The Last Call*
*The Law of Believing…*
*The Longest Pleasure…*
*The Masses Create*
*The Monkey Wife…*
*The Morning After*
*The Move…*
*The Nation Builders…*
*The New Moon's Arms…*
*The Onliest Fisherman…*
*The Open Prison*
*The Pastor's Wife*
*The Pedagogy of Action…*
*The Point is to Change…*
*The Present…*
*The Professor of Light*
*The Pursuit of Dignity…*
*The Relevance of Myth*
*The River of Singing Fish*
*The Riverman…*
*The Sacred Presence…*
*The Salt Roads…*
*The Search for El Dorado…*
*The Seat at our Door*
*The Second Shipwreck*
*The Self Lovers…*
*The Shape of…*
*The Silent Witness…*
*The Silk Cotton Tree…*
*The Sly Company of People Who Care*
*The Thieving Summer…*
*The Third Gift…*
*The Third Temptation: A Novel*
*The Thunder and the Shouting…*
*The Triple Crown…*
*The Undiminished Link: Forty Years and Beyond*
*The Unmuffled Voices of El Dorado*
*The Winds of Change…*
*The Womb in Space…*
*This Planet Earth*
*Thoughts of an old barn…*
*Thoughts of Life and Literature…*
*Thriving in the Age of Terror…*
*Time loop*
*To My Poppa…*
*Tomorrow with the…*
*Toward a New Beginning...*
*Towards the Pebbled Shore…*
*Trail of the Lost Jaguar…*
*Trances…*
*Transmigration of Souls…*
*Trapped in the Middle*
*Travel Light…*
*Tropic Death*
*Tropic Death…*
*Trust You…*
*Truths from the…*
*Twiddling Thumbs…*
*Twinkle, Twinkle…*
*Unanimous Night…*

**GEOGRAPHY**



**GEOLOGY**

*The Geology of Southern Guyana*

**GLOBAL ISSUES**

*A New Global Human Order*
*Directory of Global Professional…*
*Our Country, The Planet…*
*Shridath Ramphal: The Commonwealth and the World*

**GOVERNMENT**

*Aspcets of Organisatiional Change…*
*Constitutional Development…*
*Electoral System Reform…*
*Exploring Values for the Remaking…*
*Governance…*
*In Pursuit of Public Sector…*
*Institutional reforms…*
*Ministries of Labour…*
*Nature's Government…*
*National Development Strategy…*
*Parliament in the Republic of Guyana…*
*Procedure for the Evaluation…*
*Report of the World Bank…*
*Second Development Plan…*
*The 1891 Constitutional Change…*
*The Constitution of Guyana…*
*The Development of the …*
*The Evolution of Public…*
*The State of Urban Planning…*

**HEALTHCARE**

*A New Chaos-Based…*
*Advancing Federal Sector Healthcare*
*Caribbean Medicine Forward to Eden*
*Caribbean State, Health Care*
*MRI Guide for Technologists: A step by step approach*
*CHAOS 2000…*
*CHAOS From Cos to…*
*Conversations…*
*Chros Yuself…*
*Dementia careers…*
*Healing Our Community…*
*Health issues in the…*
*Health System…*
*Heart and Now Global…*
*Leading Cause of Death…*
*Major Diseases…*
*Nutraceuticals…*
*Our words will be there: Pandemic…*
*Passion! Healthy recipes with passion fruit*
*Power, Transnational Terrorism…*
*Profiles of female cancer survivor*
*Promoting community Mental Health…*
*Public Service Management…*
*Soaring into Magnificence…*
*Society and Health in Guyana*

*South Asian Heart…*
*The Community Development Agenda…*
*The Ecology of Malnutrition in…*
*The 'Ends' of Public Sector…*
*The Path of Practice: A Woman's Book*
*Tsunami Chaos…*

**HISTORY**

*A Brief History of the Guyana Forestry Commission...*
*A Centenary History and Handbook of…*
*A Centenary History of the East Indians in…*
*A Concise History of Queen`s College, 1844-2009*
*A Constitutional History of British Guiana…*
*A Destiny to Mould*
*A Family of Islands: A History*
*A Guide for the Study of British*
*A History of Black and Asian…*
*A History of East Indian Resistance on…*
*A History of Guyana…*
*A History of Indians in Guyana*
*A History of the Guyana…*
*A History of the Guyanese Working People*
*A History of the Queen's College…*
*A History of the Upper Guinea Coast*
*A History of the Virgin Islands of…*
*A History of Theatre in Guyana: 1800-2000*
*A History of Trade Unionism in Guyana*
*A New System of Slavery*
*A Post Slavery Nightmare*
*A Post-Emancipation History of…*
*A Pre-Emancipation History of…*
*A Question of Labour*
*A Relation of a Voyage to Guyana…*
*A Short History of the Guyanese People*
*A Short History of the West Indies*
*A Survey of Guyanese History*
*A Voyage to Demerara…*
*Absent-Minded Imperialism…*
*Account of an Insurrection*
*Africa and the Caribbean…*
*African Presence in Early Asia…*
*African Presence in Early Europe…*
*Among the Common People of British Guiana…*
*Annals of British Guiana…*
*An Illustrated History of British Guiana…*
*Anti-colonialism in British Politics: The Left and the End of Empire, 1918-1964*
*Antilles, Guyanes, La Mer des Caraïbes…*

*From Colony to Cooperative Republic*
*From Plantocracy to Nationalisation*
*Georgetown*
*Giant of the Past*
*Great Guyanese Humour: Guyana's History Through Jokes*
*Guiana: British, Dutch, and French*
*Guyana: 1838-1985…*
*Guyana: From Slavery…,*
*Guyana and the Caribbean*
*Guyana History*
*Guyana Independence...*
*Guyanese Sugar Plantations in…*
*Highlights of Guyana's History*
*Historical Information…*
*History of Barbados*
*History of British Guiana…*
*History of the British West Indies*
*History of the Colonies*
*History of the Demerara Tobacco Company, 1934-1990*
*History of the West Indian Peoples*
*History of Victoria Village*
*History, Fable and Myth in the…*
*Hogarth, Walpole and Commercial Britain*
*Hogarth's Blacks: Images of Blacks*
*How Europe Underdeveloped Africa*
*Imperialism and Colonialism…*
*In the Shadow of the Plantation*
*In Search of African History…*
*In the Tropics: Scenes & Incidents of…*
*Indenture and Abolition: Sacrifice and…*
*Indians in Guyana: A Concise History*
*Jewish Nation in the Caribbean…*
*Justice: The Struggle for Democracy*
*La Busqueda de El Dorado*
*La Verdad Sobre*
*Latin America in the 1930s*
*Lessons in Guyanese History…*
*Letters from Guiana 1796-1797*
*Letters on the West Indies…*
*Lords of the Tiger Spirit: A History of the Caribs*
*Marches of El Dorado*
*Maroons of Guyana*
*Memory, Mifration…*
*Metegee: The History and Culture of…*
*Narrative of a Five-Year Expedition*
*Natural History of Guyana…*
*Nature's Government*
*Nieuw Amsterdam in Berbice*
*Notes on the West Indies*
*Occupation to Independence…*

*Odeen Ishmael Guyana Story*
*Vol 1*
*Odeen Ishmael Guyana Story*
*Vol 2*
*Order and Place in a Colonial*
*Society*
*Passage from India to El*
*Dorado: Guyana*
*Ralegh's Last Voyage*
*Raleigh and the British*
*Empire*
*Rasta and Resistance*
*Report of the Proceedings…*
*Representations on*
*Slavery…*
*Revisiting the Demerara…*
*Scenes and Sketches of*
*Demerara Life*
*Scenes and Sketches:*
*Georgetown 1899*
*Scenes From the History of*
*the Africans*
*Scenes from the History of*
*the Chinese*
*Scenes From the History of*
*the Portuguese*
*Searching for El Dorado*
*Secret and Suppressed:*
*Banned Ideas*
*Sir Walter Ralegh*
*Slave Populations…*
*Slave Rebellions in Guyana*
*Slavery's Martyr: John Smith*
*of Demerara*
*Sources of West Indian*
*History*
*Speeches and Documents on*
*British Colonial*
*Stabroek Market and the*
*Public Clocks*
*Stark's Guide Book and*
*History of British Guiana*
*Storm Van's Gravesande:*
*The Postal History of…*
*The Rise of British Guiana*
*Story of Georgetown*
*Sugar and Slaves…*
*Sugar Cane: Hackia Sticks…*
*Sugar Without Slaves: The*
*Political Economy*
*Susanna: Unsung Heroine…*
*Sweetening Bitter Sugar:*
*Jock Campbell's…*
*Ten Days in August 1834*
*that changed the world*
*Testing the Chain…*
*The 1891 Constitutional*
*Change and…*
*The Archaic of North-*
*Western Guyana…*
*The Berbice Revolt…*
*The Berbice Uprising 1763*
*The Boy Adventurers in the*
*Land of El Dorado…*
*The British Caribbean: From*
*the Decline of…*
*The British West Indian…*
*The British West Indies*
*Sugar Industry in the…*
*The Caribbean: An*
*Intellectual History*
*The Colony of British Guiana*
*and its Labouring…*
*The Demerara Martyr:*
*Memoirs of the Reverend…*
*The Demerara Slave*
*Rebellion 1823*
*The Discoverie of the Large,*
*Rich, and Beauwtiful…*
*The Dutch in the Caribbean*
*and on the Wild Coast…*

*Colonial Emigration from the Bengal Presidency*
*Coolie Woman: The Odyssey of Indenture*
*Coping in America: The Case of Caribbean East Indians*
*Creating Their Own Space…*
*Cycles Of Civilisations*
*East Indians in the Caribbean: A Bibliography of…*
*East Indians in the Caribbean: Colonialism and…*
*Ethnicity and Indian Identity in the Caribbean*
*Evolution of Writing…*
*Fabrics of Indianness…*
*Far From mecca…*
*Footprints from India*
*From Bengal to Bush Lot to Belize: The Indentured Servants*
*From Pillar to Post: The Indo-Caribbean…*
*Global Indian Diaspora…*
*Guyana: Genesis…*
*Guyanese Writers of Indian Ancestry…*
*Hendree's Cure: Scenes from Madrasi Life…*
*Hill Coolies…*
*Immigrant #99840 and Canecutter # 7074…*
*Indenture and Abolition: Sacrifice and…*
*Indenture and Exile: The Indian Diaspora…*
*Indian Indenture in the… Indo-Caribbean*
*Indentured Labour in the Age of Imperialism, 1834-1922*
*Indentured Muslims…*
*India and the Progress of…*
*India and the Shaping of the Indo-Guyanese*
*India in the Caribbean*
*India: The Progress of her People…*
*Indian Indenture…*
*Indian Indentureship and Sunlit Western Waters…*
*Indian Village in Guyana…*
*Indians in British Guiana 1919-29*
*Indians in Guyana: A Concise History*
*Indians in the Caribbean*
*Indians Overseas in British Territories*
*Indo-Caribbean Canadians: Who's Who...*
*Indo-Caribbean Resistance*
*Indo-West Indian Cricket…*
*John Edward Jenkins The Coolie His Rights and Wrongs*
*Joseph Ruhoman's India: The Progress of…*
*Jung Bahadur Singh…*
*Kali's Feast…*
*Legacy of Slavery and Indentured...*
*Life in British Guiana…*
*Kanpur to Kolkota: Labour Recruitment for the Sugar Colonies*
*Lakshmi Out of India*
*London's Heart Probe and Britain's Duty…*

*Maharani's Misery…*
*Mohandas K. Gandhi: Thoughts, Words, Deeds: His Source of Inspiration...*
*Mother India's Shadow Over El Dorado: Indo-Guyanese Politics...*
*Passage from India to El Dorado: Guyana and the Great Migration*
*Self-Reflection….*
*Separate and Unequal: India and the…*
*Sketches of African and Indian Life in…*
*Social and Cultural…*
*Sojourners to Settlers...*
*Sugar's Sweet Allure*
*The Art of David Dabydeen*
*The Banyan Tree: Overseas Emigrants from India, Pakistan and Bangladesh*
*The Anatomy of Indian…*
*The Coolie: His Rights and Wrongs*
*The East Indian Diaspora*
*The East Indian Problem in Trinidad and Tobago... and*
*The Feast and Festivities…*
*Race War in Guyana...*
*The East Indian Odyssey…*
*The East Indians of Guyana and Trinidad*
*The Elusive El Dorado: Essays on the Indian Experience in Guyana*
*The First Crossing*
*The First Crossing: Being the Diary of Theophilus Richmond...*
*The Hindu Marriage…*
*The Indian Caribbean…*
*The Indian and Indo-Guyanese Diaspora: A British Default*
*The Legacy of Indian Indenture…*
*The Literature of the Indian Diaspora*
*The Settlement of Indians in Guyana*
*The Shadow of Dreams*
*The Sudden Disappearance…*
*The Wellsprings of Violence…*
*They Came in Ships: An Anthology of Guyanese East Indian Writings*
*They Came in Ships: An Anthology of Indo-Guyanese…*
*Those that be in bondage*
*Through Faith and Luck…*
*Tiger in the stars: The anatomy of Indian…*
*Under Attack! The Caribbean Indian…*
*Under the Southern Cross…*
*We Mark Your Memory…*
*Why Should We Be…*

**JONESTOWN**

*A New Look at Jonestown…*
*A Sympathetic History of Jonestown*
*A Thousand Lives: The Untold Story... Jonestown*
*A Will to Survive: Jim Jones' Justice and Other Short Stories*
*An Exposé of the King of the Cults*

*Awake in Nightmare – Jonestown*
*Beyond Jonestown: Sensitivity*
*Black and White*
*Cuname, Curare, and Cool Aid*
*Gather with the Saint at the River*
*Gone from the Promised Land…*
*Guyana Massacre: The Eyewitness Account*
*Hearing the Voices of Jonestown*
*Heavenly Deceptor*
*Hold Hands and Die*
*In My Father's House*
*Jim Jones and the Peoples…*
*Jonestown*
*Jonestown and Other Poems*
*Jonestown Massacre Occurs*
*Jonestown Massacre: Tragic End of a Cult*
*Jonestown: A Poem*
*New Religious Movements, Mass Suicide*
*Our Father Who Art In Hell*
*People's Temple, People's Tomb*
*Raven: The Untold Story*
*Salvation and Suicide*
*Seductive Poison*
*Snake Dance: Unravelling the Mysteries*
*Suicide in Guyana*
*The Assassination of Representative Leo J. Ryan*
*The Broken God*
*The Children of Jonestown*
*The Cult that Died*
*The Ghosts of November: Memoirs of…*
*The Jonestown Massacre: The Transcript…*
*The Onliest One Alive: Surviving Jonestown…*
*The Road to Jonestown…*
*The Strongest Poison*
*The Suicide Cult: The Inside Story of the…*
*The World's Weirdest Cults*
*Was Jonestown a CIA Experiment?…*
*White Night*

**LANGUAGE STUDIES (See also AMERINDIAN LANGUAGES)**

*A Grammar of Berbice Dutch Creole*
*Clinical Applications…*
*Dialect and/or Cultural Interference in…*
*Dictionary of Caribbean English Usage*
*Dimensions of a Creole Continuum*
*Kicking Tongues*
*Languages of the West Indies*
*The Creole Tongue of British Guiana*
*The Genesis of Discourse Grammar...*
*Use of Linguistic…*

**LEGAL ISSUES**

*Barrister for the Defence*
*Caribbean Court of Justice*
*Criminal Practice…*
*Compulsory Land Acquisition*

*Constitutional Development in Guyana*
*Contract of Service…*
*Defense Attorney*
*Development Control and Planning Law*
*Experiences of a Demerara Magistrate*
*Fundamental rights…*
*Guyana Criminal Justice…*
*In Pursuit of Justice: Fifty Years as a Criminal*
*International Criminal Justice…*
*Landlord and Tenant Law…*
*Law and the Political Environment in Guyana*
*Law of compulsory motor vehicle insurance…*
*Law of compulsory purchase…*
*Law of real property and conveyancing*
*Law of Trusts…*
*Law of Unlawful Possession…*
*Law of Workmen's Compensation…*
*Make Your Own Wills…*
*Non-contentious Probate Issue*
*Precedent in the World Court*
*Sir Lionel…*
*Strata Titles*
*The Caribbean Court…*
*The Constitution of Guyana*
*The Guyana Court of Appeal…*
*The Law of Speeding and Radar*
*The Legal Profession…*
*The Legal System in British Guiana*
*The Three Trials of Arnold Rampersaud*
*Workmen's Compensation Practice…*

**LITERATURE**

*A Handbook of Guyanese Literature*
*A History of Literature…*
*A Reader's Guide to West Indian and Black British Literature*
*A Reader's Guide to West Indian and…*
*A River Dreams Red*
*A Short Adventure Play*
*A Survey of West Indian Literature*
*African Literature…*
*An Anthology of Caribbean Poetry for Carifesta*
*An Anthology of Caribbean Literature*
*An Anthology of Guyanese Short Stories*
*Guyanese Contemporary Verse*
*An Anthology of Short Stories from Guyana*
*Beyond Sangre Grande: An Anthology of Caribbean Literature*
*Beyond Sangre Grande: Caribbean Writing Today*
*Black Presence in English Literature*
*Black Writers in Britain 1760-1890*

*Caribbean Literature: A Teacher's Handbook*
*Caribbean Women Writers…*
*Commonwealth Literature…*
*Conversations with Contemporary…*
*Dark Ancestor: Literature of the Blackman…*
*Folk Literature of the Warrao Indians*
*Frontiers of Caribbean Literature in English*
*Geography of Vote…*
*Guyanese Library and its impact…*
*Guyanese Periodicals…*
*Handbook for Teaching Caribbean Literature*
*Introdcution to Guyanese Writing*
*Jahaji Bhai – An Anthology of Indo-Caribbean*
*Johnson's Dictionary*
*Literature – Guyanese, Caribbean and Others…*
*Lutchmee and Dilloo: A Study of West Indian Life…*
*Making a Difference…*
*Making West Indian Literature*
*Novels and the Nation: Essays in Canadian Literature…*
*One captain and other literary works*
*Pandora's Headache*
*Passion and Exile: Essays in Caribbean Literature…*
*Passions of El Dorado*
*Robert Grieve The Asylum Journal Vol 01*
*Robert Grieve The Asylum Journal Vol 02*
*Shadow in the Gloen*
*Shadow Play*
*Short and Sweet*
*Song of Boatwoman*
*Ten Oxford Authors…*
*The Asylum, Volume 1*
*The Asylum, Volume 2*
*The Black Mind: A History of African Literature…*
*The Development of Land Law…*
*The Drums of Kassaku*
*The Game of Kassaku*
*The Guyana Annual 2004-2005*
*The Guyana Annual 2005-2006*
*The Guyana Annual 2006-2007*
*The Literature of the Indian Diaspora…*
*The Making of Guyanese Literature…*
*The Players of Kassaku*
*The Presence*
*The Ritual*
*The Sky's Wild Noise: Selected Essays*
*Thoughts on Life and Literature…*
*Twentieth-Century Caribbean Literature*
*Two Anthologies of Guyanese Plays*
*V.S. Naipaul and the West Indies*

**LOCAL GOVERNMENT and GOVERNMENT**

*Community Participation…*
*Governance, Conflict…*
*Modernizing the State*
*Reclaiming Development*
*The Approaches to Local Self-Government*

**MATHEMATICS**

*Algebra Revision*
*Geometry Revision*
*Statics and Dynamics*
*Trigonometry*

**MEDIA**

*Birth of Stabroek News*
*Broadcasting in Guyana*
*Media Creation…*
*Guyana's Periodicals…*
*Mass Media in 2025…*
*Notes on the Media…*
*Paramountcy of the Media in Guyana*
*Populism and the Media…*
*Strategic Communications*
*The BBC at 100…*
*Thought-Provoking…*

**MEMOIRS**

*A Glimpse of the Other…*
*A Jaguar Soul: My Guyanese-American Childhood*
*A Remigrant's Story…*
*A Silent Life…*
*A Swarthy Boy…*
*An Educational Journey…*
*An Intimate Journey…,*
*Antiman…*
*B.G. Bhagee: Memories of a Colonial Childhood*
*Beyomd the Blackboard…*
*Bishops: My Turbulent Colonial Youth*
*Boyhood Days-Book 2: A Caribbean Narrative*
*Dancing My Way to 80…*
*Demerara Sugar…*
*Dream – the Personal*
*Eight Years in Britrish Guiana…*
*Goodbye Forever Vicky.,..*
*Growing up in British Guiana: 1945-1964*
*Growing Up Guyanese…*
*Growing Up in Pln. Mackenzie…*
*Guardian Angels…*
*Guyana, The Lost El Dorado…*
*Guyana's Diplomacy:*
*I Remember That…*
*Imprints in Life's Journey*
*Inseparable Humanity:*
*Journey to Self-Discovery…*
*Anthology of…*
*Kiskadee Girl…*
*Kiss and Breathe…*
*Kite Flying in the Village: A Guyanese Girl`s Story*
*Lantern in the Wind…*
*Life of an Immigrant…*
*Marble, Grass, and Glass…*
*My Colonial Service…*
*My Heritage: Memories of Growing Up…*
*My Incredible Journey…*
*Once a Guyanese Child…*
*Potaro Dreams*
*Realizing the American*

*Recollections of Bath Estate…*
*Reflections…*
*Reflections of a Former…*
*Rejoyce…*
*Send Me My Eve…*
*Sometimes I Think About My Childhood…*
*Taken Without Consent…*
*The Demerara Martyr: Memoirs of the Reverend…*
*The Heart of the Sun: A Collection of Stories of Childhood Memories...*
*Stepping Out of the Herd…*
*The Memoirs of Lord Chandos*
*The Missionary's Wife: A Memoir of Mrs. M.A. Henderson of Demerara*
*The El Dorado Affair…*
*The Way We Were: Memories of a British Guiana Childhood*
*Some Observations…*
*The Heart of the Sun…*
*The Water Here…*
*The West on Trial…*
*Transformed and Renewed…*
*Triumph…*
*Walk About…*
*Walk Wit' Me…All Ova Guyana: Memoir of Helena Martin*
*Under the Demerara Sun…*
*Whispers in Our Ears…*
*Years of High Hopes*

**MILITARY AFFAIRS**

*A Member of the RAF…*
*Armed Forces of Latin America…*
*Armed Forces of the English-speaking…*
*Army Intervention in the 1973…*
*British Regiments…*
*Contemporary Issues in Policing…*
*Deadly Force, Colonialism, and the…*
*Domination and Power in Guyana…*
*Foundation of the GDF…*
*Lest We Forget: The Experiences of World War 2 West Indian...*
*Guyana's Military Veterans…*
*I Was There…*
*National Defence: A Brief History of the GDF, 1965-2005*
*National Defence: A Brief History of the Guyana Defence Force...*
*Reporting the War…*
*The British Guiana Volunteer Force, 1948-1966*
*The British West Indies Regiment 1914-1918*
*The Empty Sleeve*
*The Empty Sleeve: The Story of the West India Regiments...*
*The Guyana National Service, 1974-2000*
*The Guyana People`s Militia, 1976-1997*
*The History of the British Guiana Police*

*The New Road – A Short History of the GDF 1966-76*
*The Queen`s College Cadet Corps , 1889-1975*
*The Walker Brothers…*
*This is GNS…*
*World Armies*
*World Police and Paramilitary Forces*

**MIND, BODY, and SPIRIT**
*7 Days Healthy Thoughts…*
*A Life of Prayer…*
*A Weekly Encounter…*
*Another Thought*
*Ayurvedic; A Life of Balance…*
*Be the perfect you*
*Being the voice…*
*Devotions and Ailment…*
*Dfurstane's Spiritual Beliefs…*
*Gifts of God…*
*God in our midst*
*Heaven Bound…*
*Keys of Faith…*
*Life's Passages…*
*Living with Purpose*
*Morning Meditations…*
*Petals from my rose garden*
*Sunlit Stream…*
*The Best of Humanity*
*The Path of Practice…*
*The True Self*
*This Body*
*What is Man*

**MINING**
*A Hand Full of Diamonds*
*An Illustrated History of Pork Knockers…*
*Conflicts Between Multinational Corporations*
*Gold, Diamond and Orchids*
*Guyana Gold: The Story of Wesley Baird*
*Mineworkers of Guyana: The Making of a…*
*On the Diamond Trail in British Guiana…*
*Up the Mazaruni for Diamonds…*
*Venezuela…*

**MISSIONARY WORK**
*A Mission to the Indians of Orialla…*
*Indian Missions in Guiana…*
*MacNamara's Irish Colony and the US…*
*Mission work among the Indian Tribes…*
*Missionary Labours in British Guiana…*
*On sea and land on creek and river…*
*Rupununi Mission: The Story of Fr. Cary-Elwes*
*Ten Years of Mission Life in British Guiana…*

**MUSIC**
*A Scuffling of Islands…*
*Between Songs*
*Black Praxis…*
*Calypso and Society…*
*Caribbean Currents:…*
*Folksongs of Guyana: Queh-Queh*
*Musical Life in Guyana…*

*My Life as a musician…*
*My Whole Life…*
*National Folksongs…*
*National Songs Composed…*
*National Songs of Guyana*
*One Hundred Folk Songs of Guyana*
*One Hundred Years of Classical Music…*
*Rasta Lyrics*
*Ring of Steel…*
*Singing Into Jesus*
*Song of My Sou*
*Songs for a New Worldl*
*Songs of Twilight*
*Ten National Songs of Guyana*
*The Life and Works of Bill (Bhagee) Rogers...*
*Variations on Folk Songs…*
*Writings on Guyanese Music…*

**NATURAL HISTORY**

*An Essay on the Natural History of Guiana*
*A Naturalist in the Guyana Forest*
*A Naturalist in the Guianas*
*British Guiana Nature Study…*
*The Natural History of the Fishes of British Guiana*
*Land of Waters*

**NOVEL**

*A Bethlehem Alleluia*
*A Death in the Family*
*A Dip in the Sangam*
*A Harlot's Progress*
*A Journey…*
*A Kind of Homecoming*
*A Kind of Living…*
*A Little Hut in Heaven*
*A Morning at the Office*
*A Morning at the Office*
*A Morning in Trinidad*
*A Portrait of Paternalism…*
*A Shapely Fire: Changing the*
*A Tale of Three Places*
*A Tinkling in the Twilight*
*A Touch of Midas*
*A Valley in Italy*
*A Wilful Daughter…*
*A Writer Like You*
*Adoniya*
*Aftermath of Empire…*
*An Angel at the Gate*
*An Innocent Abroad*
*Another Way to Dance*
*Ariadne & Other Stories*
*Arshana…*
*Backdam People*
*Balthasar*
*Bartica*
*Benjamin, Prophet of the*
*Bubu's Street*
*Apes*
*Auntie I Don't Want You To Get Married…*
*Bethany*
*Between Bible College…*
*Between the Dash and the Comma*
*Bim: A Boy in British Guiana*
*Black Idol*
*Black Marsden*
*Black Midas*
*Blood Rights*
*Bloodlines*
*Bones*

*Born in Amazonia*
*Boy Sandwich*
*British Subjects*
*Butterflies in Paradise*
*Buxton Spice*
*Canada Geese and Apple*
*Chutney*
*Carnival*
*Carnival Girl*
*Carnival of Dreams…*
*Children of Kaywana*
*Children of the Sun*
*Choice of Straws*
*Clever Backbone*
*Companions of the Day and Night…*
*Corentyne Thunder*
*Corner Stones…*
*Cosmic Dance*
*Cosmic Disco…*
*Couvade and a …*
*Da Silva's Cultivated Wilderness*
*Dancing Between Raindrops…*
*Dark Noon…*
*Dark Swirl*
*Daughter of the Great River…*
*Dear Death*
*Dear Future*
*Demerary Telepathy*
*Dilchand Joins the Army…*
*Disappearance*
*Discussing Columbus*
*Her Darkest Hour…Distances*
*Dr. Dee Dee Dynamo's Mission to Pluto*
*East of Centre…*
*Eating Air*
*Ebedmelech*
*Eltonsbrody*
*Escape to the …*
*Essays and Fables*
*Estate People*
*Esteem*
*Eternal Tribute*
*Eternity to Season*
*Eve*
*Explainer*
*Fabula Rosa*
*Far Journey of Oudin*
*Feeding the Ghosts*
*Fetish*
*Fidel Castro is Dead*
*For the Love of My Country*
*For the love of my name*
*Fossil and Psyche*
*Frangipani House*
*From Eternity for…*
*From Silence to Silence*
*From the Heat of the Day*
*Gateway to the Dark Side: Final Book ...*
*Gather the Faces*
*Geister in unserem Blut…*
*Genetha*
*Gifts From My Grandmother*
*Glints from an Anvil*
*Grandpa's Footsteps…*
*Green Winter*
*Guiana Boy*
*Gunshots in My Cook-up*
*Guyana My Altar*
*Halfway Tree…*
*Haiki..,.*
*Happiness…*
*Hear the Gungrus Sing*
*High House and Radio*
*Home and Back*
*Honorary White*

*Reluctant Neighbours*
*Resurrection at Sorrow Hill*
*Rice and Peas…*
*Roll Play*
*Schwartzer Midas*
*Seeram's Illusions…*
*Selected Essays of Wilson Harris*
*Shadow in the Dark*
*Shadows Move Among Them*
*Shadows Move Among Them*
*Shadows Round the Moon*
*Shanti*
*Sharda*
*Shraadanjali*
*Sky Dance*
*Slippery Ochro…l*
*Sometimes Hard…*
*Son of Guyana*
*Song of the Boatwoman*
*Sources of Agony*
*Steadman and Joanna*
*Step Closer…*
*Still Close to the Island*
*Stoning the Wind*
*Stranger than Tomorrow*
*Sudden Jolts…*
*Sunlight on Sweet Water*
*Sunset's Trail*
*Suspended Sentences: Fictions of Atonement*
*The Adding Machine*
*The Age of the Rainmakers*
*The Alexin of our Cure*
*The Angel at the Gate*
*The Armstrong Trilogy…*
*The Bay of Silence*
*The Beggar…*
*The Best of Brer Anansi…*
*The Cat of Muritaro*
*The Counting House*
*The Crying of Rainbirds*
*The Dark Jester*
*The Domino Masters…*
*The Dumb and the Brave*
*The Eye of the Scarecrow*
*The Eye of the Scarecrow*
*The Far Away Girl…*
*The February 23*[rd] *Coup*
*The Flour Convoy*
*The Friend*
*The Ghost of Bellows Man*
*The Girl from Jonestown…*
*The Girl from Lamaha Street…*
*The Girl from the Sugar…*
*The Green Grass Tango*
*The Guyana Quartet*
*The Guyanese Wanderer*
*The Harrowing of Hubertus*
*The High Place*
*The Hummingbird-Tree*
*The Hungry Sailor*
*The Initiates: First Book of the Appointed Collection*
*The Friendship Shoes*
*The Integrationist*
*The Intended*
*The Jilkington Drama*
*The Journey*
*The Last Barbarian*
*The Last Ship…*
*The Late Candidate*
*The Laughing Bird*
*The Life and Death of Sylvia*
*The Life and Death of Sylvia…*
*The Long Way Home…*
*The Lost Daughter…*
*The Lost World*
*The Mad MacMullochs…*
*The Madwoman of Papine*

*The Marble Mountain: And Other Stories…*
*The Master of chaos…*
*The Migration of Ghosts*
*The Ministry of Hope*
*The Moon People*
*The Murderer*
*The Ol-Kai People…*
*The Order of the Mirror: Second Book of...*
*The Orphan of India…*
*The Other Temptation…*
*The Pastor's Wife*
*The Piling of Clouds…*
*The Promised Land and the Phoenix*
*The Return of Latchmini…*
*The Scholar Man*
*The Search*
*The Secret Life of Winnie Cox…*
*The Shadow Bride*
*The Silence of Islands*
*The Silent Witness*
*The Silver Lining*
*The Sisters and Manco's Stories*
*The Sleepers of Roraima*
*The Slow Train to Milan*
*The Small Fortune of Dorothea…*
*The Snow Line…*
*The Soldier's Girl…*
*The Speech of Angels…*
*The Spirit, the Passion and the Blood*
*The Sugar Planter's…*
*The Third Gift*
*The Third Temptation*
*The Third Temptation*
*The Thorn in the Rose*
*The Tiger*
*The Timehrian*
*The Town is Aaron*
*The Tramping Man*
*The Tree of the Sun*
*The Trumpet*
*The Turtles Dream & Keys®: Gardens Without End*
*The Twisted Circle…*
*The Undiminished Caribbean…*
*The Ventriloquist's Tale*
*The Violin Maker's Daughter,,,*
*The Waiting Room*
*The Weather Family…*
*The Weather in Middenshot*
*The West Indian Novel*
*The Whole Armour*
*The Wild Coast…*
*The Wintering Kundalini*
*The Wizard Swami*
*The Wounded and the Worried*
*There's No Place…*
*Thief with Leaf*
*This Body…*
*Those I Have Lost…*
*Three Immortals*
*Thunder Returning*
*Tide Running*
*Timepiece*
*Tomorrow is Another Day*
*Tormented Wives*
*Tradition, the Writer and Society*
*Trilogy: Carnival; The Infinite Rehearsal*
*Uncle Paul*
*Under the Tamarind Tree*
*Unlit Roads*

**ORNITHOLOGY**



**PHILATELY**



**PHOTOGRAPHIC SCENES**



**POETRY**

*For the Fighting Front*
*Forest Leaves*
*Fourteen Guianese Poems for Children*
*Fragrance of a Desert Rose*
*From Berbice to Broadstairs: Poems*
*From Mouth to Mouth…*
*From the Caribbean to England in Verse*
*Fulfilment: Poems*
*Georgetown Spies*
*Give Yourself a Hug…*
*Glorianne*
*Glossary of the soul…*
*Grass Roots in Verse…*
*Guyana Drums*
*Guyana Watan*
*Haamaaraa…*
*Guyana's Child*
*Guyanese Poetry*
*Half-Caste and other…*
*Heinemann Book of Caribbean Poetry*
*Hello New: New Poems for a New Century*
*Horizons of Life: A Collection of Poems*
*Hungry Voices Cry*
*Hunted: A Collection of Poems*
*I Din Do Nuttin, and Other Poems*
*I Had a Dream…*
*I Have Crossed an Ocean…*
*I Hear Guyana Cry*
*If Only the Gods Were Awake*
*In Flux*
*In Retrospect: A Collection of Poetry*
*Interlude: Original Poems*
*Introspection: A Collection of Poems*
*Jail Me Quickly…*
*Jaffo the Calypsonian*
*Jonestown and Other Poems*
*Koker*
*Laughter is an Egg: A Collection of Poems*
*Lazy Thoughts…*
*Leguan: A Collection of Poems*
*Leo's Poetical Works…*
*Lest We Forget: 101 Poems About the Child*
*Let's Kiss and Dance*
*Lichfield 12…*
*Life and Living: A Collection of Poems*
*Limbolands…*
*Lines and Rhymes: A Collection of Verse*
*Lotus in the Mud*
*Love's Light*
*Madib and Other Poems…*
*Maggie Harris Selected Poems*
*Mangoes and Bullets*
*Martin Carter: University of Hunger*
*Mercy Ward*
*Mira and Other Poems…*
*More Poems*
*Mother Earth…*
*My Book of Poetry…*
*My Life is Literally…*
*My Lovely Native Land*
*My New Guyana: A Collection of Poems…*
*New Ships: An Anthology of…*

*News for Babylon: The Chatto Book of…*
*No Hickory No Dickory No Dock*
*Number Parade: Number*
*Paint Me a Poem…*
*Poems from...*
*Poetry Jump…*
*Offerings…*
*On a Prayer…*
*On Watching a Lemon…*
*Our homes spring poetry*
*Our Own Poems*
*Oxford Book of Caribbean Verse*
*Performance Poetry…*
*Plain Talk: A Collection of Poems and Short Stories…*
*Poems in Creolese*
*Poems*
*Poems by Martin Carter*
*Poems for All*
*Poems for Guyanese…*
*Poems for Mary…*
*Poems from the Garden…*
*Poems in My Earphone*
*Poems in Recession*
*Poems Man…*
*Poems of a British Guianese*
*Poems of Affinity*
*Poems of Consciousness…*
*Poems of Love and Liberty*
*Poems of My People*
*Poems of Preparation…*
*Poems of Resistance*
*Poems of Resistance from British Guiana*
*Poems of Separation*
*Poems of Shape and Motion…*
*Poems of St. Agnes*
*Poems of Succession*
*Poems of Thought…*
*Poems on Guiana*
*Poems on Guyana: Verse in Reverie*
*Poems to Remember*
*Poesias Escogidas*
*Poetic Tributes to Walter Rodney*
*Poetical Works*
*Poetry Introduction*
*Poetry of KO Harrop*
*Poetry of People…*
*Poetry Jump-up: A Collection of…*
*Poetry, Introduction*
*Poetry of Psycho-realism*
*Portrait in Poetry…*
*Pure Gold and Other Poems*
*Rainwater*
*Reflections*
*Rhapsodies of Verse*
*Rhythms of Ease…*
*River Dancers…*
*Rivers of Time…*
*Rivers whisper stars…*
*Roraima: An Anthology of Poetry...*
*Sacred Stones…*
*Sacrifice: Poems on the Indian Arrival in Guyana Collected Poems 2002-2012*
*Sacrifice: Poems on the Indian Arrival in Guyana Collected Poems 2002-2012*
*Scaling Heights*
*Scaling New Heights…*
*Say it again, Granny*
*Scattered Leaves*
*Scarps of Prose…*

*Sea of Sorrows: A Poetic Anthology*
*Selected Poems*
*Selected Poems 1970-2002*
*Selected Poems of Egbert Martin…*
*Shattered Dreams*
*Shraadanjali…*
*Six Ottawa Poets…*
*Sixty Years of Loving…*
*Shoot me with Flowers*
*Slave Song: Poems*
*Soliloquies: In Verse*
*Song of the West Indies*
*Song offerings…*
*Song to Man*
*Song: Poems*
*Songs of my Soul*
*Soul Spaces…*
*Stirrings of Hope…*
*Stories and Poems by a Guyanese Village Boy*
*Stray Leaves*
*Sun's in my Blood*
*Sunrise…*
*Survival: A Collection of…*
*Talk of the Tamarinds…*
*Talking with Myself: A Collection of Poems*
*Tears of a Patriot*
*The Awakening…*
*The Break of Dawn…*
*The Cleavage*
*The Comfort of All Things: A Collection of Poems*
*The Face that Smiles*
*The Fat Black Woman's Poems*
*The Four and Other Poems*
*The Garden….*
*The Healing Place…*
*The Heinemann Book of Caribbean Poetry in English*
*The Hidden Man: Other Poems*
*The Hill of Fire Glows Red*
*The Insomnia Poems…*
*The Key: Poems from the Heart*
*The Kind Eagle: Poems of Prison*
*The Labaria Palm*
*The Listening of Eyes*
*The New Wave*
*The Penguin Book of Caribbean Verse*
*The Poem Book…*
*The Poet Cat…*
*The Poet of Guiana*
*The Presence*
*The Storm Within – An Anthology*
*The Stream of Red Tears*
*The Teenage Years…*
*The Thorn in the Rose…*
*The Time of Flambouy Trees*
*They Came in Ships: An Anthology of…*
*This Healing Place and Other Poems…*
*To a Dead Slave…*
*To Drink Your Kiss*
*To Gain A Land: A Collection of Poems*
*Turner – New and Selected Poetry*
*Twenty-Five Poems*
*Twenty-Four Poems*
*Under the Calabash Tree…*
*Under the Moon and Over the Sea*
*Underground Lines…*

*Unfathomable and …*
*Unsung Verses…*
*Verse*
*Voices in the Dark*
*Watching You, A Collection of Tetractys Poems*
*We Are One*
*University of Hunger…*
*Voiceprint…*
*Watching You, A Collection of Tetractys Poems*
*Weblines*
*West Indian Poetry 1900-1970*
*When September Comes…*
*When Kiskadees Sang*
*Where the Wild Grass Whispers*
*Wild Flowers*
*Wild Flowers and Other Poems*
*Wild Flowers and Water-Lilies*
*Winged Heart: Poems*
*Woman of the Mahabharat*
*Years of Fighting Exile*
*Yet Another Home: Poems*

**POLITICAL HISTORY**
**(See also HISTORY)**

*133 Days Towards Freedom…*
*A Commonwealth of the People: Time for Urgent Reform*
*A Destiny to Mould*
*A Political and Social History of Guyana*
*British Guiana*
*British Guiana: A Study of Marxism*
*Clement James Rohee: Selected Parliamentary speeches...*
*Guyana's Foreign Policy Towards the Twenty-First Century...*
*Justice: The Struggle for Democracy*
*More Profit than Gold*
*Our Public Security*
*Legislative Agenda: Bills, Motions and Debates*
*Peace by Pieces – United Nations Agencies and Their Roles*
*Reflections from the Frontline: Developing Country negotiations...*
*Securing Our Nation: A Compilation of Speeches made...*
*Shridath Ramphal: The Commonwealth and the World*
*The British West Indies: The Search for…*
*The Contemporary Commonwealth*
*The Co-operative Republic of Guyana*
*The Development of the Legislative Council 1606-1945*
*The Indelible Red Stain: The Destruction of a Tropical Paradise...*
*The West on Trial*
*Themes in African-Guyanese History*

*Twenty-five years in British Guiana*

**POLITICS**

*12 Years of the PPP…*
*A Destiny To Mould…*
*A Dream Deferred*
*A Dream Deferred: Guyanese Identity and the Shadow of Colonialism*
*A Great Future Together…*
*A Guide to the sources…*
*A Mouldy Destiny…*
*A Political Glossary…*
*A Time for Action…*
*A Time To Stand Up…*
*A Troublesome Man…*
*A West Indian State…*
*Against the Grain: Balram Singh Rai…*
*An Examination of National Service…*
*Anatomy of Resistance: Anti-colonialism*
*And Finally They Killed Him: Speeches and…*
*At the End of the Day, 1961-1963*
*Barbados: A Post-independence…*
*Birth of the Coop Republic…*
*Bitter Sugar…*
*Black and White*
*Black Man of Guyana…*
*Black Power in the…*
*British Guiana*
*British Guiana: A Challenge to Labour*
*British Guiana: The Case for Compromise…*
*British Guiana: Who Owns It?...*
*British Guiana's Future…*
*Caribbean Charisma: Reflections on Leadership…*
*Caribbean Revolution…*
*Change: Selected Writings…*
*Cheddi Jagan and the Politics of Power...*
*Cheddi Jagan National Assembly Speeches Vol 1*
*Cheddi Jagan National Assembly Speeches Vol 2*
*Cheddi Jagan National Assembly Speeches Vol 3*
*Cheddi Jagan National Assembly Speeches Vol 4*
*Cheddi Jagan National Assembly Speeches Vol 5*
*Cheddi Jagan National Assembly Speeches Vol 6*
*Cheddi Jagan National Assembly Speeches Vol 7*
*Cheddi Jagan National Assembly Speeches Index*
*Cheddi Jagan: Selected Correspondences*
*Cheddi Jagan: Selected Speeches*
*Clearing the Political Air*
*Coalitions of the Oppressed*
*Colombia and Venezuela and the Guianas…*
*Communism and British Guiana*
*Contemporary Politics and Economics of…*
*Counter Hegemony and Foreign Policy*
*Cultural Pluralism and Nationalist Politics*

*Guyana: Socialism in a Plural Society*
*Guyana: The Political Economy of…*
*Guyana: The Struggle for Liberation…*
*Guyana; Democracy Betrayed*
*Guyana's Elections 2020…*
*Haunting Past: Politics, Economics and…*
*Highways to Happiness…*
*History of the PPP…*
*How Europe Underdeveloped Africa*
*How the Obama…*
*How to Win Elections and Manage Political Processes*
*Ideology and Change: The Transformation…*
*Improving Public Accountability: The Guyana Experience, 1985-2007*
*Improving the Organization of Elections...*
*Indian Attitudes…*
*Introduction to Caribbean…*
*Is Imperialism Dead?..*
*Journey to Nowhere: A New World Tragedy*
*Justice: The Struggle for Democracy in…*
*Law and the Political Environment in…*
*Linden Forbes Burnham: National Assembly Speeches Vol 1….*
*Linden Forbes Burnham National Assembly Speeches Vol 2 .*
*Linden Forbes Burnham National Assembly Speeches Vol 3 .*
*Local Democracy in the Commonwealth*
*Memorandum by President Cheddi Jagan…*
*Metanoia for Guyana*
*Metegee…*
*Modern Caribbean Politics*
*Multilateral Diplomacy – For Small States*
*My Credo-Here I Stand…*
*My Fight For Guyana's…*
*National Service…*
*Nationalisation of Guyana's Bauxite*
*Next Witness…*
*No Island is an Island: Selected Speeches*
*Odyssey and Trials of the Georgetown Mayor and Councillors 1992-2012*
*Open letter to…*
*Our achievements….*
*Paramountcy of the Media in Guyana*
*Parliament in the …*
*Party Politics and Racial Division in Guyana*
*Party Politics in the West Indies…*
*Perspectives on Corruption…*
*Phoenix Force No. 47: Terror in Guyana*
*PNC Burnham and Beyond: A Pocket Book Bible*
*Pointing the way, 1959-1961*
*Political and Ethnic…*
*Politics and Public Policy in the…*

*Politics in Ethnically Bipolar States*
*Politics, Race and Youth in Guyana*
*Politics, Race, and Youth in Guyana*
*Poverty: Cause and Cure…*
*PPP Struggles…*
*Pragmatism or Opportunism*
*President Obama…*
*Price of Victory*
*Problems of Development…*
*Race and Politics Among Africans and…*
*Race vs. Politics in Guyana*
*Race, class and Ideology…*
*Race, Class, and Nationhood*
*Race, Politics, and the…*
*Readings in Government and Politics*
*Red Coconut…*
*Referendum: A Question of Human Rights*
*Report of the January 12, 1998 Violence*
*Revolt in the Tropics…*
*Rich People and Rice: Factional Politics in…*
*Road to Socialism…*
*Rooting for Labour,,,*
*Sacred Duty…*
*Shattering Illusions…*
*Something to Remember, Guyana 1980 Elections…*
*Speeches by the Prime Minister…*
*Stains on My Name, War in My Veins…*
*State Capitalism and Ideological Opportunism*
*Stolen Hope…*
*Studies in the Theory of Imperialism*
*Ten Letters to Obama*
*The Achievement of National…*
*The Bankrupt IMF Road…*
*The bauxite strike and the old politics*
*The Birth of the WPA…*
*The Caribbean, Whose Backyard*
*The Coalition Exposed…*
*The Constitution of Guyana*
*The Costs of Regime Survival: Racial Mobilization...*
*The Costs of Regime Survival…*
*The Cycle of Racial Oppression in Guyana*
*The Dark Horse…*
*The Debt Dilemma: IMF Negotiations in…*
*The DLM: Origin-*
*The failure of the Buxton…*
*The Great Paradox of Guyanese Politics…*
*The Great Republic…*
*The Guyana Contract…*
*The Haunting Past…*
*The Independence Movement…*
*Diagnosis-Ideology*
*Terror in Guyana – Phoenix Force No. 47*
*The Integrationist…*
*The Making of a President*
*The Marxian Populism…*
*The More Things Change…*
*The Morning After*
*The New Beginning…*

*Apata…*
*Ascent to Omai*
*Attitude…*
*Backfire: A Collection of Short Stories*
*Bartica: Tales from the…*
*Beauty Lies Within*
*Berbice Crossing and Other Stories*
*Black and Muddy Water…*
*Black Bush*
*Black Jesus and Other Stories*
*Black Watuh Tales…*
*Bone Soup…*
*Bound Coolie: Or the*
*Immigrant…*
*Bundarie Boy*
*Canada in US now…*
*Canterbury Tales on a …*
*Caribbean Anthology of*
*Short Stories*
*Caribbean Essays…*
*Caribbean Folk Tales…*
*Caribbean Stories:*
*Supernatural Tales*
*Caribbean tales…*
*Caribbean Verse: An Anthology*
*Chalkdust in my Eyes…*
*Choke and Rob…*
*Collection of Short Stories*
*Collins Big cat…*
*Commonwealth Short Stories*
*Cool Shade…*
*Crab-man*
*Cry of the Black Bird*
*Cyril Dabydeen Short Stories*
*David and Jonathan…*
*Deadman's Creek: Two*
*Stories*
*Der Palast der Pfauen*
*Dictionary of Guyanese*
*Folklore*
*Don't go near the water*
*Down Independence…*
*Dreams and Reflections*
*Echoes and Voices…*
*El palacio del pavo real*
*Elephants Make Good Stepladders*
*Faber Book of West Indian Stories*
*Faith and Love…*
*Famous Short Stories*
*Father's Tales*
*Fictions*
*Fictions: A Collection of Stories*
*Fish Koker…*
*Florence and Adam*
*Flowers of the Forest*
*Footprints in the Sand*
*For the Love of…*
*Frangipani House…*
*From Berbice to Broadstairs*
*From Utopia to Paradise*
*Gabrielle…*
*Garland of Stories*
*Generations…*
*Genesis and other Stories*
*Gift of the Forest…*
*Glass Forehead*
*Goatsong*
*Grass-root People*
*Green for Danger*
*Guiana Book*
*Guyana Stories…*
*Guyanese Nights…*
*Gwendolyn and Me…*
*Heart's Frame*
*Homage Stories…*
*Hot Mouth Gual…*

*House of Fear: Two Stories*
*I Live in Georgetown*
*Il palazzo del pavone…*
*In the Shadow of…*
*Intertwined…*
*Islands Lovelier Than a Vision*
*It Happened in British Guiana*
*Jogging in Havana: Short Stories*
*L'ange sur le seuil*
*L'échelle secrete*
*Labba and Creek Water: Stories from the Caribbean*
*Layers of the Rainforest*
*Le palais du paon*
*Leaves from the Tree*
*Leo's Local Lyrics…*
*Leslyn in London…*
*Life according to Ivy…*
*Longa Jornado de Oudin*
*Mental and Dictation…*
*Mojo: Conjure…*
*Monsoons on the…*
*Moongazer*
*Moriah's Journey*
*Morning of Yesterday…*
*Mr. Protestant*
*My Brahmin Days and Other Stories*
*My Undiscovered Country…*
*New Writing in the Caribbean*
*Our Wife and other…*
*Over Guiana, Clouds*
*Palacio do Pavão*
*Passport*
*Patterns*
*Penguin Book of Caribbean Short Stories*
*People of Guyana…*
*Perfect Execution…*
*Play Song Somebody: New and Selected Stories*
*Rebelle and Other…*
*Red Howling Monkey*
*Ribald Tales of Guyana*
*River Dancers…*
*Run Softly Demerara*
*Savannah's Edge*
*Selected Dozen Short Stories*
*Send Out You Hand*
*Shape-Shifter: A Collection of…*
*Short Stories*
*Some Guianese Short Stories*
*Song of the Sugarcanes*
*Stories from El Dorado*
*Stories from Guyana: A Collection of…*
*Sunstreams and Shadows…*
*Survival: A collection of…*
*Taste my Words…*
*The Amsterdam Connection*
*The Angel at the Gate…*
*The Brown Curtains*
*The Caribbean Short Story…*
*The Coming of Amalivaca…*
*The Dance of Death…*
*The Dead Don't Die…*
*The Diamond Thieves and Four More…*
*The Doomsday Earthquake…*
*The Dream of Every Heart*
*The Four Banks of the River of Space*
*The Godmother and Other Stories*
*The Guyanese Princess…*
*The Hidden Trees and Other Stories*

*The Last English Plantation*
*The Lost Love and…*
*The Magic Pot*
*The Malali Makers*
*The Mask of the Beggar*
*The Mirror That tells…*
*The Oxford Book of Caribbean*
*The Phoenix Letters…*
*The Pork Knockers and Four*
*The Return of Latchmini…*
*The Secret Ladder*
*The Shadow Behind my Rainbows*
*The Sisters and Manco's Stories*
*The Spirit, the Passion, and the Blood…*
*The Spirits of Le Ressouvenir…*
*The Sky's Wild Noise…*
*They Came in Ships: An Anthology*
*Things Guyanese…*
*Three Short Stories*
*Timepiece*
*Tiger Dead!*
*To England and Back*
*To Monkey Jungle: Short Stories*
*Trailing the Sun's Sweat…*
*Trauma: A Collection…*
*Wanderlust…*
*Waterloo and Other Stories*
*West Indian Stories*
*Windswept and Other Stories*
*Windswept and Three Other Stories*
*Witnesses and Other Stories…*

**RACE RELATIONS**

*Anatomy of Race Politics…*
*Black Paradox…*
*British Guiana: Problems of…*
*Color, Hair, and Bone…*
*Ethnic Conflict and Development…*
*Ethnic Power and…*
*Ethnicity, Class…*
*Finding Myself…*
*Fulcrums of Change: Origins of…*
*Identity, Ethnicity and Culture in…*
*In Europe's Image: The Need for…*
*Muslims in America*
*Notes on Race and Psychology*
*Party Politics and Racial Division*
*Politics, Race, and Youth in Guyana*
*Power in a Postcolonial World…*
*Power, Production…*
*Race and Empire in British Politics*
*Race and Ethnic Relations…*
*Race and Ethnicity in Guyana*
*Race and Political Discourse…*
*Race and Politics Among Africans and…*
*Race vs. Politics in Guyana*
*Race, Class and Nationhood*
*Race, Gender…*
*Race, Power, and Social*

*Racial Conflict Resolutions and Power Sharing*
*Racial Ethnic Imbalance in Guyana Public Bureaucracies...*
*Racial Identity and…*
*Sitting on a Racial Volcano (Guyana Uncensored)*
*The Cycle of Racial Oppression*
*The Sociology of Race…*
*Toward a New Beginning*
*Worlds Apart…*

**RELIGION (See also Church History)**

*24 Inspirational Messages…*
*A Day in the Life of Satan…*
*A Productive Garden…*
*A Quick Guide for Altar…*
*Advancing God's Kingdom…*
*Advancing Kingdom…*
*After God's Heart…*
*Aiming High and the Yogas…*
*Aliens, UFOs, Mars…*
*Antichrist…*
*Apostasy…*
*Attracting and Retaining…*
*Audacious Anglicans…*
*Barabbas or Jesus…*
*Be Thankful…*
*Beauty for Ashes*
*Believers are called…*
*Beyond a curse…*
*Beyond the leaves…*
*Biblical Mysteries…*
*Breaking Siege…*
*Built for Goodness…*
*Called to the 5-FLD…*
*Canadian Fiqh…*
*Caribbean Fiqh…*
*Complete in Christ…*
*Cosmic Conversations…*
*Crown-The Analysis of Life…*
*Cry No More…*
*Demon in the House…*
*Devices of the Devil…*
*Dig Deeper…*
*Divinity…*
*Effective Ministry for…*
*End of Days…*
*Enjoying Your Senior Years*
*Ethics and Professional…*
*Everyone needs forgiveness…*
*Fathers and Founders…*
*Fathers are important…*
*Fear Not, God is…*
*Fellowship at the Family Table…*
*Fight for your destiny…*
*For the Glory of Islam…*
*God Delivers his Children…*
*God Outfoxed Great Leaders…*
*Going Hard after God…*
*Gruesome to Glorious…*
*Guyana in Prophecy…*
*Handwriting on the…*
*Hard After God…*
*Hard Look…*
*Healing and…*
*Heavenly Wisdom…*
*Hinduism…*
*I am worshipping…*
*I Thank My God…*
*Ichabod…*
*Introduction to Christology…*

*Islam, Muslims…*
*Islam and Other Major World Religions*
*Jacob's Ladder…*
*Jesus and the Gospel of the…*
*Jesus Christ, a necessary…*
*Jesus's Birth, Death…*
*Keep Worshipping God…*
*Keys to Breakthrough…*
*Kingdom of Heaven*
*Keeper of Souls*
*Knowing God…*
*Leadership and Servanthood…*
*Let Your Faith Arise…*
*Life in the Secret Place…*
*Live with Precision…*
*Lord, I am not ready…*
*Magnificent Obsession…*
*Maintaining the Glow…*
*Making Church Fun…*
*Memory and Myth: Post Colonial religion...*
*Metamorphosis…*
*Ministry Made Easy…*
*Modeling Kingdom…*
*My Faith Looks Up To Thee…*
*Mystery of the Resurrection*
*No Greater Name…*
*No More Temple…*
*On Your Mark: The Message of Mark*
*Overcoming the Strongman…*
*Pray and Push…*
*Pray This Way…*
*Preaching Doom…*
*Progressively Through the Reservoir of God*
*Prosperity God's Way…*
*Purchas: His Pilgrims…*
*Putting God First…*
*Religion, Power, and….*
*Road to Armageddon…*
*Sanatana Dharma…*
*Secure the Upper Springs…*
*Shepherding God's Flock…*
*Shift the Atmosphere…*
*Shine Like The Stars…*
*Sigh and Cry…*
*Sons of God…*
*Speaking Truth to Power…*
*Strategically establishing…*
*Study Guide….*
*Surviving the Storm…*
*The Da Vinci Code Revisited: A Conclusive Refutation...*
*The Church's Impact…*
*The Diabolical Mind…*
*The Dissolution of Heaven…*
*The Face of God…*
*The Great Reset…*
*The Greatest…*
*The Heaven Jesus Gained…*
*The Hell Jesus Went Through…*
*The Hindu Concept…*
*The Modern Book of Muslim Names…*
*The Mystery of God…*
*The Pentecostal Show…*
*The Poor Man's Wisdom…*
*The Pursuit of Excellence…*
*The Revelation of Jesus…*
*The Seven Pillars of the Church…*
*The West Indian Bible…*
*Thy Kingdom Come…*
*Touching the hem of his…*
*Transfigured for…*
*Transformational*

*Leadership…*
*Treasures and Hidden…*
*Two Israels…*
*Waiting on God…*
*Way Maker…*
*What a Friend We Have…*
*When the Music Fades…*
*Where is the Babylon…*
*Why Attending Church…*
*Winning Your Battle…*
*Working for the Lord…*
*Your Prayers Matter…*

**RESEARCH**
*A Guide to Historical Research*
*A Study of the Historiography…*
*How to do better research*
*The Pressures of Text…*

**SCIENCE**
*Advanced Structured Materials…*
*Advances in Imaging and Electron Physics*
*Advances in Imaging and Electron Physics*
*Advances in Remote Sensing…*
*Bioelelectronics, Biointerfaces, and Biomedical Applications 2,*
*Cryogenic Operation for Low Temperature Electronics*
*Encyclopaedia of Electrical and Electronics Engineering Fiber Optic*
*Encyclopaedia of Remote Sensing…*
*Communications: Fundamentals and Applications*
*High Temperature Electronics*
*Ichtyology…*
*Integrated Optoelectronics (First International Symposium)*
*Integrated Passive Component Technology*
*Low Temperature Electronics and High Temp.*
*Low Temperature Electronics: Physics, Devices, Circuits*
*New Technology for Geosciences…*
*Noise and Fluctuations Control in Electronic Devices*
*Noise in Devices and Circuits I, SPIE Proceedings*
*Optoelectronics and Photonics*
*Organic Semiconductor Materials, Devices, and Processing*
*Photodetectors and Fiber Optics*
*Photodetectors: Materials, Devices, and Applications*
*Remote Sensing…*
*Sand and Gravel…*
*Selected Topics in Electronics and Systems*
*Semiconductor Device-Based Sensors for Gas, Chemical, and*
*Sensors Based on Nanotechnology*

Silicon Nitride and Silicon Dioxide Thin Insulating Films
Silicon Nitride, Silicon Dioxide and Emerging Dielectrics
Silicon Photonics—Fundamentals and Applications
Silicon-based Millimeter wave Technology
Solid-State Electronics and Photonics in Biology and Medicine,
Spatial Methods…
Springer Handbook of Electronic and Optoelectronic Materials,
State-of-the-art Program on Compound Semiconductors
Superconductivity

**SOCIAL STUDIES**

A Cathedral Inside: Odyssey of a Guyanese Family
Adventures of the Homeless…
Among the Hindus and Creoles
An Introduction To Our Social Philosophy
Building Relationships…
Building Sustainable…
British Guiana or Work and
Can children ever…
Care and Respect…
Caribbean Personhood II…
Children Make Your…
Coming Back…
Conflict and Solidarity in a Guianese Plantation
Conflict Management…
Conquering Shame…
Contributions Towards the Resolution of…
Cooperative Republic, Guyana 1970…
Divorce and Remarriage…
Domestic violence in America
Dream big and live your…,
Dynamics of a Creole System…
Dyslexia from a …
Education of HIV/AIDS…
Family and Business…
Family structure…
Finish Strong…
From Singleness…
Gender Equality in the Caribbean
Glimpses of Living Guyanese...
Global Cities-Local Places…
Groundings with my Brothers
Growing up Guyanese
Growing up in Guyana
Guyana
Guyana at the Millenium Crossroads
Guyana Diaries
Guyana: A Bed of Thorns
Guyanese
Guyanese Women
HIV and AIDS Knowledge and Stigma in Guyana
How to deal with Broken Relationships
Humans 2.0…
I am a Guyanese

*Individual and Society in Guiana*
*Indo-Caribbean Resistance*
*Inspire the Child*
*It Happened in British Guiana*
*Invest in your children's…*
*Kinship and Class in the West Indies*
*Laskhmi Out of India*
*Leadership: A Tough Call…*
*Marriage for Sale...*
*Medicine Cult: A Prescription for Side Effects and Death*
*Middle Passage: Impressions of Five Societies*
*Neighbours are important…*
*New Caribbean Man*
*Once a Guyanese Child*
*Parenting…*
*Plantations, Peasants, and State*
*Poverty and Basic Needs*
*Preparing for work…*
*Preparing for workplace…*
*Public Security: Criminal Violence and Policy in Guyana*
*Pulling the Punches: Defeating Domestic Violence*
*Rasta and Resistance*
*Remaining Calm in ….*
*Selected aspects of Guyanese fertility: Education, Mating and Race*
*Self-help Housing, the Poor and…*
*Settled on Dregs…*
*Side Effects: Death – Confessions of a Pharma Insider*
*Single Parenting…*
*Small States and Segmented Societies*
*Social Distancing…*
*Standing Up…*
*Success is Possible…*
*Suffering and Recovery…*
*Super Seniors: Beyond 65 and Fully Alive*
*Sustainable Livelihoods*
*The benefits of working…*
*The Best Ever Guide to Demotivation for Guyanese...*
*The Coloured Girl in the Ring*
*The Dynamics of Freedom…*
*The Guyana Exodus*
*The Importance of Motherhood*
*The Other Side of the Medical Coin*
*The Plural Society in the British West Indies*
*The Poor and the Powerless*
*The Principles of Stabilizing…*
*The Revelation of Love…*
*The Roles of the Christian…*
*The Roles of the Husband…*
*The Sacred Bombshell Handbook…*
*The Simple Keys to a Happy…*
*Thrive Like a Dandelion: A Self-Empowerment Journey...*
*Trading Poverty for…*
*Training Daughters…*
*Training Sons…*

*Treat Me Well…*
*Twelve Essentials for a successful marriage*
*Understanding and working…*
*Understanding Poverty and International Development Cooperation*
*Waiting for Justice*
*Waiting on Sons…*
*Welfare and Planning in the West Indies*
*Where does purpose…*
*Why do people choose to…*
*Your success will attract…*

**SPORTS**
*100 Great Westindian Test Cricketers…*
*75 Years of West Indian Cricket*
*A Time in Our History: Berbice Cricket From 1939 to 2010*
*An Abounding Joy…,*
*Blasting for runs*
*Caribbean Cricketers…*
*Clive Lloyd: The Authorised Biography*
*Cooperstown is my Mecca*
*Cricket and West Indian Identity*
*Cricket Without a Cause…*
*Cricketers Who Toured…*
*Guyanese in India, West Indian Test Cricket*
*Hand-in-Hand History of Cricket…*
*Historical and Present Day Views of…*
*I was born to learn…*
*Indian-Caribbean Test Cricketers…*
*Indo-West Indian Cricket*
*Indo-West Indian Cricketers*
*Joe Solomon and the Spirit…*
*Living for Cricket*
*Lunchtime Medley: Writings on West Indian Cricket*
*Muscular Learning: Cricket and Education*
*Nation Imagined…*
*Report of the Governance Committee on West Indies Cricket*
*Sandow's Gymnasium…*
*Sports Event Management…*
*Sportsmen and Sportsmanship - A compilation of articles*
*The Complete Record of West Indian Test…*
*Test Cricketers…*
*The First West Indian Cricket Tour...*
*The Rites of Cricket…*
*The Rise of West Indian Cricket*
*The Unforgiven…*
*West Indian Cricket…*

**TRADE UNIONISM**
*A History of Trade Unionism in Guyana*
*British Guiana: A Challenge to Labour*
*Caribbean Workers' Struggle for…*
*Cries From the Workplace: The Making of…*
*Emergence of the Caribbean Labour Movement*

**TRAVEL, EXPLORATION, and ADVENTURE**

*Zoo Quest to Guiana*

**WALTER RODNEY**

*A History of the Guyanese Working People*
*And Finally They Killed Him*
*Assassination Cry of a Failed Revolution...*
*Come Lehwe reason…*
*Groundings With My Brothers*
*Guyana Sugar Plantations*
*History of the Upper Guinea Coast*
*How Europe Underdeveloped Africa*
*Lakshmi Out of India*
*People's Power, No Dictator*
*Poetic Tributes to Walter Rodney*
*Rasta and Resistance*
*Walter Rodney*
*Walter Rodney and his times…*
*Walter Rodney Speaks*
*Walter Rodney: 1968 Revisited*
*Walter Rodney: His Last Days and Campaigns*
*Walter Rodney: Intellectual and Political Thought*
*Walter Rodney: Revolutionary and Scholar*
*West Africa and the Atlantic Slave Trade*

**WOMEN'S ISSUES**

*50 Women: 50 Years…*
*60 years of women artists in Guyana…*
*A Preliminary Study of Women Soldiers...*
*A Woman of Valor…*
*Backslider*
*Bibliography of Women Writers…*
*Blaze of Women…*
*Born with a Veil*
*Caribbean Women Writers…*
*Co-Wives and Calabashes*
*Facing the Wind…*
*Framing the Word…*
*Feminist and Critical…*
*Four Women*
*Gender, Place and Ethnicity*
*Gender Equality in the…*
*Guyanese Women…*
*Home Girl…*
*In Guiana Wilds: A Study of Two Women*
*Liminal Spaces…*
*Managing a Great Woman…*
*Media Trends…*
*Men, Women and Children…*
*Mother Imagery…*
*Strong Women Make History…*
*Sun, Sex and Gold: Tourism and Sex Work*
*The Aloneness of Mrs Chatham…*
*The Geometry of Marriage...*
*The Pregnancy Handbook for Inexperienced Mothers*
*The Wounds of Naipaul and the Women of India*
*West Indian Women…*
*What Every Woman in Public Life Should…*
*Where are you Agnes…*

*Woman of the Mahabharat*
*Women and Change in the Caribbean*
*Women and Development in the Third World*
*Women and Politics: An International Perspective…*
*Women, Human Settlements and Housing…*
*Women Across Borders…*
*Women in Caribbean History…*
*Women in Caribbean Politics…*
*Women in Guyana…*
*Women To remember…*
*Women Traders…*
*Women's Power to Heal…*
*Wordsworth's White Wife…*

**ZOOLOGY**

*Mammals of the Neotropics*
*Monkeys of the Guianas…*
*Safari South America: The Saki Monkeys*
*The River Wolf…*
*Tropical Wildlife in British Guiana*

# APPENDIX B

## DOCUMENTARIES

**Amerindians**

1. *A Photojournal of the Nine Guyanese Amerindian Tribes* (Lal Balkaran: Toronto, 2009).
2. *Cowboys and Indians: Ranching in the Rupununi* (Guyana Shield Media Project: 2000).
3. *Round Town: Rupununi Rodeo* (Friends of Guyana: 2003).
4. *The Guyanese Amerindians* [A documentary of all nine tribes]. (Lal Balkaran: Toronto, 2020).
5. *The Rupununi* [A documentary on the Geography and the People of the North and South savannahs] (Lal Balkaran: Toronto, 2020).
6. *The Third Way to Reach Remote Tribes* (Attila Jacob Peli: 2011).
7. *Wapishana Hammock* (Rupununi Weavers Society: 2000).

**Biography**

8. *Caribbean Champion, International Statesman: The Story of a West Indian Icon Sir Shridath Ramphal* (Caricom, 2020).
9. *Field A Spotlight: Sydney Allicock* (Peter Stonier: 2013).
10. *Rivers of Sound: Gordon Rohlehr's Life and Works* (Vimeo: 2014).
11. *Medicine Man: The Stan Brock Story* (2020).
12. *Yesu Persaud: The Man from El Dorado [A new documentary on business magnate Yesu Persaud to mark his 90th birthday].* (David Dabydeen, Arlen Harris, and Daniyal Harris-Vajda: 2019).

**General**

13. *A Dream for Guyana's National Heritage* (Conservation International: 1999).
14. *An Evening with West Indies Cricket Legends Alvin Kallicharran: 2005; Clive Lloyd: 2004; and Ron Headley: 2006* (Robert Lalljie: 2004-2006).
15. *Beryl Gilroy and Janice Shinebourne with Susheila Nasta* (1986).
16. *Born Blue* [Two doctors. Two weeks. No sleep. An endless number of children in need of heart surgery]. (Geordie Day: 2016).
17. *CLR James and Defining Cricket* (Robert Lalljie: 2010).
18. *Communities, Consultation & Corporate Accountability in Guyana* (CUPE National: Ottawa, 2008).
19. *Gifted Hands* (Ramesh Vanan: 2018).
20. *Grandma, Guyana, and Me* (BBC and Tiffany Sweeney: 2018).
21. *Guyana Pepperpot. A four-episode series exploring modern issues in Guyana* (2010).
22. *Guyana's Future and Challenges in Oil* [A German team explores Guyana's offshore oil discoveries and environmental risks]. (Shane Thomas McMillan; 2020).
23. *Guyana: Path to Paradise* (BBC: London, 2012).
24. *Guyana: Road to Prosperity* (Neaz M. Subhan. 2022).
25. *Historical and Contemporary Georgetown – Guyana's Heartbeat* (Lal Balkaran: 2015). Revised 2020.
26. *I Is a Long-Memoried Woman* (Grace Nichol: 1990).
27. *In Their Own Words: Black veterans of World War Two Telling Their Stories for the First Time* (Robert Lalljie: 2006).
28. *Kriiyoliiz: A young woman searches and reclaims Creolese* (Janice Imhoff: 2021)
29. *Medicine Man: The Stan Brock Story* (2020).

30. *Mr. Bickerton! Eat Your Hat!: About Guyanese linguist Professor Ian Robertson's journey to discover Berbice Dutch Creole* (Janice Imhoff: 2021).
31. *Once More Removed: A Journey Back to India* (Shundell Prasad: 2013).
32. *Poison the Lifeline* [A documentary abouth the 1995 Omai cyanide spill]. (2000).
33. *Sea Wall* (Brian Zahm: 2010).
34. *The Bastard Sings the Sweetest Song* (Christy Garland: 2012).
35. *The Black and Asian Contribution to Britain During World War Two* (Robert Lalljie: 2006).
36. *The City Voices: Ghetto Life in Guyana* (Elijah Marchand: 2013).
37. *The Commonwealth Contribution to Britain During World War Two* (Robert Lalljie: 2008).
38. *The Seawall* (Mason Richards, 2011).
39. *The West Indies Contribution to Britain During World War Two: Squadron Leader Ulric Cross* (Robert Lalljie: 2005).

**Geography**

40. *Coast Land* [A documentary describing the effects of overtopping and sea level rise (Alex Arjoon: 2020).
41. *Geography of Guyana* [A four-part series showing the Coastland, Hilly Sandy Belt, Forest Region, and Savannah Region (Lal Balkaran: Toronto, 2020).
42. *Guyana: A Photographic Journey* (Lal Balkaran: Toronto, 2008).
43. *Guyana: A Visual Journey* (Kurt Hammer: Chicago, 2013).
44. *Imbotero Research Centre: Merging Coastal communities and Science* (Alex Arjoon: 2022).
45. *Last Eden* (Dan O'Neill: 2021).
46. *Mabaruma Sojourn* (Annette Arjoon-Martins and Dave Martins: 2009).

47. *Return to the Tepuis* (Jenny Nichols: 2013).
48. *The Barima Mora Passage* (Alex Arjoon: 2020).
49. *The Rupununi Savannahs of Guyana: A Visual Journey* (Lal Balkaran: Toronto, 2012).

**Jonestown**

50. *American Justice: Jonestown Massacre* (1992).
51. *605 Adults 304 Children: An immersive and intimate documentary filmed entirely by the Peoples Temple in Jonestown, Guyana* (Michael Mahafiie: 2019).
52. *Escape from Jonestown* (CNN: Nov 2008).
53. *Guyana: Cult of the Damned* (1979).
54. *Guyana Tragedy: The Story of Jim Jones* (CBS: 1980).
55. *Hyacinth* [A kind of poetic nonfiction that revolves around a trip in 2008 to Jonestown].(Lydia Moyer, Charlottesville, 2008).
56. *Jim Jones' Guyana Tragedy: History of The Teacher* (1980).
57. *Jonestown – Nightmare in Paradise* (National Geographic: 2013).
58. *Jonestown: Paradise Lost* (History Channel: 2007).
59. *Jonestown: The Life and Death of Peoples Temple* (PBS Home Video: 2006).
60. *Pieces of Jonestown* (Aaron Oldenburg: Baltimore, 2010).
61. *Seconds From Disaster* (National Geographic Society: 2012).

**Nature**

62. *A Dream for Guyana's National Heritage* (Conservation International: 1999).
63. *Flight of the Harpy Eagle in Guyana* (National Geographic: 2011).
64. *Guyana* (Robert McManus: 2009).
65. *Guyana: Yours to Discover – Pictures of Guyana* (Mike Charles Productions, 2009).

66. *Guyana: Yours to Discover – Wild Guyana* (Mike Charles Productions: 2008).
67. *Guyana: Yours to Discover* (Mike Charles Productions: 2007).
68. *Iwokrama Canopy Walkway* (BBC: 2010).
69. *Jungle Eagle* (Nature: 2010).
70. *Jungle Fish* (Louisana Kreutz: 2012).
71. *Kanuku: Mountains of Life* (Conservation International: 2005).
72. *Monster Fish* (National Geographic: 2014).
73. *River Monsters: Lair of Giants* (2012).
74. *River Monsters: Body-Snatcher Monster* (2014).
75. *River Monsters: Man-eating Monster* (2014)
76. *The Lost Land of the Jaguar*, (BBC: London, 2003).
77. *The monkey-eating eagle of the Orinoco: A documentary on the harpy eagle* (BBC: 2011).
78. *The spectacular fierce animals of Guyana* (Real Wild: 2022).
79. *Upriver Through Guyana* (Preston King: Travels, PBS, 1994) [A documentary on Guyana's pork-knockers].
80. *Wildlife in Guyana* – a 3-part series (BBC: 2008).

**Philately**

81. *Stamps of British Guiana and Guyana since 1850* (Lal Balkaran: Toronto, 2011). Revised 2020.
82. *The Travels of the British Guiana: The World's Most Famous Stamp* (Sotheby's: London, 2014).

**Politics**

83. *Burnham Did It Again* (Granada Television: London, 1973 [A documentary of the July 16, 1973 fraudulent General Elections].
84. *In the Slky's Wild Noise* [A 1976 documentary on an interview ith Dr. Walter Rodney] (Victor Jara Collective: 1983).

85. *Raid on Democracy: A Look at the March General Election in Guyana* (Neaz M. Subhan, 2020).
86. *Songs from Walter Rodney's Choir: A new film on the life and works of the world-famous historian murdered 32 years ago.* [A world premier at the University of Dar Es Salaam, 2012]. (Robert Lalljie: London, 2012).
87. *The Making of a Prime Minister* (Granada Television: London, 1969) [Anatomy of the 1968 fraudulent General elections].
88. *The Terror and the Time* (Rupert Roopnaraine; 1979).
89. *Thunder in Guyana* (Suzanne Wasserman: Women Make Movies Distributor: New York, 2003) [A documentary on Mrs Janet Jagan (President 1997-1999) with a political history of the country from 1943 to 1997). Clips of the General Elections held between 1953 and 1997 are included).
90. *Trail of the Vanishing Voters* (Granada Television: 1969) [A documentary on the first general elections in December 1968 held after independence was attained in May 1966. It turned out to be a massive fraud].
91. *W.A.R. Stories: Walter Anthony Rodney* (Clairmont Chung: 2010).
92. *Walter Rodney Documentary: What they Don't Want you to know* (Arlen and Daniel Harris: 2022).

**Travel and Exploration**

93. ARD's travels throughout Guyana. Please see www.youtube.com for well over fifty such travels that this Essequibo-born traveller has done over the years. Each brings out the natural beauty, economic and cultural geography and way of life of the people living at each location in all ten regions.
94. *Bamazon* [8-part documentary on Guyana's pristine natural resources (History Channel: 2012).
95. *British Guiana: The Country and its industries* (British Pathe: 1933).

96. *Discover Guyana* (Discover Your World Television: Richmond Hill, 1994).
97. *Essequibo River: Hidden River. A 3-part series* (2022).
98. *Expedition Essequibo* (Blue Paw Artists: 2013).
99. *Exploration Guyana* [An exploratory journey through the jungle of Northern Amazonia. Charles Montier and two Patamona Amerindians attempt the first descent of the Potaro river from its source to its mouth]. (Charles Montier: 2011).
100. *Guyana: A Visual Essay* (Kurt Hemmer and Tom Knff: 2013).
101. *Guyana: The Lost World* (narrated in English by Cara Jones based on a Japanese expedition to Mount Roraima).
102. *Guyana: The Last True Wilderness* (Sussex Wildlife Trust: 2021).
103. *Guyana* (Robert McMansen: 2009).
104. *Into the Bush* (Esias Lord: 2019).
105. *Into The Lost World* (National Geographic: 2002).
106. *Journey to Hope* (Tania Khalaf: 2012).
107. *Jungle fish: How flying fish could save Guyana's rainforest* (Louisana Kreutz, 2013).
108. *Killers of the Rupununi* (Mutual of Omaha Wild Kingdom Series, NBC, 2019).
109. *Mount Roraima: The Lost World* (National Geographic: 2003).
110. *Nostalgic Guyana* (Equality Travel Group: Toronto, 2002).
111. *Return to the Tepuis* (National Geographic Society: 2013).
112. *Roundup in the Rupununi* (Mutual of Omaha Wild Kingdom Series, NBC, 2022).
113. *Serious Explorers – Raleigh,* a 10-part series. (BBC: 2011).
114. *The Last Tepui* (National Geographic Society: 2022).

115. *The Wild Coast: An Exploration of the Guianas* [A geographical, historical, and philosophical exploration of freedom in the three Guianas of South America. Reviewing the sites of Jonestown, escapee Papillon in French Guiana, and the freedom-loving Maroons during the bloody guerilla war in Suriname} (David Whalen: 2014).
116. *Through the Cattle Trail* (Episode 8 Season 1967. Stan Brock leads cattle through the Rupununi Cattle Trail from Surama in Northern Rupununi to Takama in the Berbice Savannahs; Mutual of Omaha Wild Kingdom Series, NBC).

## APPENDIX C
## FILMOGRAPHY

### FILMS ON GUYANA AND GUYANESE

1. *A Guiana Sumiu*. Directed by Rodrigo Van Der Put. 2019.
2. *Gift of the Forest. 1968* [A movie on Amerindian life based on a book by R. Lal Singh who spent ten years (1905-1915) among the Makushis in the North Rupununi].
3. *Green Mansions*. 1959
4. *Guyana: Crime of the Century*. 1979 [Based on the November 1978 Jonestown Mass-Suicide]
5. *Guyana Tragedy: The Story of Jim Jones*. 1980
6. *I Is a Long-Memoried Woman*. 1983 [Film adaptation of Grace Nichols's award-winning book of the same name].
7. *In Search of Jim Jones*. 1981
8. *Mustard Bath*. Directed by Darrell Wasvk. 1993
9. *Orpailleur*. Directed by Marc Barrat. 2009
10. *The Bastard Sings the Sweetest Song*. 2012.
11. *The Humming-Bird Tree*. 1992 [The BBC produced and released this film at Christmas 1992 based on the novel *The Hummingbird Tree* (1969) by literary icon, renowned poet, sportsman, and columnist Dr. Ian McDonald].
12. *The Jonestown Haunting*. 2020.
13. *The Other Fellow*. 2022
14. *The White Diamond*. 2004
15. *To Sir With Love*. 1967. This was a popular British drama film starring the late Sydney Poitier and based on the experiences of notable Guyanese E. R. Braithwaite as a school-teacher in an inner London city school during the 1950s. He wrote a book of the same name that was published in 1959 in London by Bodley Head. The British singer Lulu made her debut in the film singing its title song.
16. *Too Hot to Handle*. Directed by Jack Conway. 1938
17. *Truth and Lies*: Jonestown, Paradise Lost. 2018

## FILMS BY GUYANESE

**ABBENSETTS, Michael** (1938-2016)
*Samba* (1980)
*Outlaw* (1983)
*The Lion* (1993)
*Easy Money* (1981)
*Big George is Dead* (1987)
*Lille Napoleons* (1994)
*Sweet Talk* (Methuen, 1974)
*Empire Road* (Granada: 1979)

**BEHARRY, Len**
*Anmol Bandhan* (The Precious Knot). 1974

**CHAN, Errol**
*Jus Lyk D* (2011)
*Luck Beat Handsome* (2011)
*Roots and Soul* (2010)
*Ruth* (2011)
[He was chosen for the 2011 President Film Endowment Project in Guyana].

**CORSBIE, Ken**
*The Seawall: Tales of the Guyana Coast.* 2012

**JACKMAN, Yaphet** (www.yaphetjackman.com).
[Cinematographer]
*Adero.* 2017
*Christmas For Sale.* Directed by Yaphet Jackman. 2022.
*Delima's Delimma.* 2013
*Guiana Guyana.* 2010
*Guyana Pepperpot.* 2010
*Seawall Walker.* 2010.
*Tradition.* 2011
*USAID 50th Anniversary.* 2011

**JAGESSAR, Rohit**
*Guiana 1838.* 2004

**JAMES, Lionel**
*The Life Swap Adventure*. 2017.

**KUMAR, Harbance**
*Rainbow Raani*. 2006

**LEE, Vivian**
*If Wishes Were Horses*. 1976

**MAHASE, Richard B.**
*The Tenant's Rent's Due*. 2009

**MARCHAND, Elizabeth**
*The City Voices*. 2013

**MOHAMED, Paloma**
*Jezebel*. 1991

**PRASAD, Shundell**
*Festival of Lights*. 2010

**RAMOUTAR, Gavin**
*Antiman*. 2014

**SADEEK, Sheik**
*Song of the Sugar Cane*. 1980
[Film adaptation of the winning novel in the 1959 National Gold Medal award].

**SHIVRAJ, Mahadeo**
[Actor, producer and director].
The following were produced and directed by Mahadeo Shivraj.
*'83 Million Gees* - Written by Ronald Hollingsworth.2013
*A Jasmine for a Gardener* - Written by Churaumanie Bissundial.2012
*Appointment with Karma* - Written by Somnauth Narine.2023.
*Brown Sugar too bitter for me* - Written by Somnauth Narine. 2013
*Brown Sugar too bitter for me 2 – The Oil Dream* - Written by Somnauth Narine. 2023.

*Deception*. 2001
*Forgotten Promise* - Written by Somnauth Narine. 2014
*Good Time*. 2017
*Karma: A Love Story*. 2007
*Kicking It High*. 2004
*Master of None*. 2015
*Poker Face*. 2023
*Protection Game* - Written by Somnauth Narine. 2016
*Snitch in New York*. 2003
*The Americans*. 2013
*The Quack Doctor by the Roti Shop* - Written by Somnauth Narine. 2023
*The Smurfs*. 2011
*Till I Find A Place* - Written by Ronald Hollingsworth.2010
*Unbreakable Kenny Schmidt*. 2015

**SINGH, Ryan**
*Fried Bakes and Dumplings*. 2015 [Winner of the 'Audience Choice Awards' for *Fried Bakes and Dumplings* Greater August Town Film Festival GATFFEST 2016, in Jamaica].
*Graffiti Alley*. 2016.
*Housekeeping, IRL: The Series*. 2016
*Mom*. 2013.
[Best Documentary under 40 Minutes' Winner for 'Mom' at the Caribbean Tales International Film Festival CTIFF 2013].
*Rasta: A Soul's Journey*. 2015
*The Black Experience Project Report*. 2017

**WASYK, Darrell**
*Mustard Bath*. 1993

## FILMS IN WHICH GUYANESE APPEARED

**ALI, Jamal** (b. 1940 in Guyana)
*Black Joy*. 1977
*Open Door*. 1973
*R.H.I.N.O.: Really Here in Name Only*. 1983

**ADAMS, Robert** (1902-1965)
*Caesar and Cleopatra*. 1945
*Dreaming*. 1944
*Follow the Sun*. 1951
*It Happened One Sunday*. 1944
*King Solomon's Mines*. 1937
*Men of Two Worlds*. 1946
*Midshipman Easy*. 1935
*Old Bones of the River*. 1938
*Old Mother Riley's Jungle Treasure*. 1951
*Sanders of the River*. 1935
*Sapphire*. 1959
*The Criminal*. 1960

**AMOS-Ross, Troy** (b. 1975)
*Cinderella Man*. 2005
*Lost Girl*. 2010
*Phantom Punch*. 2008

**AUSTIN, William** (1884-1975)
*It*. 1927
*Redheads on Parade*. 1935
*The Marriage Playground*. 1929

**BAKSH, Mariam** (b.1982)
*The Banana Shell*. 2005

**BELLE, J.J** (1955-2004)
*The Last Resort of Jonathan Ross*. 1988

**BRASHER, Christopher** (1928-????)
*The Deepest Hole in the World: Documentary*. 1972
*Commonwealth Games*. 1958
*Matters of Life and Death*. 1967

**BEATON, Norman** (1934-1994)
*Desmond's*. 1989
*Real Life*. 1984
*Endgame of Samuel Beckett*. 1991

**BLAKE, Asha** (b. 1961)
[Five-time Emmy-award winning television journalist].
*Later Today*. 1999
*Life Moments*. 2002
*World News Now*. 1994

**BROCK, Stan**
*Escape From Angola*. 1976
*Galyon The Indestructible Man*. 1980
*The Corner Bar*. 1973

**CAINE, Shakira, née Baksh** (b. 1947)
*The Man Who Would Be King*. 1975
*Son of Dracula*. 1973
*Where in the world?* 1971

**CAREW, Jan** (1920-2012)
*Drama 61-67*. 1961
*Seven Songs for Malcolm X*. 1993

**CASTOR, Chris** (1896-1986)
*Moonstrike*. 1963
*No Place for Jennifer*. 1950
*Once in a Lifetime*. 1937

**CASE, Gordon** (1948-2020)
*Aggro Seizeman*. 1975
*Muscle Beach Party*. 1964
*The Day of the Triffids*. 1981

**CHANDERPAUL, Tagenarine** (b. 1996)
*'83*. 2021
[a Bollywood movie] Tagenarine Brandon Chanderpaul is a Guyanese cricketer who plays for Guyana in first-class cricket.

He is a left-hand opening batsman. He made his international debut for the West Indies cricket team in November 2022

**CHINN, Anthony** (1930-2000)
*Raiders of the Lost Ark*. Directed by Steven Spielberg. 1981
*Indiana Jones and Raiders of the Lost Ark*. Directed by Steven Spielberg. 1981
*A View to a Kill*. Directed by John Glen. 1985
*The Fifth Element*. Directed by Luc Besson. 1997

**D'OLIVEIRA, Damon**
Produced the following:
*Au plus proche,* 2011
*Bagage,* 2008
*Bonne mere*. 2008
*Brother*. 2022
*Lie With Me*. 2005
*Love Come Down*. 2000
*Poor Boy's Game*. 2007
*Proteus*. 2003
*Rude*. 1995
*Save My Lost Nigga Soul*. 1993
*Somebody is Watching Us*. 2009
*Subway Harmonies*. 2010
*The Book of Negroes* (TV Mini-series). 2005
*The Grizzlies*. 2018
*The Law of Enclosures*. 2000
*What We Have*. 2014
*Wildhood*. 2021

Acted in:
*72 Hours*. 2018
*Angel in a Cage*. 1999
*Back in Action*. 1994
*Bogus*. 1996
*Bollywood/Hollywood*. 2002
*Chilly Beach. The Canadian President*. 2008
*Deep Sleep as Angel*. 1990
*Donkey Kong Country*. 1997-2000
*Double Take. 1998*
*Exotica*. 1994

*Full Disclosure.* 2001
*Getting Away With Murder.* 1996
*Glitter.* 2001
*Jungleground.* 1995
*My Teacher Ate My Homework.* 1997
*New York Minute.* 2004
*Short Circuit 2.* 1988
*The Five Senses. 1999*
*Trial By Jury.* 1994
*Uncut.* 1997

**DICKSON, Kwesi** (b. 1967)
*Endangered Species.* 2021
*Last Passenger.* 2013
*Putas y Huevos.* 1993
*The Occupant, SAS: Red Notice.* 2021

**FOX, Rhona**
*Law and Order.* 2009
*Made in Jersey.* 2013
*United Wall Street Project.* 2014

**GALE, Peggy** (b. 1944)
*Hindsight.* 1975
*Rameau's Nephew by Diderot (Thankx to Dennis Young) by William Schoen.* 1974
*To Lavoisier, Who Died in the Reign of Terror.* 1991

**GLASGOW, Dwayne** (b. 1979)
*Friday Night Slimetime.* 2005
*Most Extreme Elimination Challenge.* 2003
*The Wayne Brady Show.* 2002

**GOMES, Marc** (b. 1961)
*As The World Turns.* 1997
*Deadly Business.* 1986
*Divas.* 1995
*Ed McBain's 87th Precinct.* 1996
*Heatwave* (also known as *Heatwave*). 1997
*Hidden Blessings.* 2000
*If?.* 2002)

*In Defense of a Married Man*. 1990
*In the Eyes of a Stranger*. 1992
*Last Wish*. 1992
*Lighting Force* 1991-1992.
*Lost!*. 1986
*Married to It* (1993
*Murder by the Book* (Or *Alter Ego*). 1987
*Murder in Space*. 1985
*Prescription for Murder* (Or *Taking Care*). 1987
*Stairway to Heaven*. 1998
*Sue Thomas: F.B. Eye* (also known as *Lip Service*). 2002
*The Crow*. 1997
*The Lake*. 1998
*Too Outrageous!*. 1987
*Unfinished Business*. 1984
*Waiting for Michelangelo*. 1996

**GRANT, Cy** (1919-2010)
*At the Earth's Core*. 1976
*Captain Scarlet and the Mysterons*. 1967
*Home of the Brave*. 1957
*Into The Wind*. 2011
*Man From the Sun*. 1956
*Roar of the Greasepaint – The Smell of the Crowd* (a musical). 1964
*Sea Wife*. 1957
*Shaft in Africa*. 1973

**GRANT, Eddy** (b. 1948)
*Idiocracy*. 2006
*Pineapple Express*. 2008
*Romancing the Stone*. 1984

**HARKISHUN, Avi** (b. 1988)
*Not Another Immigrant Story*. 2016

**HING, Cindy** (b. 1977)
*On the Town in the Palm Beaches with Frank Licari*. 2016
*Issues Reports*. 2008

**HUNTE, Muriel** (b.1925)
*Family Life*. 1971

*Great Moments in Aviation*. 1994
*The Full Monty*. 1997

**HERBERT, Leon** (b. 1955)
*Alien*. 1992
*Emotional Backgammon*. 2003
*Batman*. 1989

**HILL, Ramsay** (1890-1976)
*Everybody's Old Man*. 1936
*Midnight Lace*. 1960
*One Hundred and One Dalmatians*. 1961
*The King's Thief*. 1955
*The Ten Commandments*. 1956
*The Three Stooges Go Around the World in a Daze*. 1963
*The Unsinkable Molly Brown*. 1964

**HODIAK, Keith**
*An American Werewolf in London*. 1981
*Doctor Who*. 1983
*Dr. Jekyll and Mr. Hyde*.1978
*EastEnders*. 1992
*Full Metal Jacket*. 1987
*Revenge of the Pink Panther*. 1978
*The Bill*. 1985
*The Chinese Detective*. 1981
*The Lion, the Witch and the Wardrobe*. 1988

**HOWELL, Kafi** (b. 1985)
*The Best Man: The Final Chapters*. 2022

**HUMPHRYS, Laraine** (b. 1953)
*Carry on Girls*. 1973
*Dirty Money*. 1979
*Space*. 1999
*The Great Riviera Bank Robbery*. 1979

**HYNDMAN, Eldridge** (d.2021)
*Exit Wounds*. 2001
*Land of the Dead*. 2005
*The Sentinel*. 2006

**JOHNSON, Ken 'Snakehips'** (1914-1941)
*Oh, Daddy!* 1935

**JONES, Javon Jomo** (b. 1997)
*B00.* Directed by Teresa Lu. 2015
*Falling Water.* 2016
*Little Man.* Directed by Princeton Holt. 2014
*Perspective Chapter 2: The Misdemeanor.* Directed by Rose Troche. 2016
*Seven Seconds.* 2018
*The Cycle. Directed by Michael Marantz.* 2015

**KHAN, Mohamed** (b. 1979)
*15 Minutes.* 2007
*I am Legend.* 2007
*The Thomas Crown Affair.* 1999

**MAIR, John** (b. 1950)
*Bookmark.* 1983
*The Media Show.* 1987
*World in Action.* 1963

**MAXWELL, Charmayne** (1969-2015)
*Brownstone: If You Love Me.* 1995
*Brownstone: Pass the Lovin.'* 1994
*Midnight Mac.* 1995

**MCKENZIE, Mike** (1922-1999)
*Dream House.* 1997
*Tales of the Unexpected.* 1979
*The Stick Up.* 1977

**MEDAS, Ayton** (1917-1989)
*Crane.* 1963
*Teletale.* 1963
*The Adventures of Ben Gunn.* 1958

**MELVILLE, Pauline** (b. 1948). She is an award-winning actress and author and was a professional actress before she became a writer. Her films include:

*2 Point 4 Children*. 1992.
*Spender*.1993).
*Alas Smith and Jones*. 1990
*Blackadder's Christmas Carol*. 1988
*Boom, Boom, Out Go The Lights*. 1981;
*Brighton Rock*. 2010
*Britannia Hospital*. 1982
*Far from the Madding Crowd*. 1967
*Girls on Top*. 1985
*Happy Families*. 1985

Her television appearances include:
*How To Get Ahead in Advertising*. 1989
*Mona Lisa*. 1986
*Red Dwarf*. 1989
*Scrubbers*. 1983
*Shadowlands*. 1993
*Stuff*. 1988
*The Comic Strip Parents*. 1988
*The House of Bernarda Alba*. 1991
*The Long Good Friday*. 1980
*The Young Ones*. 1982
The Young Ones. 1982
*Ulysses*. 1967
*Utz*. 1992
*White City*. 1985

**NELSON, Vonda G** (b. 1972)
*Happiness*. 1998
*Downtown: A Street Tale*. 2004

**POUNDER, Carol Christine Hilaria or CCH** (b. 1952)
*A Touch of Hope*. 1999
*Aladdin and the King of Thieves*. 1996
*All She Ever Wanted*. 1996
*All That Jazz*. 1979
*As Summers Die*. 1986
*Avatar 3*. 2024
*Avatar: The Way of Water*. 2022
*Avatar*. 2009
*Baby of the Family*. 2002

*Bagdad Café*. 1987
*Batman: Assault on Arkham*. 2014
*Benny and Joon*. 1993
*Blossoms and Veils*. 1998
*Booker*. 1984
*Boycott*. 2001
*Cora Unashamed*. 2000
*Coriolanus*. 1979
*Demon Knoght*. 1995
*Disappearing Acts*. 2000
*End of days*. 1999
*Face/Off*. 1997
*Final Justice*. 1997
*For Their Own Good*. 1993
*Funny Valentines*. 1999
*Go Tell It on the Mountain*. 1984
*Godzilla: King of the Monsters*. 2019
*Home Gaian*. 2012
*I'm Dancing as fast as I can*. 1982
*If These Walls Could Talk*. 1996
*Jack Reed. One of Our Own*. 1995
*Leap of Faith*. 1988
*Lifepod*. 1993
*Little Girl Fly Away*. 1998
*Melting Pot*. 1998
*Murder in Mississippi*. 1990
*My Girlfriend's Back*. 2010
*NetForce*. 1999
*New Year*. 1994
*No Place Like Home*. 1989
*On The Edge*. 1987
*Orphan*. 2008
*Postcards from the Edge*. 1990
*Prizzi's Honor*. 1985
*Psycho IV: The Beginning*. 1990
*Rain*. 2008
*Redemption. The Stan Tookie Williams Story*. 2004
*Resting Place*. 1986
*RoboCop 3*. 1993
*Run Till You Fall*. 1988
*Sliver*. 1993

*Superman/Batman: Public Enemies*. 2009
*Tet Grenne*. 2002
*The Big Day*. 1999
*The Disappearance of Christina*. 1994
*The Ernest Green Story*. 1993
*The Importance of Being Earnest*. 1992
*The Line*. 1987
*The Mortal Instruments: City of Bones*. 2013
*The Tower*. 2008
*Things Behind the Sun*. 2001
*Things That Go Bump*. 1997
*Third Degree Burn*. 1989
*Unchained Memories*. 2003
*Union City*. 1980
*White Dwarf*. 1995
*Zooman*. 1995

Television films in which she appeared.
227. 1989
*American Masters*. 2007
*American Playhouse*. 1985
*Archer*. 2015
*Batman Beyond*. 1999
*Beware the Batman*. 2014
*Biker Mice from Mars*. 1994
*Birdland*. 1994
*Brothers*. 2009
*Cagney & Lacey*. 1986
*CBS Schoolbreak Special*. 1989
*Common Ground*. 1990
*Cop Rock*. 1990
*Crossing Jordan*. 2001
*Detention*. 1999
*ER. 1994-1997*
*For the People*. 2002
*Gargoyles*. 1995-1996
*Ghost Cop*. 1998
*Girlfriends*. 2004
*Hill Street Blues*. 1981-86
*Histeria!*. 1998
*Home Improvement*. 1992

*House of Frankenstein*. 1997
*If Tomorrow Comes*. 1986
*Jackie Chan Adventures*. 2003
*Justice League Unlimited*. 2004-06
*L.A. Law*. 1986-1992.
*Law and Order: Special Victims Unit*. 2001-2010.
*Lifestories*. 1991
*Living Single*. 1995
*Miami Vice*. 1989
*Millenium*. 1996-1998
*NCIS: New Orleans*. 2014-2021.
*NCIS*. 2014
*Numbers*. 2005
*Perception*. 2013
*Quantum Leap*. 1990
*Return to Lonesome Dove*. 1993
*Revenge*. 2011
*Robin's Hoods*. 1994
*Rocket Power*. 2000
*Rude Awakening*. 2000
*South Central*. 1994
*Sons of Anarchy*. 2013-14
*Static Shock*. 2001
*Sweet Justice*. 1994-1995.
*The Atlanta Child Murders*. 1985
*The Cosby Show*. 1992
*The District*. 2001
*The Good Fight*. 2021
*The Lion Guard*. 2018
*The Outer Limits*. 2000
*The Practice*. 2001
*The Shield*. 2002-2008
*The West Wing*. 2000
*The X-Files*. 1994
*The. No. 1 Ladies' Detective Agency*. 2009
*True Colors*. 1991
*Valerie*. 1986
*W.I.T.C.H*. 2006
*Warehouse 13*. 2009-2014
*Women in Prison*. 1987-1988

**RAMOS, Regan** (b. 1971)
*Diary of the Dead*. 2007
*Jigsaw*. 2017
*Polar*. 2019

**RAYE, Sol** (1934-2006)
*Desmond's*. 1989
*Great Moments in Aviation*. 1994
*Runaway Bay*. 1992

**ROSHEUVEL, Golda**
*Lady Macbeth*. 2016
*Luther*. 2010
*Silent Witness*. 1996

**ROSS, Damali** (b. 1989)
*BlacKKKlansman*, 2018
*Orange is the New Black*. 2018

**SCOTT, Brian** (b. 1960)
*Czarodziej z Harlemu*. 1990
*Jan z drzewa*. 2008

**SEMPLE, Ron Bobb** (1952-2022)
*See You Yesterday*. 2019
*Temptations. Confessions of a Marriage Counselor*. 2013
*Truth*. 2007

**SINGH, Ryan**
*Conduct Unbecoming*. Directed by Sidney Furie. 2011
*11 Blocks*. Co-directed by Matthew Bennett. 2015
*Mr. Crab*. Directed by Faisal Lutchmedial. 2011

**SOOKDEO, Diana** (b. 1969)
*The Basement Girl*. 2000
*Wild Thing*. 1987

**STEPHENS, Rycklon** (b. 1978)
*WWE Raw*. 1993
*WWE Superstars*. 2009
*WWF Smackdown*. 1999

**TAGGART, Bec** (b. 1992)
*The Umbrella Academy*. 2019

**VALZ, Ian** (1957-2010)
*The Panman: Rhythm of the Palms*. 2007
*Trade Winds*. 1993

Television films
*The Peacock Dance*. 2003
*The Plantation*. 2010

**VON EEDEN, Trevor** (b. 1959)
*Batman: The Brave and the Bold*. 2008
*Black Lightning*. 2017
*Young Justice*. 2010

**WATSON, Maiko** (b. 1981)
*Barbra James*. 2003
*Potion*. 2011
*Sugar Jones: How Much Longer*. 2001

**WEATHERS, Sam** (b. 1980)
*Hookers in Revolt*. 2006
*The Fappening*. 2015
*Vault of Terror II: The Undead*. 2015

**WELLMAN, Guy** (b. 1971)
*FBI*. 2020.
*Hawaii Five-O*. 2019
*Hilbilly Elegy*. 2020
*I Promised*. 2016

**WILLIAMS, Errol** (1951-2007)
*Echoes in the Rink: The Willie O'Ree Story*. 1997
[The only New Brunswick Film to be accepted at the 1998 Toronto International Film Festival]
*When Voices Rise: Dismantling Segregation in a Polite Society*. 2001
[Premiered at the 5th Annual Bermuda International Film Festival, where it won the Audience Choice Award]

**WILSON, Shaunette Renée**
*Black Panther*. 2018
*The Resident*. 2018
*Billions*. 2016

**WRIGHT, Letitia** (b. 1993)
*Aisha*. 2022
*Avengers: Endgame*. 2019
*Avengers: Infinity War*. 2018
*Black Panther: Wakanda Forever*. 2022
*Black Panther*. 2018
*Death on the Nile*. 2022
*Guava Island*. 2019
*My Brother The Devil*. 2012
*Ready Player One*. 2018
*Sing 2*. 2021
*Surrounded*. 2023
*The Commuter*. 2018
*The Silent Twins*. 2022
*Victim*. 2011

Television films:
*Banana*. 2015
*Black Mirror*. 2017
*Chasing Shadows*. 2014
*Coming Up*. 2013
*Cucumber*. 2015
*Doctor Who*. 2015
*Glasgow Girls*. 2014
*Holby City*. 2011
*Humans*. 2016
*I Am…*2021
*Random*. 2011
*Small Axe*. 2020
*Top Boy*. 2011

## APPENDIX D

## LIST OF PLAYS BY GUYANESE PLAYWRIGHTS

**ABBENSETTS, Michael**

**Stage plays**

- 3 one-act plays (*The blind man and the baby; Jacko come back tuh; Tiger*), National Cultural Centre, Guyana, 1991.
- *Alterations.* New End Theatre, UK 1978.
- *El Dorado*. Theatre Royal Stratford East, UK 1984.
- *In the Mood* (two acts). Hampstead Theatre, UK 1981.
- *Samba* (two acts). Tricycle Theatre, UK 1980
- *Sweet Talk* (two acts). New End Theatre, UK 1973
- *The Lion*. Cochrane Theatre, UK 1993.
- *The Outlaw*. Arts Theatre, UK 1983

**Television plays**

- *Big George Is Dead,* Channel 4, UK, 1987.
- *Black Christmas,* BBC, UK, 1977.
- *Crime and Passion,* Channel 4, UK, 1975.
- *Empire Road,* series, BBC, UK, 1978–79.
- *Inner City Blues,* Channel 4, UK, 1974.
- *Little Napoleons,* mini-series, Channel 4, UK, 1994.
- *Roadrunner,* Channel 4, UK, 1977.
- *The Museum Attendant*. BBC2, UK, 1973.

**Radio plays**

- *Alterations,* BBC World Service, UK, 1980.
- *Brothers of the Sword,* BBC Radio, UK, 1978.
- *Home Again,* BBC Radio, UK, 1975.
- *Sweet Talk,* BBC Radio, UK, 1974.

- *The Dark Horse,* BBC Radio, UK, 1981.
- *The Fast Lane,* Capital Radio, UK, 1980.
- *The Sunny Side of the Street,* BBC Radio, UK 1977.

**ALBEE, Edward**
*Zoo. Story,* Theatre Guild, Guyana, 1970.

**ALEXANDER, Lorrimer**
*Conniving at the Terminus* (A radio play in four acts), Radio Demerara, 1960s.

**AMEERALLY, Niamatalli**
*Appan jaat,* Theatre Guild, Guyana, 1964.

**ANDERSON, Megan**
*A Change of Heart,* Theatre Guild, Guyana, 1960s.

**ARCHIBALD, Douglas**
*Bamboo Clump,* Theatre Guild, Guyana, 1983.

**BALGOBIN, Basil**
*Asra,* Georgetown, Guyana, 1945.

**BASCOM, Harold A.**
*Blank Document,* a radio play, 2010. (Winner of the Guyana Prize for Literature, Drama)
*Crisis Spell,* NCC, 1989.
*Cockle House,* NCC, 1996.
*Desperate for Relevance,* Theatre Guild, Guyana, 2014. (Caribbean Award 2014 and Winner of the Guyana Prize for Literature, Drama)
*Family Budget,* NCC, 1989.
*Home For Christmas,* NCC, 1992.
*Makantali,* NCC, 1984. (Winner of the Guyana Prize for Literature, Drama)
*Philbert and Loraine,* NCC, 1992.
*Queen O'De Pack,* NCC, 1994.
*Tessa Real-Girl & The Old Fool,* NCC, 1990.
*The Barrel,* NCC, 1987.
*The Butter Line,* Lichas Hall, Linden, Guyana, 1983.

*The Handy Man,* Paul Robeson Theatre, New York, 1996.
*The Visa Wedding,* NCC, 1992.
*TV Alley,* NCC, 1988.
*Two Wrongs,* 1994. (Winner of the Guyana Prize for Literature, Drama)
*Witch Hunt for Harry Barker,* NCC, 1993.

**BENN, D.M**
*Pickpockets Anonymous,* Theatre Guild, Guyana, 1963.

**BISSUNDYAL, Chauramanie**
*Brooklyn Raani,* 1990.
*Disco Dulahin,* 1990.
*From Ganges to Demerary,* 1988.
*From Palos to Guanahani,* 1991.
*Hello El Dorado,* 1990.
*I Is a Jumbie,* 1989.
*Mad No Hell,* 1990.
*Migrant Error,* 1989.
*Trick and the Rajah,* 1986.

**BLAIR, Brenna**
*Warrior of Dignity,* TG, 2012.

**BLAZE, Ronan**
*For the Love of Aidana Soraya,* National Cultural Centre, 2006. (Winner of the Guyana Prize for Literature, Drama)

**BOURNE, Tommy**
*Hassa Curry* (A Caribbean one act play). Gray Dramatic Group, Mackenzie (now Linden), 1958.
*Mackenzie Blues* (A play in act), Mackenzie (now Linden), 1960s.

**BRAITHWAITE, Barrington**
*Legend of the Silk Cotton Tree,* playscript by Al Creighton, a play that demonstrated an interest in history, folklore, and legend, NCC, 1992.

**BUNYAN, Jay**
*Children of Two Worlds,* 1992.

**CADOGAN-TAYLOR, Sheron**
*The Ex,* Theatre Guild, Guyana, 2018.

**CAMERON, Norman**
*Balthasar*. A drama in five acts. 1931.
*Jamaica Joe*. A play in three acts. Queen's college. 1946.
*Kayssa* or *Hear the Other Side*. A play in one act. 1959.
[Presented on September 4 and 5, 1959 in observance of the author's thirtieth year as a playwright].
*Price of Victory*. A play in two parts (based on a Nigeria legend). 1965.
*Three immortals*. A collection of three plays (*Adoniya,* a play in three acts; *Ebedmelech*; and *Sabaco*), 1953.

**CAMPBELL, John**
*Dhanwattie,* a play in one scene, Theatre Guild, Georgetown, Guyana, 1966.
[Awarded 2nd prize Playwriting Competition organized by the Theatre Guild].
*Don't Look Back,* a play in one act. 1963.

**CAREW, Jan Rynveld**
**Radio plays**
*Anancy and Tiger,* BBC, UK, 1958.
*Song of the Riverman,* BBC, UK, 1968.
*The Legend of Nameless Mountain,* BBC, UK, 1958.
*The River Man,* BBC, UK, 1957.
*The University of Hunger* (with Sylvia Wynter), BBC, UK, 1960.

**Television plays**
*A Roof of Stars,* London, 1963.
*Behind God's Back,* London, 1969.
*Exile from the Sun,* London, 1963.
*No Gown for Peter,* London, 1963.
*The Baron of South Boulevard,* London, 1963.
*The Big Pride* (with Sylvia Wynter), London, 1961.
*The Conversion of Tiho,* London, 1963.
*The Day of the Fox* (with Sammy Davis), a play in three acts adapted for television, London, 1962.

*The Raiders*, London, 1963.
*The Smugglers*, London, 1963.

**Stage Plays**

*Behind God's Back*, Carifesta, Georgetown, Guyana, 1975
*Black Horse, Pale Rider*, a play in two acts, University of the West Indies, Mona, Jamaica, 1970
*Black Midas*, Theatre Guild, Georgetown, Guyana, 1965.
*Gentlemen Be Seated*, Belgrade, in the then Yugoslavia, 1967.
*The Peace Play*, Theatre Guild, Georgetown, Guyana 1987
*The University of Hunger*, a play in three acts, Theatre Guild, Georgetown, Guyana, 1966.

**CENDRECOURT, Esme**

*Captain's Party*, New York, 1930s.
*Grandpa's Pride*, a play in three acts, 1933
*New probationer*, a play in three acts, 1939
*Night in the Caribbean*, New York, 1930s.
*Romance of the Kaieteur*, a play in three acts. 1931
*Unmasked*, a play in three acts. 1944

**CHANCELLOR, Bertie W.**

*26, Tiger Bay Alley or The Lord Will Provide*, a play for radio in act.

**CHAPMAN, Grace**

*The Green Bottle*, National Cultural Centre, 1984.

**CHARLES, Bertram**

*Another Place Somewhere* (with Charles De Burst), Theatre Guild, Georgetown, Guyana, 1969.
*Human Predicament*, Theatre Guild, Georgetown, Guyana, 1970
*Papa's Idol*, Theatre Guild, Georgetown, Guyana, 1990.
*The Alexin of Our Cure*, Theatre Guild, Georgetown, Guyana, 1969.
*The End of the Affair*, Theatre Guild, Georgetown, Guyana, 1968.
*The Ties That Bind*, Theatre Guild, Georgetown, Guyana, 1990.
*Within Our Narrow Walls*, Theatre Guild, Georgetown, Guyana, 1971.

**CHATTORAM, Puran**
*A Bridle for the Tongue,* 1960.
[Performed by the Rama Krishna Group at the Inter-school Drama Festival, 1961].
*Vote For Me,* a radio play in one act, 1963.

**CHRITCHLOW, Randolph**
*Unbreakable,* Theatre Guild, Georgetown, Guyana, 2018.

**CHUNG, Geoffrey R**
*Cottage hospital,* a play in the vernacular in four scenes.

**CLARKE, Michael**
*Possessed,* NCC, 1984

**COLLIER, Dorothy**
*Harry in haste,* 1947.
*Love is blind,* 1947.
*Married,* 1948.
*Plain sailing,* 1948.
*Quiverful,* 1948.
[These five plays were written for the Marriage Course arranged by the Catholic Church's arm Sword of the Spirit]. 1947-1948

**CORSBIE, Ken**
*All Ah We,* TG 1970s.
*Dem Two,* TG, 1970s.
*He One,* TG, 1970s.
*Jack and Jill,* TG, 1980s.
*My Name is Slave,* TG, 1971.

**CRAWFORD, A.E.**
*Brief interlude.* A play in the vernacular in one scene.

**CROAL, Elsie**
*Dora's Dinner,* TGH, 1977.

**D' OLIVIERA, Evadne**
*The Sacred Jewels,* TG, 1969.

**DANNS, Ken**
*Dec 15*, TG, 1998.
(Winner of the Guyana Prize for Literature, Drama)
*French Leave*, TG, 1958.
*Living Home*, TG, 1991.
*The Man-in-Law*, TG, 1995.
*The Woman-in-Law*, TG, 1998.
*Tourist Touch Down*, TG, 1994.

**DEMERARA DRAMATIC CLUB**
*Our Boys*. 1891
*Rob Roy*. 1893
*Ye Strings of Pearls*. 1897

**DEVONISH, Hubert**
*The Starapple, the Hibiscus, and the Sugarcane Flower*, NCC, 1998.
(Winner of the Guyana Prize for Literature, Drama)

**DOWDING, Simone**
*A Treat For My Mother*, Police Officers' Mess Hall, Georgetown, 2022.Police Officers' mess Hall.

**DRAYTON, Kathy; and Joyce Trotman**
*Highlights of the Guyana Story*, TG, 1966.

**DUFF, Michael**
*Country Girl*, NCC, 2000.
*No Tricks No Loving*, NCC, 1993.
*No Tricks No Loving II*, NCC, 1994.

**FARLEY, Seville**
*Blood-Thirsty*, TG, 1960.
*Jarge-town*, TG, 1960.

**FARRIER, Francis**
*Air Partner*, TG, 1965.
*Border Bridge*, TG, 1964.
*Journey to Freedom*, TG, 1966.
*Manaka*, TG, 1965.
*Pal*, a play in one act, TG, 1963.

*Quitters*, TG, 1965.
*The Plight of the Wright*, TG, 1969.
*The Settlers*, TG, 1977
*The Slave and the Scroll*, TG, 1964.
*The Tides of Susanburg*, NCC, 1986.
*The Trumpeter* (based on the story of James Sayers Orr or "Angel Gabriel" (1800-1856), NCC, 1977.
*Two Upward Gentlemen*, University of Middlesex, London, England, 1981.
*Young Skibby*, TG, 1975.

Radio Plays
*A Family Christmas*, TG, 1964.
*Home is for Christmas*, TG, 1964.

**FORSYTHE, Victor**
*Liberty village*, a radio play, 1966.
[Winner of the Demba Radio Play Competition, 1966 on the occasion of its 50th anniversary]
*Sweet Carilla*, a radio play, 1958.
[Awarded first prize in the first National Radio Play Competition, 1958]
*To Let Room 99*, TG, 1967.

**FRASER, Winslow**
*Andel*, a play in one act, 19??
*Bacra dead ah backdam*, 19??
*Body in the Lamaha*, a play in two acts, 19??
*Death was the bridegroom*, a play in one act, 19??
*Ramona*, a play in three acts, 19??
*Winds of Change*, TG, 1970.

**GEORGETOWN DRAMATIC CLUB**
*A Wife's Revenge*, 1894.
*East Lynne*, 1893.
*Lady Audley's Secret*, 1894.

**GILKES, Michael**
*A Pleasant Career*, NCC, 1992.
(Winner of the 1992 Guyana Literary Prize for Drama)
*Cara Lodge*, NCC, 2006.

*Couvade: A Dream Play of Guyana,* NCC, 1993.
*Last of the Redmen,* NCC, 2006.
*In Transit,* TG, 1965.

**GIRDHARI, Arnold**
*Marriage For Sale.* Three one-act plays. 1984.

**GRANNUM, A.L.**
*Desire in the Dust,* TG, 1977.

**GRANT, Cy**
*Bald Prima Donna,* TG, 1971.
*Hello Out There,* TG, 1971.

**HAZEL, Harrington**
*The Big Hoax,* a play in three acts, 19??
*Gramps,* a radio play, 19??

**HEATH, Roy**
*Inez Combrey,* TG, 1972.

**HENRY, Sydney**
*Political Diversion,* NCC, 2018.

**HILL, Erroll**
*The Square Peg,* TG, 1965.

**HOLDER, Wilbert**
*It's Happening again,* a play in two scenes, 19??

**HOLLINGSWORTH, Ronald**
*83 Million Gees,* TG, 1997
*Diplomatic Blow,* TG, 1992.
*Find Another Man – Buck Pot !!,* TG, 1992.
*Marriage After Death,* TG, 1993.
*My Second Wife,* TG, 1993
*My Wife and I,* TG, 1993
*Stamping,* TG, 1996.

*Till A Find Ah Place II*, TG, 1992.
*Till A Find Ah Place III*, TG, 1994.
*Till A Find Ah Place in Sophia*, TG, 1998.
*Till A Find Ah Place*, TG, 1992.
*Viagra! Grand Dad's Day Out*, TG, 1998.

**HOPKINSON, Slade**
*Fall of a chief*, a play in nine scenes, TG, 1965.
*The onliest fisherman*, a play in one act, UWI, Mona, Jamaica, 19??

**IMHOFF, Janice**
*Love Stretched!*, 2008.
*Miss Edwards*, Festival of One-Act Plays, TG, May 2011
*The 11th Finger*, De Impeccable Palace, Brickdam, Georgetown, 2016.
*The Changing Hand*, 2008.

**JAMILA**
*Only the Brave*, 1943.

**JOHN, Errol**
*Tout*, TG, 1974.

**JOHNSON, Clayton**
*The broken egg that hatched*, a play in the vernacular in two acts, 19??

**JONES, Le Roi**
*The Dutchman*, TG, 1970.

**KING, Sheila**
*A Matter of Policy*, a radio play, 19??
*Bourdabounty*, a play in three acts, TG, 1963.
*Fo' bettin' or worse*, a two-act play in the vernacular, TG, 1966. [Awarded third prize at the 1966 Theatre Guild Playwrighting Competition].
*Hands across the river*, a radio play, 19??
*Random House*, 19??

**KWAYANA, Eusi**
*Christus the Messiah,* with the musical score by future Minister of Education under the PNC Government, Ms. Cecilene Baird, circa 1951-52.
*King on Trial,* 1981.
*Proclamation,* a play based on the 1823 Demerara Revolt, 1992.
*Queen of the Riot,* 1981.
*Rookmin Mai & Auntie Pet,* street plays, circa 1970s.
*The Promised Land,* a play in one act, TG, 1965.
[Winner of the 'Best Play' Prize in the Youth category at the British Guiana Drama Festival, 1965]

**LEWIS, Alyan**
*The legal angle,* TG, 1963.
*Summer love,* a play in four acts, TG, 1963.

**MADHOO-NASCIMENTO, Gem**
*Murder at Guiseppe's,* NCC, 2009.
*Guyanese Roots and Rhythm,* NCC, 2005.

**MANNING, Lloyd J.**
*The miracle,* a radio play, 1966.
[Winner of the 1966 Demba Radio Play competition]
*Time and tide,* a play in three acts for stage and radio, 19??

**MARTIN, Sidney**
*Energy Swankey,* a tragedy in three acts, 19??

**MARTINS, Dave**
*All in Wan,* NCC, 2006.
*Raise Up,* NCC, 1990.

**MCDONALD, Ian**
*The Tramping Man* (UWI School of Continuing Education: St. Augustine, 1969). [A one-act play published in a collection of eight Caribbean Plays titled *A Time and a Season*].

**MCLEAN, Shantal**
*The Murder,* NCC, 2018.

**MCPHOY, EION**
*Cartel Queen*, NCC, 1996.

**MCWATT, Mark**
*The Knife of Dawn*, 19??
[Based on the incarceration of political activist and national poet Martin Carter in 1953].

**MICHAEL, Ras**
*Jo-Ann*, NCC, 1986
*Lot 88 Carter's Nigger Yard*, NCC, 1987.

**MILLER, Ronald**
*Waiting for Gillian*, NCC, 1999.

**MITCHELL, Ronald**
*Happy Holiday*, TG, 1965.

**MITTELHOLZER, Edgar**
*The sub-committee*, a sketch, 1951.

**MOHAMED, Gabrielle**
*Spirits of the Mountain Crest*, NCC, 2022.
[Best Drama Guyana Prize for Literature, 2022]

**MOHAMED, Paloma**
*All For The Money*, 19??
*Anybody See Brenda*, 19??
*Benjie Darling*, 19??
*Duenne*, NCC, 1998. [Winner of Guyana Prize for Literature, Drama, 1999].
*Father of the Man*, 2000 [Winner of Guyana Prize for Literature, Drama].
*Jezebel*, 1990.
*Jezebel II*, 1991.
*Mammy*, 1990.
*Nancy Story*, 2004 [Winner of Guyana Prize for Literature, Drama, 2005].
*Reggae Marley*, 19??
*Testament*, 2008.
*The Massacuraman Man: A Folk Play For Young People*, 2003.

*The Confirmed Bachelor*. 1995.
*Trouble in Paradise*, 1996.
*Typhocious Rickatics*, 2004.

**NARAIN, Harry**
*The Eleventh Hour*, NCC, 1992.
(Winner of the Guyana Prize for Literature, Drama, 1993)

**NARAINE, Somnauth**
*Deedar*, stage version of the famous Bollywood 1951 movie, 1988.

**NOBREGA, Cecile**
*Stabroek Fantasy*, 1956.

**OGINGA, Kwesi**
*A Kwanzaa Celebration*, Community Theatre, Silver Spring, Maryland, USA, 1996.
*Burning*, Pegasus Hotel, Georgetown, 1980.
*Conversations*, Wheaton Community Center, Maryland, 1997.
*Drum Poem*, Dinner Theater, Sheraton Washington North Hotel, Washington, D.C., 2009.
*Feelings*, TG, 1982.
*From Bondage Thru Emancipation*, NCC, 1982.
*Hol' On To Yuhself*, Pegasus Hotel, Georgetown, 1980.
*Life Tells Me*, NCC, 1990.
*On The Other Side of My Mind*, Good News Theater, USA, 2019.
*Sam and Simone*, Caribbean Theater, Montgomery County, Maryland, USA, 2001.
*Shaking Hands with Shadows*, Wheaton Community Center, Maryland, USA, 1995.
*Tengar*, NCC, 1983. [Commissioned for then President Forbes Burnham's 60th Birthday Celebration].
*The Break*, NCC, 1986. [Commissioned in memory of the late President Forbes Burnham (1923-1985)].
*The Rebellion*, NCC, 1984. [Commissioned for then President Forbes Burnham's 61st Birthday Celebration].
*These Things Happen on My Street*, Good News Theater, Maryland, 2011.
*This Fish is Sweet*, Margaret Sweinhart Senior Center, USA, 2012.

*To My Son A Legacy*, NCC, 1985. [Commissioned for then President Forbes Burnham's $62^{nd}$ Birthday Celebration].
*Vagrants*, Prince George's County Community Playhouse, USA, 1996.

**PERSAUD, Darendra B.**
*Daughter's Dilemma*, a play in two acts, TG, 1963.
[Awarded first prize in the 1963 Theatre Guild's Playwriting Competition]

**PIETERS, Mavis**
*Onward Guiana*, a play in four acts, 19??

**PILGRIM, Billy**
*A Pride of Heroes*, a musical play, TG, 1977.
*Produce or Perish*, TG, 1976.
*The Purchase*, NCC, 1980.
*The Yard*, a musical fantasy, NCC, 1981.

**PILGRIM, Frank**
*Christmas reunion*, a one-act radio play, 1964.
*Miriamy*, a West Indian play in three acts, TG, 1962.
*Singing rum*, a radio play, 1963.
*Skeleton at the party*, 1954.
*The homecoming*, a radio play, 1964.

**RAMRAJ, Victor J**
*The Dead Son*, TG, 1965.
[Won the Playwright of the Year Prize, 1965]

**ROACH, Eric**
*Bel Fanto*, TG, 1974.

**ROGERS, Nigel**
*Swan Song of the Kiskadee*, NCC, 1993.
*The Haunting of Abraham Solomon*, NCC, 1996.
(Winner of the Guyana Prize for Literature, Drama, 1997)

**ROHLEHR, Lloyd**
*Thousands cheer*, a radio play in three acts, 1962.

**ROSS, Hyacinth**
*Open confession,* 19??

**SADEEK, Sheik**
*Bound Coolie or The Immigrant,* TG, 1958.
*Black Bush,* TG, 1965. [Winner of the 1966 Demba Radio Play competition]
*Fish Koker,* TG, 1961.
*Goodbye Corentyne,* TG, 1965.
*Namaste,* TG, 1965.
*No Greater Day,* TG, 1965.
*Pork-knockers,* a humour in one act and one scene, TG,1959.
*Savannah's edge,* TG, 1965.

**SAUL, Leon**
*For Better For Worse,* 1981.
*Guyana's Got Talent,* NCC, 2022.

**SCOTT, Michael**
*Death of Po'leho,* TG, 1967.

**SEAFORTH, Carol**
*Big dilemma,* TG, 1963.
[Awarded 2nd prize in the 1963 Playwriting competition]

**SEEPERSAUD, Ramdyal**
*Guiana's People,* a play in the vernacular in three scenes, TG, 1960.
*The Stalwart,* a play in five scenes, TG, 1960.

**SHEWCHARAN, Narmala**
*Janhjat: Bola Ram and The Long Story,* 19??

**SINGH, RAJKUMARIE**
*A White Carmellian and a Blue Star,* 19??
*Bohemian Interlude,* 19??
*Hoofbeats at Midnight,* TG, 1964.
*No More Kitchrie For the Groom,* TG, 1974.

*Roraima,* a radio play, 1966. [Won the 1966 Prize for the Best Radio Play in the Demba Radio Play competition]
*Sakina, I Love You Still,* 1943.
*The Sound of Her Bells,* 1970.

**SINGH, Subraj**
*Laugh of the Marble Queen,* NCC, 2019. [Won the National Drama Festival Award, 2020]
*Masque,* NCC, 2016. [Won the 2016 National Drama Festival Award for the New Guyanese Play and Best Production]

**SMITH, A. W. H.**
*Arsenic and Old Lace,* 1948.

**SMITH, Ricardo**
*Miss Phoebe or Guyana Legend,* a play with music in three acts, 1965. [Performed as part of Independence celebrations on May 28, 30, 31 1966].

**STEPHENSON, Elaine**
*Tamari,* a play in three acts, 19??

**SUBHAN, Neaz M**
*I Am Us,* NCC, 2019. [Adapted for the screen "I Am Us" The Movieshow at Caribbean Cinemas. 2020]
*When Chocolate Melts,* NCC, 2013. [Winner of 2013 Best Playwright Prize]

**TELFORD, Mosa**
*Children of baby,* 2016.
*Before Her Party*. 2018

**VALZ, Ian**
*A Passage to the Sun,* NCC, 1988.
*Antillean House,* NCC, 2004.
*Borderline,* NCC, 2007.
*Breakfast at Oranje,* St. Maarten, 2006.
*Breaking All The Rules,* NCC, 2003.
*Chiware's Revenge,* NCC, 2007.
*House of Pressure,* NCC, 1985, 2006.
*Masquerade,* NCC, 1985.

*Rhythm of the Palms*, NCC, 1990.
*Room to Let*, NCC, 1982.
*Separate Status*, NCC, 1997.
*The Peacock Dance 2*, NCC, 2002.
*The Peacock Dance*, NCC, 2001.
*The Plantation*, NCC, 2008.
*Two's A Crowd*, NCC, 1982.
*Virgin in Black*, NCC, 1989.

**VAN SERTIMA, Sheila**
*It's Brickdam*, TG, 1959.

**WESTMAAS, David**
*Old suit, new cloth*. A comedy. 19??
*The harvesters*. A play in vernacular in three scenes. 19??

**WHITE, Lloyd**
*Sunset of light or Vision over Guiana*, a play in two acts, 19??

**WILLIAMS, Vivian**
*Asylum Wedding*, 19??
*Dead or Alive*, 2000.
*Joe Flounce*, 1995.
*Run lef the Tambeh*, 1994.
*The Aids Family*, 1994.
*The Deads of State*, 1996.
*The President*, 2000.
*Zenrick and Cleopatra*, 20??

**WILTSHIRE, Rae**
*Adult*, ????
*Don't Ask Me Why*, ????

**YARDE, Sonia**
*The Colour of Race*, NCC, 2022.

--------

**Places in Guyana where plays were performed:**
NCC – National Cultural Centre, Georgetown, Guyana
TG – Theatre Guild, Georgetown, Guyana

## APPENDIX E

## COMPILATIONS AND ANTHOLOGIES

Works by Guyanese authors have been represented in the following compilations and anthologies:

1. *A Handbook of Guyanese Literature* (Guyenterprise Ltd.: Georgetown, 2007).
2. *A Reader's Guide to West Indian and Black British Literature* (Hansib: Hertford, 1997).
3. *An Anthology of Caribbean Poetry for Carifesta* (Ministry of Culture, Youth, and Sport: Georgetown, 2008).
4. *An Anthology of Contemporary Guyanese Verse* (Petamber Persaud: Georgetown, 2013).
5. *An Anthology of Guianese Poetry* (A.J. Seymour: Georgetown, 1954).
6. *An Anthology of Local Indian Verse* (C.E.J. Ramcharitar-Lall: Georgetown, 1934).
7. *An Anthology of Short Stories From Guyana* (Dido Press: London, 2007).
8. *An Introduction to Guyanese Literature* (Petamber Persaud: Georgetown, 2013).
9. *Anthology: Twenty-six stories, Fiction and Non-Fiction* (MiddleRoad Publishers: Toronto, 2017).
10. *Caribbean Dozen: Poems from Thirteen Caribbean Poets* (Walker Books Ltd: London, 2020).
11. *Caribbean Essays: An Anthology* (Evans Brothers: London, 1972).
12. *Caribbean Folk Tales and Legends* (Bogle L'Ouverture: London, 1980).
13. *Caribbean Literature* (Argosy Company Ltd.: Georgetown, 1951).
14. *Caribbean Narrative* (Heinemann: London, 1966).
15. *Caribbean New Wave*: Caribbean Writers Series (Heinemann: London, 1990).
16. *Caribbean Poetry Folktales & Short Stories* (iUniverse: Bloomington, 2005).

17. *Caribbean Poetry Now* (Hodder & Stoughton: London, 1984, 1995).
18. *Caribbean Prose* (Evans Bros., Ltd.: London, 1967).
19. *Caribbean Verse: An Anthology* (Heinemann: London, 1967).
20. *Caribbean Voices* – Volumes 1 and 2 (Evans Bros., Ltd.: London, 1966).
21. *Caribbean Women Writers: Fiction in English* (Macmillan: London, 1999).
22. *Caribbean Writers: Critical Essays* (New Beacon: London, 1968).
23. *Commonwealth Literature and the Modern World* (Didier: Brussells: 1975).
24. *Commonwealth Poems of Today* (John Murray: London, 1967).
25. *Creation Fire: A Cafra Anthology of Caribbean Women's Poetry* (Sister Vision Press: Toronto, 1990).
26. *Critical Writings on Commonwealth Literatures: A Selective Bibliography to 1970, with a List of Theses and Dissertations* (Pennsylvania State University Press: Scranton, 1975).
27. *Faber Book of West Indian Stories* (Faber and Faber: London, 1960).
28. *Guyanese Literature* (Hephaestus Books: Richardson, 2011).
29. *Guyanese Writers* (Hephaestus Books: Richardson, 2011).
30. *Heinemann Book of Caribbean Poetry* (Heinemann: London, 1992).
31. *Hinterland: Caribbean Poetry from the West Indies and Britain* (Bloodaxe Books: London, 1989).
32. *I Have a News: Rhymes for the Caribbean* (Lothrop, Lee & Shepherd Books: New York, 1994).
33. *Introduction to Guyanese Writing* (National History and Arts Council: Georgetown, 1971).
34. *Meet Me At The Four Corners: Brampton Writers Guild Anthology* (Brampton Writers' Guild: Brampton, 2021).
35. *My Lovely Native Land: An Anthology of Guyana* (Longman: London, 1971).

36. *New Caribbean Poetry: An Anthology* (Carcanet Press: 2007).
37. *New Voices of the Commonwealth* (Evans Brothers.: London, 1968).
38. *Oxford Book of Caribbean Verse* (Oxford University Press: Oxford, 2005, 2009).
39. *Oxford Book of Short Stories* (Oxford University Press: Oxford, 2002).
40. *Penguin Book of Caribbean Short Stories* (Penguin Books: Harmondsworth: 1986, 1998).
41. *Penguin Book of Modern Poets* (Penguin Books: Harmondsworth, 1995).
42. *Response* (Nelson & Sons: London, 1969).
43. *Roraima: An Anthology of Poetry from Emerging Caribbean Canadian Writers* (Createspace: Scotts Valley, 2011).
44. *Scaling New Heights: 2022 Pakaraima Writers Anthology* (Middle Road Publishers: Toronto, 2022).
45. *Selected Poetry: Caribbean Writers* (William Heinemann: London, 1993).
46. *Stories from the Caribbean* (Dufour: Philadelphia, 1965).
47. *The Cambridge Encyclopaedia of Latin America and the Caribbean* (Cambridge University Press: Cambridge, 1992).
48. *The Cambridge Guide to African and Caribbean Theatre* (Cambridge University Press: Cambridge, 1994).
49. *The Heinemann Book of Caribbean Poetry in English* (Heinemann: London, 1992).
50. *The Kykoveral Anthology of Guianese Poetry* (British Guiana Lithographic: Georgetown, 1954).
51. *The Literature of the Indian Diaspora* (Greenwood Press, Connecticut. 1992).
52. *The Penguin Book of Caribbean Verse in English* (Penguin Books: London, 1986).
53. *The Poetry of the Negro 1746-1949* (Doubleday: New York, 1949).
54. *The Routledge Reader in Caribbean Literature* (Routledge: Oxford, 1996).

55. *The Silence of Islands* (Peepal Tree Press: Leeds, 1994).
56. *The Sun's Eye: West Indian Writing for Young Readers* (Longman's Green & Co.: London, 1968).
57. *Twentieth Century Caribbean and Black African Writers* (Gale Research Inc.: Detroit, 1984).
58. *Twentieth-Century Caribbean Literature* (Routledge: London, 2006).
59. *Voiceprint: An Anthology of Oral and Related Poetry From The Caribbean* (Longman: Londoin, 1995).
60. *West Indian Narrative: An Introductory Anthology* (Humanities Press: New York, 1966).
61. *West Indian Poetry* (A.J. Seymour: Georgetown, 1981).
62. *West Indian Poetry 1900-1970. A Study in Cultural Decolonisation* (Savacou Publication: London, 1974).
63. *West Indian Poetry: An Anthology for Schools* (Longman Caribbean: London, 1989).
64. *West Indian Poetry: Studies in Caribbean Literature* (Heinemann: London, 1989)
65. *West Indian Stories* (Faber & Faber: London, 1960).
66. *Young Commonwealth Poetry: An Anthology* (Heinemann: London, 1967).

## APPENDIX C

## ABOUT THE AUTHOR

Lal Balkaran is an award-winning internal auditor and published author. He was born at Versailles on the West Bank Demerara and attended Malgre Tout RC School (1960-65) and West Demerara Government Secondary School (1965-70). He taught for five years in the South Rupununi after leaving high school and travelled throughout the country over the years. He is principally self-taught as a Certified Internal Auditor (CIA), Chartered Global Management Accountant (CGMA), Fellow Chartered Governance Professional (FCG), Fellow Chartered Professional Accountant (FCPA), and Fellow Chartered Management Accountant (FCMA). In addition, he earned his MBA from the Edinburgh Business School.

Mr. Balkaran wrote nine reference books on business and seven on Guyana. Also, he has had over fifty articles on business and a range of other areas published widely across the globe, some of which have been award-winning. He has also done eight documentaries on Guyana.

In January 2000, he established a chapter of the Global Institute of Internal Auditors (IIA) and the Institute's certifications including the flagship Certified Internal Auditor program in

Guyana – a first for the country. He was also an external examiner to the University of Guyana and the University of the West Indies (Cave Hill Campus). Mr. Balkaran has been a member of the Institute of Internal Auditors (IIA) for over 30 years and is a Past President and honourary member of the IIA-Toronto. He was a long-term member of the Committee of Research and Education Advisors of IIA Global and is a current member of the *Internal Auditor* and EDPACS Editorial Advisory Boards. He was a leading member of the **Internal Audit Advisory Board** set up by the Treasury Board Secretariat in Ottawa in 2005 under the Paul Martin Government to establish internal audit functions in federal agencies of the Government of Canada.

Lal is the only recipient of all three of IIA-Canada Awards: the 2010 Arthur J. Child's **Distinguished Service in Canada Award;** the **2012 Contribution to the Profession of Internal Auditing Award;** and the **2018 Lifetime Achievement Award.** In July 2022, he won the prestigious **Bradford Cadmus Memorial Award** from the Florida-based IIA-Global for his outstanding contributions in research, education, publications, and other activities in the field of internal auditing – the only Canadian, Guyanese, and Caribbean person to achieve this feat.

See www.lbapublications.com